W9-AEG-174

101 Best Businesses to Start

101

Best Businesses

to Start

Sharon Kahn and
The Philip Lief Group

 Doubleday

NEW YORK   LONDON   TORONTO   SYDNEY

Published by Doubleday, a division of Bantam Doubleday Dell Publishing Group, Inc., 666 Fifth Avenue, New York, New York 10103.

Doubleday and the portrayal of an anchor with a dolphin are trademarks of Doubleday, a division of Bantam Doubleday Dell Publishing Group, Inc.

Library of Congress Cataloging-in-Publication Data

Kahn, Sharon, 1950–
   101 best businesses to start.

   1. Small business—Handbooks, manuals, etc.
2. New business enterprises—Handbooks, manuals, etc.
3. Success in business—Handbooks, manuals, etc.
I. Philip Lief Group. II. Title. III. Title: One
hundred one best businesses to start. IV. Title: One
hundred and one best businesses to start.
HD2341.K28 1988   658.1'141   87-33224

Paperback: ISBN 0-385-24180-1
Hardcover: ISBN 0-385-24181-X

COPYRIGHT © 1988 BY THE PHILIP LIEF GROUP, INC.
ALL RIGHTS RESERVED
PRINTED IN THE UNITED STATES OF AMERICA

JUNE 1988

BG

To Michael

Contents

So . . . You Want to Start a Business   1

Why These 101 Are the Best Businesses   12

BUSINESS SERVICES

Auditing Specialist   18

Business Broker   23

Career Counselor   31

Janitorial Service   36

Management Consultant   41

Meeting Planner   47

Messenger Service   53

Public Relations   57

Quick Printer   62

Seminar Producer   69

Temporary Employment Service – Clerical   74

Temporary Employment Service – Professional   82

Trade Association   88

Turnkey Office   93

CHILD CARE

Daycare Center   100

Playgym   108

Sleep-away Camp   113

COMMUNICATIONS

Book Producer   120

Desktop Publisher   126

Information Detective   131
Newsletter Publisher   136
Pagers   143
Video-editing Service   149
Videographer   152

COMPUTERS

Computer Consultant   160
Computer Repair   164
Computer Trainer   168

FOOD AND DRINK

Catering   174
Gourmet Food Products   180
Gourmet Food Store   185
No-alcohol Nightclub   190
Ocean Farming   194
Pizza Parlor   199
Sandwich Shop   203
Take-out Restaurant   207

HEALTHCARE AND FITNESS

Aerobics/Exercise Instructor   214
Daycare for Seniors   219
Diet Clinic   226
Freestanding Medical Center   230
Healthclub   236
Home Healthcare   243

HOUSEHOLD SERVICES

Alarm Systems   252
Carpet Cleaner   260

Closet Organizer   264
Drycleaner   267
Grocery Shopper   271
Home Decorating Center   275
Household Management Service   279
Kitchen and Bath Design   283
Landscaper   288
Laundromat-Plus   292
Maid Service   297
Self-storage Center   302
Water Conditioning Company   307

PERSONAL SERVICES

Auto Detailing   314
Automotive Tune-up Center   318
Beauty Salon   323
Clothing Alteration Shop   328
Dating Service   332
Financial Planner   337
Image Consultant   342
Mediator   348
Personal Fiduciary   353
Private Post Office   357
Skin-care Aesthetician   361
Vocational School   365

REAL ESTATE

Home Inspector   372
Manufactured Housing Contractor   376
Real Estate Agent   381
Real Estate Appraiser   386

Real Estate Auctioneer   391
Relocation Consultant   399

RETAILING

Athletic Shoe Store   406
Children's Clothing Boutique   410
Florist   416
Garden Center   422
Large-sized Apparel Shop   426
Left-handers Store   430
Pet Store   433
Pro Athletic Shop   438
Professional Women's Clothing Shop   442
Pushcarts   446
Rental Center   451
Specialty Bookstore   457

SALES AND MARKETING

Auction House   464
Consumer Show   471
Craft Wholesaler   474
Direct Sales Company   481
Import Entrepreneur   487
Mail-order Catalog   493
Telemarketer   499
Trade Show   504

TRAVEL AND ENTERTAINMENT

Balloon Decorator   512
Bed and Breakfast Inn   516
Limousine Service   523
Miniature Golf   528

Party Planner   533
Party Rental Store   538
Tour Operator   545
Waterpark   552
"Whodunit" Producer   557

So . . . You Want to Start a Business

Tommy Crouch has been an entrepreneur almost all his adult life, beginning with the accounting firm he established in little Hope, Arkansas. When he sold his practice back in 1970, Tommy tried working for someone else, signing on as an executive at a fledgling stereo manufacturer. As the company's sales skyrocketed from $600,000 to $11 million during Tommy's eight-year stint, he recognized the tiny equity position he held gave him neither power nor wealth. "I realized that I'd never be more than a minority stockholder, so I sold my interest and tried to find something easy to do."

The first thing Tommy did was take his family on a Myrtle Beach, South Carolina, vacation, where they played the area's elaborate miniature golf courses. When he returned to Hope, Tommy bought and managed an apartment building. "After a couple of years, I decided I needed something more exciting," says Tommy. "I kept thinking about those golf courses." In 1983, he called the Myrtle Beach Chamber of Commerce, which gave him the phone number of a course designer. The first of four Gator Golf Courses was born and Tommy was on his way to the miniature golf hall of fame.

Tommy Crouch, like the other three hundred or so entrepreneurs profiled in this book, passed beyond the dreaming stage to that of actually building a business. Motives for starting a company differ, but all these business venturers return to the same theme: the sense of satisfaction that comes from owning a business of one's own. "You're in control of your destiny," says Howard L. Shenson, a management consultant from Woodland Hills, California. "You control the earning potential and life style." Adds Ruby Burgis, who operates Personal Home Care maid service from an Atlanta suburb: "I like being creative, coming up with ideas that I don't have to ask my boss to ask *his* boss to okay."

But you can't ignore the downside: Starting a business is a shaky undertaking. Tommy Crouch was one of the lucky ones because each of his ventures has brought success. But, depending on whose statistics you cite, half of all new American enterprises fail within one year of startup, and another 20 percent close their doors within the first five years.

Nevertheless, venturers need only look around them for encouragement. The small-business climate is alive and well, and the United States has rarely seen such a fervor of startup activity. The Commerce Department considers 95 percent of all businesses in the country small businesses. Independent firms contribute a similar percentage of the country's gross national product. Each of those companies was started by an entrepreneur with a dream and drive.

Independent business people who have survived and prospered —often after repeated attempts and disappointments—point to three factors that make or break a business: the business idea, the owner's commitment and personality, and capital.

THE RIGHT IDEA

101 Best Businesses to Start will help you come up with the right idea for a business to meet your personal needs. To prosper, your startup must fill a gap amid all those goods and services that bombard customers, and it must fill that gap for years to come. Some ideas for new businesses are tried and tested, and if competition is sparse—or if you can offer an appealing twist on a theme—a business idea does not have to be completely original to fly. For example, laundromats have been around for years, but new theme laundries that combine cleaning clothes with an entertaining diversion (like pool or a singles bar) are adding spice to the old industry and money to entrepreneurs' pockets.

Hint: In choosing a business, stay away from fads—you will only find your services obsolete a few years down the road. Instead, evaluate the needs of the community you hope to serve. Look at the local demographics and trends. Washington Grocery Service, a shopping service, was born when its co-founders were batting around ideas on "how we live in America and how we could base a business on that," says Linda Baker. "People work too much. They need help in their lives. We can give them some relief."

Look at other businesses in your area to determine if competition has already locked up the opportunities. If you think there's room for at least one more entry, decide how to set yourself apart. "Create a strategic difference," counsels Michael Knuppe, proprietor of AAAAA Rent-A-Space self-storage centers in San Leandro, California.

WHAT IT TAKES

Every business is nourished by a specific set of skills, of course, and our profiles detail the training and personality traits that each industry requires. However, in general an entrepreneur needs the following traits:

- Self-confidence and assertiveness
- Boldness, courage, optimism, and the willingness to take controlled risks
- A capacity for hard work: discipline, diligence, and perfectionism
- Ambition, persistence, determination, and commitment to a goal
- Leadership ability, decisiveness, efficiency, and the ability to delegate authority
- Team spirit and concern for others
- An ability to solve problems: resourcefulness, inventiveness, and organizational aptitude
- Flexibility and adaptability
- Honesty, integrity, and a commitment to high standards of quality
- Street-smarts, intelligence, and good judgment

Perhaps most important, you also must love your company. Can you picture yourself in the driver's seat for sixty to eighty hours a week? Will your family and others in your support system back you 100 percent of the time? "To succeed, pick something you love and are gifted at," suggests Jeannie Gehring, president of Slender Center diet service in Madison, Wisconsin. She, for one, remains "an adolescent in love. I love the advertising, accounting, nutrition, speaking, and counseling aspects of the business. I've never had a day I wasn't roaring to get to work."

CAPITAL

Every entry in *101 Best Businesses to Start* leads off with high and low startup capital requirements. Of course, the better capitalized businesses reach profitability faster (and are therefore more fun) than those that squeak by from day-to-day. When capital is scarce, entrepreneurs use a variety of ploys to hold down initial costs. "Learn to improvise and improve," says Erika Zimmerman, whose Erika's Hair-U-M Inc. beauty parlor operates from Darien, Illinois. For example, Dennis Sheaks bought used equipment to outfit Joe Peep's New York Pizza. Donna Porter says some of her best advertising at Playful Parenting of Lancaster (Pennsylvania), a children's gym, comes from enrolling her tots in charity olympics events. Innumerable sole proprietorships operate from home until it's time to hire a second person. And many businesses hire part-time or commission labor who receive pay only when the work comes in the door.

To be on the safe side, overestimate your expenses and time until breakeven and underestimate your profits. Don't forget to factor in living costs. Most experts suggest socking away enough savings to support your family for a full year, or securing another source of income, such as a working spouse might provide, that can pay the household bills.

An accountant can help you project your business's expenses, revenues, and cash flow. When calculating startup and operating costs, make sure to include the following: the cost of leasing, buying, renovating, and building your place of business; furniture, equipment, and supplies; gas, electric, water, and telephone utilities; garbage collection, janitorial, maintenance, and extermination; inventory; payroll; professional dues and continuing education; promotion and advertising; credit card fees; licenses and permits; bad debt; taxes; and insurance.

Funding comes in as many guises as there are businesses. The first place to look, of course, is your own savings. If you can cover only part of your expenses from cashing in your pension plan and raiding your bank book, approach friends and family. Charles Grove, who designs $300,000 to $1 million miniature golf courses like the ones Tommy Crouch operates, says it's not unusual for a young company with $42,000 to get into the business. "They get their in-laws involved, and a couple of neighbors put up money, which creates a viable financial base to approach the banks. Then the couple sets up a corporate structure with the provision that they can buy the others out."

Small-business owners rarely go beyond family and friends for financing. Commercial banks won't risk lending money to startups, although sometimes entrepreneurs can secure personal loans. The Small Business Administration once represented a ready lending source, although its kitty has dwindled in recent years.

Very large (and very promising) startups can sometimes approach venture capitalists and limited partners. Occasionally, startups with massive potential convince investment bankers to float an initial public offering of their stock, enabling them to sell shares to public investors. However even these funding sources expect the principals to pour substantial home-grown capital into the new business.

TO BUY OR START

Once you determine what sort of business you want to run, consider whether to buy a company or start from scratch. Both options have advantages and disadvantages: For better or worse, an ongoing business will have all its operating systems in place. You inherit either adept or incompetent employees along with either a ready-made clientele or customers who never seem to pay their bills. If you do your homework well, however, an ongoing business's operating history should give you an idea of future risks and profits.

Ironically, while buying an existing company may be more costly than starting from your own base, you may need less cash initially. Most small-business purchases are leveraged buyouts, meaning the seller accepts a down payment and the buyer pays the remainder of the cost from the business's cash flow over three to five years. Thus, a $100,000 buyout may require just $33,000 in cash.

If you buy a reputable franchise, you eliminate even more of the risk since the parent company guides your every step. Some franchisors offer financing, and sometimes banks will even loan against a franchise purchase. However, you not only sacrifice a percentage of your future profits, you also lose a degree of independence when signing on as a franchisee.

Starting from scratch is the scariest option. Those individuals who succeed with their own idea, however, shape every aspect of the business from store decor to corporate structure. Startup costs are not as high since you pay neither a seller nor a franchisor.

CORPORATE STRUCTURE

For tax and legal purposes, you can set up a business in a number of ways. To limit your personal liability, you can incorporate. While the owner of an unincorporated business accepts complete personal responsibility for all of the business debts and contractual promises, incorporation limits the extent to which creditors can attach a business owner's personal wealth.

Successful businesses pay greater taxes through the incorporation route, however. The corporation is taxed on the business's profits before it pays shareholders the portion of profits (dividends) due them. Shareholders then owe taxes on their personal profits as well.

To avoid the double whammy of paying corporate and personal taxes, ask your advisers about a subchapter S corporation, which is available to certain smaller operations. In such a structure, the corporation channels all profits directly to the shareholders and pays no taxes. Instead, its owners declare their share of the corporation's income on their personal tax returns. Subchapter S corporations thus offer the advantages of limited liability while avoiding the disadvantages of double taxation on corporate profits.

Single-investor operations often opt for a sole proprietorship structure, which cedes the entrepreneur complete control over every aspect of the business. The business pays no corporate tax since all profits are considered personal income. However, sole proprietors also assume complete responsibility for the business's obligations.

In a similar manner, partnerships distribute all the rights and responsibilities of ownership among the shareholders. Each partner reports his or her share of the business's profits as personal income and shares the liability for losses incurred by the business. Limited partnerships provide a variation on the theme; one shareholder (the general partner) assumes unlimited liability for all business obligations as well as the greater portion of control over operations. The investing, or limited, partners share a smaller amount of responsibility, determined by the size of their investment in the business.

CALL ON THE BEST

Erika Zimmerman doesn't try to operate Erika's Hair-U-M alone. In addition to top stylists, she hires the best bankers, bookkeepers, and attorneys she can find. "If you try to do your book work on your own, you'll end up a nervous wreck," she says. "Your mind's not on what it should be: running your business."

An experienced lawyer and accountant can advise you on which business structure best meets your needs. They can help you file the necessary documents within the required deadlines, and also help you make your way through the paper blizzards precipitated by your trying to obtain licenses, permits, insurance, workers' compensation and sales tax registration, and a federal employer identification number. Professionals can help in tax planning and setting up the best possible accounting systems. The right accountant can show you how, by determining inventory and plant depreciation properly, you can greatly reduce your taxes. But most important, your lawyer and accountant can help you structure a business plan.

THE BUSINESS PLAN

Brian Ford, audit partner in the Philadelphia office of Arthur Young and co-author of *The Arthur Young Business Plan Guide* (Eric Siegel, Loren Schultz, and Brian Ford, John Wiley & Sons, New York, 1987, $22.95) admits that many entrepreneurs tackle business-plan writing only to impress financiers. "That's a big mistake," he says, pointing out that a business plan serves as a blueprint for operating a company profitably. "If I had independent means to start my own company, the first thing I'd still do would be to write a business plan." Business plans allow the writer to focus thinking on each aspect of the company's operations, from distribution to competition to marketing. Often, entrepreneurs recognize mistakes they've made on paper in time to correct them in practice.

Don't skimp in putting together the business plan. Many plans for even small businesses run thirty to sixty pages or more. The experts say a business plan should contain the following elements:

* A clear, concise statement of your business—its name, address, age, product, goals, financial condition, and prospects

* A description of the products or services you offer—how they are manufactured or supplied, how they compare to competitors' offerings, and what patents, copyrights, or other protection against competitors you hold

* An overview of your market—conditions in the industry, the economy, and your region; your competition and future competition; your target customers

* Your marketing strategy—your pricing, sales, distribution, and customer services; your advertising and promotion plans and how they will increase sales

* An outline of your company's management—personnel structure, management expertise of yourself and other key employees, business organization, and staffing

* A statement of your business's sources of financing and plans for repayment of loans

* A review of your company's financial condition and a preview of its future financial state: startup costs and breakeven date; past statements (for purchase of an ongoing concern) and projected statements, including balance sheets, profit-and-loss statements, cash-flow charts. Experts recommend monthly or quarterly breakdowns for the first one to two years, and quarterly or annual projections through five years

In addition, if you intend to use the business plan as a document with which to secure financing, your lenders or investors will want to see a two-to-three page executive summary at the very top of the business plan. The summary condenses all the information you include in the rest of the plan into a quick-to-read abstract. It concludes with the amount of financing you're seeking and a brief statement of what it will be used for.

HOME

Unless you are a sole proprietor who conducts business from a spare bedroom at home or at the client's premises (for example, an auditing specialist or image consultant), you'll need to find an appropriate location and arrange to lease or buy it and to build or renovate the premises. Like all the other aspects of starting a business, construction always takes longer and costs more than projected, so cushion your opening date with a delay in mind. When selecting a site, evaluate the traffic volume and customer accessibility. Check out your neighbors within a several-block radius. While retailers might be hurt by a direct competitor, many storekeepers say complementary businesses build traffic flow.

Ask yourself what your customers expect of you and pick a site with that in mind. Jennifer Kahnweiler, a Cincinnati, Ohio, career counselor, felt the Fortune 500 clients she wanted to land would respond to an upscale image, so she went for premium space. "In the beginning, I took shared offices in an executive suite to cut overhead and tap into clerical services," she says.

While you won't want to pay for surplus space, be sure to find a location that allows for the growth you project. When renting, negotiate to pay only for usable space (landlords often charge for square footage under columns and other such nonspace). Ask for the right to sublet or sell your lease. Protect yourself against unreasonable rent hikes, and make sure that the lease gives you enough time to establish your business in its location. As a rule, don't commit more than 10 percent of your projected sales volume to your rental expense.

HELP WANTED

When recruiting employees, as when searching for investors, many small companies rely on family. When family members display talent, drive, and desire, merging home and business represents the best of all worlds since you keep profits and goals within the family. Joan LaGreca left her job as a bank officer when she became pregnant just in time to handle billing and other paperwork for her husband Sal when he set up his personal fiduciary practice in Edison, New Jersey.

Beware, however. Although your spouse and children might represent a convenient source of help, make sure that each contributes to the business. Countless small businesses have disappeared because they made do with sub-par help when they should have hired the best. Businesses that choose professional, loyal, responsible, competent, hardworking, creative employees stand a much greater chance of prospering. Treat your staff with fairness, pay employees well, and reward individual contributions to the business.

Especially in the beginning, absentee management usually proves a disaster, so expect to put your time in on the floor. "You can't hire a manager and expect them to do things like you would," says Dorothy McNish, whose Elecia Michelle Inc. children's clothing boutique operates out of Little Rock, Arkansas. "No employee is as interested in your shop as you are."

On the other hand, if you don't want to spend your entire life locked inside your business, train competent people to handle any emergency and all day-to-day operations. At some point, the owner's best contribution should be managing the big picture. Business schools stress that any entrepreneur who can't leave for six weeks and come back never had a business in the first place.

THE CUSTOMER SEARCH

Like it or not, every entrepreneur is a salesperson. Starting before you open your doors and continuing throughout the life of your business, you will need to devote a great deal of energy to attracting customers. Each industry requires a different approach. Retailers buy advertising and places of entertainment invite the local media to review their services. Caterers and party planners throw grand-opening galas and invite local businesses that might use their service. Consultants and financial planners cold-call on individuals who would benefit from their expertise. "You can't sit waiting for the touch of Midas," says Erika Zimmerman. "Make things happen. Send brochures. Talk to your local paper and explain that you're just starting out."

No seasoned entrepreneur downplays the importance of ongoing marketing and sales efforts. You may want to hire outside or internal professionals to help in this area. Experienced advertising agencies, public-relations firms, and marketing consultants can contribute the extra visibility that will give your business an edge on competition.

Even those small companies that rely on word-of-mouth advertising say it pays to help pass the word along. Some place ads in the Yellow Pages or classifieds in pennysaver newspapers. You might also consider telemarketing and distributing flyers either by stuffing them in mailboxes or handing them out at the supermarket.

CALL FOR HELP

101 Best Businesses to Start will help you consider what some of the most promising businesses offer in the realms of wealth, excitement, and life style. This book will give you glimpses of what people like and don't like about their chosen fields so that you might envision yourself in a similar company. But don't stop here. Bear in mind the statistics on failure and tap the wealth of help that is available for the asking. Some aid costs money, of course, while other assistance is inexpensive or even free. The libraries are full of information on the specifics of starting a business. Books cover every aspect from writing a business plan to marketing. Big-Eight and smaller accounting firms offer advice in the form of brochures and personal guidance. Don't neglect distributors, suppliers, and others who have a stake in your success. You can also call on the Small Business Administration, local chambers of commerce, industry trade associations and publications, and universities and colleges for help both on starting and running a venture.

Those who start their own business risk failure, of course. On the other hand, if you do succeed, you'll be in control of what management consultant Howard Shenson calls your "destiny." Whatever else you experience in the course of running your own business, you'll have the satisfaction of knowing you tried. "Don't be a shoulda, a woulda, a coulda," says Frank Contaldo, who operates Bantam Investment Group, an Elk Grove Village, Illinois, business brokerage firm. "The difference between making a career change to IBM and buying or starting your own business is you're investing in yourself. You'll make the money if you're good at what you do. The glory," he concludes, "goes to the one in the arena."

Why These 101 Are the Best Businesses

To be in the running as a "best" business in *101 Best Businesses to Start,* a startup had to promise one of the following products or byproducts (and many promised several):
- Wealth, at least more than an individual with an appropriate background to start a company in a particular field could make working for someone else
- Independence, or the freedom from work-place restrictions
- Fun (or glamour or stimulation or creativity)
- Ease of entry and operations

WHO WANTS TO BE WEALTHY?

Everyone fantasizes about making millions, and we've included some individuals whose businesses surpassed their own expectations. Take Matt Zale, who opened his first Athlete's Foot store in Greenwich Village in 1977 as a twenty-four-year-old kid with no retailing experience. In 1987, his thirty-six-unit chain exceeded sales of $10 million and projected sales of $20 million within the next few years.

With such examples to lead the way, we heard plans from individuals who envision replicating their concept in nationwide chains or franchises, in fields as diverse as flower boutiques, maid services, and pizza shops.

Many businesses provide healthy salaries but don't generate real wealth until they are large enough to sell or to take public. Gary Penrod, who grew Building Services Industries into a $12-million-annual-sales janitorial service, enticed a British buyer to spend more than $3 million for his company.

However, while most entrepreneurs expect to make more money than they ever could earn working for a boss, true wealth rarely is the overriding motive for launching a business. For most venturers, starting a company involves creating a job—a dream job.

I DO IT MY WAY

In the course of over three hundred interviews for *101 Best Businesses to Start,* we heard the recurring theme that independence is the real prize of starting a company. Instead of the nine-to-five drudgery of working for someone else, a business of your own presents a way to control your hours, your environment, and the tasks you perform. We interviewed individuals who said entrepreneurship means never having to say "I'm sorry" to a boss, or never asking for time off in the middle of the week to go skiing or to stay home with a sick child. Founders talked about the joy of making their own decisions: experimenting with a creative merchandising technique, turning down work from unruly clients, working in Palm Springs in the winter and Maine in the summer. "I'm free to make my own mistakes," said one business broker. "I probably make half a dozen bloopers a day—and some are big enough to have gotten me fired if I made them working for someone else. But the creative freedom I have lets me try a lot of unorthodox approaches that work, too. That's why I've about tripled the salary I made before I started my firm.

IT'S GOTTA BE FUN

Founders typically bemoan the long hours, the sacrifices and hard work that goes into turning their startup into a profitable concern. Then, whether we were interviewing someone in the entertainment field (water slides) or in a business where the fun potential is less obvious (temporary-help agencies), entrepreneurs went on to tell us of special compensations: "No two days are ever the same. I'm always doing something new. When I'm at my lowest, something goes right and I experience a real high." Some people were even less restrained in their enthusiasm: "I'm having a ball! I love the reaction of my customers, my family, my friends." Most of all, they love knowing that they went for it, whether they succeed modestly or spectacularly. "Now, when I'm ninety years old looking back over my life, I'll never have to regret that I didn't try to create my own destiny," said one woman.

Fun, of course, means different things to different people. But realize you'll spend more time with your business (particularly in the startup years) than with your family, your leisure activities, or your other passions. The experts have good reason to warn against transforming a hobby into a business unless you also have the managerial and organizational expertise to carry it off. However, nobody can make a hateful business successful, at least not in the long run. You've got to love what you do to make it worthwhile.

IT'S SO EASY

Finally, many individuals confine their businesses to just one part of their lives, rather than making them the domineering, overpowering force. These more "holistically" minded people chose operations in which they could either minimize their hours (as, say, artisans or management consultants), or could hire outside managers to run them in their absence. Some entrepreneurs forgo profits to spend more time with family or to pursue hobbies. Others see the company's smoothly meshing gears as an opportunity to turn their energies to other startups. "This business is simple enough, once I get it rolling, to call in a competent manager," said one entrepreneur. "Sure, I'll check everything closely once a week, but I can use the rest of my time to start the second unit in the chain."

BUT WHAT BUSINESS WILL I START?

Many individuals aren't really sure what business to start—but they know they're in love with the concept of entrepreneurship. In fact, as the post–World War II baby boomers age, and as women increasingly enter the work force, this description will fit more and more people as they come to see in entrepreneurship the alternative to scaling the corporate ladder. The higher a person climbs in a corporation, the more heated grows the competition, simply because there are few positions at that level. In 1975, every midcareer vacancy in corporate America had an average of ten candidates. By 1985, twenty people vied for the same spot, and by 1995, forty to sixty candidates will be competing for that vacancy. The answer for increasing numbers of Americans who see their top-management dreams blocked by too many competitors? Instead of slugging it out in a corporation, they're starting their own businesses.

If you aren't positive which business you want to start, don't apologize: As long as you pour the same enthusiasm into a venture once you pick your star, you can be as successful as the individual who always knew which field to enter. However, you may be faced with your own lack of expertise, so you'll probably look for a business that's easy to enter and provides minimum risk. If possible, try on a career before you plunge into entrepreneurship: If you'd like to become a tour operator, take a job with an existing operation for a few months at least. If producing seminars attract you, line up a gig while you're still drawing a paycheck.

The Box Score

A note on the numbers at the top of each chapter: Each figure represents a comfortable average. Just as some startups may squeeze by on less initial capitalization and others may require more, revenues, profits, and breakeven time will also vary. The revenue and profit spreads assume the venture has already passed the breakeven mark listed at the top of each entry. In other words, a business listing "annual pre-tax profits" of $40,000 on $200,000 in revenues assumes the company has already operated for the six to eighteen months typically required to break even. "Staffers needed for startup" represents the minimum to open shop, an entrepreneurs may want to employ more help.

The concept of profits varies from industry to industry, as well as geographically. Some companies pay their founders handsome paychecks, leaving practically nothing for profits, while other entrepreneurs forgo salaries almost entirely. We've tried to follow industry norms where possible. For example, most retailers pay themselves $20,000 to $40,000 a year, leaving profits of just 1 to 2 percent of revenues. On the other hand, particularly in the beginning, sole proprietorships in service businesses typically dispense with salaries and regard everything left after expenses as profit.

Business

Services

Auditing Specialist

> *"I get the dumbest, wildest answers to my questions [about why vendors overcharge clients]. I get satisfaction out of sending a five-page letter back, stating 'The reality is . . .' then watching the refund come in." – Doug Arnold, Doug Arnold & Associates*

Low Startup Investment: $0 (home-based)

High Startup Investment: $20,000 (computerized office)

Time Until Breakeven: Immediate to six months

Annual Revenues: $50,000-$3 million

Annual Pre-tax Profits: $45,000-$1 million

Staffers Needed for Startup (including founder): One

Do you thrill in paper trail chases? Do you know your PBXes from your PVCs? Is a fifty-fifty split of a juicy refund from the utility company (or insurance or telephone company, etc.) worth a little confrontation? Then don your detective trenchcoat. If you have expertise—or the aptitude to pick up expertise—in areas where vendors bill by byzantine methods, check out auditing. The practices differ by industry, but auditors typically receive half of the refunds, which sometimes soar into seven figures, all because they uncover overcharges that often date back years.

THE CASE OF THE MISSING VOICES

Take, for example, the classic case of the Houston hospital. Doug Arnold, who operated Doug Arnold & Associates from the Dallas suburb of Garland, first sniffed a refund when he noticed the telephone company charged the hospital for five direct connections to the local fire department. When the receiver is raised, the phone automatically rings the fire department. That part wasn't suspicious. But, "every connection carried charges of voice-grade circuits, meaning the operator can talk with the fire department," explains Doug. "Now, why do you need voice lines when the entire fire station had just ten people?" Upon investigation, Doug discovered four out of the five circuits carried mere fire alarm capability, with no voice interaction possible. That meant his client should have been paying a lesser charge ever since the circuits were installed in 1978. The refund: $35,000.

That wasn't Doug's biggest case by a long shot, although his refunds average between $20,000 and $40,000. In 1982, he set the Texas record for a refund when he won $458,000 for the County of Galveston—"enough of a refund to get the district manager for that account shipped to Siberia," Doug recalls. Nor did the hospital have the oldest paper trail. Doug once traced a mischarge on equipment rented by a Houston shipping firm back to 1952. "There's no statute of limitations pertaining to refunds," he explains. For his average $30,000 refund, Doug might spend only a day at a client's site eyeballing the equipment, another two to three days scouring the books, and two to three days (sometimes more) negotiating with the vendor.

IT'S ALL IN BLACK AND WHITE

Auditors don't perform magic to come up with these refunds. Any office manager or accountant who has the patience to sort through regulatory tariff information—and recognizes the specific equipment involved—could conduct an audit. All you do is check bills against equipment to verify that clients possess what they're charged for, and check charges against what the law (or the contract with the vendor) allows. Fraud is rarely an issue. More likely, overcharges result from mistakes.

Of course, it's not as easy as all that. Auditors do best in fields infamous for rate confusion because billing differs depending on usage, package deals, or date of installation. "A good example is telephone switching equipment," says Doug Arnold. "If the telephone company installed it in 1976, it has one set of rates; the identical equipment installed two years later has a different set. When the sun comes up in the east, prices go this way. When it's a blue Monday, prices go that way. We're talking about a constant game between the telephone operating companies and the regulatory bodies." In addition to telecommunications, industries as varied as utilities, freight forwarding, property taxes, and insurance all support auditors.

You can get into the business for the price of your education, because you can work from your dining room table until you grow large enough to bring on employees or diversify into other areas, such as consulting. The best way to acquire the knowledge you need is by working for the vendors you eventually will audit. When Doug Arnold took an aptitude test with the military, he found he was destined for something electronic. After his military stint, Doug worked for such telecommunications employers as Western Electric and Southwestern Bell in capacities ranging from manufacturing to installation to talking with the government about rates. When he decided to solo in 1981, Doug spent his $500 startup kitty to fly to Astroworld in Houston where he had lined up his first job. That first job provided a $24,000 refund—"And half was mine," says Doug.

WAITING CAN PAY

A client who requests consulting or detailed inventory accounting might pay expenses or an up-front fee. Most auditors, however, earn by commission—meaning they don't get paid unless they uncover overcharges. Doug says not to worry about getting paid since just about any big utility overcharges most customers somewhere along the line. However, you may have to worry about when you will get paid. You don't pocket your fee until after the vendor pays the refund. Luckily, most cases are settled relatively quickly out of court, usually by pointing out to a vendor the genuine mistake that took place. After all, vendors don't want to lose a valued customer. While your client sees the refund as an unexpected windfall, the wait can sometimes be painful for you—it's your source of income. Be sure to stash away enough living and marketing dollars to cover the lean times. Doug counts on three months to a year delay, for example, when uncovering AT&T overcharges.

Payment by commission works for auditors for two reasons: They usually earn bigger amounts than clients would agree to as a fee, and, because they don't pay for your services up front, clients are more willing to take you on. They simply have nothing to lose and everything to gain. Actually, that reasoning goes only so far if you're pitching an in-house expert, like the communications manager of a large mail-order firm. "If I could get a large company like American Airlines or Sears to let me work through their system, I could retire this time next year," says Doug Arnold. "But how is a communications expert going to explain a million-dollar refund to senior management? They believe they'll be held accountable for the company spending the money in the first place."

THE HARD SELL

To land that account, explain that in-house experts are managers—not watchdogs, which is your bailiwick. The fault lies with the vendor, not with the manager who mistakenly overpaid.

The territoriality one encounters with in-house personnel makes a sell harder than some newcomers expect. If you hire someone to sell for you, make sure they have a good working knowledge of auditing, since clients see no tangible product when they first agree to your services. The salesperson has to guess what refunds are possible before most clients will open up the books. "We learned about selling the hard way," says Doug. "Twice we brought in people to solicit business, and they basically stirred up dust—collected names of people who I could call back." Doug decided it was cheaper to have secretaries make such cold calls. "We circled names in the phone book of hospitals with two hundred phones and telephone answering services. Then I made follow-up calls from those that appeared interesting."

ASKING THE RIGHT QUESTIONS

When making those cold calls to potential clients, questions like these get the most accurate returns:

- Do you own the system or rent it? (Renting returns better refunds every time.)
- Is your company at a single office, or do you have other locations, too? (The more complicated the system, the better.)
- What kind of accessories are involved? (Hope for lots of them.)

• How long has the system been in place? (Long-term overcharges add up.)

• How many local and toll lines do you have? (More, again, is better—and long-distance is best.)

"From a few questions I pull an estimate out of thin air that usually comes within 30 percent of the refund," says Doug Arnold. Although he turns down audits on accounts where he suspects the refund will be too small to pay for his time, he "never found an account that wasn't entitled to something back."

Because of the resistance from telecommunications managers in large companies, Doug targets city governments for most cold calls —unless he gets a hot tip. Here's how that works: "Sometimes I get a call from a phone company salesperson who fears the service department is about to ruin an account. I call the account and say I heard through the grapevine that something could be in error, and would they like me to help? If I get that salesperson out of hot water, the next time he or she has a drink with buddies who have a problem, I get a referral."

JACK OF ALL TRADES

Audits can also lead to other business. For example, consulting provided nearly half of Doug Arnold's 1987 revenues of $350,000 to $3.5 million (depending on whether he lands a huge California city account he's bid on, and whether some big claims are paid before the year is over). He does everything from marketing his own telecommunications software to installing microwave systems. Utility auditors often consult on energy efficiencies.

Some auditors branch out into other specialities. For example, if you audit personal property insurance claims, you can cross over into property tax audits—or hire somebody who knows the ropes.

SOURCES

Industry Association

Society of Telecommunications Consultants 1 Rockefeller Plaza, Suite 1912 New York, N.Y. 10020 (212) 582-3903

Business Broker

> *"Everyone talks about the American Dream—we're sitting on top of it. We dole out opportunities and, if the job is done right, the sellers love you, the buyers love you."* – Frank Contaldo, Bantam Investments Group, Chicago

Low Startup Investment: $10,000 (small-town office)

High Startup Investment: $100,000 (franchise in city location, with advertising)

Time Until Breakeven: Six months to one year

Annual Revenues: $100,000-$1 million

Annual Pre-tax Profits: $40,000-$300,000

Staffers Needed for Startup (including founder): One to three

Frank J. Covich, who consults for individuals who want to become business brokers, quotes first-hand evidence that his clients have chosen the best of all fields: "Brokers continually see what's for sale in all sorts of industries. It's a funny thing, but none of the people we've helped get into brokerage leave to enter any of these other businesses." The secret attraction, according to Frank Covich, is that, "You can make a lot of money in brokerage, and, unlike a hardware store, you don't pay a million dollars for inventory."

According to the Department of Commerce, fast-track Americans are an antsy lot: One out of every four U.S. businesses changes hands every five years. Enter a new breed of expeditor to match buyers and sellers of small and, increasingly, medium-sized businesses, ranging from card shops to used car dealerships. As a field, business brokerage has been around since the mid-1970s and is still tiny in comparison to its related sibling, real estate, which boasts one hundred fifty thousand offices nationwide. Tom West, president of International Business Brokers Association, and publisher of *The Business Broker Newsletter,* estimates fewer than three thousand full-time brokers hang their shingles across the country.

But the money that changes hands in business sales is enormous. Compared with real estate, which counts $250 billion in annual sales, all business transfers (including those not sold through brokers) generate $300 billion. Estimates on the number of brokered businesses vary widely, but Tom West guesses between 25 and 50 percent of company sales are handled by brokers. And another thing: business brokers command 10- to 14-percent commissions, compared to 6- to 7-percent realtor fees. They still occupy a relatively new niche, however. "One of the biggest negatives we face is people not knowing what business brokerage is," says Leonard Ostroff, who opened The Ostroff Group in Cherry Hill, New Jersey, in 1981. "I'm looking forward to more competition to help get the word out."

AN OPPORTUNITY FOR PROFESSIONALS

Len Ostroff talked with numerous brokers while shopping for a business he planned to finance with severance pay from a chemical engineering position. He found a wide range of ability among brokers, some of whom he deemed unprofessional. "I had all that money on the line," he grimaces, "and no confidence in the brokers I dealt with. There was a real need for somebody to do it right." Len believed he understood how to structure deals that would please both buyer and seller. So, instead of plowing his cash into a buyout of his own, he opened a small office and began brokering.

While they don't necessarily recommend such a seat-of-the-pants approach, Frank and Robert Contaldo managed to get their start without even an office. In 1980, after selling their chain of three restaurants themselves when they became disillusioned with the brokers they contacted, the brothers launched a VR Business Broker franchise they call Bantam Investments Group. With their cars doubling as offices and a part-time employee to answer their home phones, they pounded pavements in search of sellers. They knocked on doors of pizza shops and clothing stores, asking entrepreneurs if they might consider selling. Once they lined up sellers, they advertised those businesses in newspapers.

Half a dozen years later, with eight salespeople ensconced in comfortable digs in the tiny Chicago suburb of Elk Grove, Bantam now sells more dry cleaners and pet shops than any broker in the VR network. With more than three hundred units operating in 1987, the VR parent company, based in Needham, Massachusetts, is the largest franchisor in an industry that is nearly 30 percent franchised.

HALF A MILLION

On the upside, the top brokerages draw annual commissions in the $500,000 ballpark, says Tom West, who founded United Business Investments a generation ago and served as president of VR before starting *The Business Broker Newsletter* in 1984. That top-of-the-line brokerage might split commissions fifty-fifty with salespeople, and deduct overhead of about $5,000 a month. That leaves the boss $190,000 as profit—more if he or she brokers some sales personally. For instance, Len Ostroff himself generated two-thirds of the $300,000 The Ostroff Group achieved in gross commissions in 1986.

While the majority of brokerages are two-or-three-people shops, the trend is toward multiple offices. Regardless of the number of storefronts, the owner collects half of all fees, so expansion is a nice plan for those who can manage from afar. For example, Ian Mac-Lachlan opened Business Team Inc. in San Jose in 1982, and added two more California offices by 1987, for total gross sales of $12 million and $1 million in commissions, making his company, according to Ian, one of the largest in the country.

THE BIG ONE

Tom West calls the business brokerage field seductive. Even when prospects seem low, brokers stay in business for the same reason people fish: There's always the possibility they'll hook the big one . . . the deal just around the corner with a $400,000 commission. Allowing that such deals occur, Tom advises firms that don't break into the black within a year or so to reassess. "This is not a business where persistence always pays off," he says.

Nevertheless, don't give up on the challenges. Len Ostroff reports he sees some pretty weird businesses. "You listen to twenty buyers and think it will never sell," he says. "Then somebody comes in and says, 'I'd love to have that business.' "

YOUR RESUME

Those in the business have a hard time delineating exactly what prepares a person for brokerage. Seventeen states require real estate licenses, but a several-month-long course takes care of that stumbling block. A couple of organizations provide training and support services for fees around $20,000. Structured Approaches International, Frank Covich's outfit, specializes in making brokers out of financial planners, who Frank says are already comfortable with numbers. While franchises have no product to sell other than a few weeks of training, some forms, and referral networks, Ian MacLachlan advises those truly unfamiliar with brokerage to buy a franchise. "Some training is better than none at all," he says. He also argues that, since some franchise names carry credibility, you could attract commission-paying customers more quickly than with a sign that reads "John Smith Brokerage." But franchising gets to be expensive if you get too successful. "You don't want to give away another 6 to 8 percent of your commissions as a franchise fee," says Ian.

Len Ostroff offers would-be brokers the same advice he gives buyers who ask him to find a business in any other field: Go work for an established brokerage before flying solo.

CHARACTER

Good brokers generally share certain character traits. Chief among them:

▪ They understand numbers and the law as they apply to business sales. "You have to be able to read a P&L statement—and know that it stands for 'Pretend & Lie,' not 'Profit & Loss,' " says Frank Contaldo.

• They are good salespeople. Much of a broker's time revolves around selling buyers on the merits of particular businesses—and convincing owners to sell.

• Brokers are good negotiators. "You have to deal forcefully with attorneys, accountants, buyers, and sellers," says Tom West.

• They are empathetic. "Somebody wrote a list of the ten most traumatic events in life, and retirement ranked second," says Len Ostroff. "Consider you represent an entrepreneur who built a business over fifteen years. He doesn't want the wrong person to take over his baby, and, if you can't justify divesting, he'll never, ever sell."

Finding all these requisites in an employee may rank on the probability scale with finding oil in your backyard, especially considering just a handful of schools offer courses in business brokerage. "Because it's a growth industry, we don't have a large pool of experienced people to draw from," explains Ian MacLachlan. His solution includes ex-CPAs, ex-bankers, and ex-business owners whom he trains in-house. Following the industry norm, all forty of Ian's people operate on a strictly commission basis, which holds down operating costs since you don't have to budget salaries. "We operate more on a partnership basis than as employer/employee," says Ian.

IT COMES DOWN TO SELLING

Clients fall into two groups: buyers and sellers. Referrals from attorneys and accountants make up sizable portions of both, but you'll spend a great deal of effort coming up with prospects. To track down sellers, "walk, talk, knock, and sell," counsels Frank Contaldo. Although he sees a trend toward telemarketing, Tom West agrees "there's nothing like going to talk to the small-business community. When it's snowing outside, that business owner remembers you when he thinks about chucking it all and moving to Florida."

Lure buyers aboard the easy way: Simply advertise the properties you have to sell. If the particular convenience store they targeted doesn't work out, chances are you have another prospect that might. If not, you can subscribe to business-listing services to come up with likely properties. For a fee, listing networks provide names of franchise and private companies for sale all over the country. In less formal arrangements, brokers who provide leads to colleagues generally split fees.

Most brokers charge 10- to 12-percent commissions, payable by the seller, with $4,000 to $10,000 minimums for smaller transactions. In 1986, Tom West said the average sale involved a $125,000 business. Additionally, many brokers handle deals worth millions. "We call them mergers and acquisitions, but it's really the same thing," says Ian MacLachlan. Like many of his colleagues, he is shopping more large deals. "There's truth to the old argument 'There's no more work in putting together a big deal than a small one,' " says Tom West. And, a solid, larger business with better records may be an easier sale. But the best part: The commissions are higher.

MAKING MATCHES

Ian MacLachlan finds that about four months will have elapsed between getting a listing and closing the sale. But that's an average. Some listings stay on your files for eighteen months, while others sell before you complete the paperwork, particularly if you have a ready stable of buyers. Although Ian concentrates on California sellers, Business Team works buyers all over the country, spending $5,000 a month to advertise in *The Wall Street Journal* as well as local newspapers. For large sales, some brokers contact competitors in a given industry who might buy the particular business they have on the block as a way to expand.

THE PERFECT FIT

According to Tom West, 90 percent of buyers who use brokers are first-time owners with zero idea of what particular business they want. The broker becomes an analyst who delves into a buyer's personality in order to find the perfect fit. "People make decisions emotionally," says Tom, based on the type of life style and environment they want rather than on how much money they can make. For example, because you like gardening you might prefer a flower shop even though you could make more money in a computer-repair business. Tom recalls the client who answered an ad for a liquor store. "The salesperson found he had six dogs and sold him two pet shops instead."

Frank Contaldo profiles buyers using interview forms made up of fifteen to twenty questions. "We ask why they want to buy a business, who will run it, what are their interests." How much money buyers have in hand ranks close to the bottom of Frank's list. "The only way we handle sales is through seller financing," he insists. The buyer puts 25 to 40 percent down, and the seller takes the rest in monthly installments that the buyer meets through his new business's cash flow. Buyers like seller financing because they can afford better deals. "The seller makes a lot of money, because he is paid interest," says Frank.

TRENDS

Business brokers predict some fine-tuning of their industry as it matures. The larger acquisitions that brokers now target are attracting large, established real estate and financial specialists. Len Ostroff, for one, happily anticipates this particular trend. "When I'm ready to sell, they'll be ready to buy me out," he grins.

In addition, brokers are becoming both more specialized and more diverse. For example, some are signing up to represent particular franchisors. Others are narrowing their scope to unique niches, such as country inns or professional practices, but aiming for buyers and sellers across the country.

Most of all, business brokerage is becoming more professional. "Five years ago, there was more of a used-car atmosphere," says Ian MacLachlan. "A more professional breed of people are coming in, systematizing the business."

SOURCES

Industry Associations

International Business Brokers Association, P.O. Box 247, Concord, Mass. 01742 (617) 369-5254

Institute of Certified Business Counselors, P.O. Box 30695, Walnut Creek, Calif. 94598 (415) 945-8440

Publication

The Business Broker Newsletter, P.O. Box 247, Concord, Mass. 01742 (617) 369-5254

Consultants/Certification Groups

Interstate Companies, P.O. Box 2008, Myrtle Beach, S.C. 29578 (800) 527-5056

Structured Approaches International, 1225 River Rd., Suite 2D, Edgewater, N.J. 07020 (201) 886-7345

Business Centers of America, 1940 E. Camelback Rd., Phoenix, Ariz. 85016 (602) 277-4991

Referral/Listing Services

National Association of Independent Business Brokers, 120 Mountain Ave., Bloomfield, Conn. 06002 (203) 243-1125

Franchise Broker Network, 3617A Silverside Rd., Wilmington, Del. 19810 (302) 478-0200

Nation-List Headquarters, 1660 S. Albion St., No. 407, Denver, Colo. 80222 (303) 759-5267

Career Counselor

> *"I get vicarious pleasure through my clients' successes. I have the privilege of living all kinds of different careers through them." – Susanne Parente, Susanne Parente Associates*

Low Startup Investment: $2,000 (home-based)

High Startup Investment: $15,000 (office with clerical help)

Time Until Breakeven: Six weeks to two years

Annual Revenues: $60,000 (solo)-$500,000 (solo at low end, with associates at high end)

Annual Pre-tax Profits: $50,000-$100,000

Staffers Needed for Startup (including founder): One

"If you think of your father, chances are he joined a corporation and collected a gold watch when he retired forty years later," observes Betsy Harrison, president of Career Development Corporation, Rochester, New York. "But our generation places more value on self-worth and challenge—which means we change jobs relatively frequently. Meanwhile, the corporation no longer can guarantee lifetime jobs. These two forces have absolutely turned society upside down." And, in the process, created a whole new field: career counseling.

Catalyst, a New York City–based network of counselors, considers career counseling a three-step process:

▪ Self-evaluation, in which the counselor helps a client evaluate skills, aptitudes, and interests through tests and discussion.

▪ Research into occupations and careers.

▪ Preparation for job hunting, including framing the résumé and honing interview skills.

In addition, some centers steer clients to industry contacts and even provide access to job listings.

But don't confuse career counseling with employment agencies. "We don't promise a job, even though we have a 98-percent success ratio," says Susanne Parente, president of the firm bearing her name in Westfield, New Jersey. "We're here to help identify goals and directions."

WHO NEEDS YOU?

Two types of clients pay your bills: individuals and corporations. "Individuals are primarily professionals making a mid-life career switch, people entering retirement, students right out of college, and women returning to the work force," says Jennifer Kahnweiler, of Kahnweiler Associates, a 1986 Cincinnati startup. For individuals considering plunging into a new career, Jennifer combines counseling with aptitude tests to help the client decide which avenues to pursue. Then her staff researches the industry to give clients answers to questions they need to get started. What is a typical day like? What skills do you need? What money can you expect? Who can you contact to tell you more? Who are the prospective employers in this part of the country?

Career counselors command anywhere from $50 to $100 an hour to point individuals in the right direction. Unless the situation teems with some special problems, figure on spending four to eight hour-long sessions with each client.

Corporations provide bigger bucks than individuals because they buy $1,000 to $2,000 seminars for a group of employees, or they put you on retainer to help a more-or-less steady stream of employees. In a seminar setting, you might talk with employees when layoffs are inevitable. Topics include how to write résumés or deal with the depression that typically accompanies the pink slip. The corporation also may pay you to tackle career problems for individuals, particularly in two areas: outplacement (or helping laid-off employees adjust and find a new job) and spouse relocation (or helping the spouse of a new employee find work in the area). In spouse relocation, you may still be paid by the hour, but many outplacement counselors ask for 15 percent of the employee's last annual salary.

OUTPLACEMENT

Fired or laid-off employees typically have suffered emotional wear-and-tear that counselors address before launching a job search. "People need to understand their anger or frustration," says Jennifer Kahnweiler, who counts a psychologist among the associates at Kahnweiler Associates. "People who lose jobs often feel a loss of identity," nods Sue Parente. "We help them put things in perspective. We help them realize they're performing a function—they are not their job."

Such delicate advising explains why the industry's professional societies and the approximately eighteen states that require a license say you need a master's degree in counseling psychology in order to call yourself a career counselor.

After you've made what Sue Parente calls "the warm and fuzzy" psychological approaches, you counsel former employees the same way you do others who question their careers. Take spouses, for instance.

TRAILING SPOUSES

In 1985, 28 percent of companies responding to a study conducted by Merrill Lynch provided some sort of spouse relocation. With the growing number of dual-career couples, "even those companies that don't offer spouse relocation know that in the future they will have to make it attractive to spouses if they want to move their employees," says Jennifer Kahnweiler. For that reason, she follows up six months after firms turn down her first get-acquainted calls.

To attract corporate clients, call on those employers in town who are branches of large corporations that tend to transfer employees. Jennifer watches the newspapers to see which firms are relocating to Cincinnati. Then she sends the personnel department letters along with a brochure explaining her company, recommendations from other clients, and even articles about the career counseling industry. "The field is so new, we still have to do a lot of education on what career counselors actually do," she explains.

The career counselor helps the spouse of the transferred employee with résumé writing, interview skills, and the task of identifying contacts in the new town. Some get involved in relocation counseling (see Relocation Consultant). Career counselors place a high value on networking. "We put clients in touch with individuals who know a lot about a field," explains Jennifer. "The President of Women in Communications might know which Cincinnati companies are good to work for in the journalism field, for example." She says most people are surprisingly willing to take time away from busy schedules to chat about their areas of expertise. They're flattered that you value their experience enough to ask their advice.

In addition, counseling firms introduce clients directly to employers. Kahnweiler Associates maintains a data base that lists area employers and the skills each looks for. Susanne Parente establishes formal working relationships with particular employers and employment agencies who expect to see résumés she pre-screens. "They're happy to get résumés from me because we don't charge them a fee."

BUILD AN IMAGE

Some career counselors start from a home office, particularly if they conduct seminars on many corporations' facilities. But you'll probably want to move into an office as soon as you can afford one so you can see individuals more comfortably. Jennifer Kahnweiler rented an executive suite where she had access to clerical help who type client résumés. "We felt we needed premium space to project a professional image, particularly to corporate clients," says Jennifer. She hired an artist to design a logo, letterhead, and brochures.

As you grow, you'll need additional counselors. Jennifer subcontracts with five independents rather than putting them on salary. That way, she only pays them when she needs them to handle the client load.

Income for solo practitioners generally tops out around $60,000, because fees for the most part are hourly. While that's certainly not bad, you can make more by running some group sessions, which pay more than one-on-one counseling. But career counselors expect even more opportunity in the future. "Within five years, anyone who's starting now will have a booming business," predicts Sue Parente. "This is particularly true because we're seeing a marked increase in the number of men who relocate when their wives take transfers. They're increasingly asking for spouse location as a legitimate demand. It's a sad comment on society, but maybe because they're men, they get it."

SOURCES

Industry Associations

American Association for Counseling and Development, 5999 Stevenson Ave., Alexandria, Va. 22304 (703) 823-9800

Catalyst, 250 Park Ave. S., New York, N.Y. 10003 (212) 777-8900

Janitorial Service

> *"Contract cleaning is a very easy business to get into. After the first few years, I had a very high income and was interesting enough to attract a foreign investor." – Gary Penrod, Hawley Group*

Low Startup Investment: $4,000 (solo operator)

High Startup Investment: $75,000 (buying a small operation or starting with a half dozen employees)

Time Until Breakeven: One month to two years

Annual Revenues: $50,000-$15 million (one-person operation at low end, regional contractor at high end)

Annual Pre-tax Profits: $35,000-$1.5 million

Staffers Needed for Startup (including founder): One

A large interstate chemical conglomerate asked Gary Penrod, a former high school English teacher, to figure out why turnover was so high and the results so inadequate in the company's in-house cleaning department. We're talking hundreds of thousands of square feet of office and industrial space that a couple hundred employees cleaned every night, so the stakes were high. That assignment changed Gary's life. "I went in with the crews at night. I found people with a second grade education who were illiterate and knew they had no chance of advancement. There was no upward mobility for these people." It was hardly shocking they couldn't work up enthusiasm for pushing a broom the rest of their lives.

Gary Penrod made two recommendations: Bring in educational consultants to teach the cleaners how to read; or disband the in-house janitorial crews in favor of outside contractors whose business involves dealing with constant turnover and low motivation.

THE MILLIONAIRE JANITOR

Gary made those recommendations in the late 1960s. In 1970, he borrowed $3,700 for equipment and payroll and "listened to my own advice. I started a contract cleaning company." Although it took him a few years to hook his former employer as a client, Gary offered office cleaning services in two states within the first year. By 1984, his Building Service Industries, Wilmington, Delaware, grossed $12 million and employed sixteen hundred in eight states as far flung as New York and Texas. That was the year Gary sold the company to a British group for a figure "in excess of $3 million." He also stayed on to help the new owners acquire similar contract cleaning services throughout the U.S.

The Building Service Contractors Association International says to expect janitorial services to grow faster than just about any other business sector during the next ten years. The U.S. Department of Labor predicts a 15.1 percent increase in janitors between 1987 and 1995, when the total will hit 3.38 million. Not only are there more buildings to clean, but more of them are being cleaned by professionals. The association reveals that businesses spent $45 billion in 1986 on day-to-day cleaning chores. And outside contractors claimed 30 percent of the market. "The bankers and chemical producers who are our clients don't want to deal with the problems" inherent in the cleaning industry, says Gary Penrod. But one company's poison is another's opportunity.

A SLUSH FUND

If you plan to start with several contracts, you'll need equipment, marketing, an office, and payroll. (Traditionally, contractors bill on the last day of the month, so plan on meeting weekly payrolls before you ever see a dime of reimbursement.) To do it right, industry experts recommend $50,000 in seed capital and a similar line-of-credit to help you grow. Most of that goes for buying heavy-duty cleaning implements. You can also buy existing contractors for about 40 to 50 percent of their annual revenues.

But you can start for less if you're willing to grow slowly; namely, do all the cleaning and marketing yourself, using a home-based office. Some individuals even start part time, hanging on to daytime jobs and cleaning at night. "I wouldn't rule out what I and hundreds of others did—start with virtually no cash and hang on to make a company work," says Gary Penrod. Indeed, *Venture Magazine* ranked four janitorial companies among the ten cheapest franchises on its 1986 Franchisor 100 list. Franchises start at $3,600 —and many franchisors provide financing. Several even throw in a few contracts to get you started.

In fact, profits are best in those early days because your only expenses involve lining up contracts and buying the supplies and equipment you need to clean. Some franchisees claim one-person outfits net 70 percent of sales (not counting the owner's salary). But you're limited to the few jobs one person can do, so annual revenues may hover around the $50,000 mark. To expand, add another cleaner, which immediately cuts profits in half. Put on a few staffers and you'll need supervisors, office space, possibly a warehouse, and a sales force to sustain the whole bunch, which explains why the bigger companies are thrilled to pocket $1 out of every $10.

A CLEAN SWEEP

To boost those margins, many contractors add other services, ranging from carpet dying to parking lot maintenance. Not only will the additional services improve your bottom line, but many clients like "one-stop shopping." If you clean draperies twice a year, they won't have to hire an outside service. If your supervisor checks the factory's gauges when the plant is closed on weekends, the client won't have to pay an employee to perform that chore.

While you can certainly advertise in the "Business Services" listings of newspaper want ads and in the Yellow Pages, the spoils usually go to the aggressive. "I used to take Sunday afternoon rides looking for real estate signs announcing new buildings, then call on the landlords," recalls Gary Penrod. In other words, dig up potential clients and ask to bid on their cleaning contract.

Make the proposal professional. You might call a building's contractor to learn what materials it contains. Then contact the chemical manufacturer to find the best way to maintain that particular llama-wool-blend carpeting. Show off your expertise by stating how you plan to care for a client's computer room. If you run across a company that does its own cleaning, point out you may be able to polish floors and dust word processors for less than an in-house cleaner because you have trained personnel and buy supplies in bulk.

Once you quit vacuuming yourself, expect labor to eat up about 55 cents of every dollar you bring in. Really efficient firms in non-union areas usually bid around 60 cents a square foot per year. But before bidding, check out all the variables. "It takes longer to clean ten thousand square feet where five hundred people work than the same space with two hundred people," says Gary Penrod. "Also, determine if the space is carpeted, how old it is, and how it's heated and air conditioned. Are you dealing with an insurance office where you'll have to pick lots of staples off the floor or an executive suite that's basically clean?"

REVOLVING DOOR SYNDROME

Expect your biggest headache to be employee turnover—200 to 300 percent a year isn't unusual. Cleaning personnel often are transients—students or their parents who quit as soon as school is paid for. Few people see janitorial work as a career, so they lose nothing by quitting when another opportunity arises. "Nobody aspires to be a cleaner," recognizes Gary Penrod. "That's not so much a problem as a fact." The turnover is the reason corporations gave up in-house cleaning in the first place, remember?

You may hold on to people longer if you pay above minimum wage and train for advancement. Recruit employees by offering to transport crews to outlying corporate parks that are far from most employee's homes. Some companies praise the loyalty of handicapped and older workers.

High technology may eventually change the way we clean our businesses. Robots already sweep a few Japanese factories. The steam jets that hospitals use to sterilize operating rooms could be adapted for scouring bathrooms. But those solutions are probably years away from large-scale implementation. Meanwhile, there's still time for entrepreneurs to apply some elbow grease.

SOURCES

Industry Association

Building Service Contractors Association International, 8315 Lee Highway, Suite 301, Fairfax, VA. 22031
(800) 368-3414

Publications

Services, 8315 Lee Highway, Suite 301, Fairfax, Va. 22031
(800) 368-3414
Building Services Contractor, 101 W. 31st St., New York, N.Y. 10001
(212) 279-4455
Sanitary Maintenance Magazine, 183 Madison Ave., New York, N.Y. 10016 (212) 685-6010

Management Consultant

> *"There's a saying: Once a consultant, always a consultant. People who leave the business come back. They've tasted a life that can't be reproduced any other way."* —John Hartshorne, Institute of Management Consultants

---

Low Startup Investment: $500 (working for existing clients)

High Startup Investment: $5,000 (office and advertising)

Time Until Breakeven: Immediate to one year

Annual Revenues: $50,000-$250,000

Annual Pre-tax Profits: $40,000-$200,000

Staffers Needed for Startup (including founder): One

Three consultants are standing on a street corner when a man stops to ask the time. The first consultant answers, "Do you want it in Eastern Standard or Greenwich Mean?" "What time do you want it to be?" asks the second. The third consultant borrows the man's watch before quoting him the exact time.

INFORMATION IS YOUR RAW MATERIAL

Perhaps a profession has really arrived when it's large enough to have insider jokes. ACME, an industry trade association, estimates sixty thousand management consultants practiced in 1986—compared with just forty-five thousand two years before. Counting consultants of all sorts (including management consultants) Howard L. Shenson, who calls himself "a consultant to consultants," says four hundred thousand individuals doled out advice-for-pay in 1986, including between one hundred twenty-five and one hundred fifty thousand part-timers. He sees no reason why a breathtaking 22-percent annual growth rate shouldn't continue over the next couple of decades.

Why such growth? Today's corporations buy outside expertise as an accepted part of doing business. In some cases, companies that slashed staffs during the recessionary early 1980s decided to stay lean; instead of staffing to middle-management capacity, they hire occasional consultants for special projects and troubleshooting.

As the economy is now based on services, not manufacturing, information has surpassed capital as the most important ingredient for business success. As a consultant, information is your raw material.

LOW ENTRY, HIGH POTENTIAL

Finally, consulting is a growth industry because so many people want to consult—and it's one of the easiest fields to enter. All you really need is expertise and enough savings to pay for the groceries until fees start coming in. "It's wasteful to have a separate office," says James H. Kennedy, editor of *Consultants News*. "Working from your home is not only acceptable, it's become trendy," adds Howard Shenson, who notes that clients expect consultants to visit their offices anyway. Even if you want a secretary, computer, and office, figure on spending $5,000 instead of maybe $500 for a home-based solo operation.

Also, subcontracting with other consulting firms represents a popular entry route. The client hires you through an established firm, which pays you a fee as an independent contractor. You are in demand either because of your special expertise or because you complement their already overburdened staff. The seasoned consultants oversee your work while you hone skills and make contacts. Subcontracting arrangements also free you from the sometimes dreary task of marketing.

If you do well, the business is good for the ego. Says John F. Hartshorne, executive director of the Institute of Management Consultants: "There is a satisfaction in solving complex problems and seeing situations turn better for your clients." Where else does the ego get such stroking? Heads of corporations pay handsomely for your insights. According to surveys performed by Howard

Shenson's newsletter, *The Professional Consultant & Seminar Business Report*, the average consultant bills $856 *a day*.

There's no question: The leafy part of the carrot is green. John Hartshorne says high-powered executives who move into consulting can match their previous level of income, at the very least, and many do far, far better. "$50,000 is a floor," adds Jim Kennedy. Howard Shenson supports Jim's claim, figuring the typical consultant clears just over $86,000 a year before taxes but after deducting business expenses.

YOUR FIRST CLIENT: YOURSELF

Your first consulting job should be for the face you see in the mirror. "Do a self-audit," says Jim Kennedy. "Is your knowledge industry-specific, or do you have functional knowledge? In other words, do you know the fast food business, or are you a treasurer who could work as well in a bank as in a fast food restaurant?" Your answers will steer you to provide the right types of services for the right kinds of clients.

Aside from expertise in your chosen area, you should possess good communication skills. An MBA isn't essential, but some sort of graduate degree looks good on a résumé, and management experience is necessary. A job often boils down to problem solving— taking apart a teaser and putting it back together in a new way, or extracting new meaning from old information. Consultants are the kind of people who like crossword puzzles.

Even though most experts counsel you to start your consultancy by drawing up a business plan, Howard Shenson suspects up to one-third of management consultants skip over this important step. "People don't grow up thinking, 'I'm going to be a consultant.' Typically they are asked to consult while they're employed and find that it's psychologically and financially rewarding." While such a haphazard approach may bring in extra bucks while you're on another job, take a more serious approach if you make a full-time commitment to consulting. Write down your strengths and goals— and update them regularly.

While Howard Shenson's research suggests four out of every ten consultants start part time, he also speaks from experience in this regard. In 1969, he was teaching management and applied economics at California State University in Northridge. After a couple of moonlight assignments, Howard launched a full-time practice from a spare bedroom in his home. Two years later, he managed fifteen consultants, when a new specialty reared its soon-to-be beautiful head. "People began to ask me how to get into consulting," he recalls. So he developed a seminar on the subject, and decided that consulting on consulting was a lucrative niche. He returned to solo practice, thereby giving up the headaches of overseeing other people's work. By 1986, Howard had presented either his one-day $95 program, or his two-day $485 workshop to fifty thousand people, not to mention having generated additional income from books, newsletters, and lectures.

MARKETING

John Hartshorne suggests approaching your own boss before you quit to give you at least one rent-paying customer. Jim Kennedy vividly recalls when he was fired on Decoration Day, 1957. "My employer said, in lieu of severance, we'll give you $50 a day for the next two months to consult." Such an arrangment may be a cheap way to get out of severance pay. But the situation benefits the new consultant as well, since each assignment provides credibility when approaching new clients.

Before grabbing helter-skelter for clients, consider your most likely prospects. For example, don't bother approaching the Fortune 500. "Large companies look for name brands and won't hire solos," says Jim Kennedy. "If something goes wrong, the purchasing authority wants to say he got the leading authority in the field." (Although solo practitioners make up the backbone of the management consulting field, bigtimers play as well. Chicago-based Arthur Andersen & Co. employed 6,450 professionals in 1985, generating worldwide consulting revenues of nearly half a billion dollars.)

Mom-and-pop companies aren't a good bet either. "They can't afford you," says Jim Kennedy. Instead, expect most of your clients to be medium-sized companies.

Next, consider geography. Even if you're willing to eat a lot of airline food, travel is expensive and time consuming. At least in the beginning, limit your clients to an affordable radius.

Once you identify a likely client group, become known to the right people. Direct mail of classy-looking brochures followed up by telephone calls can't hurt. But it helps if the client knows your name in advance and, in fact, "holds you a little in awe," says Howard Shenson, who advises consultants to develop an image. Image building comes through visibility: lecture before the Kiwanis Club or the National Hardware Association; write articles for *Byte* magazine or *Inc.*

Even after you line up a client, the road show still goes on. "Unlike the law, for example, where [steady clients provide] work on a retainer basis, your commitment is to complete a project," warns John Hartshorne. "You have to generate additional business to carry you after the first project is long finished." Once a project is completed, however, extend your usefulness—and your client's fee—by offering to tackle new projects for the same company.

SPIN-OFFS

As a consultant, you're not limited to on-the-job consulting, however. Howard Shenson sees "informational products" (a/k/a books, lectures for which you receive a fee, and newsletters) as excellent marketing tools as well as great income builders. "A consultant is like a dentist," he says. "The moment a dentist stops filling and drilling, he has to stop billing. Products like books provide an income even when consultants are not consulting."

If you ever decide to get out of the seminar business, Howard says you can make three to five times your seminar's net annual profit by selling to a publishing or seminar company. "In other words, if you net $75,000 a year, you might sell for $225,000 to $375,000."

SOURCES

Industry Associations

ACME Inc., 230 Park Ave., New York, N.Y. 10169
   (212) 697-9693
Institute of Management Consultants Inc., 19 W. 44th St.,
   New York, N.Y. 10036 (212) 921-2885

Association of Management Consultants Inc., 500 N. Michigan
    Ave., Suite 1400, Chicago, Ill. 60611 (312) 266-1261
Society of Professional Management Consultants, 163 Engle St.,
    Englewood, N.J. 07631 (201) 569-6668

Publications

Consultants News, Templeton Rd., Fitzwilliam, N.H. 03447
    (603) 585-2200
Consulting Opportunities Journal, 5000 Kaetzel Rd.,
    Capland, Md. 21736 (301) 432-4242
The Professional Consultant & Seminar Business Report,
    20750 Ventura Blvd., Suite 206,
    Woodland Hills, Calif. 91364 (818) 703-1415

Consultants

Howard L. Shenson, 20750 Ventura Blvd., Suite 206,
    Woodland Hills, Calif. 91364 (818) 703-1415
Hubert Bermont, P.O. Box 309, Glenelg, Md. 21737
    (301) 531-3560
The Consultants Brokerage, Box 4604, Mountain View, Calif.
    94040 (415) 964-2929
Consultants National Resource Center, 5000 Kaetzel Rd.,
    Capland, Md. 21736 (301) 432-4242

Meeting Planner

> *"Although you work on a meeting for a year, the response time for gratification is short between the actual event and the Monday night reviews. You know when you have a hit."* – Carl Mischka, CEM Enterprises

---

Low Startup Investment: $5,000 (solo, operating from home)

High Startup Investment: $25,000 (with an associate, from an office)

Time Until Breakeven: Three months to one year

Annual Revenues: $90,000-$5 million (large firm)

Annual Pre-tax Profits: $70,000-$500,000 (large firm)

Staffers Needed for Startup (including founder): One

MEETING PLANNER SCENE 1:

You've just breakfasted on the balcony of the resort hotel where you booked your client's Caribbean meeting. Soft breezes stir the notes you've made detailing which seminar speakers agreed to attend. You reach for the phone; the skipper of the schooner that you're considering for an evening cruise during the three-day conference invites you to come to the harbor after your appointment with the caterer. Speaking of the caterer, you decide to switch that clams casino order to shrimp cocktail for the opening cocktail party.

MEETING PLANNER SCENE 2:

Another hotel room, another city. This time it's Chicago in February, and you're on the phone negotiating with a limo service to pick up conventioneers stranded at the airport by the taxi strike. Of course, if the blizzard arrives, ground transportation won't matter since O'Hare will close anyway. That may be just as well, since the convention hall says your booking begins Thursday—not tomorrow as you told attendees.

Is the life of a meeting planner glamorous? You bet. You stay in the best hotels and eat at fancy restaurants. All the vendors lavish you with VIP treatment because they want your clients' business. It's no wonder that you're popular: A survey of the forty-five hundred members of Meeting Planners International, the industry trade group, indicated planners directed over $4 billion in meeting-related expenditures during a one-year period ended in July 1986.

Is the life of a meeting planner stressful? To say the least. You're at the mercy of catastrophes you can't control, like weather and personalities. That doesn't count those glitches that are worth worrying over because human error can creep in—like making sure two thousand attendees' name tags are spelled correctly.

"Meeting planning is a lot more complicated than planning a wedding or party," warns Carl E. Mischka, who runs CEM Enterprises from his Newport Beach, California, home. "A meeting planner is like the conductor of an orchestra who also composed the piece." And that's just one symphony. Meeting planners typically work on several projects simultaneously. Respondents to the Meeting Planners International survey planned an average of forty-six meetings a year. Some larger firms coped with two thousand.

JOB DESCRIPTION

What does a meeting planner actually do? Everything depends on the clients' needs and your own specialties. But here's a sampling from a much longer laundry list of meeting-planner functions compiled by The Convention Liaison Council:

- Establish meeting design and objectives.
- Select and negotiate with site and facilities.
- Budget.
- Handle housing and transportation.
- Plan the program.
- Establish registration procedures.
- Manage exhibits.
- Manage food and beverage.
- Select speakers.

- Schedule promotion and publicity.
- Produce and print meeting materials.

You might plan everything from educational seminars for five hundred to a twenty-member board meeting to an international junket for a franchise group. Carl Mischka offers a number of planning services at CEM (an abbreviation which, coincidentally, works equally well for "Conferences/Events/Meetings" as it does for Carl's initials). "Sometimes we do everything including program design, or sometimes just site selection," says Carl, who started CEM in 1982 after stints planning numerous meetings for a textbook publisher he worked for and then publishing the now-defunct *Meeting Site Selector* magazine. In addition to managing client events that attract from twenty-five people to twenty-five hundred, he also produces his own trade show—for meeting planners, no less. Typically, the client pays a planner to manage an event, but Carl puts up his own capital for the meeting-planner trade show, which he recovers from exhibit fees. (For an in-depth look at trade show producers, see Trade Show.)

Some planners specialize in particular functions, like registration or publicity, while others concentrate on specific industries or a particular region. One Nashville-based planner, for example, offers convention services to meetings booked in her city. After all, what out-of-towner knows the area sights and services better than a native? She collects referrals from the chamber of commerce, convention bureau, and hotels.

Those planners who tackle just one particular industry usually branch out over time as a contact in one field recommends them to a colleague in another area. For example, planners who started organizing computer-company events because they know the industry's arcane jargon, might soon offer their services to the artificial intelligence community. If you manage three large meetings for $25,000 each every year, you've got a good living wage. Add on special services, like audio/visual presentations and market-research projects for your industry niche, and income moves into six figures.

CLIENT HUNTING

There are two paths to signing up meetings to plan: through others in the industry or directly through your own clients. Most planners are one-to-five person firms, and often subcontract when they're overloaded or a job requires some special skills. So let competitors and in-house meeting planners know your areas of expertise. Also, talk with convention and hotel managers and ask for referrals. In the beginning, you might offer to handle limited functions—just junkets for spouses whose partners are attending the trade show, for example.

But once you have a track record, you'll probably want the income that comes from developing your own major accounts. Telemarketing and direct mail set the stage for in-person interviews, followed by formal proposals. Call on groups who mount their own meetings and try to interest them in farming out duties. Some presentations require elaborate audio/visual or slide shows and four-color brochures, so you might want to set aside some capital for marketing.

If both you and the client remain interested after the get-acquainted session, next comes the formal proposal. Depending on the complexity of the meeting, the number of functions you'll take on, and the budget at stake, proposals range from a couple of pages to a twenty-page thesis. Here, you detail your plans, including exactly what you'll do for the client and what duties the client will keep in-house.

Meeting planners ideally like twelve months to pull together a large meeting. Like everything else, a meeting is easier the second time around because you learn the personalities and industry. If you pitch an annual event, write a renewable clause into your contract that gives you a shot at producing the event next year.

The client will expect you to bring in the meeting on budget, which means you negotiate down such items as hotel space and transportation. Some planners take commissions from airlines, hotels, and ground transport, which allows them to hold down their own fees to the client. Other planners argue that the practice creates a conflict of interest and take fees only from the client. At any rate, "After the negotiations, you need a good working relationship with vendors," says Carl Mischka. "Then everybody has the same client and goal: to make the meeting work."

OUTSIDERS WITH CLOUT

You can still get paid while you train by handling meetings on staff at a large corporation. But meeting planning is evolving from an in-house function to a field dominated by entrepreneurs. Increasingly, big business, trade groups, and professional societies are turning to outside professional meeting planners, which creates a lot of opportunities for you to hang your own shingle.

The switch away from in-house meeting planning partially involves economics. In addition to fees to hotels, convention centers, transportation companies, and the like, which the client fronts, a typical New York planner charges $25,000 (sometimes paid in installments during the planning process) to set up a three-day convention. Others take a percentage of the gate, if we're talking about a for-profit trade show, on top of a flat fee. Even so, those groups that once carried a planner on staff say it's cheaper to contract with a planner once or twice a year than to pay a staffer's full-time salary and benefits.

But corporations are jumping out of the meeting planning business for another reason. Executives are recognizing that meeting planning requires a whole stable full of skills that professionals handle better than someone who doesn't plan meetings for a living. As meeting planning moves from a field of part-time dabblers to full-time professionals, and as more meetings are called every year, opportunities look bright—if you don't mind taking Chicago in February along with Caribbean breezes.

SOURCES

Industry Associations

Meeting Planners International, INFOMART, 1950 Stemmons Freeway, Dallas, Tex. 75207 (214) 746-5224
Local Chapters, MPI

Convention Liaison Council, 1575 Eye Street, Suite 1200,
Washington, D.C. 20005 (202) 626-2764

Publications

The Meeting Manager, INFOMART, 1950 Stemmons Freeway,
Dallas, Tex. 75207 (214) 746-5224

Meetings & Conventions, 1 Park Ave., New York, N.Y. 10016
(212) 503-5700

Successful Meetings, 633 3rd Ave., New York, N.Y. 10017
(212) 986-4800

Corporate & Incentive Travel Magazine, 488 Madison Ave.,
New York, N.Y. 10022 (212) 888-1500

Meeting News, 1515 Broadway, New York, N.Y. 10036
(212) 869-1300

Messenger Service

> *"You can get off on the 'rush.' Drivers play a game: I know it takes an hour and ten minutes to get from Miami to Broward. Let's see if I can take this short cut and get there in an hour without speeding." – Kathy Bready, ASAP Courier*

Low Startup Investment: $0 (a home-based service using the family car)

High Startup Investment: $75,000 (to set up an office, hire drivers, and lease cars)

Time Until Breakeven: Immediate to six months

Annual Revenues: $25,000-$750,000 (multiple or super-busy locations)

Annual Pre-tax Profits: $20,000-$90,000

Staffers Needed for Startup (including founder): One

When something absolutely, positively has to get there—and overnight's not fast enough—messenger services speed to the rescue. The hotshot attorney, knowing the case is finished unless the brief gets to the courthouse across town by 3 P.M., calls a courier. The frazzled Akron sales department, fearful of losing a $25 million deal unless the Phoenix office okays a contract before the competitor takes over, needs two services: one to pick up the important envelope and deliver it to the Akron airport; another to meet the plane in Phoenix and rush it to the powers that be.

One thing's for sure, says Kathy Bready, who started ASAP Courier Corporation, Miami, Florida, in 1983: "You're certainly never bored." Everybody in our busy world needs everything yesterday. When you're not dashing across town on some cliffhanger, you're delivering paychecks or other papers too important to be entrusted to the mail.

Since starting a messenger firm required no particular expertise and zero capital, Kathy began her firm just as a way to finance medical school. "I was a chemistry major. What did I know about business?" she asks. She needed money for tuition and living expenses, and knew complying with an employer's hours while attending medical school was out of the question. "My boyfriend noticed the major utility in town was using high-hourly-wage people—paying them maybe $16 an hour—to deliver documents regularly. He suggested I bid on the delivery."

LOADED SALARIES

Sixty dollars later, Kathy was incorporated. She had some stationery printed and wrote to the utility company using the key argument that still brings in business. Kathy explains: "Employers think they're paying someone a salary anyway, why shouldn't they send them on a delivery? But they forget to calculate the benefits, sick leave, pension plans—those extras that put salaries way out of proportion to a $5 or $8 delivery charge."

Landing the utility helped ASAP take off faster than a speeding messenger. The regular revenues her first customer provided allowed Kathy to market her services to other companies that were heavy messenger users. Now her business covers all of Florida from Jacksonville to the Keys. Kathy estimates 70 percent of the revenues, which amounted to more than $400,000 in 1987, come from steady, repeat clients.

The difference between success and failure in the messenger business usually boils down to whether you line up standard runs, or deliveries that you schedule on a regular basis. Knowing that First Bank needs its receipts transferred every afternoon at four provides two benefits: Such regularity assures you of a revenue base, and it also helps you better schedule drivers and pick-ups in the same areas of town. Even before starting, call on large companies that have branch offices nearby to suggest you handle their interoffice mail.

Most courier services make just handshake arrangements with major clients, but you might consider actual contracts. A contract guarantees cash flow. The drawback: You must lock in your price for the year or two of the contract.

STREET SMART

You can start a messenger service with virtually no overhead if you operate from your home and use your own car. Some inner-city services prefer bicycles or public transportation, which are faster than cars on crowded streets. Some Manhattan messengers even use skateboards. An expensive office adds little since you get practically no walk-in traffic. Instead, most customers come either from Yellow Pages advertising or solicitations. Employees don't need an office, either, since most operate on the run. Even as you add a driver or two, a home-based dispatcher can relay most locations either by phone or by radio. ASAP functions in Jacksonville and Miami with no physical presence at all. Customers simply call the company's Miami dispatch center on a toll-free line. The dispatcher, in turn, alerts local messengers where to pick up and deliver.

As you add more drivers and clients, however, an office provides a place for clerks to do the billing and payroll. But keep the office on ground level so drivers can leave their cars double-parked while they dash in to pick up a package for delivery.

An office also adds credibility as you pull in more clientele. Kathy Bready opened her first out-of-state office in Reading, Pennsylvania, her old home town, in 1986. Why so far from Florida? "I wanted to give my grandfather something," she explains. Her $45,000 budget covered a small storefront, expenses for eight drivers and dispatchers (including Granddad), and some marketing and advertising.

INDEPENDENTS

Kathy's drivers aren't really employees at all, but independent contractors, a distinction that can make or break a delivery service. You're liable for employees, meaning if a driver has an accident in your company car, guess who gets sued. But independent contractors supply their own cars, which drivers register and insure under their own names. If you want the benefits of a "moving billboard," pay the drivers $50 a month to display a sign containing your company logo and phone number on their cars.

ASAP splits each delivery fee fifty-fifty with drivers, with bonuses for longtime messengers. Paying a commission rather than a salary makes bookkeeping easier since Kathy doesn't deduct taxes, and it also creates a better driver. "What makes a minimum wage employee in your car go faster during an eight-hour shift? Commissioned drivers are motivated, because the more deliveries they make, the more they earn. As soon as they drop off something, they call the dispatcher to ask what's next."

Solo operators who make their own deliveries can earn astounding profits—70 percent to 90 percent. Overhead basically amounts to gas, an answering service, and marketing to round up customers. Adding personnel boosts revenues, because there are only so many deliveries a single entrepreneur can make. The overhead of an office and a payroll, however, cuts profits dramatically. You can still keep 20 percent of the gross as profits—if you're tough with both drivers and clients. If a driver fails to show up for a shift with no excuse, Kathy Bready may not provide a second chance. "If you've got three nine o'clock runs and your fourth messenger doesn't show up, you have to send out a supervisor. Then what do you do if you get a rush order?"

Kathy also cuts off clients who don't pay after 120 days. "When you're young, you love to hear the phone ring, and you even jump for clients who don't pay. But you soon learn that doesn't make sense," she says.

Incidentally, the boyfriend who suggested Kathy's messenger business had other good ideas as well. He's now married to her. And what about medical school? "Now that the business is successful, I have the time to go back. I might still become a doctor," says Kathy. On the other hand, "It's exciting to run a business. Maybe I'll expand ASAP. Maybe I'll franchise."

SOURCES

Industry Association

Association of Messenger Services Inc., 270 Madison Ave., New York, N.Y. 10016 (212) 532-8980

Public Relations

> *"When you work for a company, you never know if an enhanced fee is a measurement of you or the firm. When you build client relationships yourself, there's never a question of who's responsible. And that's a lot more fun." – Robert Amen, Robert Amen & Associates*

Low Startup Investment: $500 (home base)

High Startup Investment: $5,000 (office in metro area, some marketing)

Time Until Breakeven: One to nine months

Annual Revenues: $50,000-$5 million (solo at low end, fifty to one hundred employees at high end)

Annual Pre-tax Profits: $40,000-$500,000

Staffers Needed for Startup (including founder): One

When Carol Cone wanted to snare the prestigious McDonald's Restaurant of New England account, she spent almost $40,000 in time and expenses to prove her Boston-based firm had the enthusiasm to sprinkle new glitter on the account which another public relations agency had gripped for twenty years. One of her ploys: a skywriting plane that played off McDonald's advertising theme to splash across the sky: "It's a great time for a great PR agency—Cone & Co." Carol Cone got the job.

Public relations is part show-biz, all right, at least the type of PR that Carol Cone practices. Your job involves carrying a client's message to the media or directly to the public. Sometimes you use quiet press releases and gentle persuasion. Other times you set up special events or other eye-catchers as part of an overall program meant to develop an image or theme that will stick in consumers' minds. One of Carol's more visible programs helped push the Rockport Company from an obscure maker of walking shoes to the acknowledged leader in this burgeoning new field. The program, which included securing an endorsement of its walking shoe by the American Podiatric Medical Association and hiring a medical spokesperson, culminated with one man's walk across America. Rob Sweetgall's 11,208-mile hike grabbed coverage on ABC's "Good Morning America," in *The Wall Street Journal* and *Parade* magazine, as well as in lots of local spots. Of course, Carol tipped them all off to what a great story an interview with Rob would make.

INVESTOR RELATIONS

On the other end of the PR spectrum sits Robert Amen, of Robert Amen & Associates, Greenwich, Connecticut. His idea of razzle-dazzle is a coffee-and-croissant buffet for security analysts at New York's Pierre Hotel. "I consider myself a corporate and investor relations consulting firm," explains Robert. Instead of promoting new consumer products, he reaches institutional investors to talk about a client's stock.

Investor relations is possibly the fastest-growing niche within the swiftly expanding public relations field. The membership of The National Investor Relations Institute grew 54 percent, from 1,200 in 1984 to 1,850 three years later. The reason: Corporations, skittish over the mass of corporate takeover attempts in the 1980s, are paying more attention to their shareholders, particularly the large shareholders.

Before he set up shop in 1981, Bob Amen already had an investor relations background, having worked in that capacity for several corporations as well as with a Wall Street firm that specialized in proxy solicitations. If you enter this PR niche, come equipped with a legal or financial background. "You need contacts in the financial field and financial knowledge," explains Bob, who adds that journalism expertise is handy in other areas of public relations. In addition, if you understand a particular field well and know which publications like which stories, you can turn that experience into PR for your industry. As you grow, increase your knowledge of other industries.

THE ACCOUNTS

PR agencies generally have two types of clients:

* Project accounts that need to get across a particular message. These relationships last anywhere from a few weeks if all you do is distribute a press release and arrange any follow-up with reporters, to several months if you promote a product roll-out that might involve luncheons and media coverage in several cities. Of course, agencies generally hope the project will lead to the second type of client.

* Retainer accounts that pay a set fee over a longer period. You handle a client's ongoing public relations, which includes keeping the media appraised of newsworthy events, and might develop into writing annual reports and employee brochures. "Retainer clients are crucial so you can plan ahead," says Bob Amen. "They provide cash flow, the continuity that allows you to hire a staff or budget for the future." Robert Amen & Associates had ten retainers in 1987, which provided the bulk of its $750,000 in billings.

To attract those retainers, call on corporations in your areas of expertise and ask to pitch a campaign. Even firms with an in-house PR department may need to farm out particular functions, like developing the West Coast image for a New England–based company.

Don't neglect your company's own PR. Some firms send press releases on new accounts or staff promotions to advertising and industry publications. Success breeds success, so don't be shy about letting others know you landed a big account. You can also host a cocktail party to launch your firm or to celebrate your first anniversary. Invite the press as well as current and potential clients. Also, don't hesitate to network: Meet potential clients through trade organizations or host a seminar on the value of PR. Without being too pushy, let clients know you can perform similar services for their corporate friends. "Some firms in investor relations link with bankers or lawyers," says Bob Amen. "If you handle their PR, they recommend you to their clients."

MAKING TALENT PAY

If you secure enough clients, you can make a good living in PR. Overhead is low: Once you start hiring associates, your biggest expense is for salaries. A solo practitioner can expect to keep the bulk of billings for profit and salary; the owner of a larger firm with many account executives and a lavish office can still earn 10 percent of the gross as profits in addition to a salary that easily moves into six-figures.

In the beginning, many general public relations agencies start at home with a word processor and a telephone. But if image is particularly important, you might need a classy office address. Bob Amen felt he needed an office to attract Fortune 500 clients who might balk at paying high fees to a home-based business. Even so, Bob spent only about $1,000 to set up shop and hire a part-time secretary. You also must pay for your clients' mailings, for phone calls and travel to meet with out-of-town media, and for expenses (such as research) incurred on special projects. But you usually can bill those expenses on top of your fee.

The bigger PR firms gravitate toward larger cities because traditionally that's where the clients are. If you specialize in investor relations, you gain a big edge by locating near New York, since at least 60 percent of the assets managed by institutional investors congregate on the Eastern Seaboard. But more general boutiques can round up clients any place businesses need public relations. "If a company deals with press releases that have to be cleared every week or two, it makes sense to be close to the client," says Bob Amen. "You may even have an advantage if you know the local culture and can also deal with the national press in New York and the trade press in Chicago and the entertainment media in Los Angeles."

Most observers expect PR agencies to flourish in the future for two reasons. Corporations increasingly see the value of public relations, even to the point of switching dollars once allocated for advertising to PR. "Today, the skills of persuasion and communications are indispensable for executive leadership," writes *Public Relations News,* which estimates that 70 percent of a chief executive officer's time goes for PR and PR-related matters.

Meanwhile, as contradictory as it seems, those same corporations that can't live without PR are paring their in-house staffs as part of the overall cost-cutting climate. That move leads to the second reason why agencies will flourish. Instead of staffing a PR department, corporations increasingly contract with outsiders to handle their media contacts. Observers say that a large portion of the thirty thousand new PR jobs that the U.S. Department of Labor predicts for 1990 will go to independents rather than corporate departments.

SOURCES

Industry Associations

The Public Relations Society of America Inc., 33 Irving Place, New York, N.Y. 10003 (212) 995-2230

National Investor Relations Institute, 1730 M St. N.W., Washington, D.C. 20036 (202) 861-0630

Publications

O'Dwyer's Directory of Public Relations Firms, 271 Madison Ave., 12th Floor, New York, N.Y. 10016 (212) 679-2471

Public Relations News, 127 E. 80th St., New York, N.Y. 10021 (212) 879-7090

Quick Printer

> *"It's gratifying to see an idea in someone's head turn into a beautifully printed piece, then see that piece go out in the mail to thousands of people."* – Juanita A. Ohanian, Nebel Printing

---

Low Startup Investment: $50,000 (basic storefront)

High Startup Investment: $250,000 (large franchise shop)

Time Until Breakeven: One to three years

Annual Revenues: $200,000-$2 million

Annual Pre-tax Profits: $25,000-$500,000

Staffers Needed for Startup (including founder): Two

There's no doubt about it: We're now in the Information Age. Although computers once promised a "paperless office," information means paper. Businesses published an estimated twenty-five hundred *billion* pieces of paper in 1986. By 1990 a projected 4 trillion pieces will be produced.

The quick-print industry owes its vitality to all that paper, with special thanks to a fidgety society that wants those copies yesterday. The U.S. Commerce Department calls printing and copying "the fastest-growing segment of the business services sector," which, in turn, ranks among the fastest-growing parts of the economy. Noting that quick print shops billed nearly $4 billion in 1986, *Quick Printing Magazine* predicts 15-percent annual growth for the next several years at least.

YOU NEED TO BE SMARTER

Once the technology became available to print anything a customer desired inexpensively and quickly, entrepreneurs caught on fast. Quick printers duplicated shops as fast as a supercopier churns out copies. Doug Roorback, editor in chief of *Quick Printing Magazine*, estimates that twenty-five to thirty thousand shops operated across the U.S. in 1986.

The stats, meanwhile, prompt some observers to ask about competition. Kenny Fisher, a/k/a Kenny the Printer, who in Irvine, California, runs what may be the world's most successful quick printing shop, counts two hundred quick printers in his county alone. But he's not complaining. "Quick printing is a super opportunity if you're smarter than the competition. I take serious money out." Indeed. Kenny's 1986 revenues of more than $2 million gave him 25-percent profits. That doesn't count the $150,000 or so he makes as a consultant nor the speaker's fees he commands for spilling his secrets at industry conventions.

Doug Roorback expects continued demand to more than compensate for the growing numbers of printers. "It's a common mistake to interpret competition as oversaturation," he says. While he counsels newcomers to pick location carefully, avoiding areas where large numbers of good printers already reside, Kenny Fisher believes, "There must be two thousand opportunities around the country. There's room for competence."

Nevertheless, gone are the days when speed alone guaranteed success. Photocopying and one-day turnaround of stationery and other printed material will probably always remain the foundation for the industry. But today's typical quick-print shop also offers services ranging from four-color and laser printing to facsimile transmission and word processing. According to the National Association of Quick Printers (NAQP), after a median of 5.5 years, entrepreneurs tend to classify themselves as "quick/commercial" printers as they add equipment and graduate to bigger, more complicated jobs.

EQUIPMENT FOR SALE

If you follow the typical growth curve, NAQP says you can expect to average 47-percent higher sales in your second full year of business than your first. Your fifth year should triple revenues of the startup year. In 1985, the average quick-printing company, regardless of age or number of units, recorded $449,700 in sales and $65,500 in net owner's compensation (salary plus profits).

The need to dish out a full buffet of services has upped the startup ante, since you must buy a smorgasbord of equipment. A full-service franchise or larger urban units with state-of-the art equipment, such as high-speed and multicolor copiers, could run to $250,000. But you can still open a small storefront with basic equipment for $50,000. "A lot of independents start with used equipment, or lease and pay for their equipment through cash flow," explains Doug Roorback. In addition, franchises, which open one of every three print shops, typically finance equipment packages. You put down 40 percent and pay the rest in monthly installments.

Juanita A. Ohanian spent just $10,000 for used equipment to outfit Nebel Printing Inc., in the D.C. suburb of Rockville, Maryland, in 1978. She reasoned that, because her background was in office management and accounting rather than printing, she might initially buy the wrong machinery out of ignorance. "Three to six months later, I started seeing things I needed," she recalls. "Because I wasn't hocked to the hilt, I could get loans to buy what I really needed." By 1986, Juanita had $600,000 worth of equipment, including a couple of original presses that she says actually appreciated in value. Revenues that year: $1.7 million with a growth potential of $5 million by 1991.

WHERE DO COMPETITORS BLOW IT?

Kenny Fisher advises a microscopic exam of your market before setting up shop. "Talk with owners, employees, association people. Buy copies you don't need. Match stories," says Kenny, who spent two-and-a-half years talking to over one hundred printers before opening Kenny the Printer. After this grand overview of the industry, zero in on your particular community. "Find out where the competition is blowing it," says Kenny. "If you can complement what's being offered, you can make a lot of money." For example, if nobody yet offers laser-printing, you might sew up the market for customers who want to design their own ads on a Macintosh. Extras such as delivery services and credit card sales also attract customers.

For newcomers wanting a quick tutorial on the industry, Kenny Fisher and other printing consultants tell what they know for a fee. In addition, trade organizations offer seminars. Finally, in addition to high schools, some community and four-year colleges—notably the Rochester (New York) Institute of Technology—offer vocational programs.

SUCCESS FORMULA

A 1985 National Association of Quick Printers study revealed five basic characteristics shared by all top-dollar volume quick printers. The most successful operators

- Have a stronger and more consistent management profile
- Target small businesses as their chief customers
- Avoid price wars with competitors and emphasize quality and timeliness of service
- Locate in business areas of major metropolitan areas
- Use more aggressive marketing techniques

None of these traits requires you to be a printer. In fact, franchisors fondly insist that a knowledge of printing is superfluous to running a print shop. Los Angeles–based Postal Instant Press says 98 percent of its franchisees had no previous knowledge of the printing business. "I hire technical people who run the presses and do camera work and typesetting," concurs Juanita Ohanian. "There's no way one person can do all those things anyway. I still can't run a press."

However, if you don't know printing, you should know how to manage a business. Kenny Fisher frequently advises clients to "fire themselves off the presses" and "start using your brains instead of your hands." Consider Kenny's challenge: In addition to dealing with "prima donna pressmen and equipment that breaks down, you have to deliver a perfect product on time to a customer who doesn't even know what he wants." That, dear printers, is a full-time managerial job.

MINDING THE STORE

Kenny insists the entrepreneur should be on hand to manage the shop. He multiplies his own presence by bringing in his family: His wife Susan handles payroll while his mother operates a copier, and his teenage son helped open the shop. Now that the operation emcompasses ten thousand square feet and thirty employees, closed-circuit TV cameras scan the plant floor, allowing Kenny to materialize whenever a problem surfaces.

While printers expand up, many argue against expanding out, maintaining that their shops are not reproducible. With one shop, overhead is more or less fixed and any volume beyond a certain point goes straight to the bottom line as profits (the "gravy principle"). You'll do better with one shop doing $500,000 than two stores doing $250,000 each, because when you add an outlet you must double your personnel and equipment.

In addition, whether five hundred miles or five blocks separates your shops, you can't be everywhere at once. It's unrealistic to expect a manager without a piece of the action to match the drive of owner/operators. For single-shop owners, a 1986 *Quick Printing Magazine* survey estimated net owner's compensation (salary plus profits) averaged 16.6 % of revenues of $354,900 or $59,000; multiple shop owners averaged 3.3 outlets each, generating combined sales of $973,000 and net owner's compensation of just 10.6 %, or $103,000. The $103,000 is more than $59,000, however.

VOLUME EQUALS $$$ IN YOUR POCKET

When drumming up action, look for a steady client base of small and medium businesses instead of an independent business person who wants business cards printed. The local department store needs flyers every month, and its marketing department requires weekly reports for the Monday morning staff meeting. To build volume, Nebel Printing particularly courts large accounts whose printing needs come in steady streams rather than one-time spurts. However, since no client makes up more than 10 percent of the shop's volume, losing one wouldn't hurt too much, says Juanita Ohanian.

In addition to direct mail and personal calls on local businesses, Nebel buys the largest-size ad the Yellow Pages offer. Kenny Fisher doesn't like to talk about the specifics of his ad campaigns, holding that that would give competitors too many good ideas. But he wholeheartedly believes in marketing, and says why: "My ad budget is at least half of what startup competitors gross. It's suicide to go into business in my territory. They can't duck my momentum."

QUICK-AND-DIRTY BECOMES QUICK-AND-CLEAN

Operators say finding competent, reliable employees remains their biggest challenge. Kenny believes many operators don't do enough to entice the few well-trained craftspeople around. "You can tell minimum-wage people how to fry a hamburger, but quick-print shops have to hire tradespeople who know how to run a press," he says. Many printers provide on-premise apprenticeships. Both Kenny and Juanita pay wages above the industry norm to attract good help.

Automation may help solve the employee shortage. "It's not far-fetched that someday we'll have copying machines we just talk to," says Juanita Ohanian. "Manufacturers are making printing presses that are easier to clean up. You can probably wear a suit and tie to clean the presses soon."

Technology promises to transform the young industry at an even more furious pace. In addition to high-speed and multicolor copying, perhaps the most touted innovation turns a quick printer into a full-fledged, small-scale publisher. So-called desktop publishers (see Desktop Publisher) use a word processor to custom design a page, which the operator prints instantly on a laser printer. A high-speed copier takes over to run off the finished product. If old Gutenberg would be astounded by the print shop of today, he would be utterly flabbergasted by next year's possibilities.

SOURCES

Industry Associations

The National Association of Quick Printers, 1 Illinois Center, 111
E. Wacker Dr., Chicago, Ill. (312) 644-6610

The Graphic Arts Technical Foundation, 4615 Forbes Ave., Pittsburgh, Pa. 15213 (412) 621-6941

The Printing Industries of America, 1730 N. Lynn St., Arlington,
Va. 22209 (703) 841-8100

Publication

Quick Printing Magazine, 3255 S. U.S. 1, Fort Pierce, Fla. 33482
(305) 465-9450

Consultants

Kenny Fisher, Kenny The Printer, 17931 Sky Park Circle, Irvine,
Calif. 92714 (714) 250-3212

Tom Crouser, Crouser & Associates, P.O. Box 1396, St. Albans,
W. Va. 25177 (304) 722-6333

Seminar Producer

> *"High school teachers accept $20,000 a year because there's a great deal of satisfaction in teaching. But if you're in the right field, you can teach professional seminars, achieve the same level of satisfaction, and make significantly more money."* – Jack Tumminello, The 1st Seminar Service

Low Startup Investment: $0 (home-based specialist with a ready client-audience)

High Startup Investment: $10,000 (includes marketing and arranging for seminar space)

Time Until Breakeven: Immediate to one year

Annual Revenues: $25,000-$25 million

Annual Pre-tax Profits: $20,000-$3 million

Staffers Needed for Startup (including founder): One

Case Study: When Jimmy Calano was fired from his job producing seminars, he was indignant. The then twenty-four-year-old had produced seminars since his college days and had no intention of letting some employer knock him out of the business he knew best. Undaunted, Jimmy hooked up with a partner, twenty-seven-year-old Jeff Salzman, who owned a Boulder, Colorado, advertising agency. In 1982, they hired their first instructor to do a three-city tour. The seminar was called "Image and Self Projection for Professional Women."

The pair posted "Sold Out" notices on two of those first three seminars, and grossed $220,000 during their first year. But such success is nothing compared to what's happened since. In 1986, Boulder-based CareerTrack grossed over $26 million, primarily on seminars costing clients $48 a shot. In 1987, Jimmy and Jeff were projecting $32.5 million in revenues while lining up participants as far away as Australia. In addition to advising young executives on "Stress Management" and "Business Writing," their sixty trainers wax profound on consumer topics such as "How to Find and Keep a Mate."

Okay, class, what lessons do we learn from Jimmy Calano's true-life experience?

A) The seminar business can be cut-throat.

B) The seminar business offers easy entry.

C) The seminar business has a huge and ready market of students.

D) The seminar business can be hugely profitable.

E) All of the above.

If you answered E, take a gold star and enter the wonderful world of seminars.

THIRST

Jimmy Calano knew by instinct what Jack Tumminello, president of The 1st Seminar Service, a Lowell, Massachusetts, seminar broker, confirms through experience: "The thirst for knowledge and know-how is enormous," says Jack. "The number of seminars is going to grow."

The 1st Seminar Service makes a living by matching its list of seminar providers with individuals and corporations craving instruction on particular topics. The service estimates some four thousand "seminarians" discoursed on about twenty-five thousand topics in 1987. Counting those courses that enjoyed multiple runs, Americans attended one hundred thousand seminar sessions in 1987. *Training* magazine estimates corporations alone spent nearly $2 billion to send employees to seminars in 1986, a 10.5-percent increase over the previous year. Counting all forms of in-house training, John Naisbitt writes in *Reinventing the Corporation* that "corporations spend nearly $60 billion a year on education and training . . . about the same amount spent on education in the nation's four-year colleges and universities." That's a lot of seminars.

Because the audience is there, and because seminar production is a relatively cheap business to get into, there seems no end to the types of people entering the seminar business: Nonprofit trade associations, like The American Institute of Electrical Engineers, sponsor curriculums for particular industries; universities experiencing declining student enrollments give courses not only on campus, but in cities far from home; and corporations disguise sales calls as seminars, using desktop-publishing workshops to hustle computer software, or tax-planning sessions to push municipal bonds.

Even entrepreneurs profess more than one motive: Seminars often generate substantial income, and, if you're a consultant or other professional selling your expertise, they also introduce you to potential clients. Entrepreneurs interviewed for other chapters of this book praised seminars as reputation builders in such varied fields as garden-center retailing and financial planning.

FILLING THE CLASSROOM

Getting started in the seminar business is dead simple—if you have a course that someone agrees to pay for. Just show up with whatever teaching materials you use, which may be no more than your notes and a gallon of water to keep the vocal chords in working order. Assuming you're a dynamite educator with a hot topic, word-of-mouth can carry you a long way. You may eventually hire an assistant or a whole staff to give similar seminars. Or you may branch out with audio or video tapes.

But, chances are, clients won't drop out of the sky like raindrops. "We find the biggest problem is not finding people to teach, but putting people into their sessions," says Jack Tumminello. "The average marketing cost for producing a seminar is 30 percent to 60 percent of sales." The lst Seminar Service offers one aid. It serves as a clearing house for anyone who wants a particular seminar. The service earns a fee from the producer by putting the customer in touch with the right producer.

Depending on your topic and your audience, you have several choices on how to market. Newspaper ads and even flyers handed out on the street attract consumers interested in "How to Achieve Happiness in Ten Minutes a Day." If you have a very specific but useful topic, like data processing for Digital Equipment Computer users, cold calls to corporation training managers might be best. You might try direct mail for seminars meant for more general, but still targeted groups, like medical doctors who want to learn the latest malpractice news. But direct mail costs can be stiff—figure $25,000 for a fifty-thousand-piece campaign. Expect to attract no more than 1 percent of that mailing (five hundred people), which means each student has to fork over $50 just to pay for the marketing. If you want to pay for the meeting facilities, the instructor, and make a profit, better plan on charging a lot more than that!

THOSE WHO CAN'T MARKET, TEACH

Or, you don't have to market at all. Instead, sign on with seminar producers like CareerTrack or the American Management Associations who contract with instructors. According to Jack Tumminello, depending on which course and how often you teach, an independent instructor can earn $25,000 to $100,000 a year.

The flip side of this suggestion calls for marketeers who don't have specific expertise to sell rather than teach a seminar. The instructor doesn't put up a cent, but contributes expertise. The marketeer, or producer, must find the audience and facilities. But, since the instructor is an independent contractor, producers don't worry about payrolls; instead, they just pay the instructor from the proceeds of the seminar. "Usually the organization taking the risk —whoever's doing the marketing—gets the larger percentage of the proceeds," says Jack.

The typical provider conducts eight to twelve programs a year, all focused on an area of expertise. "You can have half a dozen topics that apply to data-processing people, but don't try to address finance people, because then you have to market to a whole new group," advises Jack. But if you build a curriculum for one group, hopefully they'll come back for additional seminars over the years.

Of course, CareerTrack provides the exception to that rule, since it markets to everybody in cities of fifty thousand or more. In 1987, it scheduled over three thousand seminars for a half-million people. Although the courses often enjoy free publicity in newspaper "What's Going On" columns, CareerTrack relies almost exclusively on brochures sent through direct mail to line up participants. "It's not that advertising doesn't work," explains Gillian Goodman, corporate communications specialist. "It's just that direct mail works so well for us."

CareerTrack seminars attract two hundred to five hundred people per session, often held at a hotel conference room. "The average class is not a workshop," admits Gillian Goodman. The company needs the volume to reach breakeven because it charges only $48 per participant.

If your topic is general, such as "Basic Supervision Skills," you may be limited to a gate price of less than $200. But if you have a special expertise in high demand, such as "Robotic Engineering," you can charge $600 to $1,200 for a similar-length program. In this case, the generic seminar needs to draw fifty participants to produce the same revenues as a ten-participant robotics program.

Overhead for a seminar producer can be minimal—an office staff, marketing, a registrar at the course site, and the cost of staging each seminar, including the instructor and renting meeting facilities. Some producers cut deals with hotels and line up accommodations as well. For a busy producer who counts on repeat business, profits can approach 65 percent of revenues.

In addition to live-instructor courses, technology offers new outlets to the seminar business. CareerTrack sells each of its seminars as four-hour, $39.95 audio tapes meant to turn a commuter's car into a university on wheels. And other companies have gone the step further to videos, which teach everything from "Assertiveness Training" to "Auto Mechanics." Computer-aided instruction teaches children about algebra and professionals about new surgical techniques. The latest—but undoubtedly not the last—frontier: laser videos that allow a student to interact with a taped instructor.

SOURCES

Industry Association

American Society for Training & Development, Box 1443, Alexandria, Va. 22313 (703) 683-8100

Publication

Training, 50 S. 9th St., Minneapolis, Minn. 55402 (612) 333-0471

Temporary Employment Service – Clerical

> *"If you're an action-prone person, you've picked the right business." – Delores Pass, Associated Temporary Staffing*

Low Startup Investment: $45,000 (primarily for payroll)

High Startup Investment: $200,000 (includes computer and advertising)

Time Until Breakeven: Six months to one year

Annual Revenues: $250,000-$5 million

Annual Pre-tax Profits: $12,000-$500,000

Staffers Needed for Startup (including founder): Two to four

The temporary employment industry appears anything but temporary. In 1986, 767,000 people filled temporary jobs on any given day—a sizzling 125-percent increase over the 340,000 temporary slots counted by the Bureau of Labor Statistics in 1978. Five million people worked as a temp sometime during that year—more people than live in the state of Maryland. That rate of growth is three times faster than service industries show as a whole, and over eight times that achieved in the entire nonagricultural sector. Projecting a conservative 5-percent annual increase, the government expects 1.1 million daily jobs to await temps by 1995.

Let's take it from the employer's standpoint: By 1986, nine out of ten companies contributed to a national temp payroll of $7 billion. Rather than hire for the peak times, business has learned to staff lean and mean, preferring to bring in temps rather than lay off workers they can't always afford to pay. "The last recession was a lesson on over-hiring," says Sam Sacco, executive vice-president of the National Association of Temporary Services (NATS).

AN EXPANDING PIE

In addition, the pool of temporary workers has gone beyond clerical help. By 1986, 37 percent of the temporary pie belonged to medical, professional, and industrial jobs. Everybody from biochemists and engineers to bartenders got into the act, hiring themselves out in a manner once confined to low-paid, pink-collar office help. (See Temporary Employment Service—Professional.)

A temporary-help service basically acts as a matchmaker between companies that need short-term labor and individuals who want a job—but not full time or forever. The temporary firm pays the worker weekly, and in turn bills corporate clients for each hour its employees are on the job.

Despite what sometimes looks more like war than competition among the nation's twenty-six hundred companies (some seventy-six hundred offices all told), "Anybody can succeed with a temporary employment company if you have enough capital," insists Philip D. Cox, president of StaffAmerica Management Group Inc., a consultancy specializing in the temporary help industry.

THE CASH-FLOW MONSTER

You need capital to pay for your success—too much of a good thing can be expensive since temp services must meet their payroll before they collect from clients. Phil Cox recalls a client who, six weeks after launching her firm, billed fifteen hundred hours a week at $8 an hour. "That sounds great until you realize she had to pay all those workers $12,000 every week and might not collect from her clients for another thirty or sixty days," says Phil. The moral of the story: Be sure to put together a line-of-credit or slush fund to cover payroll until the cash starts rolling in. Phil's client found a banker who bailed her out with an emergency loan.

Some will disagree, but Phil Cox insists starting a temporary-help firm "appears more difficult than it really is." In addition to meeting early payrolls, your greatest challenges are caused by the rush of startup variables. Those chores include everything from the usual site selection and penetration of market, to more industry-specific problems, such as recruiting a reliable labor pool. However, Phil insists that an owner who methodically completes a checklist of fifty or so tasks will create "the proverbial snowball."

Once the systems for recruiting help and attracting clientele are rolling, "the retained earnings generated can accumulate very rapidly," explains Phil. In other words, once you build a steady pool of temps and a steadier corporate client base, you do little to collect the money that comes in. Your job, after all, is to manage the schedules of others who do the work.

Investors are starting to catch on: Stock of public temporary-service companies has sold for thirty times earnings, compared to just thirteen times for the broad market, as measured by the Standard & Poor Corporation's 500 index. Larger companies, too, are getting in on the action. They pay premium prices for established firms. By buying existing client and personnel lists, the newcomer drastically reduces the startup period. Phil Cox cites the entry of big players as a positive trend for entrepreneurs. "Build up the business to $3 million or so, then go to the gobblers and sell," he advises.

JUGGLING

Getting to that $3 million, however, isn't as easy as it may sound. Particularly in the early stages, a temp entrepreneur manages diverse details—and the company's life depends upon it. Along with organization, timing is everything. For example, don't recruit too early, or thirty applicants may ring your phones off the hook asking where their jobs are; by the time you have clients lined up, those temps may be working elsewhere.

You—or your team—must possess the personality and ability to manage a business that requires three distinct sets of skills:

▪ Sales. Particularly in the beginning, selling corporate clients on the merits of temporary staffing in general, and your shop in particular, involves hours of cold-calling and telemarketing. It pays to pinpoint your prospects and cater to them. For example, Sharon Bredeson custom trains temps at Staff-Plus Inc., a Minneapolis company she founded in 1973 to handle the specific word processing systems used by Fortune 500 companies in her area. Because clients know a Staff-Plus temp doesn't waste time and make mistakes learning their systems, "we don't have to knock on doors," says Sharon. "Clients come to us."

▪ Personnel. "We use every source of recruiting: newspapers, speaking at women's clubs, tying in with educators," says Delores Pass, president of Jacksonville, Florida's Associated Temporary Staffing Inc. Weeding out the incompetents and keeping a steady supply of workers represent ongoing challenges. Temporary workers, by definition, are unreliable since they don't want to work full time. "It's frustrating to deal with their schedules," admits Delores. "You expect three word processors and find that only two are interested in working on a particular day." The only solution is constant restocking of the personnel pool.

▪ Administration. After checking an employee's time card, a paycheck has to be cut, taxes and insurance deducted, and bills sent to the client, with reports made to the government. Manpower Inc., the world's largest temporary-help service, applied for entry into the Guinness Book of World Records for filing 460,348 W-2 forms for 1985. President Mitchell S. Fromstein says the company completed the forms the only way possible: "With temporary help, of course!"

With so many different aspects to juggle, the ability to organize and manage is key. Before you recruit clients or interview employees, establish the mechanics that will keep you running. Create forms to take job orders and interview. If you try to place employees based on scribblings you make on pieces of paper, you're lost.

THE ELECTRONIC ROLODEX

While some startups rely on index cards and a well-thumbed Rolodex to track employees and clients, Sharon Bredeson entered the twentieth century by computerizing Staff-Plus. Recruits automatically test in word processing skills when they fill out applications on a keyboard. The computer puts information on each individual into a data base, which instantly confirms which temps are available when clients call. Companies that spend more than $500,000 annually with Staff-Plus tie in by modem. By punching in what they require in terms of skill, amount of time, and location, the client can, in essence, hire its own temp.

Sharon Bredeson declines to put a price tag on efficiencies gained by computerization, such as cutting paychecks and bills electronically. But she says computers place employees faster and don't lose applicants who are unavailable for a couple of weeks in dusty file cabinets. Sharon figures the computer system justified itself four months after installation in 1985. "We have half the staff of noncomputerized companies," she says.

BECOME A CORPORATE ARM

The paper a computer spews out will transform the temp agency of the future into an indispensable outside arm of corporate personnel departments, predicts Sharon Bredeson. Staff-Plus, which employed twenty-five hundred people in 1986, sends clients quarterly reports breaking down their use of temporary labor. Graphs show how much each department spent on temps, and for what reason: illness, special projects, etc. Providing detailed information is one service that sets Staff-Plus apart from the competition, says Sharon.

To attract clients, focus advertising in the Yellow Pages, newspapers, and local business journals. Visit the people in charge of hiring. Tell them about your particular strengths, stressing how quickly you can get someone on the job after a company's 9 A.M. panic call. If you train temps in a particular word processing skill, say so. In addition, explain the benefits of hiring temporaries on a regular basis. For example, the National Chamber of Commerce estimates that nearly 38 percent of all business expenses relate to such hidden costs as fringe benefits, absenteeism, and recruitment —debits which hourly rates don't duplicate. A company pays for only the temp's hours on the job.

HELP WANTED

The temporary-help industry's potential may depend not on finding enough business—corporate clients increasingly are pre-sold on the concept—but on rounding up enough workers interested in part-time jobs. "Recruiting is directly tied to the unemployment rate, which is expected to fall as baby boomers assimilate into the work force," says Delores Pass, whose Associated Temporary Staffing was considered one of the 500 fastest-growing companies in America by *Inc. Magazine,* with $15.9 million in 1985 sales. A year later her twelve-office company grew by another $9 million. Like an increasing number of temp agencies, Delores provides temps with a whole line of benefits to lure them aboard, ranging from holiday and vacation pay to profit sharing and health benefits.

NATS's Sam Sacco says the field must target untapped work forces to overcome the labor shortage. "Stress older workers," he recommends. "People retire earlier, are more mentally acute, have experience and reliability." Like the retired, housewives and some handicapped individuals "may consider themselves unemployable because they don't want to work full time." It's your job to persuade otherwise.

Training is another big applicant draw. With 70 percent of Staff-Plus's business dedicated to word processing instead of other clerical duties like typing, Sharon Bredeson routinely trains temps on various software packages. Such a move benefits both the temp firm and the employee since Staff-Plus's word processors command $15 an hour, versus $7 for typists.

MILLION-DOLLAR SHOPS

Consultant Philip Cox estimates that more than 70 percent of a typical client fee goes to pay the wages of temporary employees. Once it lays out administrative expenses and employee benefits, the average temp shop pulls in profits of just 3 to 5 percent, according to NATS. The good news is volume can grow quickly. "It's very hard to get to $2 million in a flower shop, but it's not uncommon in temporary help," says Phil. In 1986, the average Uniforce franchisee billed over $1 million (based on fifty-six offices contributing systemwide sales of $62 million). Delores Pass says her busiest offices bill $2 million.

Startup costs vary wildly. Sharon Bredeson, who has cased Austin, Texas, where she plans to expand, expects opening a top-of-the-line computerized office will cost $200,000. That capital will pay for business insurance, computers, and a respectable facade needed to lure clients, in addition to advertising for the temporaries. Says

Sharon: "A Fortune 500 company is not going to do business with Mom and Pop unless they can guarantee the resources," meaning the temporaries. She plans a crash advertising campaign to bring in lots of workers. On the low end, Phil Cox says a small startup can roll for $45,000 and break even within nine months.

Once your first office pulls in its first million, you might think about opening satellites in other cities. Delores Pass, for example, operates in six cities along the East Coast. As large players get bigger and permanent placement agencies open temp departments, the competition is getting warmer. But, as employers increasingly accept temporary help as another tool in the arsenal of doing business, the industry still sees elbow room for newcomers.

SOURCES

Industry Association

National Association of Temporary Services, 119 South Saint Asaph St., Alexandria, Va. 22314 (703) 549-6287

Publications

Office Magazine, 1600 Summer St., P.O. Box 1231, Stamford, Conn. 06904 (203) 327-9670
Office Systems, 941 Danbury Rd., P.O. Box 150, Georgetown, Conn. 06829 (203) 544-9526
Personnel Journal, 245 Fischer Ave. B2, Costa Mesa, Calif. 92626 (714) 751-1883
Personnel Administrator, 606 N. Washington St., Alexandria, Va. 22314 (703) 548-3440

Consultants

StaffAmerica Management Group Inc., 1061 E. Mountain Dr., Santa Barbara, Calif. 93108 (805) 969-2996
GMF Management Group, 70 Charles Lindbergh Blvd., Uniondale, N.Y. 11553 (516) 222-2299
Transitions Unlimited, 2211 Norfolk, Rt. 700, Houston, Tex. 77098 (713) 529-6345

Temporary Employment Service – Professional

> *"Physicians are limited to what they can do one on one, doctor to patient. As a manager, I can have a broader impact and improve the lives of many more individuals." – Dr. Alan Kronhaus, Kron Medical Corporation.*

Low Startup Investment: $2,000 (assuming an agent arrangement)

High Startup Investment: $50,000 (putting aside money for an office and payroll)

Time Until Breakeven: One to nine months

Annual Revenues: $1.5 million-$20 million

Annual Pre-tax Profits: $400,000-$5 million

Staffers Needed for Startup (including founder): One

Like many great ideas, The Lawsmiths struck Eric Walker when he was least expecting it. The engineer was visiting an attorney friend, Robert Webster, when Bob's sister stopped by. "She mentioned she was a lawyer who freelances," recalls Eric. "I asked about temporary agencies and she said there were none in the legal field.

"If we were doing this story as a comic strip," he continues, "that's where the light bulb would go on." Eric knew temporary-employment services existed not only for clerical workers (see Temporary Employment Service—Clerical), but also for engineers, nurses, and accountants. After Bob's sister left, the two old friends kept talking, a discussion which led to the formation of The Lawsmiths in 1985, a San Francisco–based temporary employment service for lawyers.

A ROSE IS A ROSE

According to the National Association of Temporary Services, in 1985 the technical/professional and medical fields contributed more than 20 percent of the 5 million temporary workers in the country. Niches for accountants, marketing specialists, draftspeople, and other professionals—which barely existed a few years ago —represent the fastest-growing segments of the burgeoning temporary-services industry.

Rather than "temp," doctors and clergy prefer the term *locum tenens,* which the dictionary indeed defines as "a substitute physician or clergyman." But, just like a word processor, professional temporaries want to work only three days a week, or only during the summer. Most employers won't hire a nuclear plant designer for a day when their own happens to call in sick, but that's part of the beauty of the professional side of the temporary service industry: Instead of rotating your employees daily, as do clerical agencies, a doctor or lawyer or chief executive stays on the job for weeks at a time. Dr. Alan Kronhaus, an internist who founded Kron Medical Corporation in Chapel Hill, North Carolina, estimates his temps average four weeks on a job, although rare assignments last two and a half years. Longevity on the job eliminates much of a temporary service's expense of employee placement. Another plus to running an agency for professionals is that, instead of collecting fees from a hodgepodge of clients, professional services take aim at very specific employers, such as hospitals or financial departments within Fortune 500 firms.

NEW MATH

Like their clerical cousins, most temporary professionals are on the temp service's payroll; the service pays its employees directly and bills clients for work performed by the temp. A difference at this juncture involves basic arithmetic. A top-of-the-line word processor might command $600 a week. Kron Medical charges between $2,000 and $3,900 a week for its doctors, depending on their specialties, which include pediatrics, internal medicine, radiology, and pathology. In turn, the company pays salaries competitive with doctors starting out in group practice, which range from about $60,000 for a family doctor to $135,000 for an anesthesiologist, if they work full time—or $1,150 to $2,600 for a forty-hour week.

Okay, you may provide far more aid to professional employees than a clerical firm does, which cuts into profits. For example, Kron Medical covers medical malpractice insurance and pays for air transportation and lodging on assignments, since it places M.D.s all over the country. It even helps them apply for licenses in various states. Nevertheless, Kron's high price tags allow much higher pre-tax profits than the clerical temp agencies achieve.

Kron Medical, with 1986 revenues of $12 million, now bases its forty-five full-time staffers in a $4 million building that bears the company's name. But Alan Kronhaus launched the company from a spare bedroom. Despite modest beginnings, startup cost $30,000, primarily for payroll until clients reimbursed Kron Medical for the M.D.s' salaries.

A STARTUP SHORT CUT

Eric Walker and his partner detoured around the costly startup phase with two ingenious maneuvers. The Lawsmiths kept overhead to nil and, more importantly, signed its lawyers as independent contractors rather than employees. In effect, The Lawsmiths acts as an agent, negotiating an hourly rate with clients and billing for the lawyers. The attorneys wait for payment until The Lawsmiths is paid, and the firm bypasses the cumbersome task of withholding taxes. "This arrangement means we don't have to have a slush fund to pay people before we are paid," says Eric. The entrepreneur warns that establishing your temps as independent contractors is a complicated legal procedure. Some states forbid the arrangement and the IRS studies the contractor–temp firm relationship closely. "Check with a CPA or attorney who is familiar with recent tax law changes to make sure you meet the federal and state requirements," Eric insists. "Penalties are harrowing—you can end up liable for all the taxes not withheld, even if you can prove the employee paid taxes."

The Lawsmiths' attorneys take home a minimum of $25 an hour. The firm tacks another $10 to $15 on top of that fee as its cut. Says

Eric: "It doesn't take many people working to make a decent income if we get $10 to $15 an hour."

Indeed. At any one hour in 1987, about twenty Lawsmiths' lawyers rendered services to legal departments of large corporations or helped sole practitioners whose workloads got out of hand. If twenty people work forty hours a week, fifty weeks a year, The Lawsmiths accumulates fees of $400,000 to $624,000—after paying the lawyers.

To make things even more attractive, The Lawsmiths claims that expenses total near zero. "Be visible to the rest of the world, but start with as low overhead as possible," counsels Eric Walker. To cut costs, he and his partner work from their homes. In the beginning, a call-forwarding telephone service, costing only $18 a month, gave The Lawsmiths a business phone listing in the Yellow Pages. The partners spent $500 on stationery, business cards, and mailings, plus a similar amount to print a brochure. "Pay a design firm to do your brochure layout right," says Eric. "Don't reek of rinky-dink."

The principals do their own billing and correspondence with a personal computer and use a letter-quality printer. Other expenses include lunches to entertain clients and rent on a conference room several times a month. "Clients never see your place of business since you call on them at their offices," explains Eric. "But you need a place to interview the temps." The half-hour interviews help weed out perfectly capable lawyers who make lousy temporary attorneys. Experience, top-notch schools, and letters of recommendation can't answer the gut question of who makes a good temporary. "The personality type has to be 'street-smart,' " he says. "If an employer asks for a quick summary, the temp can't spend days on a long legal treatise." To interview attorneys, The Lawsmiths schedules a dozen interviews in a single day and spends $80 to rent a conference room from a turnkey office concern.

Some states require at least one partner to have a degree in the service you provide. Alan Kronhaus, who still practices one half-day a week, says his medical background helped convince clients he understood the type of doctor they needed. He stresses that dealing with payrolls, billings, and interviewing both clients and professionals requires some business knowledge as well. "If you don't have a business background, team up with someone who does," he advises.

FINDING THE CLIENTS

Kron Medical mails about a quarter-million letters a year to nudge hospitals and group practices to hire its doctors. The company suggests clients might need a fill-in physician until they hire a surgeon or pediatrician full time, or until their own employee recuperates from an illness or injury. Other practices just can't afford a year-round associate when the bulk of their business comes during beach weather or ski season.

Rather than Kron's national focus, The Lawsmiths court a local base of corporations and small legal practices that hire temporaries to ease their workloads. To alert clients to their service, Eric Walker and Bob Webster spend hours calling heads of corporate legal departments. Eric figures he has thirty to sixty seconds to make his initial pitch, merely explaining how the temporary concept works.

"You have to have explanations at your fingertips," he warns. "People say: '$40 an hour amounts to annual salaries of $80,000—I don't pay my full-time employees that.' You have to jump in and invalidate that method of comparison right away. Explain the overhead factor—benefits, vacations, taxes usually amounts to 33 percent on top of wages. That's a hidden cost that they don't pay temporaries."

TRACKING DOWN THE TEMPS

Temporary services advertise for employees in professional publications. The Lawsmiths averages one résumé a day from a one-inch classified ad in the San Francisco Law Journal. Eric says many of his firm's regular attorneys have families and don't want to commit to long hours on a continuing basis. Others are sole practitioners who need supplemental income. Kron Medical runs ads in key national medical journals. Many of its temps have just completed medical training and aren't sure where they want to settle, or even what specialty they want to practice. Kron offers them an opportunity to sample. Some are part-time physicians, like the missionary who works in Third World countries half the year.

As temporary help becomes more accepted in the professions,

service firms see lots of room for expansion, geographical and otherwise. The Lawsmiths plans offices for Los Angeles and New York, and Alan Kronhaus has far-reaching, if somewhat mysteriously phrased, plans for Kron Medical Corporation: "I'd like to conceive and implement other innovations in the organization and delivery of medical services."

SOURCES

Industry Association

National Association of Temporary Services, 119 S. Saint Asaph St., Alexandria, Va. 22314 (703) 549-6287

Consultants

StaffAmerica Management Group Inc., 72 LaVuelto Rd., Santa Barbara, Calif. 93108 (805) 969-2996

GMF Management Group, 70 Charles Lindbergh Blvd., Uniondale, N.Y. 11553 (516) 222-2299

Transitions Unlimited, 2211 Norfolk, Rt. 700, Houston, Tex. 77098 (713) 529-6345

Trade Association

"Running the trade association gives me an opportunity to stay in an industry I love, but lets me get out of the trenches." – Jane Booras, Executive Suite Network

---

Low Startup Investment: $10,000 (a home-based startup, renting a small mailing list)

High Startup Investment: $50,000 (researching industry names from scratch, adding staff, and providing a newsletter or other service)

Time Until Breakeven: Six months to three years

Annual Revenues: $50,000-$2 million

Annual Pre-tax Profits: $10,000-$300,000

Staffers Needed for Startup (including founder): One

Aerobics instructor Kathie Davis was complaining to her husband Peter that professional conferences she attended frustrated rather than informed her. "The trade associations were for coaches, or club owners, but nothing for instructors. We needed safe, new information on how to teach classes, and services such as insurance. We needed a way to share ideas."

In 1982, the aerobics industry was still new. Its members were scattered; some owned salons while others worked part time in health clubs or in a YWCA. And nobody, but nobody, talked to competitors. The Davises realized if they waited for aerobics' instructors to band together to form a trade association in the usual way—where a number of leaders call a conference and everybody chips in money for lobbyists or research—they might see one around the year 2000.

For Kathie and Peter Davis, the proverbial light bulb flashed on with thousand-volt strength. That night, "we figured out we should start the trade organization ourselves, and the next morning we got our business license," explains Kathie. A couple of weeks later, Peter resigned as a tennis coach at the University of California, San Diego. "We just never doubted it would work," says Kathie.

Five years after startup, the International Dance-Exercise Association Inc. (IDEA) boasted twelve thousand members and thirty-five full-time employees. While Kathie Davis declines to talk about revenues or profits, dues alone would bring in well over a half-million dollars a year.

"PROFIT" IS NOT A DIRTY WORD

Virtually every established business group has at least one trade association. Meeting-prone industries, or those which need lots of representation in Washington, have many splinter groups. While the majority still operate as not-for-profit representative bodies, an increasing number of founders say they intend to make a bundle. "I was afraid that many people would object to our designation as a for-profit group," admits Jane Booras, executive director of the Executive Suite Network (ESN), the association that represents turnkey offices (see Turnkey Office). "But what better incentive do we have to do a good job? We have to renew the member's confidence every year before they sign on with us again." Not only do members accept that reasoning, "I think many relate to us better because they're small business people and so are we," says Jane.

Most established trades already have an association, although you can buy one just as you can any other business: Jane Booras purchased ESN in July 1986, nine months after it was founded by the National Association of Secretarial Services, itself a for-profit group. However, the opportunities lie not with entrenched industries, but in startup fields. In the course of researching this book, we found numerous brand-spanking-new trade groups (most operating in a for-profit mode). On the other hand, many fields are still stranded, waiting for an enterprising entrepreneur to take control of the situation and help unify the industry.

Unless lobbying represents a major part of your *raison d'être*, you can start a trade association as easily in Podunk as you can in Washington, D.C. IDEA operates from San Diego, and ESN hails from

Dallas. We contacted organizations for this book in places as diverse as Moline, Illinois (The American Rental Association) and Albuquerque, New Mexico (The Association of Commercial Mail Receiving Agencies). Until you need staff, an executive director can operate from home—and even part time if you don't mind starting slow. Your initial costs will involve marketing: identifying potential members and giving them a reason to join. That reason might be a newsletter or an upcoming convention.

WHO NEEDS YOU?

Before quitting your job to start a trade association, conduct some market research to see if industry members are numerous and interested enough to support you. Kathie and Peter Davis researched aerobics—sort of. They invested $10,000 in a twenty-thousand-name mailing list of health clubs and hired an editor to put together an eight-page newsletter with tips on dos-and-don'ts, nutrition, and injury prevention. "Then we sent a flyer asking people who were interested to send us $1" to cover the mailing costs, says Kathie. The five hundred replies, representing 2.5 percent of the mailing, amounted to an overwhelming endorsement since similar solicitations mostly garner less than a 1-percent response rate. With the first newsletter, the Davises offered annual newsletter subscriptions for $20, or memberships in the new IDEA for $32. Those who joined the association got the newsletter for free.

Kathie and Peter didn't realize how lucky they were that their industry even *had* a mailing list. Many fledgling fields aren't so readily identifiable and the trade organization has to build a data base from scratch. In fact, one profit-making activity most trade associations eventually spin off involves renting their member list to manufacturers or publications interested in addressing their targeted audience.

Jane Booras still copes with how to reach her industry. "No list exists of executive suites," she complains. "You can't even find them listed that way in the Yellow Pages." Within eight months of taking over ESN, Jane had identified twenty-three hundred turnkey offices across the country. "In some cases, we found them listed under 'Secretarial' or 'Office Space' in the Yellow Pages. Also, we asked members to tell other suites about us."

SPIN-OFF $$$

Many trade associations are lucky to break even on membership dues. But your membership roster provides a group of people with very specific focus, people who have already proved how keen their interest in what you have to offer is by forking over dues. Once you build a membership base, you can sell that captive audience all manner of services, often beginning with a convention.

Conventions serve two functions. They provide a much needed forum where members network, meet suppliers, and hear experts; and, eventually, they can make lots of money for the trade association. (See Trade Show.)

Most new associations start with newsletters or some form of communication to members. Early in its history, IDEA changed its newsletter into a full-fledged magazine called *Dance Exercise Today.* Not only does the magazine format provide more space to inform readers, it also finds its support in revenues from advertisers ranging from Reebok shoes to Lincoln-Mercury cars. Most trade organizations also sell reference and marketing material, including audio and video tapes.

Once you let members know you're available on a continuing basis, decide what service is most crucial to your particular industry. If you decide to include the service as a member benefit, it can act as a powerful enticement to join the association; if you charge extra for the service, it can add money to your coffers.

What the aerobics industry most needed was liability insurance. Now, an IDEA member can purchase $100,000 worth of insurance through the association for yearly premiums of just $150. Kathie Davis estimates similar coverage would cost an independent anywhere from $500 to $1,000.

The turnkey office group, on the other hand, sorely needed a referral network. When a new suite joins ESN, its name immediately goes into the continually updated directory which the association sends to anyone interest in renting turnkey offices. If a corporation needs satellite offices in a half-dozen sites, it calls ESN for referrals. Although the network is free both to the corporation and to the turnkey office, it is an expensive undertaking since ESN must print directories and maintain a toll-free number. But because it is a valuable service, ESN can charge relatively hefty dues of nearly $300 a year.

Jane Booras, who ran an executive suite herself for fifteen years, also consults. Not only does consulting provide extra income, "It also keeps me in touch with the day-to-day concerns of the industry. It helps what I do on a national basis," she says.

SUGGESTION BOXES

How do you know what your members most need? Ask them, and ask other people who follow your industry. Set up an advisory panel of industry leaders early on to get feedback and to associate opinion-makers with your association. They often consider the publicity as payment enough.

IDEA created an advisory board of medical experts. "We found ten professionals from various fields—a nutritionist, cardiologist, an exercise physiologist, a doctor in sports medicine," Kathie Davis recalls. "That was one of the smartest things we did, because we had no track record. People didn't know who we were, but these professionals added credibility."

It is absolutely possible to run a trade association without ever stepping foot in the field it represents, if you're willing to invest in lots of quick industry education. But outsiders will battle uphill. Former operators empathize with their members because they've been there. And vice versa. Members, particularly in new fields, like to know the president of this new club they're joining has earned the right to the crown.

SOURCE

Industry Association

The American Society of Association Executives, 1575 Eye St., N.W., Washington, D.C. 20005 (202) 626-2727

Turnkey Office

> *"I like being in the background, making my tenants' businesses work. I get a charge out of knowing they couldn't get things done if I weren't here."* – Barbara Hildenbrand, Hildenbrand Associates

---

Low Startup Investment: $15,000 (five offices in a low-rent district)

High Startup Investment: $200,000 (same space at a more expensive site)

Time Until Breakeven: Six months to two years

Annual Revenues: $75,000-$500,000

Annual Pre-tax Profits: $10,000-$100,000

Staffers Needed for Startup (including founder): One

When Barbara Hildenbrand's boss quit to start his own marketing company, he asked his former secretary to do his typing from her home. "I was out of a job anyway, so I said why not?" she recalls. Soon the boss took office space in an executive suite and began to sell word processing, "which was mainly me typing twelve letters an hour from home."

I CAN DO THIS

Barbara Hildenbrand decided that barely making a living wage for typing day and night made little sense. But her boss had taught her some valuable lessons. As the former secretary helped cope with his startup details, "I saw the mystique go out of starting a company," she recalls. "I felt this isn't hard, I can do this." He also introduced her to the concept of turnkey offices, also known as executive suites or business centers.

Executive suites are small one- or two-person offices that a tenant rents, complete with receptionist, furniture, common areas such as conference rooms, and optional extras such as typing services. According to Jane Booras, executive director of the Executive Suite Network, an industry trade association, each of the two to three thousand such turnkey offices across the country "generates a generic office environment." One-person proprietorships or branch offices "need space, but not the one thousand square feet a developer wants to sell."

Intrigued by the concept, Barbara called the real estate offices at Las Colinas, an office-and-residential development under construction near her Irving, Texas, home. "I signed the standard lease for fifty-two hundred square feet at $6,000 a month. I didn't know enough to negotiate. I met with their space planners, and we put in eighteen offices."

In March, 1980, Barbara had a $72,000 annual commitment—and nobody to pay the rent. It was then she realized she had bought herself not just a typing job, but also a sales job. As the building's construction dragged on, she met with prospective tenants in coffee shops and pointed to the hole in the ground that was going to be their office.

A real estate broker saw a tag line on the bottom of the construction sign that advertised executive suites and became her first tenant. The development's real estate office also referred some tenants, and Barbara got another referral from the local chamber of commerce soon after she had joined. But lining up tenants was only one of many challenges. Income also depended on selling her typing and telephone answering services to outside clients. A Yellow Pages ad brought in some business for the answering services, and notices pinned to university bulletin boards generated some typing.

By August, nine of her eighteen offices were rented. Barbara, wearing hats of office manager, receptionist, typist, and space salesperson, had gone through $3,000 in savings, $4,000 from a bank loan against her car, and $4,000 from her parents. "I was so scared I broke out in hives," until, somehow, during the last two weeks in August, she rented seven more offices. By year-end, she had hired a receptionist/typist and rented an additional eight hundred square feet. This time, however, Barbara's real estate client negotiated the lease and got her better terms.

Today, Hildenbrand Associates Inc. operates forty-seven offices from eleven thousand square feet. Rent has escalated to $17,000 a month, and Barbara's payroll covers one part-time and three full-time employees. Revenues for 1987 topped $380,000 with expenses—including Barbara's own salary—of about $360,000.

THE DEVELOPER CONNECTION

Barbara Hildenbrand's success story is being duplicated in turnkey offices across the country. "You see basically three scenarios," says Jane Booras: "An entrepreneur takes a lease on anything from two thousand square feet to a whole floor, then subleases to tenants. Or developers see executive suites as a way to incubate tenants and bounce them to larger space, so they divide a floor and hire somebody to run them. Or finally, developers contract with secretarial services who run the space on a joint venture basis."

Jane Booras says five offices in a low-rent industrial space might cost as little as $15,000, assuming the telephone system is already in place. You can rent furniture, or even have tenants rent their own if you're on a shoestring. However, larger space in a high-rent district can go for many times that amount. Lease commitments usually run five years, so make sure you have either tenants lined up or a cushion to pay the rent.

Some landlords like the idea of executive suites, gambling that small business tenants will grow and buy larger space in their buildings. Barbara Hildenbrand estimates that former tenants now occupy thirty-five thousand square feet in and around her building. With such trading-up potential in mind, you might talk some developers into favorable rent terms, or ask landlords to throw in an extra, such as maintenance.

WHO WILL YOU RENT TO?

Once you have the space, you have to fill it. In addition to tapping real estate and civic contacts, Jane Boorhas recommends targeted direct mail. "Decide who the best clients are according to your location and expertise," she advises. For example, a downtown executive suite may appeal to financial types or attorneys. Or you might have a word processing system that allows you to write press releases quickly, which might appeal to public relations firms.

Another client source is the Executive Suite Network, which lists members in a directory and provides a toll-free telephone service to companies wishing to locate turnkey office space in distant cities.

Selling turnkey office space differs from selling commercial space, because you're selling your services as well as an address. Point out the benefits. Tenants make no capital investment in furniture or secretarial and reception personnel. Clients can be in business overnight since everything is already in place. They don't have to make long-term commitments. While many executive suites ask for six-month or one-year leases, Barbara Hildenbrand leases month to month and requires no contract. "I found even those companies that sign a lease leave when they're ready," she shrugs. "Also, it's a selling point to say you just have to pay me a month's rent." Those tenants who are branch offices of out-of-town corporations also have to pass leases through legal departments, a procedure that can take as long as the duration of the lease.

SERVICE MENU

When you sell space in an executive suite, you sell convenience. A large menu of services provides two advantages: first, it attracts clients, and, secondly, it adds profit centers. Barbara Hildenbrand, for example, gets about half her revenues from rent. She prices office space high enough to cover rent on common areas, such as conference rooms, hallways, and the reception area. Secretarial and answering service income, both from tenants and off-premise clients, provides about 12 percent of revenues. A similar amount comes from Telex and facsimile services. The rest comes from what she calls "miscellaneous": markups on photocopies, postage, and office supplies.

Keep in mind your biggest expense beyond rent is personnel. Typing is a necessity for your tenants, but you may barely cover a typist's salary from what you can charge. However, you can get better markups on telephone answering services since a receptionist can answer calls for dozens of clients. If you buy a software package to handle your billing, you might offer to do client billings as well.

By offering a number of special services, your client base encompasses more than your tenants, although they represent your captive audience. Barbara Hildenbrand also offers an incoming mail service for $20 a month to entrepreneurs who want a snazzy business address, but operate out of their homes. "One client is an interior designer who needs a place to receive fabric samples and the image our address gives her."

While offering services other than office space boosts income, it also adds an unknown element to your business. You always know how much rent to expect, but you never know how much typing you'll have from week to week. The period between Thanksgiving and New Year's may be dead, for example. One solution is to keep your staff lean and hire temporaries for busy periods.

You also sell a tangible ambiance. Barbara Hildenbrand points out that clients are typically one-person shops who would miss the social interaction of an office if they didn't talk with other tenants and her staff. "I tell the phone room crew to talk with the tenants. If you're not on the phone, talk about the game last night or your vacation. It's not goofing off, it's PR. The tenants don't realize it, but we babysit a lot."

Because you "incubate" startup entrepreneurs until they leave for larger quarters, executive suite managers say they see all sorts of interesting new businesses. Barbara Hildenbrand's former boss— the one who introduced her to turnkey offices in the first place— actually took space in her complex. "First he leased my smallest office, then he ended up with two of my largest spaces," she says. "He finally moved out because he needed more space. Then he signed on with my answering services."

SOURCES

Industry Associations

Executive Suite Network, 17304 N. Preston Rd., Suite 800, Dallas, Tex. 75252 (800) 237-4741

National Association of Secretarial Services, 100 2nd Ave. S., Suite 604-S, St. Petersburg, Fla. 33701 (813) 823-3646

Publications

Office Magazine, 1600 Summer St., P.O. Box 1231, Stamford, Conn. 06904 (203) 327-9670
Office Systems, 941 Danbury Rd., P.O. Box 150, Georgetown, Conn. 06829 (203) 544-9526

Consultant

Jane Booras, 17304 N. Preston Rd., Suite 800, Dallas, Tex. 75252 (800) 237-4741

Child Care

Daycare Center

> *"Other people might see grubby clothes and running noses. But I think kids are absolutely charming. They are hysterical. It is so exciting to watch their development. Children know so much, even as babies."* – Jamie MacIntyre-Southworth, The Learning Tree Association

Low Startup Investment: $25,000 (opening in a church or municipal facility)

High Startup Investment: $1.5 million (building a large structure)

Time Until Breakeven: One to two years

Annual Revenues: $200,000-$1 million

Annual Pre-tax Profits: $20,000-$150,000

Staffers Needed for Startup (including founder): Five to ten

Society has not experienced such high numbers of mothers in the work force since Rosie the Riveter went home at the end of World War II. The U.S. Census Bureau counted 36 million working women in 1985, a year in which the country's birthrate had reached a twenty-year high. That means 8.9 million kids under age six had working moms, a figure that won't top-out until around 1995 when the Census Bureau expects 14.6 million preschool-age children will have mothers who are not full-time homemakers. The National Association for the Education of Young Children (NAEYC) estimates that licensed programs grew 72 percent from 133,000 to 229,000 facilities between 1977 and 1985, and industry insiders predict a 15-percent-a-year climb until 1992. Even then growth should continue as more parents accept daycare over other child-care alternatives.

Operators in most parts of the country simply don't worry about advertising to sign up enrollees; many for-profit centers have waiting lists of children clamoring to get in at tuitions ranging from $50 to as much as $200 a week. In 1986, *Venture Magazine* reported that licensed centers cared for just half of all children needing such supervision. Demand simply outstrips supply. "Some children are signed up months before they are born," reports Jamie MacIntyre-Southworth, whose five Learning Tree schools in Pittsburgh generated revenues of $800,000 in 1986. Her schools were so successful, she opened another two facilities in 1987.

THE GOOD-CAUSE SYNDROME

If you're successful, you can expect easily to garner 10-percent pretax profits. Given that norm and the country's demographics, the industry's reputation for lousy profits is downright confusing. Roger Neugebauer, editor of the *Child Care Information Exchange,* a publication aimed at daycare directors, suspects that "the profit motive is not as strong for a daycare operator as someone who is in the business of selling knick-knacks." Because "daycare operators may enter the business with a good-cause syndrome," perhaps many fail to stress cost-savings and to pursue opportunities that could add substantially to the bottom line.

Many observers claim anyone who doesn't make a comfortable living from daycare suffers from a lack of business sense. "A lot of elementary school teachers are really dissatisfied with their jobs and think they can just open a daycare center," observes Jamie MacIntyre-Southworth, who taught early-childhood education on the university level before launching the first of her schools in 1976.

Although teachers may start the majority of daycare centers, many team with partners who have some business expertise. Teacher Kay Koulouras, director of Perry Kay Nursery School and Kindergarten in Southfield, Michigan, concentrates on managing her center's fourteen-person staff and curriculum, but turns over business chores to her husband Perry, who has a management background. This division of labor is one reason Kay says her school has been successful. "My husband takes on most of the bookwork responsibilities," such as filling out federal tax forms, she explains.

FAMILY AFFAIR

Daycare, more than many other businesses, often assumes a family flavor. During various stages in Perry Kay's twenty-five year history, Kay Koulouras's mother cooked, her mother-in-law watched the grandchildren, her father-in-law did the gardening, and her sons earned allowances for cleaning the facilities. "It's a nice human story," says Kay. "But it also helped us cut costs."

The enormous 316-child Council Oaks Learning Campus in the Tulsa suburb of Broken Arrow, Oklahoma, goes a step further in its division of responsibilities by installing a business manager to run each facility. "The education people are free to concentrate on education," says President Jim Seawright, an architect who opted to build the school after a client backed out of the project. Of the narrower range of responsibilities, he says, "The teachers love it. They don't like to worry with the payroll, accounting, scheduling."

The $1.5 million that Jim Seawright's limited partnership raised to open his first school in 1986 brushes the highest costs of entering daycare. With seed money of $20,000 to $50,000, you can rent and furnish a church basement or renovate a house to accommodate fifty children, which Jamie MacIntyre-Southworth suggests as a threshold for breaking even. To build your own facility, at least quadruple that figure. "A good number of kids is sixty to eighty," she says. "Too many facilities with more children are just warehousing." Some operators gain reputation and experience by first offering family care out of their homes.

A STARTUP QUIZ

With no national guidelines to follow, you'll run across different requirements for licensing, building codes, and certification depending on your state. Local social or human services divisions of state government can provide legal guidelines for starting a daycare center. In addition, check with one of the three hundred fifty early-childhood associations across the country affiliated with NAEYC for more tips on starting a center.

Beyond legal requirements, the entry decisions you face come in great big clumps. In taking the following "test," recognize that not all answers are clear cut. What's right for one neighborhood and one operation may receive failing marks in a different situation. Nevertheless, questions to consider include these:

▪ Should you apply for government funding? A time-consuming, laborious process, some warn, but government funding can help you break even faster, particularly if you locate in a disadvantaged area.

▪ Should you accept babies? Parents of infants literally scurry to find facilities, and you can charge more for little ones than for their older siblings. The downside: infants suffer higher health risks, and you need a greater staff-to-child ratio to care for non-toilet-trained babies.

▪ Will purchasing a facility rather than renting pay off in the long run?

▪ Will serving lunch be worth the extra personnel and insurance costs involved in running a kitchen?

▪ Should you offer transportation? Many parents view transportation as a big enticement, but keeping vehicles on the road is expensive. Kay Koulouras recalls the emotional relief she felt when Perry Kay dropped its bus service: "I was not comfortable till the last bus came back every day."

THE PERSONNEL DILEMMA

As with any service company, personnel remains the most costly part of doing business in a daycare center. Kay Koulouras reserves 65 percent to 70 percent of her facility's annual budget to meet the payroll costs of her professionals, all trained in early childhood education. No one expects personnel costs to shrink. But operators say daycare has barely explored ways to cut costs and make money through implementing procedures that other industries take for granted. Consider computerizing some administrative functions, for example, or join a central commissary kitchen that services several schools. One dietitian can prepare meals for several schools and scout out discounts for buying in bulk.

In addition, utilize your assets—namely your building and teachers—for longer hours. Offer services beyond babysitting. For example, Council Oaks' offerings range from music, dancing, and karate instruction, to scuba diving lessons in the school's indoor-outdoor pool. Parents pay for these ancillary services on top of tuition fees, which are $65 a week for a five-year-old and $78 for an infant. "If both parents work, their time is limited," explains Jim Seawright. "They just don't have time to take a child for ballet lessons after they come home from daycare. Our job is to cut down on the taxicab effect."

Council Oaks, which accepts kids aged six weeks to twelve years, also rents out its gymnasium to neighborhood groups a couple of nights a week. Some operations increase revenue by staying open late for parents who work night shifts. Latchkey of University Place in Tacoma, Washington, attracts some twenty-five students to a "kids' night out" once every three months. For $10 each, the children attend a Friday night slumber party, complete with popcorn, video cassettes, and dance marathons; the parents get the night off; and the center averages a $150 profit.

Jamie MacIntyre-Southworth looks for her edge by attaching her centers to hospitals, an affiliation that provides many advantages. For one thing, the facilities furnish a ready pool of enrollees: some 90 percent of the four hundred kids enrolled in Learning Tree schools are offspring of hospital staffers. Perhaps more important, the hospitals help foot the bills in various ways. In addition to outright subsidies or deductions from paychecks of parents who wish to participate, one hospital provides rent-free space and maintenance. "In that center," says Jamie, "we charge parents just $50 a week."

CASHING IN ON EMPLOYER CARE

Learning Tree's hospital connection acts as a variation on the theme of employer child care. Once touted as an enlightened employee benefit, daycare programs operated by the boss have not materialized to any serious degree. In 1986, the Conference Board of New York City, reported that out of 6 million U.S. businesses, "only three thousand gave support to employee child-care needs." Working parents should not lose hope, however. The Employee Benefits Research Institute forecasts child care as *the* benefit of the 1990s.

Instead of operating a business they know nothing about, however, many employers turn to people like Jamie MacIntyre-Southworth. These corporations subsidize for-profit centers rather than open their own. Barbara Willer, director of information services at the National Association for the Education of Young Children, calls on-premise employer care just one of many options favored by employers. "In one common situation, various employers form a consortium and contract out child care to a central center," she says.

START AND SELL

In daycare, bigger often means better—or at least more profitable (as long as you don't sacrifice quality for quantity). If you cater to masses of children either in one location or in separate centers, you can buy bulk quantities of everything from crayons to apples to cleaning services. When you employ dozens and collect tuition from hundreds, you need—and can afford—tools like computers for bookkeeping. Economies of scale lead many operators to expand before their first center hits profitability. Jim Seawright says that even before Council Oaks opened, he lined up investors for the second of the fifteen to twenty centers he plans by 1988. With eager investors waiting, "Financing is just not a problem," he insists.

Despite the advantages of size, daycare remains an industry of small operations. In 1986, the five existing national chains managed fewer than 15 percent of all for-profit centers. However, the National Association for Child Care Management singled out an entire mid-sized segment of new companies in 1986, each of which plans to open anywhere from seventy-five centers to two thousand by 1990. While many of those new facilities will start from the ground up, adding one new center at a time, "there are now a number of entrepreneurs whose game plan is to build up their child care companies to a certain size, then sell," the association reports. In fact, a number of brokers specialize in finding daycare buyers and sellers, a resource you might tap to get in quickly or when it comes time to sell.

LICENSING AND THE FUTURE

Most entrepreneurs expect stricter government guidelines in the future. And, at least publicly, most say that professional operators have nothing to fear. Guidelines are minimums, after all, and many centers set far higher standards than does the government. "We exceed guidelines so far that we won't be affected at all by increased licensing," says Jim Seawright. Jamie MacIntyre-Southworth is more vocal in her support of licensing: "I can take you to five places where people keep half a dozen children in the basement and tell fire department inspectors they are all grandchildren or nephews," she fumes. "Children lose their lives and are damaged emotionally by programs run by individuals who have no understanding of the business."

The national demand for child care seems poised to grow beyond the mid-1990s. The Market Compilation and Research Bureau reports that within six months of the birth of their babies, 63 percent of new mothers currently return to work. The National Association of Child Care Management sees continued demand in Southern California, Florida, the Central Atlantic States, and Eastern Massachusetts, but reports at least temporary overbuilding in Chicago and Seattle. As with any other startup, check out the competition before moving in. If advertising to attract enrollees appears heavy, or if tuitions seem uniformly low, you might want to locate elsewhere.

Barbara Willer at the National Association for the Education of Young Children has no doubt that in the future greater percentages of parents will opt for licensed daycare over other options, such as one parent remaining at home or leaving a child with a relative or neighbor. "The decrease in numbers of babies will be offset by a larger percent of children in group programs," she predicts. "Economic conditions dictate that both parents work." And, as daycare becomes more commonplace, she suspects parents increasingly value the social experiences daycare provides to their children.

Even the financial community appears impressed with daycare and its potential. In late 1985, *Money* magazine named Kinder-Care Learning Centers, which operates more than one thousand facilities across the country, as one of the "twelve stocks that should stand the test of time."

SOURCES

Industry Associations

National Association for the Education of Young Children, 1834 Connecticut Ave., N.W., Washington, D.C. 20009 (202) 232-8777

National Association for Child Care Management, 1255 23rd St., N.W., Washington, D.C. 20037 (202) 452-8100

Child Care Action Campaign, 132 W. 43rd St., 2nd Floor, New York, N.Y. 10036 (212) 334-9595

Publications

Child Care Information Exchange, P.O. Box 2890, Redmond, Wash. 98073 (206) 883-9394

Day Care Information Service, 4550 Montgomery Ave., Bethesda, Md. 20814 (301) 656-6666

Consultant

Resources for Child Care Management, P.O. Box 669, Summit, N.J. 07901 (201) 766-9237

Playgym

> *"I love watching the parents' excitement over the things their children learn. It's so much fun to watch the parents of infants when their babies crawl for the first time."* – Donna Porter, *Playful Parenting of Lancaster*

Low Startup Investment: $15,000 (operating out of community facilities)

High Startup Investment: $100,000 (outfitting your own large gym)

Time Until Breakeven: Six months to two years

Annual Revenues: $30,000-$500,000

Annual Pre-tax Profits: $10,000-$150,000

Staffers Needed for Startup (including founder): Two

If parachute play doesn't delight you, then the silly pool surely will. These are a couple of favorite activities that Playful Parenting, a Sinking Spring, Pennsylvania, franchise, devised for parents and their six-week- to six-year-old kids.

In Parachute Play, half-dozen four-year-olds pile into the multicolored parachute while their moms and dads hold the edges high. Giggles turn to uncontrollable, down-in-the-tummy laughter as the parents circle, lifting the parachute to create bubbles that the children scramble to break. Each time a kid tries to climb out, she tumbles back and the laughter reaches higher. (This event teaches concepts of space and volume.)

The Silly Pool: Sometimes bright red jello cubes fill the wading pool. Sometimes it's rice, tortilla flour, or cooked spaghetti. Turn a bunch of six-month-olds loose in the silly pool with plastic utensils to scoop up the "yuk." Then take bets on who has more fun: the babies or their parents. (This event teaches tactile and sensory awareness.)

TYKE-SIZED PHYS ED

Playful Parenting is part of a new phenomenon of businesses that offer improved physical fitness for very young children. There's always been Little League and Girl Scouts for boys and girls of grade-school age. But these new programs start with massaging activities for children as young as six weeks. Parents today are open to the idea of child fitness programs because they're worried about warnings that our children spend too much time in front of the tube and because physical education has withered in budget-strapped schools.

Some programs are full-fledged children's gyms, with equipment, activities, and instruction. Sportastiks, a program franchised out of Champaign, Illinois, that takes children age eighteen months to eighteen years, estimates that 5 percent of its children are "serious gymnasts," some bound for the Olympics, according to Bev Hayasaki, president of the company and wife of vice president Yoshi Hayasaki—who just happens to be twenty-time U.S. National Champion in Gymnastics.

But rather than train superbabies, most gyms (including Sportastiks) emphasize the fun and learning of physical education. Explains Bill Caplin, proprietor of My Gym Children's Fitness Center, a five-unit chain headquartered in Santa Monica, California: "There's a need for competition, but not in the ages we work with. We lay the foundation for physical education with cooperative sports and games—for instance, two children hold a ball between their tummies in a relay race. They have to learn sharing and working together to make the game work."

Some programs involve parents as equal participants, and aim to strengthen the parent-child relationship along with the little one's biceps. This is particularly appealing to working professionals who crave quality time with their children but are a little inhibited about where to start. Gary Siebert, president of Playful Parenting, often recites statistics indicating "the average American mother spends less than four minutes a day playing with her child, and the average

American father spends less than thirty seconds a day playing with his child."

All the fitness programs emphasize social and cognitive skills along with the physical ones. "We change the room decor with each five-week session," says Donna Porter, who operates Playful Parenting of Lancaster from the top floor of a Landisville, Pennsylvania, firehouse. "This session, the emphasis is on letters, so we have alphabet designs throughout. When we do the letter 'E,' we pretend we're elephants and swing our 'trunks' during the 'Make Believe' session."

BEVERLY HILLS OR CHURCH BASEMENTS

Startup costs depend on the type of facility. Franchises of Gymboree, Burlingame, California, sometimes set up in churches or YMCAs where rent is almost negligible. The company's franchise literature says $20,000 will buy you play equipment, insurance, and rights to two franchise locations. Playful Parenting centers range from mall locations, where the rent alone might run $60,000 a year, to franchises in existing daycare centers, where the primary expense is equipment such as tumbling mats and hoola hoops. Its brochure says to expect to pay $25,000 for equipment and set-up, and have access to another $10,000 to $20,000 for advertising, insurance, and working capital.

Bill Caplin chose a Beverly Hills site for his second My Gym. "For us, exposure is important. We're the Cadillac of the children's fitness industry and need to look the part." My Gym spends a lot of money on equipment, as well, ranging from a ceiling mechanism to lower swings and rings to a custom-designed, crawl-through castle. Keep in mind that above all, the exercises have to be safe and fun.

Charging $80 for eight one-hour classes, My Gym targets the higher end of the income spectrum. Says Bill: "We're getting more nannies these days. Both parents are working, and the nannies bring the children for social interaction with other kids."

Operators of less expensive programs agree that the better educated the parents, the more likely they are to enroll their children. "A lot of my parents are doctors or schoolteachers, who recognize the value of what we do," says Donna Porter, who charges $30 for a five-week session. The lesson: Look for neighborhoods with professional parents.

BE AGGRESSIVE

The big challenge is spreading the message that organized fitness programs that combine social and mental games beat taking the kids to the park. If you can't afford advertising, let local reporters know about your program. You may get great publicity through articles describing toddlers who slide, bounce, climb, and crawl. "You have to be pretty aggressive about getting out in the community and making yourself known," says Donna Porter. She calls several families every night, picking numbers from the phone book, to let them know about her center. She also rounds up some of her toddlers and their parents to participate under the Playful Parenting banner in charity events, like the Baby Olympics benefit for the March of Dimes.

Bill Caplin sends mailers to schools and invites parents into My Gym for open houses. "You can also send an instructor to a school with portable equipment," he suggests. Daycare centers looking for ways to entertain their charges might welcome you with open arms.

Such an outreach program can also provide a few extra bucks. You can arrange to visit a daycare facility once a week and give classes all day long to different age groups. Give the center a percentage of the customer fees, and the school director likely will welcome you aboard. You'll probably convert some of those children into regular members at your facility, too.

While classes will provide the bulk of your revenues, use your facilities for such extras as birthday parties and even summer camp. "Business is a little slower in the summer because some people take their children to the pool instead of coming to us," says Donna Porter. On the other hand, "Kids in nursery school come to us only during the summer." Her camps run three hours a day, and parents can sign up for one to four weeks.

For entrepreneurs who really think big, consider what happened with Gymboree. The company generated $10 million in 1986 through three hundred fifty franchise centers. In addition to exercise classes, Gymboree keeps the fun—and revenues—rolling with such extras as videos, books, dolls, clothing, and toys. In 1985, twelve years after setting up the first Gymboree class in a San Raphael, California, community center, *Fortune* magazine put founder Joan Barnes's personal net worth at over $2 million.

But before you think big time, you must build a name—and an income—with your gym. Recognize you're dealing with little people who have yet to learn the fine points of walking, much less tumbling, somersaults, or more advanced techniques. Make sure you staff accordingly. Bill Caplin limits My Gym's classes to fifteen children, and puts three teachers on the floor. Donna Porter needs only one teacher for about ten kids since parents participate, spotting for their own children. "But you can't just hire teachers off the street. Both my part-time instructors have degrees in education and experience with handicapped and preschool-aged children."

YOU GOTTA LOVE 'EM

Bill Caplin, still a bachelor, loves playing with the children. "I was a camp counselor and taught phys ed at a Catholic school. But teachers are underpaid and not appreciated. So, wanting to combine my love of sports and children, I went to work at a children's gym." After running somebody else's gym for while, he decided to open his own. Now he owns two My Gym Children's Fitness Centers, a partner owns two, and his brother-in-law runs another—and Bill talks of franchising.

Like so many people who deal with children, Donna Porter acknowledges her satisfaction with her work goes far beyond the $30,000 or so she expects to make in 1987, her first year after buying the business from another Playful Parenting franchisee for $30,000. A bookkeeper by training, Donna once ran a daycare program from her home and wanted to work with children again. "But I wanted something people chose to come to, rather than felt they were forced into."

Donna finds a personal fulfillment working with her families. "From the time I was four years old, I always wanted lots of children," she says.

Playful Parenting's franchise brochure quotes President Gary Siebert: "A hundred years from now it will not matter what my bank account was, the sort of house I lived in, or the kind of car I drove—but the world may be different because I was important in the life of a child."

Sleep-away Camp

> *"I remember one child I spent three years teaching to swim— he was a real rock, but he finally learned. Camp directors get the same gratification as teachers. I began working with children when I was seventeen as a dishwasher at a camp and have never stopped since."* – David Glaser, Camp Trywoodie

Low Startup Investment: $75,000 (leasing a small camp in an unpopulated region)

High Startup Investment: $1.5 million (buying a large facility near a big city)

Time Until Breakeven: Three to ten years

Annual Revenues: $100,000-$1.2 million

Annual Pre-tax Profits: $15,000-$250,000

Staffers Needed for Startup (including founder): Five to fifty

Expect some trade-offs when you run a sleep-away camp. For every food fight you break up, there's a child arguing that you're the best darn counselor in the history of camps. For every mosquito bite, there's a star twinkling at midnight. For every homesick camper, there are half a dozen others vowing to return next year.

CHILDREN AND MOTHER NATURE

For better or worse, you can divide a camp's attractions into two categories: children and nature. Jeffrey Solomon runs the New

York City–based National Camp Association advisory service, which matches children and camps in much the same way travel agents recommend vacations. "Were you a camper?" he asks. "Camp is something only people who've experienced it can appreciate. Nothing takes the place of the interaction with other kids and the growth a child goes through during those weeks. Camping provides a special moment in time. Watching a shy, insecure child blossom benefits the camp director as much as the child."

Observers say camps are prepping for a resurgency. The industry suffered declining enrollments in the 1970s and 1980s as fewer children fit into the five- to fifteen-year bracket. But all that's changed as the first members of today's baby boom exchange their toddler status for childhood. The first beneficiaries—summer day camps for preschoolers—have already seen full enrollments. "It's not unusual to see day camps with five hundred, six hundred kids," says David Glaser, a camp consultant who ran Camp Trywoodie, a sleep-away camp in Hyde Park, New York, for thirty years. Now, day-camp grads are starting to pile into sleep-away bunks.

SETTING UP CAMP

There are three ways to enter the camp business: starting from scratch, leasing a camp, or buying an existing facility. Each approach has its ups and downs:

▪ You can still find thirty to one hundred acres of virgin wilderness just perfect for your Camp Sky Blue Waters—if you can convince parents to send their children to Montana or other faraway sites. When starting from scratch in more populous, less remote areas, expect to spend upwards of $1 million for land and to construct facilities sufficient to feed, house, and entertain the two hundred campers that comprise a mid-sized camp.

Of course, not all camps offer the cookie-cutter activities of swimming, horseback riding, computers, and belt-making. If you delete horseback riding, you've saved a couple hundred thousand and reduced stiff insurance costs as well. (Insurance is a growing problem in the industry, and some camps have cut back on some high-risk programs to reduce premiums.) If your property's lake meets the local health department's specifications for swimming, you won't have to dig a $100,000 pool. Particularly if you offer a specialty, such as foreign languages or football, you may start small and grow as your income allows. Also, "Opening within one hundred fifty miles of New York City will probably cost ten times what a Midwest camp costs," says David Glaser.

▪ If you lease a camp site, expect the annual rent to equal about 10 percent of a purchase price. Leasing is good for property owners who keep title to the land while turning over use of a site to a camp operator. This arrangement is good for you if you want to see how well a particular site draws campers, or if you want a less expensive introduction to the business. The American Camping Association accredits both camps and sites. While accreditation is not mandatory, the seal of approval tells parents your camp meets certain minimum standards.

▪ Buying an existing camp is, by far, the most common entry point to the camp business. This solution isn't cheaper than starting with an uncleared forest (if you can find one), but you might break even faster since, along with swimming pools and tennis courts, you inherit a list of children who attended last year. If the camp has a good reputation, at least half the campers may return for a second year. Also, check to see if the camp is accredited. You can always apply for accreditation, but the process takes one summer and the American Camping Association may ask you to make costly improvements.

You also may need less hard cash to buy an existing camp than to start from scratch. If the owner agrees to finance, you may put one-third down and pay the balance over five years from the camp's cash flow. Also, buying an existing camp presents innumerable benefits for entrepreneurs who have never worked in the field before. Systems are already in place and you can sometimes work out a "transition period," where you come on as camp director while asking the old owner to stay on for the first season. That way, you become familiar with the camp and the parents get to know you.

You also can shop for bargains among non-operating camps. During the lean years, a number of camps closed down. Because you'll have to spruce up the camp and recruit and accredit from scratch, you may be able to buy an abandoned site for half the price of an operating camp.

Dave Glaser sold Camp Trywoodie in 1986 for around $650,000 to an adult religious group which adapted the grounds for a retreat. The 200-camper operation had provided annual gross revenues of

$300,000 to $400,000 for years, but Dave was in his sixties and his longtime partner was ill. It took two years to find a buyer, says Dave, because "camps just can't put an ad in the paper. You'd lose parents if they think that you're going out of business." So if you're in the market to buy a camp, check with camp owners (many know what's going on with competitors), brokers who specialize in camps, and the American Camping Association.

YOU WORK FOR A LIVING

Once you have a facility, figure on working not just the two summer months when your camp is operating, but another nine or ten months as well. "The easiest part of my year was always summer, because then the staff helped," says David. As many as thirty percent of camp operators have other careers (many are teachers), and squeeze in such duties as recruiting staff and campers and property maintenance. In addition, a few brave souls court out-of-season business. "Particularly camps near population centers can attract corporations for retreats, or religious groups," says Jeff Solomon. A few operators winterize buildings and market to groups all winter long.

Recruiting begins as children hug their counselors goodbye and receive a registration form for next year. You can send campers (and parents) newsletters updating them on the new gymnastics program you plan, or mail out yearbooks containing pictures of last year's staff-camper softball game. If 50 percent of last year's kids promise to return this year, you're half way to capacity. You can ask for a deposit on tuition (which averages $2,400 to $3,400 nation-wide for eight-week sessions), and use part of that capital for marketing.

Camps find new recruits through three basic sources: advertising, camp fairs, and referral agencies. Most northeastern camps consider Sunday's *New York Times* the top forum for their ads. Camps in other parts of the country zero in on large city publications. If you run a specialty camp that attracts children from all over the country, you can also advertise in specialty publications. For example, tennis camps might advertise in *Tennis Magazine*, and camps for overweight children could check out weight-watcher magazines. Newspaper ads generally start in early January, and some camps that offer four-week sessions advertise into the summer.

Camp fairs, which often take place in January and February, represent an increasingly popular expo for your wares. Organizers, which might be the local YMCA or other youth groups, sell booths for $100 to $400 and invite parents to bring children by to see what different camps offer. At the fair, give out brochures and fact sheets on your camp, and collect names of potential campers for later follow-up.

Private referral agencies, such as the one Jeff Solomon runs, charge camps between 10 percent and 15 percent of the total tuitions paid by campers they place. Instead of merely listing what camps are available, the agencies match a child's interests, geography, and budget to a particular camp. The American Camping Association performs the same service for accredited camp members for a $350 annual fee. When you're working on 15-percent to 20-percent profit margins, you barely break even on referrals. However, next year, if those same children return on their own, you make your full profit.

Parents rarely part with tuition without some convincing. Once you snare an inquiry, ask to visit children's homes. Bring along slides or video tapes of last year's highlights, or, if you're selling your first season, at least bring photos of the facilities. You can invite parents to drive out if your camp is close enough to a population center. One Catskill Mountain operator rents a New York City hotel suite during the spring when parents are busy comparing camps. Then he invites families to stop by the hotel to see video presentations of canoe trips and drama classes.

RECRUITING GUIDES

Your other recruiting chore involves finding staffers. Most camps operate with one employee per every three or four campers. That includes counselors, nurses, cooks, and special instructors. To find employees, check with the American Camping Association's staff placement service. You can also run your own ads and contact college employment offices.

Your best new employees, however, may be former campers. After all, they know what camping is all about—and they know your own camp's particular charms. If your camp is as much fun as it should be, you won't have to sell them on working for a summer or two. They'll come to you. For example, when the kids found out he had sold Camp Trywoodie, Dave Glaser says he fielded some pretty nasty reactions. "They were angry with me, saying they wouldn't get the chance to work for me as counselors."

SOURCES

Industry Association

American Camping Association, Bradford Woods, 5000 State Rd., 67 North, Martinsville, Ind. 46151 (317) 342-8456

Publication

Camping Magazine, Bradford Woods, 5000 State Rd., 67 North, Martinsville, Ind. 46151 (317) 342-8456

Consultant

David Glaser, 10 Covey Rd., Hyde Park, N.Y. 12538 (914) 229-2971

Communications

Book Producer

> *"Book producing is a perfect fit for an eclectic mind. For me, there's a book in everything. The business gives the opportunity to explore." — Sue Katz, Sue Katz & Associates*

Low Startup Investment: $1,500 (to put together a book proposal and page layout from a home office)

High Startup Investment: $30,000 (for an office and assistant)

Time Until Breakeven: Six months to two years

Annual Revenues: $75,000-$1 million

Annual Pre-tax Profits: $10,000-$200,000

Staffers Needed for Startup (including founder): One

Quick, what do the following books have in common? The *Joy of Sex, What They Don't Teach You at Harvard Business School,* and *Items from Our Catalog.* Number one, each was a bestseller. Number two, each and every one was created by a book producer, a/k/a book packager.

Book producers perform many functions, depending on the project, so the definition is still somewhat hazy. But the approximately two hundred independent producers of books in 1987 (compared with maybe fifty at the turn of the decade) do for books what movie producers do for films: Just as independent Hollywood producers hire script writers, actors, and put up part of the capital to entice a major studio to take a film under its wing, book producers hire writers, contract with designers and editors, and sometimes line up printers to deliver bound books to publishers. In other words, they take an idea for a book and nurture it into something a publisher wants to buy. Producers deliver anything from edited manuscripts to camera-ready copy and artwork to finished books to publishers.

The big difference between producing and publishing is that producers leave distribution to the publishers' massive networks.

FROM OBSCURITY TO RESPECTABILITY

A decade ago publishers often distrusted producers as purveyors of slap-dash balderdash; today, they increasingly welcome book producers aboard, almost as respected co-publishers. The reason for the 180-degree turn? Unencumbered with bureaucracy, producers often turn out books faster and cheaper than traditional publishers. The average producer has five to fifteen books in the works at any one time, while a single editor at a publishing house is responsible for more titles than that. As a producer, you can devote more attention to a project, generally producing books more efficiently and for less than a publisher could.

Your edge comes by being better equipped to tackle particular projects than anyone else. A number of book producers specialize in particular areas—and their books on do-it-yourself woodworking or financial management show their expertise. Or you can specialize in books that require sophisticated design and production techniques. If a publisher produced such four-color, illustrated books, they likely would need to price the book out of the market just to cover their costs.

Think you might like to enter the world of book producing? A publishing background makes life a lot easier since, according to a *Publishers Weekly* article, producers, or "packagers," wield "knowledge of almost all facets of publishing: contracts, selling, rights, editing, production, design, finance, etc. The packager completes about 80 percent of the publishing functions, whereas the in-house editor handles 15 to 20 percent."

Sue Katz, who launched Sue Katz & Associates Inc., in 1982 from her New York City home, had worked on both the sales and editorial end with such publishers as Holt, Rinehart & Winston, Bantam, and Scholastic. She also had a master's from Columbia University in business, which proved invaluable in putting together such titles as *Forecasting Revenues and Planning Profits.* "My original idea was to do marketing consulting for publishers, but I had a portfolio of ideas for books that I kept coming back to," Sue recalls. In the past, if her employer vetoed an idea, her only route was to drop it. "Now I had a chance to influence those ideas—but I had to get them sold."

BOOK PRODUCING FOR NONPUBLISHERS

Even you haven't spent years in publishing, you might consider entering the field if you have an organized mind, can write a quality book proposal, and have expertise in an area where publishers are clamoring for books. While you provide the specific industry expertise, you'll probably want to enlist a partner who can play all the right notes in the publishing world. And don't restrict your expertise to a single book. "Look at the broad market," advises Sue Katz. "Not just books, but newsletters and audio/visual. For example, a retailer might say, 'Retailing is a very "today" business. Maybe I could generate a newsletter on hot store designs.' Or, 'I know retailing is taught in schools. What books do they need?' "

Also, take a few courses on publishing procedures and read such industry publications as *Publishers Weekly*. Every publisher treats producers differently, but boning up on the publishing world at least helps you learn the lingo. Once you can convince publishers you have the know-how, you'll have an easier time selling your wares.

MAKE AN OFFER

The first step in selling a book is putting together a proposal. Proposals run twenty-five to one hundred pages or more and include a chapter-by-chapter outline, a sample chapter or two, and a biography of the author. Include any data that will sell the book, initially to the publisher and ultimately at the bookstore. Figures on the success of similar books or on the public's growing interest in a subject help convince a publisher that your project will sell. While too many books on a similar subject suggests a glutted market, beware of the project that has *no* competition: Perhaps publishers just don't think a book on the subject will sell.

Above all, make your proposal look professional. "Book producers might spend more money on slicking up the proposal than a writer would," says Sue Katz. "You should have more marketing information. We fuss a fair amount with the presentation."

Sue warns that for every proposal you sell, several others never see a publisher's imprint. Especially in the beginning as you develop a reputation, "you have to be very agile and know the moment to let go." On the other hand, you also have to know when to push an idea. Sue recalls the origins of the *Rock Video Book,* which she ultimately presented in camera-ready form in 1984. "The idea was born when I was watching MTV. Soon after, I met a writer who would be perfect: she was rock music critic of *Stereo Music Magazine.*" Sue bounced the idea of a book on the new music video phenomenon off an editor she knew at Bantam. Although he expressed interest, he had moved to Simon & Schuster by the time the proposal was ready. Sue had faith, however, that he'd still be interested, and sent him a mock-up of the book (meaning a cover and page layout design) along with the proposal. Simon & Schuster bit —and eventually published the book.

"If you include art, a mock-up could cost $250 to $750," says Sue. If the proposal is never sold, the designer accepts that as a kill-fee. However, the designer usually bets that a publisher will buy the book. Then the mock-up fee acts as a downpayment on the larger project.

Writers are a different story. In some cases, producers write the sample chapters themselves. Or you can contract with a freelance author to supply the sample chapters in return for expenses, usually phone bills and possibly travel fees. Like the designers, the writers hope to land a larger contract when a publisher buys the book. Knowing that many proposals never result in contracts, Sue Katz usually pays a writer a flat fee to produce sample chapters. "Sometimes it's embarrassing how small," she admits.

Once you sell the proposal, writers either sign on for a flat fee, or receive a percentage of the advance and royalties (a fifty-fifty split between packager and author is common). You either subcontract other functions, such as editing and proofreading, or perform them in-house.

ROYALTIES

Publishers pay producers in three stages. First comes the advance— or rather half the advance, since the second installment comes only after you deliver the completed project. The third stage occurs after the book is in the bookstores, when the royalties start rolling in.

Here's how it works: Let's assume you receive a $20,000 advance against royalties, which means you won't receive any further royalties until your advance is earned out. If the book sells for $20 in the bookstore and you've negotiated a 10-percent royalty fee, then ten thousand copies must be sold before your royalty payments kick in. In addition to the advance and royalties, many packagers also negotiate a flat production fee which pays for producing mechanicals.

In a variation on the theme, producers who specialize in books that require production expertise often charge publishers a per-unit production cost, much as a printer charges a publisher for books. Say a producer can deliver a full-color book for $3 per unit, using an overseas printer. The producer charges a flat rate of $3.50 per book. To offset these relatively slim profit margins, some producers retain the right to sell the book in foreign markets. Since they've already paid the expenses for color separations, producing the foreign edition costs far less than what a U.S. version costs, assuring higher overseas profits.

HOW LONG IS A PIECE OF STRING?

Producers try to cover their expenses with the advance and production fee, and make their profits on royalties. How much can a producer make? "Remember everything you've heard about what writers get paid?" says Sue Katz. "Some books get miniscule advances, others get millions. There's just no rule-of-thumb."

Some producers expand their base of acting as the middleman between writers and publishers. To increase profits and keep the creative juices flowing, Sue co-authored (as well as packaged) *Having a Love Affair with Your Own Husband (Before Someone Else Does)*. Others co-venture projects with other book producers. The approach gains them expertise and valuable publishing contacts, while multiplying their projects and visibility. "I did a co-venture on *Sports Widow's Revenge*, an event book for wives of sports fanatics," says Sue. "My co-producer was familiar with sports, so I didn't have to research that aspect of the book."

While publishers, with their vast distribution networks, remain the most common source of producers' income, lucrative contracts are to be found elsewhere. You can produce premium editions—a giveaway pamphlet, for example—for a corporation or association related to a particular book. Or you can package books for non-publishing companies like industry trade associations. Philip Lief, producer of *101 Best Businesses to Start,* finds that producing books for an association requires just as much work as producing for a publisher. But, he says, "You're guaranteed the sale of a certain quantity, which takes some of the risk out of the business."

Whether you produce books for publishers or private organizations, industry analysts predict that producers will play an increasingly important role as publishers merge into huge conglomerates. Publishers suffer from pared-down staffs while their marketing departments demand more "big" books. "Producers have the opportunity to produce books that are financially successful because we don't have to worry about the financial and editorial constraints that are normally found in a publishing house," explains Philip Lief. Given book producing's 150-percent growth rate in the past ten years, chances are there's room for creative entrepreneurs to carve out a niche.

SOURCES

Industry Association

American Book Producers Association, Fourth Floor, 319 E. 52nd St., New York, N.Y. 10022 (212) 982-8934

Publication

Publishers Weekly, 205 E. 42nd St., New York, N.Y. 10017 (212) 764-5154

Desktop Publisher

"I've always like writing. Now I get the same sort of high from design—a creative high." – Sharon Bobbitt, Publications Plus

Low Startup Investment: $10,000 (equipment only)

High Startup Investment: $15,000 (includes advertising)

Time Until Breakeven: Three months to one year

Annual Revenues: $25,000-$200,000

Annual Pre-tax Profits: $20,000-$100,000

Staffers Needed for Startup (including founder): One

In 1986, Malcolm Ross dumped a twenty-year career in chemical research to become a desktop publisher. He traded in a monthly paycheck for freelance jobs wherever he could find them. Instead of having the swanky offices and staff backups of a large corporation, he works from his Gaithersburg, Maryland, home and doubles as his own receptionist and typist. He gave up security to enter a field so green most potential clients don't even know they need him.

Malcolm Ross is pioneering in the new industry of desktop publishing by producing brochures, advertising, and other company correspondence for corporate clients. Additionally, he also publishes his own newsletter devoted to desktop publishing, The Electric Page. Did he make the right choice? "Oh Lord, yes. I don't want to be a manager again, but I'm growing so fast I'm now looking at premises outside my home." Acknowledging the inevitability of his success, he sighs: "Sooner or later, I guess I'll have to hire some help." In 1987, Malcolm expected his Electro Graphic Services Inc. to gross $120,000.

DEFINITION, PLEASE

Market-research firm Dataquest forecasts that by 1990 the desktop publishing equipment market will have exploded from 1985 sales of a puny $2.5 million to $5 *billion*. Desktop publishers are no more than micro-or personal-computer users who employ new, very "friendly" technology to compose designs on-screen rather than through paste-up, typesetting, art creation, or the like. Then, desktop publishers go one step further by reproducing near typeset-quality printouts of what they've envisioned on the screen. While some entrepreneurs use laser printers hooked up to their computers to produce a final copy, others hire a printer to deliver the final step of printing.

Just as you don't have to understand the mechanics of a car to drive one, you don't have to know the first thing about Silicon Valley to stage an Apple or IBM desktop operation. But Malcolm Ross explains the process clearly in a monthly newsletter he sends to fourteen hundred clients or potential clients: "The laser in the printer is made to 'paint' a picture of your computer file on the drum of what is really a photocopying machine, by scanning back and forth at high speed while the drum rotates. Toner, similar to that used in photocopiers, is attracted to or repelled from the im-aged ('painted') or un-imaged areas of the drum. From there the toner is transferred to a piece of paper as it is fed past the rotating drum." To make copies, you take the "camera-ready" image to a printer who runs off duplicates.

Suffice it to say the pseudo-typography you produce on $10,000 worth of equipment contained on the top of your desk is profes-sional enough to satisfy some major magazine and book publishers. Unless you scrutinize the type with a jeweler's eye, you probably wouldn't guess that it wasn't typeset.

A TOOL OR AN END IN ITSELF?

Desktop publishing is fast finding favor with advertising firms and large corporations to produce everything from company newsletters to menus to advertising flyers. Malcolm Ross pockets two sets of clients: corporations like Holiday Inn and the World Bank, which hire him as a consultant to guide them through the rudiments of a desktop operation so they can publish in-house; and small businesses, which ask him to design and print brochures, flyers, letterhead, and other paraphernalia, and for whom he acts as the publisher. "Basically, we're talking about designing direct mail," he explains. "Clients? Dry cleaners, church associations, or anyone who needs to get the word out on meetings and services."

Sharon Bobbitt, whose Publications Plus performs similar services from her Evanston, Illinois, home, knows of a dozen desktop publishers in the Chicago area. Six months into her venture, she's matching the salary she made as AT&T's Chicago manager of public relations. Sharon's plans include branching into magazine publishing on her Apple Macintosh. "The machine makes up for my lack of eye-hand coordination," she explains. "Previously, I didn't have the freehand ability to create my own layouts and designs."

Whether you see desktop publishing as a means to another end, such as newsletter publishing, or as the basis of a business, such as designing brochures for local businesses, you can probably get started for less than we indicate here, simply because hardware and software prices continually fall. In addition, the computers simultaneously get easier to use and offer more sophisticated options. You may want to rent an IBM or Macintosh from a computer-leasing store to see which you like best. Also, you may want to update your equipment in a year or two as manufacturers spring glitzy surprises on the market.

You'll gain expertise daily, so don't let a little thing like computer illiteracy slow you down. A short course on the subject given at a community college might help, but the best thing to do is get in there and practice. Fluency comes within a month or two. "The Macintosh seemed to take my gloves off," says Malcolm Ross. In addition to using it to design flyers for the Main Street florist, he uses his Mac for writing his newsletter, for facsimile transmission, forecasting and spread sheet analysis, data management, and other aspects of running his own business.

KNOCK-KNOCK

If you work from the spare bedroom in your house, how do you let customers know they need you? Malcolm joined two Maryland chambers of commerce where he "hit people over the head with a two-by-four—anything to let them know I was here." He sends his monthly newsletter to those small and large company contacts he made. The Electric Page contains a hodgepodge of desktop publishing news and information on Electro Graphic Services. Malcolm says on any given issue, anywhere from .5 to 5 percent of newsletter recipients call to ask about his services.

Sharon Bobbitt relies on contacts and references. In one coup, she took AT&T work with her when she left her job. "Large companies are downsizing their public relations departments and don't have the staff to take on new chores," she explains. Another early client was the Women's Business Development Center, a nonprofit group that advises small business. "It was invaluable to have a real client while I was learning," says Sharon. "I didn't charge them much, but I got a lot of referrals through them."

You also might ask printers and office supply stores to refer you to their patrons. Some might prove hostile, particularly small printers who offer similar services. But many may recommend you to clients as a less expensive alternative to typesetting shops.

If you decide to specialize, you may want to advertise directly to businesses in a particular industry. Direct-mail or trade publications can alert all the lawyers in North America that you can design their legal forms, for example.

Most desktop publishers begin with a variety of income sources. But Malcolm Ross, who consults as well as publishes, suspects aggressive promoters can take the desktop publishing business in almost any direction they want. As we said before, the field is so new, it's up to the participants to create the rules—and the opportunities.

SOURCES

Publication

Publish; PC World, MacWorld, all published by
PCW Communications Inc., 501 2nd St., Suite 600,
San Francisco, Calif. 94107 (415) 546-7722

Consultants

Electro Graphic Services Inc., 14430 Pebble Hill Lane,
Gaithersburg, Md. 20878 (301) 294-9079
The Byte Works, Suite 6C, 207 E. 30th St.,
New York, N.Y. 10016 (212) 532-3590

Information Detective

> *"I'm a curious person and like accumulating all this information. I like never knowing what the next search is going to be." – Katherine Ackerman, Katherine Ackerman & Associates*

Low Startup Investment: $5,000 (a home office)

High Startup Investment: $20,000 (an office with one employee)

Time Until Breakeven: Three months to one year

Annual Revenues: $25,000-$10 million

Annual Pre-tax Profits: $20,000-$2 million

Staffers Needed for Startup (including founder): One

Andrew Garvin was in his final classes at the Columbia Graduate School of Journalism in 1968, and he was bored. The professor was saying something about journalists conveying information, so Andy scribbled a couple of circles on his notepad, representing people who need information. He drew a few more circles, which stood for information sources. Then he sketched a large circle and connected spokes to each of the small circles. The big circle? That was a kind of information supermarket where users could shop for every piece of information they'd ever need. Those doodles provided the rough draft for FIND/SVP Inc., the information clearinghouse that Andy Garvin founded the next year in his New York City studio apartment with $12,000.

THE INFORMATION EXPLOSION

The conglomerate United Technologies says that the world's knowledge is doubling every eight years. Gasp! But, thanks to the data-base explosion, thousands of entrepreneurs and major corporations can track the information through libraries of facts they are compiling. Maybe a client needs to know what products competitors are researching in the artificial intelligence field. Or which state has the greatest population of Arabian horses. The single salient piece of information you need is out there—if you know which data-base haystack contains your particular needle. Information detectives dig up whatever facts clients need to know. They primarily search through computerized data bases, but also leaf through reference books and publications, and interview experts. "If you know where the sources are, then you know where the answer is," explains Natalie Berliet, president of American Connection Inc., the Stamford, Connecticut, firm which specializes in finding information for French businesses.

Investment banker Stuart-James, which underwrote a $3.78 million public offering in October 1986, for FIND/SVP, at the time estimated the information services industry at $11 billion, and projected industry growth to $35 billion by 1990. In addition to inhouse corporate or university libraries, most of the three hundred to five hundred purveyors of information are one-person research outfits, like Natalie Berliet, who operates from her home. But a few entrepreneurs have parlayed their talent for weeding out information into substantial dollars.

MAKING MILLIONS

Take Andy Garvin, for one. In 1970, his first full year in business, FIND/SVP took in revenues of only $6,459. But he hung in there. By 1985, the company had $7.8 million in revenues. Its investment banker wrote, "In the next three to five years, FIND has the potential to generate annual revenues of $30 million to over $75 million." At the time the company went public, the forty-one-year-old president's annual cash compensation amounted to $113,931, and his stock was worth $890,420. As the asking price of the stock rose from 7 cents to 16 cents a share within six months, Andy became—on paper, at least—a millionaire.

FIND/SVP boasts more than one thousand subscribers. (The second part of the company's name stands for *s'il vous plait,* or "please" in French, and refers to a French research firm with which FIND is affiliated.) These clients—from individuals and publications to major corporations—pay a monthly retainer that averages about $500, based on hourly rates of about $70. For larger projects, they pay additional sums.

KEEPING BUSY

But most small independents charge by the hour, usually in the $50 to $70 range. Although many of their clients return for a repeat performance, their information hunger can't feed a retainer. Assuming you are busy, you could make $100,000 a year as an independent following paper trails. But most information detectives say you can't live on searches alone.

"There still is not enough demand to fill the whole day with searches," warns Katherine Ackerman, a former reference librarian at the Chicago *Tribune* who operates Katherine Ackerman & Associates in East Lansing, Michigan. Kathy consults, teaches data-base research at a community college, and writes articles on information retrieval for computer publications. "I work at lots of different things, both out of choice and necessity," she says. In addition to generating income, extra activities like conducting seminars provide contacts—people who later may hire you to dig up details. In your search for clients, you might give a talk at a civic organization, or for a professional group that could use your services.

If you start from a spare bedroom, overhead needn't run more than $5,000 for a computer, printer, modem, and some training. Many of the data-base vendors offer one- or two-day courses, although you need a good deal of practice to become proficient in your searches. If you choose to rent an office, add another researcher or two, or market heavily, that startup figure can easily double or quadruple.

Because you become such a repository of information on all sorts of fascinating topics, you might think of hocking your expertise to a larger audience through selling over-the-counter research reports. Each search for a specific client is strictly confidential, of course. Based on the trends in questions coming in from clients, however, FIND/SVP also researches on spec. It compiles data in report form and sells to a larger audience. For example, its bimonthly catalog lists a two-hundred-page, $1,275 analysis of "The Changing Pasta Market," and a $995, two-hundred-page study entitled "The Maturity Market: Americans 55 and Over." In addition, FIND/SVP sells reports from other researchers, such as a one-hundred-page, $1,275 look at the international bath-and-shower products market from Euromonitor Publications.

MAKE YOURSELF UNIQUE

If you can pinpoint a large enough speciality customer base, go for it. Your expertise differentiates you from bigger competitors like FIND/SVP, and also makes marketing easier. Natalie Berliet sent letters of introduction to companies in France announcing her service.

As far as the future goes, "nobody's sure what the new technology [CD-ROM, or "compact disk, read-only-memory"] will do to information retrieval," admits Kathy Ackerman. CD-ROM technology can store two-hundred-thousand pages on one disk and allows less experienced researchers to search at a fixed rate without connecting to an expensive data base. The less expensive, easier solution to data searches could crimp the entrepreneurial information business if more corporations create their own in-house research libraries. Instead of having their own firms, independents may take jobs with corporate America. "But the spread of the new technology could also make people more aware of their information needs," says Kathy. It could be the information-detective business is poised for its own explosion.

SOURCES

Industry Association

Information Industry Association, 555 New Jersey Ave., N.W.,
Suite 800, Washington, D.C. (202) 639-8262
Special Libraries Association, 1700 18th St., N.W., Washington,
D.C. 20009 (202) 234-4700

Consultant

Katherine Ackerman & Associates, 403 Oxford St.,
East Lansing, Mich. 48823 (517) 332-6818

Newsletter Publisher

> *"Every renewal means subscribers are reappointing me. People are telling me I do a good job everyday." – William E. Donoghue, Donoghue Organization Inc.*

Low Startup Investment: $10,000 (a five-thousand-piece direct mail campaign, no staffers)

High Startup Investment: $65,000 (eighty-thousand-piece mailing)

Time Until Breakeven: One to three years

Annual Revenues: From pocket money to millions, depending on price and number of newsletter titles published, and ancillary services offered

Annual Pre-tax Profits: Varies. Due to accounting practices, most newsletters show a loss while still providing substantial cash-flow. Spinoff products and services can be hugely profitable.

Staffers Needed for Startup (including founder): One

If you have a passion for chocolate, or if you absolutely hunger for the latest scoop on artificial intelligence, you may well subscribe to a newsletter on the subject. The Newsletter Association, an industry trade group, estimates that publishers produced at least eleven thousand different for-profit newsletters in the U.S. in 1986, twice the number posted five years ago. And the Newsletter Clearinghouse, a company that tracks newsletters, sees no reason why a 12- to 15-percent annual growth rate shouldn't continue. "There is an incredible need for specialized knowledge that newsletters address," says Paul Swift, managing editor of the Clearinghouse's *Newsletter on Newsletters,* an $84-per-year semi-monthly diary of the industry. Adds Michael L. Kibler, director of member service at the Newsletter Association: "People have such demand for great amounts of information, especially on their jobs. They don't have time to wade through a 120-page magazine when an eight-page newsletter covers what is crucial to their needs."

WHAT'S NEWS

The industry owes the start of its growth to Lyndon Johnson. In the 1960s, scores of newsletters surfaced to follow the ever-changing bureaucracy of the Great Society's new government programs. Even the deregulated society of today needs newsletters to explain what Washington's up to. For example, *Chemical Waste Litigation Reporter* reports on environmental law for $990 a year, and the *Washington Letter on Latin America* sells for $295 annually. In the 1980s, though, newsletters moved from snitching on the government to giving hints on making money. Investment letters include such titles as *Howard J. Ruff's Financial Success Report* ($129 a year) and *The Stanger Review,* a $6,000-per-year sheet which reports on partnership investing.

If you think you have a dynamite idea for a newsletter, consider the size of your audience and the price it will pay for your information. If all of America will buy your letter, you can make millions by charging a few cents a copy. But if you can round up only a hundred readers, each one must shell out thousands of dollars before you get rich. Business letters can command much higher rates than consumer letters and they therefore prosper with a much smaller subscription universe. Not only do executives view your letter as crucial to their livelihood, but they can charge it to their office expense accounts.

A SKI CHALET IN ASPEN

Newsletter publishers are a satisfied lot because, unlike most of the laboring world, they choose their own working hours. Thanks to the telecommunications revolution, you can write a newsletter from any setting—a ski chalet in Aspen or Waikiki Beach—and, using a modem, send your copy to a printer miles away. Paul Swift reports that he even knows of one letter that is published from prison.

Running a newsletter requires varied skills, from conducting interviews to dealing with printers to keeping track of subscribers. But there's no shortage of places where you can learn the basics. In addition to many university journalism departments, both the Newsletter Association and the Newsletter Clearinghouse offer regional seminars and manuals on all aspects of newsletter publishing.

A SMITH-CORONA IN THE KITCHEN

Newsletters offer especially easy entry. "I started by banging out a one-page letter on a Smith-Corona in my kitchen." Many letters begin in the moonlight as would-be publishers keep a daytime job until their idea takes off. Husband-and-wife teams commonly begin with one spouse holding onto a job for the sake of a paycheck until success is assured. You can even print professional-looking letters on a relatively inexpensive laser printer (see Desktop Publishing). And, if toiling at every task—from writing the copy to buying paper—becomes too time-consuming, you can always hire college students or other part-timers to stuff envelopes.

Two types of people write newsletters: journalists who tap into a good subject area and experts who sell their insights to the world. William E. Donoghue is of the latter species, a financial consultant who earned his living by advising corporations on how to invest their money before he entered the newsletter business in 1975. That year, an obscure financial letter interviewed Bill Donoghue on the fledgling money-market field, a business Bill says he helped create. Although the letter claimed only one hundred or so subscribers, each contributing just $114 a year, Bill saw the potential and bought the newsletter for $14,000. He then changed its name to *Donoghue's Money Fund Report,* and improved the quality of information. "I started in my living room with one employee on a word processor," recalls Bill.

Bill Donoghue says he expanded too quickly with the first stirrings of success. He added too many staffers and moved to expensive quarters. With direct-mail costs gobbling cash, he soon found himself $100,000 in the hole. "I brought in creditors and showed them my furniture, explaining my mother had a lien on that." He cut his staff and watched a glacial-paced turnaround begin as subscribers started to trickle in.

Despite its rough beginnings, the newsletter took off because it was a great idea. A decade after Bill took it on, *Donoghue's Money Fund Report* boasted one thousand corporate and institutional subscribers. At $595 per subscription, it generates revenues of $500,000 a year. Bill did not stop there, however. His Donoghue Organization Inc., based in Holliston, Massachusetts, now encompasses two other financial letters as well as a syndicated newspaper column and books with such titles as *No Load Mutual Fund Guide,* and *William E. Donoghue's Lifetime Financial Planner.* In 1986, sales from the entire Bill Donoghue parcel of projects topped $5 million.

GROWTH COSTS MONEY

As Bill learned, growth costs money. Lucky entrepreneurs have succeeded with startup capital of $10,000, which is enough to launch a five-thousand-piece direct mail campaign. But Michael Kibler recommends a $65,000 ante that includes a $20,000 first-year salary for yourself or an employee; $500 to hire an artist to design an attractive format; $8,000 to print the newsletter and direct-mail solicitation pieces; $3,000 for postage; and $28,000 to rent mailing lists for eighty thousand people. You'll eat up the rest in phone costs, the lawyer's fee for incorporation, and other necessary incidentals.

Your biggest cash drain comes from lining up subscriptions. According to the industry rule of thumb, you should expect to spend $1 to attract $1 in new subscriptions. In other words, a newsletter that sells for $100 will spend $100 on direct mail to sign on each reader. A startup newsletter often sends out twenty-five to thirty thousand solicitations—and a 1-percent rate of response is considered excellent.

A NATURAL TAX SHELTER

Tax laws, however, cushion the blow from these initial costs. "Publishing is a natural tax shelter," explains Bill Donoghue. Even though you receive a lump-sum payment with each subscription, you don't declare the income until you deliver the product. Under these rules, a reasonably creative accountant can legally achieve both steady cash flow and paper losses at the same time. For example, assume you receive a check for $120 in December for a one-year subscription to your monthly newsletter. You declare a first-year income of just $10, because you mail out only one letter that year. You defer the other $110 to the next year, when you actually mail the other eleven issues. At the same time, you can write off the $120 spent to entice that subscriber aboard the year you shelled it out, and spend the entire amount received as soon as you have it in hand.

You usually know whether you're in for the long haul when it's time to ask for renewals twelve months after startup. A newsletter that fulfills its editorial promise can expect three out of four subscribers to sign up for another stint. Instead of $1, you may spend just a nickel for every $1 worth of second-year subscriptions. At that point, you make 95 cents out of every dollar sent in by subscribers. While some of that money goes for overhead and to finance new subscriptions, a sizable portion is profits.

Gene Cowell, whose *Island Properties Report* outlines the opportunities in Caribbean real estate, suggests that small publications use index cards to track the comings-and-goings of subscribers. However, if you publish a larger letter that shuffles readers monthly, you should either buy a computer or sign on with a fulfillment house that will keep track of subscribers and mail your letters for you. You can get names of fulfillment houses from the Newsletter Association or The Newsletter on Newsletters.

Publishers should never quit prospecting for new subscribers. You can buy lists of potential subscribers from brokers and trade associations for between $40 to $100 per thousand names. To pull in readers, Gene Cowell advertises in travel and real estate publications. Bill Donoghue peppers his numerous books and interviews with promises to send a free copy of his newsletter to anyone calling a toll-free telephone number.

You can also sell your own list of subscribers to other (noncompeting) publishers. In fact, if you ever decide to stop the presses and quit publishing, another publisher probably will buy your business strictly for the value of your readers' names.

THE LETTER IS JUST THE BEGINNING

The fun begins when renewals start to arrive regularly. With little overhead, you can use a newsletter as a base to spin off everything from seminars to books to related letters. "Any serious publisher does ancillary business," says Michael Kibler of the Newsletter Association.

Your subscriber becomes a resource to tap, a proven customer who is willing to spend money for facts, figures, insight, or gossip. Because ancillary books or workshops draw on information already gathered for the newsletters, even modest sales can return juicy profits. "Use your mailing list as much as possible," recommends Gene Cowell, whose subscribers periodically receive flyers touting books he's written about a specific aspect of Caribbean real estate, such as an in-depth look at the tax laws and property value in Jamaica.

In addition to the usual books and conferences, the forty-employee Donoghue organization parlayed its *Donoghue's Money Fund Report* into a computerized, on-line duplicate that sells for $2,500— nearly five times the price of the newsletter. But his most recent spin-off may prove to be the most lucrative. In the summer of 1986, Bill decided to go beyond advising readers where to invest by offering to do their investing for them: He registered as an investment service with the Securities & Exchange Commission. Following the practice of other investment services, Bill invests clients' cash for 2 percent of the initial sum invested. Within a month of announcing the service in his newsletter, the entrepreneur was awash in $3 million of subscribers' cash.

Even if you don't handle other people's money, you need to build your reputation carefully. Newsletters give the impression of authority; you're expected to voice informed opinions. Publishers report that subscriber mail asking for direction and relating their own insights is heavy. Be careful that you don't damage your reputation by sticking your neck out only to have it broken. "It's ego gratifying," says Gene Cowell. "You become an instant expert in your field. You become a club president."

Observers say newsletters will continue to present good opportunities for publishers who can carve out niches. To scout out competition, check *The Newsletter Yearbook Directory* published by the Newsletter Clearinghouse, the *Oxbridge Directory of Newsletters,* and *Ulrich's International Periodicals Directory,* which are available in many libraries. Research the other eleven thousand newsletters all vying for your reader's attention and, as Bill Donoghue counsels, "identify a market with a real 'need-to-know,' not 'nice-to-know.' "

SOURCES

Industry Association

The Newsletter Association, 1401 Wilson Blvd., Suite 403, Arlington, Va. 22209 (703) 527-2333

Publications

The Newsletter on Newsletters, 44 W. Market St., P.O. Box 311, Rhinebeck, N.Y. 12572 (914) 876-2081

Newsletter Profit Report, 7315 Wisconsin Ave., Suite 601N, Bethesda, Md. 20814 (301) 951-9393

Pagers

> "My problem: I can't pass up an opportunity. And in the
> communications business, there are all kinds of opportunities.
> There's a magic to it." – Michael Bowman, American
> Mobilphone

Low Startup Investment: $200,000 (for a small market)

High Startup Investment: $1 million (multi-markets)

Time Until Breakeven: One and a half to three years

Annual Revenues: $50,000-$5 million (small market [two hundred
subscribers] at low end, multi-markets, [twenty thousand subscribers]
at high end)

Annual Pre-tax Profits: $17,500-$2 million

Staffers Needed for Startup (including founder): Two to fifteen

On October 15, 1950, the first beep from a commercial pager
spurred a New York City physician to call an answering service. For
the next couple of decades, every time a beep sounded in a dark-
ened theater, a medical doctor sprang into action. But pagers aren't
just another medical instrument anymore. By 1986, when the Telocator Network of America counted 5.5 million paging subscribers,
less than half belonged to the medical field. "I deal with insurance
agents, plumbers, sales reps—people who have to keep in touch,"
says Michael Bowman, president of Birmingham, Alabama–based
American Mobilphone Inc., which operates a seven-city paging network with 1987 revenues of more than $5 million. But Mike thinks
beeper companies have barely scratched the potential market. "The
challenge is to cross over into the consumer market. And I think we
can do it."

So do a lot of other experts. Depending on who you talk with, the paging industry could grow anywhere from 20 percent to 35 percent a year until the turn of the century. The service and sales sectors will snatch up millions of those 125 million beepers, but much of the growth will come from moms and dads who want to stay in touch with their teenagers. One national paging company even marketed a rhinestone-studded pager as a Mother's Day gift. Entrepreneurs are betting some subscribers will have one pager for their business phone and another to catch those home calls that just can't wait for an answering machine playback.

NO MYSTERY ABOUT IT

Here's how paging works: A caller activates the beeper by dialing a number attuned to a specific radio signal. Within sixty seconds of receiving the call, the paging company's computer automatically transmits a signal to the subscriber's beeper. Subscribers generally can choose beepers in the following categories: (1) tone only (when the beep sounds, the subscriber knows to call the office); (2) digital display (using a touch-tone phone, the caller punches in a seven-digit number which appears on the subscriber's pager); or (3) tone-and-voice (the caller leaves a verbal message after the beep). Most networks lease pagers for $13 to $30 a month, depending on competition and the technology a subscriber orders. You can also sell the pager outright and just charge $8 to $15 a month for the service.

Only a handful of manufacturers make pagers, but about fifteen hundred companies handle transmissions, service, and repairs. In the beginning, most startups were entrepreneurial, although such big players as Southwestern Bell have gobbled up as many large-city frequencies as they can buy.

Before you jump into the frenzy, recognize one thing: although the market is vast, the territory is finite. As Michael Bowman explains: "Radio frequencies are a natural resource, like land. Only so many exist. When they're used up, there just aren't any more." According to Clifford Bean, telecommunications marketing manager for market researcher Arthur D. Little Inc., "Most of the big markets are taken, but I still see niche opportunities in smaller markets (trading areas with 1.5 million population or less) and in new frequencies the Federal Communications Commission (FCC) began offering in the 900 megahertz band in 1987."

CASHING OUT

This limited number of radio frequencies means a small window of opportunity exists to set up a paging network from scratch. If you don't grab whatever frequency is available today, somebody else might. Of course, most everything has a price, and many operators prefer to buy already operating networks anyway. They say somebody else has fought through the regulatory red tape and signed up a base of subscribers.

Mike Bowman, who continues to oversee American Mobilphone, says he may be selling his newest offshoot. In 1987, after American Mobilphone's investors declined to expand further, he personally acquired frequencies in four Florida cities under the corporate name Coastal Express. Was it worth the hassle? At the time of this writing, "I haven't even bought any equipment yet, and I've already had four offers to sell."

Most mature systems sell for between $900 and $1,200 per subscriber, minus whatever debt is outstanding. Although he is still contemplating offers, Mike expects to invest about $400,000 to get Coastal up and running. After about eighteen months, he foresees fifteen hundred subscribers and annual revenues in the $500,000 ballpark. At that point, he'll think about selling. "I could triple my money in a year," he figures.

Even if you decide not to cash out, paging is still lucrative. Operators talk of 35- to 40-percent pre-tax margins. A company in a large market might earn $350,000 on revenues of $1 million. Blanket a couple of neighboring cities, and triple those figures. If you start in a small town, your potential is less, of course, and you may want to offer other business services, too, such as telephone answering or typing, to boost revenues.

DOING IT FROM SCRATCH

If you decide to start your own paging business from scratch, you'll follow six basic steps:

- Finding the frequency. This task involves some fancy detective work because the FCC doesn't lift a finger to help you find which signals are untapped. "Finding available frequencies is like trying to find out how many people make over $50,000 in Philadelphia," says Mike Bowman. "The IRS knows, and the information is public, but good luck finding it."

Ah, but some enterprising entrepreneurs will come to your rescue—for a price. FCC search firms will comb the records for you. Or, for about $2,500, you can buy computer software, which can be updated for $125 a month, that follows the market. Mike Bowman was scanning such a program when he found not one, but four adjacent Florida cities with available UHF signals. He couldn't believe his good fortune because, as Mike explains, "Paging works best when you can tie up an entire trade pattern." For example, American Mobilphone's signals cover both Birmingham and Huntsville, cities where its customers often travel on business.

- Conducting an engineering study. Before you claim a signal, you have to prove to the FCC that your transmissions will service customers without damaging other reception. To conduct a study, you need an antenna, so contact a local radio television station and ask to lease space on theirs. (It's too expensive—and absolutely unnecessary—to build your own when perfectly good towers exist in every market.) Then, hire an engineer, such as those who advertise in the *Telocator Bulletins,* who charge $300 to $500 for a channel interference study.

- Filing with the FCC. Retain a law firm, preferably one in Washington that specializes in telecommunications. They'll complete all the paperwork and file with the FCC for somewhere between $800 and $2,000. In fact, most firms can also do the frequency search and hire the engineer.

- Sitting out the FCC. It can take three to six months before you get an FCC go-ahead. The agency files a public notice that you've requested a signal, and gives other interested parties thirty days to ask for the same frequency. In popular markets, as many as five competitors might counter file, although one competitor is more likely. Lotteries decide duplicate filings. Coastal wasn't challenged in Tallahassee, and won lotteries for Fort Walton, Pensacola, and Panama City.

- Construction. From the date you receive the FCC okay, you have twelve months to get your system on the air—or you lose your license. In addition to the tower, which you've already secured, you need a paging terminal (which can run $80,000 to $130,000); at least one transmitter, depending on how hilly the terrain is ($20,000 each); and pagers ($150 to $200 each).

▪ Lining up customers. Mike Bowman estimates it takes 2,200 customers to break even in the mid-sized markets he targets. With two sales representatives lining up an average sixty subscribers per month, he breaks even in about a year and a half. If you don't want to spring for salaries, you can pay commissions, or base-plus-commission.

YOU'VE ONLY JUST BEGUN

Whether you buy an ongoing network or operate a new frequency, you have to service the equipment. In-house technicians are costly, but you can buy five-year warranties from manufacturers for about $30 a pager, or sign up with repair depots for a monthly commission. There is a drawback to this last route, however. As Mike Bowman explains, "It forces you to have more inventory than you rent because some pagers are always in repair." He suggests fifteen hundred beepers for every one thousand subscribers.

You also need to ensure that "the transmitter is transmitting and the terminal is terminalling," says Mike. Until you reach maybe five thousand subscribers, a full-time technician is a luxury. Instead, put an engineer from a local radio or TV station on retainer to service any problems that might arise.

You can expand not only in volume, with a wider and wider audience of subscribers, but into other technologies as well. For example, many paging companies install and service mobile car phones. On the more "glamorous" side, some carriers are examining beeper broadcasting. They transmit stock quotes or news updates.

Mike Bowman says to expect technology that will change the way we look not only at pagers, but at communications altogether. "We may evolve a different type of phone, or an inexpensive plug-in device for a normal phone that will allow callers to send messages to subscribers' phones." Another expected innovation is synthetic voice transmission: The caller just talks into a phone, and the paging company's receiver prints out those words in written form.

SOURCES

Industry Association

Telocator Network of America, 2000 M St. N.W.,
Washington, D.C. 20036 (202) 467-4770

Publications

Telocator Bulletin, 2000 M St. N.W., Washington, D.C. 20036
(202) 467-4770
RCR Publications, 1725 Marion St., Denver, Colo. 80218
(303) 832-6000

Consultant

Michael Bowman, American Mobilphone Inc., 100 Oxmoor Blvd.,
Birmingham, Ala. 35209 (205) 942-2337

Video-editing Service

"I might edit one project on the environment, another on labor unions, followed by another on scholarships at black colleges." – Carol Slatkin, Carol Slatkin Video Services

Low Startup Investment: $6,000

High Startup Investment: $20,000

Time Until Breakeven: Three months to one year

Annual Revenues: $50,000-$100,000

Annual Pre-tax Profits: $40,000-$70,000

Staffers Needed for Startup (including founder): One

When Carol Slatkin decided to get into video after graduating from Clark University in the 1970s, she had no technical expertise. In fact, the only experts anywhere were a few television engineers who were pioneering video-tape production.

Her skills developed along with the technology. Carol joined a small film organization and learned to shoot and edit before taking a partner and opening her own Washington, D.C., firm in 1980. They bought a portable broadcast-quality camera and editing equipment and did a little of everything. But Carol found her calling in editing—taking the raw tape others shoot and distilling it into a strong statement. By 1987, she and her partner had taken different routes, and Carol Slatkin Video Services today concentrates almost exclusively on editing tapes for the business world.

MULTIPLE CHOICE STARTUP

The video-cassette recorder has spawned a whole set of new careers. In addition to videographers who shoot events (see Videographers), a cadre of professionals edit video, record sound, and add special effects to video tapes. As a video editor, you have three choices:

▪ You can join an organization as an in-house editor, an increasingly common job at large corporations and trade groups.

▪ You can invest a million or two in sophisticated on-line editing facilities and start your own business.

▪ Or you can set up an off-line editing facility to do basic editing tasks as a freelancer. You can buy equipment to edit broadcast quality half-inch tapes for around $6,000; to edit three-quarter-inch tapes, you'll need $10,000; to add such touches as wipes and dissolves, figure on spending $20,000.

If you choose one of the first two routes, you don't need to read this. An in-house job is a great place to learn the basics. (These days, as schools are finally catching up with the technology, you can also get a video education on campus.) If you've got the capital to put together an on-line facility, chances are you're either well-versed in the business or can hire people who are. So let's concentrate on Carol Slatkin's specialty: off-line editing.

OFF-LINE

"With off-line editing equipment, I do the rough work," Carol explains. "I might get forty twenty-minute tapes that I narrow down to one by cutting and splicing. Then I hire a narrator and add original or stock music." Some customers want to go no further than that. Most on-line editors charge $15 to $50 an hour; some tack on an equipment charge of around $100 a day. Companies that hire a freelance editor might expect to spend $5,000 to $10,000 on a fifteen-minute tape. With that kind of fee structure, a busy and ambitious off-line solo editor could make $60,000 a year. Add employees to do the grunt work and concentrate instead on bringing in more jobs, and revenues will multiply.

For those who want a more polished product, Carol takes the tape to an on-line editing facility where she masterminds the final touches. "Each frame in a video tape has a number. I tell an on-line editor using computer technology like a fine razor blade exactly where to cut the frames." In addition, on-line equipment can add such ornamentation as dissolves and digital effects. On-line facilities charge around $300 an hour, so you need to know exactly where you want each filigree.

If you're editing in a smaller town, you may need to snap up all jobs that come along. But Carol specializes in business tapes, lining up steady work from about ten regular clients, including independent producers, public relations companies that produce tapes for their clients, trade associations, corporations, and charitable foundations. "D.C. is perfect because of all the international associations" that bring steady repeat business. "They all want to make videos to go along with their brochures explaining who they are."

Carol refers less lucrative consumer jobs, like weddings or parties, to other freelancers who concentrate on them. Most consumer videographers edit their own shoots to hold down expenses. But those who don't own their own editing equipment often rent facilities from editors, a practice that brings in extra income when you aren't using your equipment.

Although many video editors work from their homes, Carol shares office space with other video and film editors. She believes corporate clients perceive her business as larger and more credible because of the arrangement.

Like the equipment it works with, the video profession is still evolving. In many cases, you still must convince customers to fork out the thousands needed to produce and edit a video tape. But don't be tempted to offer a cut-rate special and churn out unprofessional quality. "The community of video professionals is small, and people see your work," Carol warns. "You're only as good as your last show."

SOURCES

See Videographer

Videographer

> *"I've never had one day like the previous day. I speak to a variety of people and most are interesting. I grow and change with the times."* – Jerry Fried, Ace Audio Visual Co.

Low Startup Investment: $1,000 (operating from home with rented equipment)

High Startup Investment: $200,000 (renting an office and buying sophisticated equipment)

Time Until Breakeven: One month to two years

Annual Revenues: $25,000-$1 million (high end includes sales generated by employees)

Annual Pre-tax Profits: $10,000-$300,000

Staffers Needed for Startup (including founder): One

ACTION: You pull back from the white lilies to the lilac softness of the bridesmaids. You glance at your sound equipment when Aunt Minerva begins singing "Oh Promise Me." As you zoom in on the groom's sober handsomeness, you nod to your assistant in the corner to pan the crowd. The camera catches the tears on Granny's cheeks and the giggles from the nephews in the second pew. As the organ sounds the opening chords of the "Wedding March," you direct your video recorder at the rear of the chapel.

ROLL 'EM: You point the camera at Rutherford Beauford Smythe, the richest curmudgeon this town has ever seen. He recites the bit about being of sound mind and body in a straight forward manner, but leans forward with a gleeful gleam in his eyes when he mentions his brother and only living heir. "Just wanted to let you know, Rodney, that I meant it when I called you a good-for-nothing. You may have bamboozled mother, but not me. You're not getting a cent of my millions, because I'm leaving it all to The Society for Siamese Cat Research."

VIDEO FOR FUN AND PROFIT

Video technology has opened opportunities to a new group of professional videographers. Some assignments require highly skilled artistry, such as taping a high school talent contest where baton twirlers and disco dancers perform under rotating lights. Other situations—taping a legal deposition or an interview for a video dating service, for instance—mostly demand a steady hand or a tripod and some bright lights.

The possibilities in video production are limited only by the imagination. In addition to traditional filming forums, such as recording news and entertainment events, videographers now tape business events, like a stockholder's meeting, and consumer specials, such as a bat mitzvah. In the legal realm, states increasingly allow video-taped depositions and "day-in-the-life-of" tapes that show how an injury affects an accident victim's daily routine. Realtors show clients videotapes instead of driving them from house to house. Manufacturers send training videos as part of their product package. Trade associations and universities, job applicants and video dates—everybody sees video as a vehicle to get their point across.

HERE'S THE RUB

Video possibilities may be unlimited, but to turn them into a living wage, you've got to convince buyers they need your service. Because using video in most fields is so new, potential customers may never have considered hiring a video professional to immortalize their event. Videographers may spend as much time educating the public about their services as they do on assignments.

As a videographer operating in the early days of the video revolution, you've got a choice. You can either work part time at video taping, or you can create full-time opportunities by selling as if your livelihood depends on it.

WEEKEND WORK

Especially if you concentrate on the consumer end—taping parties, weddings, or even household possessions for insurance purposes—you can start part time. Most assignments fall on weekends anyway. Charlene Canape, author of *How to Capitalize on the Video Revolution* (Holt, Rhinehart and Winston, New York, 1984, $16.95), recommends teaming up with other providers of party services. You can ask to display a discrete sign in their windows, or have them recommend your services to clients. "Bridal shops, florists, tuxedo rental shops, jewelers, printers, and beauty salons are all places that will be frequented by young people with wedding bells in their futures," she writes. "To reach people who are thinking of throwing a party, try delicatessens or gourmet food stores that might cater the event."

You can track down the party givers yourself. Check the society pages of your newspaper for engagement announcements and synagogue records for upcoming bar and bat mitzvahs. Match their names with addresses from the phone book, and send them a flyer explaining your services.

You don't need much capital to start because companies rent equipment. As for the advantages of renting, "You're always assured of getting the most up-to-date machines," writes Charlene Canape. "You never have to worry about repair and maintenance. You don't have to worry about storing your gear or insuring it."

The disadvantage: Renting can be expensive. When you build enough volume to warrant purchasing equipment, select brands that will be compatible with pieces you plan to add later. In addition to the basics (a camera, player, and color monitor), you may start with lights and sound equipment and a van to lug around all the paraphernalia. If you don't want to spring for editing equipment right away, you can rent editing facilities—or even farm the work out to editors (see Video-editing Service)—for $25 to $75 an hour, depending on how fancy you want to get. Outfitting a sophisticated production and editing studio, and hiring an assistant or two, might push startup costs to $250,000.

JUMPING IN WITH BOTH FEET

If you decide to enter video production full time, chances are you've studied the technique either in college or with a production company. Some manufacturers provide fairly sophisticated training as well.

While consumer taping can be lucrative, the anniversary or sweet sixteen party you tape is a one-time affair. Likewise, business or legal taping may offer repeat business from a few clients, but probably not enough to pay all the bills in the beginning. So don't specialize in your first year. Instead, start with a variety of assignments from as many avenues as possible. If you keep your sales hat on the same rack with your creative hat, you may come up with video opportunities potential clients haven't thought of before.

There are three ways to make money in this business: charge a lot for single assignments, resell the same tape many times, or cultivate repeat customers. Single windfalls come primarily to those who build massive reputations. Clients include cable networks and local television stations that need extra footage. Multiple sales—beyond commercial hits like aerobic tapes—require marketing imagination. For example, Gruenberg Video Group Inc., New York City, sells video yearbooks to high school students. Entrepreneur Paul Gruenberg trains student crews at various schools to tape events during the year. He hires freelance editors to pull visions of proms and pep rallies into a final, $30 product, complete with background music and clips of newsworthy events of the year.

TAPING ATTORNEYS

But most videographers look for repeat business: for example, relationships with attorneys. If you pursue the legal market, first bone up on what's acceptable in your state. Some states don't allow video wills. Others restrict what can be taped during a deposition, or the manner in which it can be photographed. For example, most courts prefer a stationary camera to zooms and fade-outs.

To tap the legal market, mail an introductory letter to lawyers whose names you've rented from a local bar association or chosen from the Yellow Pages. You can advertise in local legal journals, although Jerry Fried, president of Ace Audio Visual Co., Woodside, New York, warns that telemarketing or direct mail can be expensive. "I feel our service is need-based. When the customer needs the service, they look you up in the Yellow Pages." Ace advertises in the Yellow Pages under legal services, video taping, and audio/visual equipment.

Once you get an attorney's attention, delineate the advantages of video: For example, you can tape patients who are too sick to appear in court. If there's reason to suspect a will may be contested, an attorney might suggest a video version. The judge can decide whether he or she was competent when making the will by seeing and hearing the deceased.

In addition, "Most [legal] videographers say the best way to get started is by associating yourself with a court reporting service" that takes depositions, says Charlene Canape. "Most lawyers still insist that a written record be kept in addition to the video record."

CRACKING THE CORPORATION

Many large companies already have a video department. However, many are understaffed and rely on freelancers, especially for complicated professional work. To crack the corporate market, call on both the video department head and head of marketing. Also, check in with public relations companies who can recommend you to their clients.

Video seems tailor-made for some markets. When you offer to tape real estate, point out how much time agents waste shuttling home buyers from house to house. If you want to tape job résumés, advertise in the university newspaper and check with the school's placement office.

VIDEO BARTERING

In the beginning, you may have to tape a few events for free so you'll have sample video tapes to show. Why not offer your services to professionals whose help you could use? For example, tape the accoutrements and handiwork of a caterer who might recommend your services. Record a party for an advertising company executive who will help you design your brochures.

When taping an event, "get specific marching orders from the person who commissioned the tape." *How to Capitalize on the Video Revolution* continues: "Are there certain activities (a toast, a receiving line, the arrival of an important guest) that you must be sure not to miss? Are there certain people who should be photographed more than others?" Visit the scene ahead of time to see what lighting is needed. If you're shooting a wedding, check with the church to make sure your equipment is permitted.

As video equipment becomes easier to use, more consumers and corporations will tape their own events. But, "a video involves more than just letting the camera roll," says Jerry Fried, referring to "script writing, setting up scenes, adding titles in the editing, setting up locations." Just as shutterbugs who squeeze off millions of shots turn to professional photographers for formal portraits, it's a sure bet that video hobbyists will call on the professional videographers of the future.

SOURCES

Industry Associations

Women in Film & Video, 27 W. 20th St., New York, N.Y. 10011 (212) 206-8555
Film Councils & Organizations in most large cities

Publications

Videography Magazine, 50 W. 23 St., New York, N.Y. 10011 (212) 645-1000
Millimeter, 826 Broadway, New York, N.Y. 10003 (212) 477-4700
Knowledge Industry Publications, 701 Westchester Ave., White Plains, N.Y. (914) 328-9157
Broadcast Week, Box 5727-TA, 2500 Curtis St., Suite 200, Denver, Colo. 80205 (303) 295-0900

Computers

Computer Consultant

> *"I went into consulting as a way to control my time. I may spend sixty hours a work week now, but I might take a four-day weekend to go skiing. If I suspect a client will be more demanding than I care to tolerate, I just don't accept the assignment. My goal? Controlling my life."* – Peggy Morgan, Morgan Systems Inc.

Low Startup Investment: $0 (consulting for existing clients)

High Startup Investment: $5,000 (an office and advertising)

Time Until Breakeven: Immediate to one year

Annual Revenues: $50,000-$250,000

Annual Pre-tax Profits: $40,000-$200,000

Staffers Needed for Startup (including founder): One

In 1983, Peggy Morgan began selling a unique product: gray matter, the unique knowledge she'd accumulated about computers. She'd learned "information systems"—a/k/a computers—on the corporate fast track at Sun Oil, and in academia, teaching at Temple University. "I could not have considered starting this business five years earlier because computers were just becoming accessible to smaller businesses. The vast majority of my clients are under $20 million [in sales] and the vaster majority are under $10 million. They just could not have afforded computerization before."

COMPUTERS FOR EVERYONE

Well, now nearly everyone sees benefits in owning a computer. As the cost of processing vast amounts of data falls and the use of computers as a standard tool of competition rises, far smaller companies than Peggy Morgan's clients latch onto IBMs and DECs and

Wangs. The most prevalent problem: They haven't the slightest idea which system best serves their needs or what to do with it once they bring in aboard. Enter the likes of Peggy Morgan and a growing cast of computer specialists. "If a company spends $35,000 or $50,000 for a computer, they might need to spend that much for a professional to develop strategies to use it," Peggy explains. "Many companies can afford that as a one-time fee, but can't afford that salary every year."

Computer consultants serve two basic functions:

▪ They select the appropriate computer system, including which peripherals, networks, and software to buy (a one-time project for a consultant).

▪ They integrate the computer into day-to-day management (a situation the client may call you back for).

"Essentially," says Peggy, "a computer should make a business so much more productive that it pays for itself. We help people realize the profit potential in computers."

OVERHEAD IS ZILCH

As a consultant, you don't build any inventory, so you can start inexpensively. (See Management Consultant.) Unlike your clients who need more sophisticated hardware, you can start with a personal computer, which you probably already have since you must be a hacker or information expert to consider this sort of business. Since clients expect you to visit their job sites, a spare bedroom or den can provide your office. Your biggest costs will involve marketing.

You have to target appropriate corporate customers and let them know you exist. Like Peggy Morgan, who started Morgan Systems Inc., from her Cherry Hill, New Jersey, home, you'll identify your best prospects as mid-sized companies. Fortune 500 companies probably will hire an on-staff expert, and startups and mom-and-pop businesses can't afford you.

Decide if your expertise cuts across industries: Can you recommend a system as easily for a school as for a chemical distributor, or are you more comfortable dealing with a specialty, such as accounting packages for financial departments? Geography may play a role in identifying clients. For example, if your specialty involves robotics, your factory customers may be scattered across the country. However, generalists may have all the business they can handle within commuting distance. Keep in mind that you don't want to eat up your startup capital with travel expenses.

While your job as a consultant is to complete a specific project, many computer experts forge ongoing relationships with corporations. Many clients find it far cheaper to pay a consulting retainer, good for the few hours a month worth of questions or programing, than to hire a staff person. Set up flexible fee schedules and let clients know how you can help them in day-to-day management.

NETWORK

What computer expertise you don't possess, you can usually buy. Get to know other computer experts around the country and in your area. Many college professors, for example, freelance as consultants. Depending on how much input you provide, either subcontract, by putting the freelancer on your payroll, or simply locate the right specialist for your client and fade into the background. Even though you may not receive any remuneration for recommending a specialist, keep in touch with the client. This approach builds good will both with clients and with other consultants who may bring you in on cases where *your* expertise can shed light.

Those first contracts will be the hardest, because clients want references. However, even after you're consulting to capacity, never forget that new business represents next month's paycheck. "When you start, you market like crazy." recalls Peggy Morgan. "Then you get so busy with one or two clients that you forget that consulting is cyclical. When those jobs come to an end, you're in the hole with nothing. Gradually, you learn to say, 'Dumbo, all this comes to an end without bringing in new jobs.' "

Peggy figures she fills only half her week with "billable hours," consulting for clients. She spends up to 15 percent of her time in administrative functions, like billing. About the same number of hours is devoted to "practice development"—for example, keeping up with products and researching and lining up seminars that she gives for university classes or for chambers of commerce. Practice development can also provide revenues. You can make your reputation by writing articles for computer magazines or publications geared to your field of expertise. And, if you have a better way to explain, say, a particular software package, consider writing a book. In addition to the royalties or fees, these projects provide dividends when a reader or audience member calls.

Peggy Morgan devotes the other 20 percent of her time to marketing. "At my strung-out busiest, I still need to court clients," she explains. "If my billable hours fall off, I devote more time to marketing." Peggy stocks a file drawer with folders on prospects she gets from talking to clients or even from the telephone book. She sends brochures and personal notes to the decision maker in charge of computers at each corporation, and follows up with phone calls.

TO GROW OR NOT TO GROW

Many computer consultants choose to stay one-person operations. The whole attraction of consulting, they say, is going solo, leaving the hassles of corporate life. However, an individual consultant is limited to the number of billable hours in a day. The owner of a large computer-consulting firm gets a hefty percentage of the fee generated by each associate. Despite the "user friendly" movement and the help large computer manufacturers provide, business's growing dependence on number-crunching and computer productivity translates into an increasing demand for computer consultants.

SOURCES

Industry Associations

Independent Computer Consultants Association, 443 N. New Ballas, P.O. Box 27412, St. Louis, Mo. 63141 (314) 997-4633
ACME Inc., 230 Park Ave., New York, N.Y. 10169
      (212) 697-9693
Institute of Management Consultants Inc., 19 W. 44th St.,
      New York, N.Y. 10036 (212) 921-2885

Publications

Consultants News, Templeton Rd., Fitzwilliam, N.H. 03447
   (603) 585-2200
Byte, 70 Main St., Petersborough, N.H. 03458 (603) 924-9281
Business Computers Systems, 275 Washington St.,
   Newton, Mass. 02158 (617) 964-3030
Datamation, 875 3rd Ave., New York, N.Y. 10022
   (212) 605-9400
InfoWorld, 1060 Marsh Rd., Suite C-200, Menlo Park, Calif. 94025
   (415) 328-4602

Computer Repair

> "Business can set finite goals over a five- to ten-year period: grow, expand, sell, and move on. Computer repair offers a big equity opportunity for technically oriented entrepreneurs." – Alan Andrus, National Computer Service Network

---

Low Startup Investment: $10,000 (home-based startup)

High Startup Investment: $100,000 (office with staff)

Time Until Breakeven: Six months to one year

Annual Revenues: $50,000-$20 million

Annual Pre-tax Profits: $25,000-$4 million

Staffers Needed for Startup (including founder): One

Two kinds of people get into the $20 billion computer repair field: manufacturers and so-called third-party service companies. The biggies like IBM still control about 90 percent of the business, but independents are marching away with a larger piece of the growing computer pie every year. The reason is simple enough: The corporations who sign the multi-million-dollar maintenance contracts would rather pay less money for better service—a package entrepreneurs can offer.

YOU DON'T HAVE TO KNOW COMPUTERS

Two other kinds of people get into the third-party computer repair field: technicians and everybody else.

"Say you're an IBM service representative," says Joseph O'Donnell, who once was one, before he began running the Mt. Laurel, New Jersey, Office of Service Inc. "If you can offer your clients a better deal [either a less expensive contract or better, quicker service—or both], they may guarantee you won't go out of business." For example, clients who know your work may pay their first six-month contract in advance. Or they may stockpile their own parts so you don't have to buy inventory. Meanwhile, concentrate on signing on more clients until you generate enough contract revenues to support yourself. In any event, you can probably hold startup below $10,000 by stocking the most necessary parts and operating out of your home.

In addition to the technicians, there is everybody else. "More important than technical knowledge is personality and an orientation to a high level of service," says Joe O'Donnell. Sales types who line up the accounts contribute as much to a computer maintenance business as the repair whizzes, and many entrepreneurs have built fortunes by managing the operation while hiring their technicians.

Besides, computers are increasingly easier to repair, thanks to manufacturer safeguards and software that tells you exactly what's wrong when you insert it in a particular machine. "Instead of diagnostic knowledge, you need logic—if I pop out this board, this will happen," says Joe. "Then you send the old board back to the manufacturer. With a little education, a good business person could be a fairly good technician."

BUILD AND SELL

Most newcomers specialize in a particular type of machine and its peripherals, and try to saturate a geographic area. Service Inc., which focuses on IBM machines within a fifty-mile radius, develops new accounts through referrals from computer consultants, telemarketing and direct mail (to executives of companies that use computers), and personal contacts gleaned from joining chambers of commerce and computer-user groups.

While several national repair companies exist (including some big enough to go public), as well as companies that tackle most any brand computer on the market, the more common scenario depicts a company growing to local capacity on one manufacturer's computer, then selling. "When you have to subcontract with independents in other areas, you've probably reached $15 million to $20 million in sales," calculates Alan Andrus, president of the National Computer Service Network, a trade group. At that point, a company has employees and office expenses that allow pre-tax profits of 20 percent of revenues—up to $4 million on $20 million gross. "Those companies at the upper end usually sell for one times annual revenues," suggests Alan. In other words, if your company grows to $20 million in sales without partners or substantial debt, you might walk away in ten years with $20 million. "There's tremendous opportunity in this field," states Alan, who is also president of one of the larger players, Grumman Systems Support Corp., in Woodbury, New York.

THE RETAINER

Some computer-repair firms service home computers—usually if the customer brings the PC to the shop and leaves it for technicians to work on during spare moments. Many also charge by the hour for customers who don't want a contract. But the lifeblood of a third-party repair company is the steady cash flow that business contracts bring.

While competition from other independents isn't yet a concern for most entrepreneurs, you still have to give clients reasons to spend $200 to $2,000 every month with "Moe's Computer Repair" instead of with Hewlett-Packard. "You have to know which hot buttons to push," says Joe O'Donnell. Price is one button, as is the immediate and quick service many startups promise. Service Inc. trains its telephone operators as troubleshooters. "Thirty percent of problems can be fixed over the phone by knowing how to operate the machines," says Joe. "The client has the machine operating immediately."

PRESSURE FROM ABOVE?

In the mid-1980s as computer sales leveled off, many manufacturers began stepping up their maintenance efforts to bring in revenues. Some third-party firms filed suits against the manufacturers, alleging that the big guys refused to sell them parts and told falsehoods intended to drive them out of business. However, most observers see this adversarial posture as temporary. "If the computer market grows again, the manufacturers will concentrate on pumping out products," says Alan Andrus. In down-cycles, customers look for the most inexpensive contract they can find to maintain their products. "The third-party side of the business is almost a recession-proof business," says Alan.

"The potential for sharp entrepreneurs with contacts and a knowledge of the business sounds almost too good to be true," adds Joe O'Donnell. For example, Service Inc. is negotiating a repair contract with a fast-food chain. If it lands the business, the company will triple its revenues overnight.

SOURCES

Industry Associations

National Computer Service Network, c/o Grumman Systems Support Corp., 90 Crossways Park Dr., Woodbury, N.Y. 11797
(516) 682-5300
United Service Network, 3540 Tilden, Orange, Calif. 92669
(714) 639-1162

Publication

Computer/Electronic Service News, Box 428, Peterborough, N.H. 03458 (603) 924-9457

Consultant

Coordinated Services, 531 King St., Littleton, Mass. 01460
(617) 486-0388

Computer Trainer

> *"Computer training allows me to blend my technical and business background with my love of teaching. It's a nice marriage."* – Lawrence Grodman, QED Information Sciences Inc.

Low Startup Investment: $1,000 (setting up a home office)

High Startup Investment: $10,000 (includes marketing or establishing a learning center)

Time Until Breakeven: One month to one year

Annual Revenues: $50,000-$10 million

Annual Pre-tax Profits: $40,000-$3.5 million

Staffers Needed for Startup (including founder): One

In the dinosaur age of computers (circa 1960), virtually every penny that corporate America spent on computers bought hardware and some rudimentary software. Today, industry experts estimate that 95 percent of the money U.S. companies budget for computers goes for salaries. What happened? Over the period of swift evolution, the price of hardware fell drastically, placing computers in every company with six zeros after its name. Compared with yesterday's elite circle of computer eggheads who understood the working of every last silicon chip, today's computer users range from secretaries to lawyers.

Despite the proliferation, we are still in the early days of the computer revolution. And the fact is, many nascent computer users would as soon sleep on a bed of nails as sit down at a PC terminal. Enter computer trainers: A growing number of educators who teach everything from basic word processing to intricate maneuvers around data bases. And technology still changes so rapidly that even skilled technicians need constant brush-up courses. "We protect that investment in salaries," explains Lawrence K. Grodman, president of QED Information Sciences Inc., a Wellesley, Massachusetts, firm that trains intermediate and advanced computer users.

THE WAYS TO GO

QED uses the seminar or workshop format, in which an instructor explains computer dos-and-don'ts first hand to a department of employees. Other trainers range from solo practitioners who teach executives one on one, to video producers with tapes explaining spreadsheet analysis, to software houses distributing disks for operators who use the computer to learn about computing. "We estimate roughly 5 percent of the amount a company spends on computing should go for training," says Larry Grodman, an early software specialist who set up QED in 1971. "For professionals, that works out to about ten days a year."

DON'T BYTE OFF MORE THAN YOU CAN CHEW

Manufacturers offer some training, and some larger trade schools have entered the business. But there's still plenty of room for the newcomer, especially if you carve out a specialty, such as how to write software, or how best to get computers to communicate with each other. "If you try to teach too many things, the cost of marketing and sales can drive you out of business before you ever get started," warns Larry Grodman.

His point is well taken: You must isolate your market and let potential customers know you're in business. You may be lucky enough to line up clients through industry contacts, and therefore restrict advertising to word-of-mouth. If that's the case, you can probably get into business for the pocket money required to set up a home-based office.

However, drumming up clients (a/k/a/, marketing) costs money. In addition to sending a sales staff on cold calls to corporations, QED mails brochures that resemble university catalogs—and cost as much to produce. (Smaller educators can print an inexpensive flyer that fits in a business-size envelope.) Because QED addresses employees who are already well-versed in computing, it advertises in computer trade magazines, like *Byte*. However, if you target a more general audience, opt for more general business magazines, like *Inc.* or *Venture*.

If your scope is more regional, check out the host of local business publications that now blanket large cities, like *Crain's Chicago Business,* or *New Jersey Business.* You can also hook up with a community college or seminar producer. In addition to income from tuitions, you make invaluable contacts by teaching classes. If one of your students also works for a corporation, you may find yourself invited to teach the rest of the staff in-house.

HOW MUCH DOES IT COST?

Startup costs also depend on the type of teaching you envision. Shooting and duplicating a video training guide will run at least $10,000, not counting the cost of placing it with users. QED conducts about half its training at "learning centers," or permanent classrooms it operates in a half-dozen cities across the country. "Our people conduct courses for corporate clients on a subscription basis," explains Larry Grodman. "The 165-member companies pay an annual fee that entitles them to blocks of student-days." Tuition varies with how many hours a corporation signs up for, but open enrollment runs about $300 a day. QED charges $2,000 a day to send an instructor to teach in-house, regardless of the number of employees who sign on.

If you instruct at the client's address, overhead is truly minimal. Most of QED's training takes place in the Eastern U.S., because that's where the company concentrates its marketing. But Larry Grodman doesn't think twice if he gets a request to train in Trinidad or Ireland. "We don't open an office, we send a person for a week or two, so it's very inexpensive. We've trained all over the world. How else is a staff in Lagos, Nigeria, going to get training except to contract with a company like ours?"

ACCORDION-STYLE CURRICULUMS

Once you create a rapport with a client, why not expand your curriculum? If you're competent in data processing, point out that employees could use instruction. If you're weak in an area where a client needs help, offer the course anyway; call in a "guest" lecturer and split the fee. "About two-thirds of our staff are independent contractors," explains Larry Grodman. "Most are private computer consultants who see their relationship with QED as a steady source of income." The flip side of this lesson: Let other training firms know you're available for courses in your specialty.

QED also offers management courses to heads of computer departments. These nontechnical seminars have little to do with IBMs or Wangs. But, remember the lesson of the railroad firms that failed to realize they were transportation companies and missed the opportunities in air travel? In other words, once you are big enough to diversify, recognize you are an educator, not just a computer trainer.

But chances are you will have your hands full teaching just computer courses. As computers continue to filter to increasing numbers of staffers who never touched a keyboard, and as manufacturers dream up one innovation after another for even experienced users, the computer education field presents lifelong opportunity. "It's a dynamic, technical environment that offers no end to growth," says Larry Grodman. "This company I founded can go on long after I'm dead."

SOURCES

Industry Association

Independent Computer Consultants Association, 443 N. New Ballas, P.O. Box 27412, St. Louis, Mo. 63141
(314) 993-1188

Publication

Data Training, 38 Chauncy St., Boston, Mass. 02111
(617) 542-0146

Food
and Drink

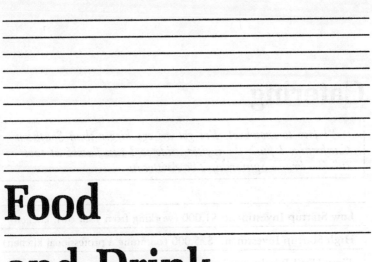

Catering

> *"I love to showboat. I've got an ego bigger than Southern California. I push the waiter aside so I can flambé at tableside."* – Frank Spinarski, The Aristocats

Low Startup Investment: $1,000 (working from your own kitchen)

High Startup Investment: $75,000 (outfitting a professional kitchen)

Time Until Breakeven: Immediate to nine months

Annual Revenues: $200,000-$2 million

Annual Pre-tax Profits: $50,000-$1 million

Staffers Needed for Startup (including founder): One

Ginger Swallow's Creative Cuisine catered three parties in the Houston area in every week of 1986, but soon she hopes to do just five events a year. In fact, "One bash a year would be fine—as long as it's the right bash." Her definition of the "right bash" owes more to economies of scale than snobbery. "I want to feed parties of thirty . . . forty . . . fifty thousand people." At $50 a head, revenues mount quickly. Ginger's two-year-old, single-person shop hasn't reached those heights yet, but the effervescent hostess has catered some Texas-size shindigs. In 1986, for example, she did six parties for between fifteen hundred and twenty-five hundred people, and in the first month of 1987 she booked $110,000 and $140,000 affairs.

The best part of it all, Ginger admits in an undertone, "I usually keep two-thirds of the revenues as profits. That's what's left after I pay for food, help, and transportation."

THE SWEETNESS OF THE BOTTOM LINE

Two-thirds?? That's pre-tax profits of $66,666 on a $100,000 dinner! These figures aren't so hard to believe when you realize that Ginger employs tactics that keep her overhead to zip, which gives her a richer bottom line than the average caterer. For example, her house serves as an office and she hires employees and even a kitchen in a nearby bankrupt restaurant only on days she actually caters events. But even operators who invest in $50,000 kitchens and full-time chefs, even those who spend heavily to promote their service to corporate clientele, allow that catering profits are the best in the entire $185.6 billion food and beverage industry. "Once you deal with enough masses, your profits can be 25 percent of revenues. In some cases, you'll do 50 percent," says Frank Spinarski. With those figures in mind, in 1986 he left a swank hotel chain where he was director of catering to launch The Aristocats catering outfit in Huntington Beach, California.

The National Restaurant Association reported that social caterers brought in revenues of $1.4 billion in 1986 and projected a 6.1-percent increase for 1987. Those figures, however, may grossly under-represent the industry since many home-based caterers don't even list in the phone book. Ginger Swallow shuns a phone listing, reasoning that anybody hosting hundreds of people will hire by reputation, not by Yellow Pages. "I don't want the kind of occasional business that such advertising would bring," she insists. "I want to be known as the caterer in the Dallas area to come to for large bashes."

SANDWICHES BY CONTRACT

But extravaganzas are certainly not the only route to the catering hall of fame. If you can carve out a reputation in any one area, you can do quite nicely. For example, anyone connected with the wedding business in the Washington area knows Love at First Bite. Consultant Jay Treadwell recommends lining up six-month contracts with corporations, a move that brings in continual business from executives who don't have time to go out to lunch.

Despite the one-shot profit potential in $800 filet mignon birthday dinners for six people, which the Aristocats occasionally caters in an individual's home, Frank Spinarski says, "Corporate is where the bread and butter is." Not only do they throw bigger and more expensive parties, corporations party more often.

To tap that corporate sector, Frank Spinarski took along a client list of eight thousand area corporations when he left his former position at the hotel chain. (You also can find corporate names through chambers of commerce.) "We called everyone on that list to see if their company used caterers," he recalls. "Probably one thousand people in the county consistently use caterers. We call every one of them regularly, asking 'When will you use us?' " Such cold calls bring in meager business at first, but once the corporations hear of the other fantastic parties you host, they start responding positively. Frank says that now of the thirty contacts he makes during a typical week, six or seven book parties.

MAKE THEM TALK ABOUT YOU

Word-of-mouth is undoubtedly worth more to caterers that to restaurateurs. Anxious brides or corporations throwing parties for new product send-offs "are not going to risk embarrassment by trying an unknown caterer," says Jay Treadwell. "They ask for recommendations." Your reputation as a fabulous restaurant chef may be recommendation enough. Ginger Swallow worked as corporate chef for a wealthy Texas real estate couple famous for their flamboyant soirées. All the banks and real estate brokers and corporate execs knew Ginger because they'd attended her parties.

But those entering the field with less visible credentials say there are as many ways to create reputation as there are parties to throw. "Build a party into your startup costs," recommends Jay Treadwell, who was formerly the general manager of Ridgewell Caterers, the Washington giant which regularly feeds the White House along with the rest of Capitol Hill society. Make that give-away party an impressive showcase for your talents. Beef Wellington and baked Alaska for one hundred guests may be prohibitively expensive, but you might do something special with cocktails and canapés. Spend the money for an ice carving or a baked Brie that your guests will remember. And rent the local museum garden or another enticing locale to lure influential people. "If you plan to specialize in weddings, invite florists, department store heads, musicians, people in charge of places that book weddings," explains Jay. "The bride will ask those people to recommend a caterer. The answer might be, 'I went to a fabulous party this caterer gave last month.' That's all the recommendation you need."

Especially while building a following, don't cut corners. "Compensation comes in all ways, not just dollars and cents, but sometimes in reputation," says Ginger, who adds, "I give stuff away. It may not be worth 10 cents of my time to add edible flowers, but it's a way to sell my company." If you can't get a client to pay for the frills but enough influential guests are attending, you may wish to add carved pineapples anyway. Look at it this way: such extra attention is cheaper and more effective than advertising.

TO BUY OR RENT

Unlike many other businesses, you can start as big or as small in catering as your pocketbook allows, because you can buy your own elaborate facilites, or rent just about anything you need. Jay Treadwell figures $100 per square foot will outfit an institutional kitchen. (Caterers do most actual cooking on-site, either with equipment they bring or facilities supplied by the clients. But you need a kitchen for "prep work," like cutting vegetables.) Heavy-volume jobs require a truck and temperature-controlled holding cabinets. You either rent china, linens, and other staples, or buy them outright and keep the cut that would otherwise go to the rental agency.

Anticipating monthly revenues of $50,000 (after nine months in business, they are halfway there), Frank Spinarski and his partners invested $50,000 in their kitchen and hired a full-time chef and secretary. But you can get by with far less. Ginger Swallow catered her first $22,000 party using her own pots and pans and rented kitchen space. She invested $5,000 of her $15,000 profits from that first affair in equipment meant to enhance her signature. For example, "I hired carpenters to make a huge, fancy cheese board shaped like a cowboy boot" to serve forty-pound blocks of cheddar at Tex-Mex barbecues.

While you can certainly administrate from a spare bedroom, consider Health Department regulations before actually cooking from home. You're legally considered a restaurant when you cater. But many places rent their kitchens. Some large city restaurants advertise their facilities for caterer use. In addition, don't forget church or school kitchens. "If you offer something special, like cooking a treat for the kids, you might get a good deal on using the school kitchen after hours," says Jay Treadwell.

As for personnel, a freelance legion makes its living by working for caterers. Ask party planners or banquet managers to recommend servers or ice carvers. Says Ginger Swallow: "If I go to a restaurant and see somebody I like, I approach them—the chef, the bartender. . . ."

WHO DOES IT

Restaurateurs are the most obvious converts to catering, but marketing types who hire culinary experts are sprinkled throughout the field. Jay Treadwell warns against underestimating the business aspects of catering. "The restaurant business is 70 percent food-oriented, with the rest going for service, organization, etc. Those figures flip-flop in catering; 30 percent food and the rest delivery, transporting the food, lining up rental equipment, juggling personnel." In catering, organization counts.

Another handy trait is a smooth manner. On the one hand, you must deal professionally with corporate clients and party planners who expect a receipt for every shrimp. But you also must assure parents of the bride that you'll be on time and everything will be beautiful for the special day.

You don't have to limit your business to gastronomy. Ridgewell Caterers, which expected revenues of between $15 million and $17 million in 1987, was begun in 1928 by the cook of the French Embassy and the butler of the British Embassy to supply all the accoutrements, like china. Party rentals are still a big part of the business. Ridgewell's, now headed by identical twin brothers Jeff and Bruce Ellis (grandsons of the founders, who fell in love and were married), did not build its kitchen until 1970. "People like one-stop shopping," says Jay Treadwell. "You can rent items from a rental store, but act as a coordinator on flowers, tents, whatever. In all likelihood, it's a profit center for the caterer and a relief for the client."

Never lose sight of the fact that people come to a caterer for the unusual. If they wanted the restrictions of a set menu, they would go to a restaurant. "Outline menu possibilities, but leave the impression that you can do anything," advises Jay.

And make suggestions. Ginger Swallow recalls an aviation company that requested a Tex-Mex picnic for twelve hundred. Instead, "I suggested an international theme, and we ended up with cuisine from six countries, including a luau with a huge pig in honey sauce and steaks branded with the company's logo. My fee went from $5,000 to $35,000." The meeting planner moved the party into an airplane hanger, and added a band, Vegas tables, and a limousine containing a Joan Collins look-alike; his fee leaped from $3,500 to $10,000. The client? "They were ecstatic," says Ginger. "They threw a party everybody remembers."

SOURCES

Industry Associations

National Association of Catering Executives, 2500 Wilshire Blvd., Suite 603, Los Angeles, Calif. 90057 (213) 487-6223

National Institute for Off-Premise Catering, 1341 N. Sedgwick, Chicago, Ill. 60610 (800) OFF-PREM

National Restaurant Association, 311 1st St., N.W., Washington, D.C. 20001 (800) 424-5156

Publications

Special Events Magazine, 20048 Cotner Ave., Los Angeles, Calif. 90025 (213) 477-1033

Catering Today Magazine, P.O. Box 222, Santa Claus, Ind. 47579 (812) 937-4464

Consultant

Jay Treadwell, Optimum Services, 5420 Grove St., Chevy Chase, Md. 20815 (301) 656-6389

Gourmet Food Products

> *"The public writes recipes to me: 'Last night, here's what I did with your chutney.' I really enjoy the feedback."* – Duggan Peak, Duggan's Own

Low Startup Investment: $30,000 (developing products and exhibiting at a tradeshow)

High Startup Investment: $100,000 (establishing a small factory)

Time Until Breakeven: Six months to two years

Annual Revenues: $250,000-$5 million

Annual Pre-tax Profits: $40,000-$2 million

Staffers Needed for Startup (including founder): One

Duggan and Robert Peak were setting up their booth at the San Francisco Food & Wine Show in May 1985, when the enormity of what they were doing hit Duggan, a former restaurant manager and the creator of Duggan's Own products, which range from a Poppy Perfect salad dressing to a cucumber dill vinegar. "Robert had just left this prosperous advertising agency and we had moved to Oregon, hundreds of miles away from my restaurant contacts in Southern California." She looked over at their baby, whom they had smuggled into the show, hoping the officials wouldn't notice and throw them out. "It felt like opening night, and I was scared. I looked at Robert and said, 'My God, look what we've done.' "

As the doors opened at 9 A.M., throngs of wholesale buyers from department and specialty stores clogged the aisles, leaving Duggan Peak no more time to worry. The couple had transformed their booth into a pastel kitchen. The look, unusual in contrast to the sterility of most booths, attracted crowds right away. Robert had created progressive packaging in airy grays and pinks, a memorable departure from the homespun clichés of most specialty foods—the burgundy bonnet topping the jar of marmalade. And Duggan had tasted every oil, vinegar, and salad dressing in California when concocting an all-natural, really different taste. By 10:30, Robert was discussing terms with the buyer from Nieman-Marcus when Duggan felt someone grab her hand. "You don't want to go exclusive with Nieman-Marcus," he said. "I'm from Macy's."

"We thought we'd be okay if we sold two thousand cases during our first year," recalls Robert. "We sold that many our first show." During their startup year, the couple hit sales of $1 million—and profits of $420,000. Within two years, sales had tripled as Duggan's Own grew from fourteen products to fifty-nine.

YOU'VE GOTTA BE SPECIAL

First the bad news: For every Robert and Duggan Peak success story, failures in the specialty food business abound. Your family recipe has got to be really special to compete with giant conglomerates that unleash entire R&D departments on $4 mustards. "Individuality is really important," says Robert. "Do some research to come up with something unique either in the packaging or product." Adds Morris Kushner, a consultant who has introduced more that six hundred items during his career, including the first capucino mix, and the first crouton to America: "If you can get the customer to pick up and read your label, you're half way home."

A tip on the label: In addition to conveying a quality image, many food manufacturers add a recipe either on the packaging or tied around the bottle's neck. After all, the more customers use your marinade, the sooner they will be back for more.

LANDING ON THE SHELVES

The first customer you must sell is the merchant. In the old days, food entrepreneurs sold to local clientele and watched their distribution expand as their fame slowly grew. "We used to take new products to the corner grocery to get an idea of how they would sell," says Morris Kushner. That approach is increasingly difficult as supermarket chains muscle corner groceries out of existence. Some specialty food stores still take samples on consignment, but numerous supermarket chains now charge a $3,000 "slotting fee" to introduce new products.

Now for the good news: Research firm FIND/SVP estimated the gourmet/specialty food market at $8 billion in 1986, and projected 12-percent annual increases through 1990. Morris Kushner adds to that picture: "When I first started, specialty products looked at 5 percent of the population. Now we can target 18 to 20 percent— that's the number of families with gross incomes of $35,000 or more. The first thing they can afford is good food. 'Tonight,' they say, 'we can eat like the Rockefellers.' "

SUPPORTING CAST

This new interest in top-of-the-line consumables has catalyzed an entire industry to help entrepreneurs introduce the latest in shiitake mushrooms and coriander marinades. Perhaps the most important new aid is the growth of tradeshows: These allow mom-and-pop operations to go national (or international) immediately by attracting the attention of department and specialty stores that buy in bulk. Although specialty food shows have been around for a generation, recently their popularity has exploded. The International Fancy Food & Confection Show took over two hundred thousand square feet at New York's Javits Center in 1987, double its size from four years earlier, placing it among the top 1 percent of all tradeshows in America. The Peaks attended nine shows in 1987, including jaunts to Tokyo, Paris, and West Germany. "Shows literally showcase your products," explains Morris Kushner. "Brokers and distributors will see your products and latch onto you."

Food brokers do not take title to your herbal cheese sticks, but merely act as your sales representative with accounts all over the country. For enticing retailers to buy your products, brokers receive 2.5- to 5-percent commissions. You handle the shipping and accounts receivable. Food distributors go a couple of steps further for their 25- to 30-percent fees. They act as middlemen by actually buying your product and shipping it to retailers they sign up.

SOMEONE'S IN THE KITCHEN

Two avenues exist to produce the products: You can do it yourself or hire a co-packer. Duggan and Robert Peak chose the initially more expensive route of operating their own factory. "To hold our overhead low, we moved from Los Angeles to Oregon," says Robert. The manufacturing plant they rented included acreage where they grow basil, tarragon, thyme, and marjoram to supplement herbs grown by local farmers. The couple's first $5,000 went for show fees and labels for their sample jars in the San Francisco show. Then they proceeded to invest $75,000 from savings to meet those increasing orders. "During our first six months, every time we got a check from a client, we would rush to the bank and get cash for more inventory," recalls Robert.

The Peaks chose to manufacture their products so they could control quality. More commonly, entrepreneurs manufacture through co-packers who agree to maintain high standards by strictly adhering to recipes supplied by the food's creators. "You take the recipe to someone who produces it under your label," explains Morris Kushner. "A co-packer buys vinegar and oils in tankfuls for all their customers, so volume provides savings."

As a rule of thumb, expect to "keystone" your products—double the cost of producing the item to wholesalers, who then tack on another 50 percent at the shelf. For example, if your overhead, including food and packaging, labor, rent, and delivery, amounts to $1 per jar of wild mushroom pâté, charge wholesalers $2 and consumers $3. "That strategy should cover all the essentials and leave a few pennies for advertising and new-product development," says Morris. Costs should fall as your volume increases; some overhead items, like rent, remain stable no matter how many cases you churn out a day, and bulk buying actually lessens per unit food costs. "Volume production will bring the $1 cost down to maybe 87 cents, which allows you to give a product a shot with a coupon or a ribbon on the top of the jar after a few months," says Morris.

KEEP THOSE PRODUCTS COMING

Savings also frees up cash for new-product R&D. "Nowadays, you don't stand a chance with one item," warns Morris. "You have to build an image with pizza, onion, avocado—all the salad dressing flavors under one label."

Specialty food retailers and suppliers deal regularly with cottage manufacturers, so don't try to pretend you have General Foods' resources. Buyers want assurances you can deliver as promised and suppliers want to know you can pay on time—so don't make promises you can't keep. Possibly because they projected a professional image in their packaging and with their factory, Robert and Duggan Peak had no trouble lining up suppliers. "People gave us credit —vinegar and olive oil companies put us on net thirty-days," says Duggan, still amazed. "Some shipped their first order COD, then established a line of credit."

Retailers likewise were helpful. "Our first orders were all prepaid or COD," says Robert. "Some large orders can't do that, but department-store buyers said they knew we were just starting and offered to pay us the day after they got the goods."

Today, Duggan laughs recalling her anxiety at the first show. "But you know, this was supposed to be a kind of early retirement for us," she says. (Duggan is in her late twenties, Robert is in his early thirties.) "Everything happened so fast. We were bitten by success."

SOURCES

Industry Association

National Association for The Specialty Food Trade Inc., 215 Park Ave. S., New York, N.Y. 10003 (212) 505-1770

Publications

Showcase Magazine, 215 Park Ave. S., New York, N.Y. 10003 (212) 505-1770

Fancy Food & Candy, 2700 River Road, Suite 409, Des Plaines, Ill. 60018 (312) 824-7440

Consultant

Morris Kushner, 4865 Louise Ave., Encino, Calif. 91316 (818) 789-8885

Gourmet Food Store

> *"The suppliers I deal with are generous, innovative, sparkling people, in love with what they do. You see this kind of passion because specialty foods is an industry made up of cottage industries. The participants provide companionship of the highest order." – Elaine Yannuzzi, Expression Unltd.*

Low Startup Investment: $50,000 (small boutique with limited offerings)

High Startup Investment: $150,000 (large gourmet market)

Time Until Breakeven: Two to four years

Annual Revenues: $300,000-$3 million

Annual Pre-tax Profits: $30,000-$600,000

Staffers Needed for Startup (including founder): One to three

---

Walking through the big burgundy barn that houses Expression unltd. offers quite a sensory experience. More than one hundred varieties of crackers line its shelves, as well as one hundred twenty-six jams, forty-five mustards, and spices from unpronounceable regions. The bright colors of thirty-eight flavors of jelly beans vie with the warm earth tones of twenty-three whole-bean coffees in burlap sacks. The take-out food section sends odors wafting through the aisles. Generous samples of goat cheese and Swiss vegetable pâté mean nobody leaves Expression hungry. Located on a remote country road in the Wachung Mountains of Warren, New Jersey, forty miles from New York City, the store sells one ton of cheese every three days.

"Six or eight years ago, specialty food stores didn't exist," says Elaine Yannuzzi, who owns what many consider the ultimate in specialty food stores. "Meats were available in old-fashioned German delis, and you could get a dozen of the more pedestrian cheeses at the supermarket. But nothing like this existed."

EXPRESSION THROUGH FOOD

In fact, Expression unltd. began without a single food item in sight. "Things were different in 1970; a woman expressed herself through her children and her home," explains Elaine Yannuzzi, who stocked the original Expression with a stitchery department, children's toy area, decorating section, and gourmet cookware corner. In the mid-1970s, Elaine added cheese to complement the cookware, and soon inserted other gourmet items. Today, all the old departments except cookware are gone, and cheese represents 30 percent of the store's sales. Revenues amounted to millions in 1986, and, with the addition of take-out foods, 1987 sales jumped by at least one-third. (See Take-out Restaurant.)

Nobody knows the true size of the gourmet or specialty food market, because an exact definition of specialty foods doesn't exist. Is the Brie that you could only buy in specialty cheese shops a decade ago still considered a specialty food even though you now can choose from a half-dozen Brie brands at the A&P? But, as an indication of the industry's growth, Packaged Facts Inc., a New York market research firm, suggested the gourmet trade it placed at $8 billion in 1985 will rise to just over $14 billion by 1990. Another firm, Frost & Sullivan, estimates a core market of 3.5 million gourmet customers, and another 10 million "light users" of gourmet products.

WHY WE EXPERIMENT

The reasons for Americans' new taste for gourmet foods include
- Increasing popularity of home entertaining
- Less time for food preparation coupled with higher incomes (well over half of all homemakers also work)
- Improved refrigeration and transportation that provides fresh, exotic fruits and vegetables year round
- Increased preference for "all-natural" foods made *sans* preservatives, salt, or sugar
- Availability of hundreds of new products that are expanding Americans' diet to include salmon pâté and radicchio

However, along with this heightened receptivity to specialty foods comes new competition. In addition to increasing numbers of specialty food boutiques, every supermarket in the country now has its gourmet food selection. To bring customers through your doors, you must create an experience they just can't get in a fluorescent-lit supermarket that stocks dog food and detergent along with the arugula and extra virgin olive oil.

If your startup budget is skinny, you can open a one-thousand-square-foot true specialty store: just teas or cheeses. Carry only a handful of companion items like biscuits or a balsamic-flavored vinegar. By addressing such a narrow market, you become known to the area's aficionados. You may eventually send out a catalog to attract mail-order customers for your chocolate truffles or whole-fruit jellies.

A GENERALIST IN SPECIALTY FOODS

Rather than creating a niche in a particular food category, Expression unltd. goes to the opposite extreme by providing the last word in specialty food shopping. Although Elaine Yannuzzi earns 80 percent of her sales from just 20 percent of her products, she carries thousands of items to create an atmosphere that brings customers from a hundred-square-mile radius. "We carry a line of Indonesian spices that maybe fifty people travel from around the area to get at Expression. We do special orders on really odd items," she says.

To choose which items to stock, Elaine shops the massive Fancy Food & Confection Shows twice annually. The show's 2,200 booths "overwhelm a person just starting out," she warns, "but I assure you [choosing a product mix] really does become manageable after a few years." Her first criterion in deciding whether to stock a particular item involves taste. "A specialty mustard sells for $3.50 to $5, compared with 79 cents in the supermarket. The taste has to say 'Oh, wow!' "

She continues, "if price is very much out of line, we'll still stock a superb product, but in lesser quantity till we see how it sells."

365 TURNS A YEAR

Because specialty foods retailers look for fast inventory turnover, you don't have to pile up debt to stock your store. "You don't bring in a spring line of sportswear that takes three months to turn," points out Elaine. "Try for weekly or bi-weekly turns on jarred foods, and daily turns on prepared foods." Use proceeds from this month's sales to buy next month's. Stash additional funds for prime buying times, like before Christmas.

Of course, to get such fast turnover, location is crucial. A specialty food store's 40-percent margins, while vastly superior to the 10-percent margins a supermarket copes with, just don't support mall locations. But try to get the most visible spot your pocketbook allows. Expression unltd. broke this cardinal rule; Elaine Yannuzzi located her shop in a building she already owned because it needed a tenant—even though she was miles from nowhere. After struggling a few years, she overcame the disadvantage of her remote site; now, during Christmas season, Expression needs a police officer to direct traffic out of its backroads parking lot. "But 'location, location, location' is a good rule," admits Elaine. "Rules make life easier."

To combat its isolation, Expression advertises weekly in New Jersey's largest newspaper, as well as in other papers less frequently. In addition, the store employs a full-time public relations manager to call on caterers, corporate customers, restaurants, and other clients who get discounts for buying in bulk.

SAMPLING BOARDS

Once you get customers into the store, you still have to sell the foods. Because many of your items are unusual, they can be intimidating. (Question: Does blackberry sauce go over ice cream or lamb? Answer: Both.) The thirty-five year-round and sixty holiday-time Expression employees taste each new item and learn about its origins so they can answer customer questions. To provide customers with a first-hand experience, the store gives away 350 pounds of cheese, chicken salad with water chestnuts, and chutney a week in samples. On weekends, one employee does nothing but refurbish the sampling boards. Elaine Yannuzzi asks manufacturers to provide as many free samples as possible, arguing that a smear of basil mustard on a pretzel can sell a whole jar. Even with help from food packagers, she still spends $150,000 a year on freebies.

Specialty food stores walk a thin line between offering the foods that customers know they want, and exposing them to an ever-increasing number of new treats. A specialty food customer is, almost by definition, adventurous: Your job is to create an atmosphere conducive to experimenting. "Even though an item may be unknown to a customer, they are secure because they know we select with care and feeling," says Elaine Yannuzzi. "Specialty food stores sell confidence. We sell a spiritual thing lingering behind the products."

SOURCES

Industry Association

National Association for The Specialty Food Trade Inc., 215 Park Ave. S., New York, N.Y. 10003 (212) 505-1770

Publications

Showcase Magazine, 215 Park Ave. S., New York, N.Y. 10003 (212) 505-1770

Fancy Food & Candy, 2700 River Road, Suite 409,
Des Plaines, Ill. 60018 (312) 824-7440

Consultant

Morris Kushner, 4865 Louise Ave., Encino, Calif. 91316
(818) 789-8885

No-alcohol Nightclub

> *"I never talk about how beautiful the club is, but I swell with pride when others talk about it. It allows me to continually create."* – Chuck Fazzino, Top Brass Nightclub

Low Startup Investment: $50,000 (stark, small club)

High Startup Investment: $500,000 (elaborate, big-city spot)

Time Until Breakeven: Six months to four years

Annual Revenues: $300,000-$3 million

Annual Pre-tax Profits: $90,000-$1 million

Staffers Needed for Startup (including founder): Five

Chuck Fazzino, a one-time drummer, made his living for a dozen years by designing the lighting systems for some of the premier nightclubs in New York City. He loved the glamour and intensity of the business, but when it came time to open his own club in 1987, he took a flyer on a risky new concept that is catching hold across the country: nightclubs without booze. Saying he wanted "a place my eight-year-old daughter could come to," Chuck adds healthy business reasons for his decision: "The National Council on Alcoholism says per capita consumption of alcohol has been declining since 1980. And there's the liability question."

Although the law Chuck Fazzino refers to isn't yet enacted in

Yonkers, New York, the New York City suburb where the Top Brass resides, he has no doubt it's coming. "In other parts of the country, a bar and bartender are responsible if a client took their last drink with you. God forbid they kill somebody, you're liable. You can be sued."

You can't be sued if you don't serve alcohol, though.

TEEN CLUBS

To date, most no-alcohol nightclubs cater to the underage set. Take, for instance, Up the Creek, the Boulder, Colorado, success story managed by an eighteen-year-old. Its seventeen-drink menu includes Puberty Punch (orange juice with sweet-and-sour mix) and Black Hole (ice cream, banana, strawberries, and chocolate). Up the Creek's customers average just fourteen and a half years old.

You can make a bundle by getting known as the in-spot for high schoolers. But some nightclubs have no intention of restricting their appeal to teens. Some Florida clubs located near campus pull in a freer-spending college crowd. One Long Island, New York, club contacted church groups and let an Alcoholics Anonymous chapter know about its no-booze policy. Its clientele averages well over twenty years old. A Los Angeles club serving only mineral water offers a variation on the theme by catering to health conscious types. While some doubt the general public outside of California would support such a specific concept, some enterprising entrepreneurs have made their fortunes by setting up fruit-juice bars in health clubs.

Top Brass hopes to bring in greater numbers of full-fledged adults. They first arrive for the club's 110-seat café, where they dine on such sophisticated cuisine as grilled shrimp with cilantro. Then they stay for the nightlife. "For some reason, kids tend to be destructive—burning rugs, gum on the floors," says Chuck Fazzino. "We try to weed out the destructive kids and get a complement of middle-aged patrons." In addition to advertising in publications that customers aged thirty and older read, Top Brass hopes its growing reputation as a place for private parties will attract a more mature crowd.

DO IT WITH LIGHTS

Opening a no-alcohol club is easier and less costly than a traditional bar. Chuck Fazzino estimates his insurance costs are 35 to 45 percent below what he would pay if he served spirits. Additionally, he did not have to fork over $2,500 to $4,500 for a liquor license that might take six to eighteen months to be approved by the state.

Particularly if you aim at the younger, less sophisticated set, you can paint the walls black and allot most of your startup capital to a good sound system and your rent. Any large structure okayed for this purpose by the fire department can be converted. You don't need an elaborate bar set-up unless you offer a great many frozen and mixed drinks. Since lighting will be low, choose seating for durability and easy maintenance rather than subtle charm. "Our club is all done with lighting," says Chuck Fazzino, who describes Top Brass as having "a high-tech, theatrical look." For example, the lights that splash the ten-foot-high, fifty-foot long wall behind the bar change colors three times a night. "The bar goes from deep blue to hot red to stars over the course of the evening," says Chuck. Flickering lights outline the railing around the five-thousand-square-foot dance floor. Instead of painting the club, Chuck just changes the color of the light bulbs every three months. "It's important to constantly renovate so the look doesn't get stale. Otherwise the regulars might look for a new club."

MUNCHIES

Elizabeth Bassford, food and beverage director at Top Brass, says it's a good idea to sell food since "people like to nosh while they drink." If you don't want to invest in a full-service restaurant, offer finger-foods. Instead of hiring a chef, your servers can microwave frozen individual pizzas. Instead of investing in fragile and expensive china, use wicker baskets to hold mozzarella bread sticks.

The profit on such $3 nonalcoholic drinks as a Sweet Georgia Brown (seltzer, vanilla syrup, coffee ice cream, and brown sugar, topped with whipped cream) surpasses even those 100-percent and higher margins on Bloody Marys and gin-and-tonics. But no-booze clubs also sell a lot of $1.50 Cokes and nonalcoholic beers with lower tickets. In addition, patrons on an allowance may not spend as freely as customers with a salary, so your bar tab could be lower than clubs that serve alcohol. A no-alcohol club could take a few months longer to break even than traditional bars.

THE GATE

One solution is to set an entrance fee and rely on volume. "We make our money at the door," says Chuck Fazzino. Top Brass, a twelve-thousand-square-foot former skating rink, can hold one thousand people. Even if weekday business is slow, once you reach weekend capacity, revenues flow faster than beer on tap with such volume.

To reach that capacity, however, you may need to pump out a fair share of promotion. In addition to advertising in newspapers and publications that singles read, such as city magazines, Chuck Fazzino recommends "spoon-feeding the press." Every feature story is worth a thousand ads. A good, well-known band also brings in clientele. While you may have to guarantee a floor in addition to a percentage of the take, many bands command their own followings.

Few observers expect liquor-free clubs to surplant their spirited cousins. But increasing numbers of entrepreneurs see room for both versions. Indeed, some traditional clubs are getting into the act by scheduling no-alcohol nights. Some operators see the traditional bars as competition while others suspect they just whet patrons' appetites and prime their customers for the no-alcohol style of nightclubbing.

SOURCES

Publications

Beverage Industry Publications, 747 Third Ave., New York, N.Y. 10017 (212) 418-4135

Beverage Media Ltd., 161 Ave. of the Americas, New York, N.Y.
10013 (212) 620-0100
Beverage Retailer Weekly, 250 W. 57th St., New York, N.Y. 10019
(212) 582-1370

Ocean Farming

> *"I love the ocean and the quality of life in Maine. It's a gas to go out on the boats. The fishermen are great people to work with—hardworking and honest."* – Endicott Davison, Great Eastern Mussel Farms Inc.

Low Startup Investment: $10,000 (contracting with fishermen and us-
ing existing production and marketing facilities)

High Startup Investment: $1 million (buying your own boat and mar-
keting in-house)

Time Until Breakeven: One to five years

Annual Revenues: $25,000-$20,000 million

Annual Pre-tax Profits: $15,000-$3 million

Staffers Needed for Startup (including founder): One

Aquaculture may be the business opportunity of the 1990s—but
you need to be a gambler. Those who make it in fish farming make
it big; it's not uncommon to see 80-percent profits and sometimes
200-percent return on investment within a few years.

Industry observers say it might take just two decades for aquaculture, which generated sales of over $1 billion in 1986, to capture
the entire burgeoning seafood market, which amounted to $16 bil-
lion in 1986. Says one analyst: "The same way farmers pushed
hunters and trappers out of the forest, aquaculture will supplant
fishing." Let's consider just one state and one shellfish: aquaculture

landings of mussels increased by 600 percent in Maine between 1981 and 1985, when production amounted to eight hundred thousand pounds.

Even as aquaculture takes a larger percentage of the market, demand for fish is leaping right out of the water: The National Marine Fisheries Services says per capita seafood consumption amounted to 14.5 pounds in 1985, compared with 10.9 pounds in 1966. Some observers say a health-conscious America will consume thirty pounds of fish per person by 1990.

With those enticements, why shouldn't we all go into aquaculture? According to one analyst, "Maybe only one in one hundred is going to make it."

BEARS IN THE WATER

Why so bearish? Consider just a couple of things that can go wrong in aquaculture. If you're operating from tanks, you must pump in oxygen: too much or too little is lethal. If you seed your runway with too many shrimp, the creatures simply devour each other. Then there's disease, algae, pollution, and a host of other variables. Most fish take two to three years to mature. If something goes wrong after the growing cycle is 95 percent completed, fish farmers have to start from scratch.

In the ocean, you also worry about natural predators: "One day we were sitting in boats watching a flock of eider ducks land on a cove so thick you could walk on them," recalls Endicott (Chip) Davison Jr., who operates Great Eastern Mussel Farms Inc. from the Maine yachting haven of Tenants Harbor. "We thought that was interesting until we realized what had happened. We'd put sixty tons of mussels into that farm and the ducks ate up all sixty tons in a week." (The dual solution to this Hitchcockian bird problem was "scarecrows"—dummies in yellow rain slickers on mock boats—and a permit to shoot a certain number of ducks each season.)

Then there's the enormous cost of most aquaculture. Most consultants recommend developing at least one hundred acres, at $10,000 an acre, to make any money farming trout or catfish. You can cultivate prawns in above-ground raceway cultures on a fraction of the acreage, but the necessary technology eats up the same $1 million. One way around drowning in startup costs is ocean fishing.

INFRASTRUCTURE

Thanks to a growing infrastructure you can lean on to harvest, process, and market your fish, you can get into ocean farming in a small way. For one thing, you don't have to pay for raw materials: the infant fish and the fish food come courtesy of Neptune. "The Atlantic Ocean is a huge food-production facility with plankton and other food sources not gobbled up by anything," explains Chip Davison, a one-time paralegal with the Manhattan district attorney's office. "Maine still leases only about seven hundred acres off its coast—with more than six hundred thousand left. There are a million other places in California, Canada, and other seacoasts where you could do this kind of thing."

Chip Davison farms mussels. He and his partners spent $250,000 in 1978 to develop the farming procedures, to set up a facility to process the mussels, and to establish a marketing organization that now sells thirty-six hundred tons of mussels a year to restaurant chains, grocers, and seafood markets around the country. If you've got big bucks and marketing ability, model your technique on Great Eastern, growing a different fish species or locating in another part of the country. If you want to enter aquaculture in a smaller way, line up fishermen who already have the boats and know-how to farm your fish and contract with producers and marketers like Great Eastern to package and sell them.

You can farm mussels by dangling them off of ropes, or you can do it Chip Davison's way: Around July 4 each year, infant mussels naturally settle about two thousand per square foot on the intertidal zones in Maine. The density knocks out a high percentage, and many others don't survive predators and sun. Working with local fishermen, Great Eastern scoops up tons of the "seeds," and "transplants" them to more optimum growing conditions in coastal waters it leases from the state. Maintenance of the beds, which primarily means fending off starfish and eider ducks that feast on mussels, is up to the fishermen who co-lease the waters. The fishermen, using their own boats, harvest the crop a year or so later, selling them to Great Eastern at the market price. Because the sea acts as a natural holding pen, you don't have to bring up the mussels until you have a buyer lined up.

You could stop there, but Great Eastern goes a step further and makes its mussels "pot ready." "We built a plant where the mussels spend twenty-four to forty-eight hours in large tanks to purge out the grit and mud," explains Chip. "Then they run on inspection belts where we weed out mussels with pearls or shells that look bad."

From there the still living mussels go to Great Eastern accounts all over the country. Farming, says Chip, makes seafood dependable. "Traditionally, the price fluctuates depending on supply. If the weather is bad, you don't deliver. We've solved those problems." He points to the hundred or so herring plants boarded up along Maine's coast. "In the past, we fished a species until it ran out. The herring might not return for ten years. We weren't willing to spend the money to market mussels unless we could guarantee we'd have a product to sell a year from now." Barring an oil spill or natural disaster, Great Eastern's accounts can expect a steady supply of mussels at a steady price year-round.

THE LAW OF THE SEA

If you want to farm the ocean, the first thing you do is make friends with the fishermen. "Traditionally, if someone's fished a certain area, that's theirs," says Chip. Before the state grants leases, Great Eastern presents its intentions at a town hall hearing. The state decides if the company's plans would interfere with traditional fishing rights as well as access. Because of its public relations efforts, Great Eastern spends about $3,000 to secure a lease that the state sells for only $15 an acre. "We only have rights to harvest the product we plant and anything that interferes, like starfish. Fishermen can't drag for scallops on our lease, because that disrupts the mussels. But they can fish for lobsters."

Once you get a lease, if you own a boat and have some expertise, start farming. Or, advises Chip, "contract with a fisherman to seed your property and monitor it on a year-round basis. Give him a percentage of the profits, and then let somebody like us handle the marketing."

Returns all depend on the yield, but, assuming you harvest a crop at all, Chip Davison says to expect at least 20-percent pre-tax profits, and more likely 40-percent or 80-percent, since you haven't spent much to plant the fish in the first place.

Fish farming isn't new. It probably began in China four thousand years ago. Today, the U.S. gets almost all its catfish and trout from farms, and part of such other species as salmon, bass, and oysters. Most experts say it's only a matter of time before virtually all our seafood comes from farms. The question remains: Who will sink in aquaculture and who will swim?

SOURCES

Industry Associations

National Fisheries Institute, 2000 M St., N.W., Suite 580, Washington, D.C. 20036 (202) 296-5090

State Department of Agriculture, aquaculture divisions
  National Mussel Marketing Association, P.O. Box 212, Plaistow, N.H. 03865 (603) 382-1801

World Aquaculture Society, 341 Pleasant Hall, Louisiana State University, Baton Rouge, La. 70803 (504) 388-3137

Publications

Aquaculture Digest, 9434 Kearny Mesa Rd., San Diego, Calif. 92126 (619) 271-0133

Aquaculture Magazine, Box 2329, Asheville, N.C. 28801 (704) 254-7334

Consultants

Aquaculture Consulting & Development Corp., Box 208, Avenida de Diego 106, Santurce, P.R. 00907 (809) 728-0905

Aquaculture Concepts Inc., P.O. Box 560, Waimanalo, Hawaii 96795 (808) 545-5622

Pizza Parlor

> *"It's a fast-paced business because you see customers for no more than twenty minutes at a time. Pizza is the fastest-growing segment of the restaurant business. The most fun part of what I do is the potential for growth." – Dennis Sheaks, Joe Peep's N.Y. Pizza*

Low Startup Investment: $50,000 (small take-out)

High Startup Investment: $400,000 (sit-down franchise)

Time Until Breakeven: One to four years

Annual Revenues: $150,000-$2 million

Annual Pre-tax Profits: $60,000-$300,000

Staffers Needed for Startup (including founder): Four

Here's a statistic bound to please pepperoni producers everywhere: 10.8 percent of all U.S. restaurants in 1987 served pizza. According to *Pizza Today* magazine, 12 percent more pizzerias served up slices in 1987 (forty-three thousand restaurants from coast to coast) than the previous year. With approximately one out of four belonging to a franchise, the rest range from elaborate shops (like the one topped by a Leaning Tower of Pisa emblazoned with "PIZZA" in two-foot-high letters, which grossed an astounding $2.25 million in 1986) to tiny take-outs that provide 40-percent profits to Moms and Pops.

A SLICE OF AMERICANA

The credit for the insatiable pizza hunger lies both with a better product and with today's life styles. "Fifteen years ago, pizza was greasy kids' stuff," says Paula Werne, *Pizza Today* associate editor. "High school kids liked it, but their mothers didn't. Today we're rid of the grease and have turned pizza into a healthy food with the four different food groups—milk (cheese), bread (crust), vegetables (toppings like spinach and tomato sauce), and protein (sausage and pepperoni)."

Product improvements made pizza acceptable; product convenience made pizza flourish. Unlike other fast food customers, pizza eaters call ahead for take-out, or have Dominos deliver it to the door in less time than it takes to bake a pizza at home. "Families are converting that one night a week they used to go to McDonald's into a night at home with take-out and the VCR," says Dennis Sheaks, who attributes 46 percent of Joe Peep's N.Y. Pizza's orders —and 57 percent of its dollar sales—to delivery. And never mind what Burger King says, pizza operators invented "have it your way" fast food. Want a slice instead of a seventeen-inch pie? No problem. Hold the anchovies, add extra cheese? Sure thing.

NOT A LOT OF DOUGH

Pizza restaurants are like a raw canvas: You can create anything you want on the basic concept, ranging from an inexpensive take-out to an elaborate chain. If you want to start small, you can set up a two-oven take-out operation in a reasonable location for $50,000 or less, compared with ten times that figure for most fast food franchises or a sit-down restaurant. The difference boils down to the degree of difficulty involved in the operations. Pizzerias sell simple products (even those that add antipastos and sandwiches) that require little expertise, equipment, or décor.

Dennis and Diane Sheaks bought used equipment when they moved Joe Peep's N.Y. Pizza into larger quarters in North Hollywood, California, ten months after buying the restaurant for $70,000 in 1985. "Toasters or automobiles have lots of moving parts to wear out," says Dennis, "but an oven is just a big insulated box with gas controls. Ovens are like wrenches—they never wear out."

The functional, unassuming look the Sheaks chose for Joe Peep's not only kept opening costs to $80,000 (including renovation to add plumbing), but also created a "fun atmosphere" that involves customers, says Dennis. "The kitchen is separated from the order area only by a low-level counter. The customers watch their pizza being made."

As for ambiance, you can install Tiffany-like lamps and stained glass, or go for a minimal look. Dennis Sheaks invites customers to scribble graffiti on the walls—anything that has to do with Joe Peep's or pizza—during the twenty-minute wait while their order cooks. "People stand on each others shoulders or bring in a friend who's never been here before to show what they wrote in the past. It's a form of entertainment."

Because they require little space, pizzerias can sometimes afford expensive mall locations, or retrofit buildings other restaurants would shun. For example, some gas stations abandoned during the oil crisis of the 1970s were reborn as pizzerias.

Delivery doesn't have to be expensive, either. If you don't want to spring for your own vans, hire drivers with their own cars and insurance and reimburse them on a per-mile basis.

STAND OUT

Despite the presence of national chains, independents do quite well in the pizza business. However, if you choose to go it alone, recognize you'll never match Pizza Hut's advertising budget. Therefore, you have to have something going for you: location, product, price, or atmosphere. Dennis Sheaks offers a top-notch pizza at a premium price. "Domino's large pizza costs just 75 percent of Joe Peep's biggest size," says Dennis. "But Joe Peep's is twice as big. If you don't give value, gear for low-income people who only have $4 to spend anyway, or very high-end customers, looking for an avant-garde style."

Let's assume you and your spouse run your pizzeria with two employees and operate with a 30-percent food cost and average strip-shopping-center rents. If you gross $200,000 a year, $80,000 or so will find its way into your pockets.

In a different scenario, you might shoot for the heights. As Dennis Sheaks sees it, if you don't mind plowing hours and profits back into operations there's plenty of room for expansion. For himself, he envisions a ten-unit Joe Peep's chain, possibly followed by franchising. His first step is to perfect a pilot restaurant. And the

Sheaks are well on their way to that goal: Joe Peep's grossed $750,000 in 1986, its second year under the couple's management, compared with just $200,000 when they bought the restaurant. Joe Peep's still sells the same secret-recipe pizza that had already earned the restaurant a loyal customer base. The difference, says Dennis, boils down to marketing.

"The first thing we did was capture on our computer the name and address of everyone who came into the restaurant," explains Dennis. "Then we created a VIPeeper Club." (To join, all you have to do is sign up.) Each month, Joe Peep's sends discount coupons or announcements of "members-only" parties to sixteen thousand members. While the mailings cost $2,500 a month, that's far below the thousands more it would cost to reach those people by television or even newspaper.

Joe Peep's also proclaims it will deliver "anywhere in the world, except South Africa." Dennis warns this is an expensive strategy, because for every driver he sends on a fifteen-mile journey, additional employees must handle local deliveries. But he's thinking ahead. "We've already got customers ten miles away from this store. I'll open my second store on the periphery of my customer base. Those existing customers will establish the new store through word-of-mouth advertising."

That second store is the second step in a pizza empire, says Dennis, who holds an MBA and ran his own management consulting firm before buying Joe Peep's. As he points out, "I figure I'm more qualified than Ray Kroc was when he started McDonald's."

SOURCES

Industry Associations

National Association of Pizza Operators, Box 114, Santa Claus, Ind. 47549 (812) 937-4464

National Restaurant Association, 311 First St. N.W., Washington, D.C. 20001 (800) 424-5156

Regional restaurant associations

Publications

Pizza Today, Box 114, Santa Claus, Ind. 47549 (812) 937-4464
Restaurant Business Magazine, 633 3rd Ave., New York, N.Y. 10017 (212) 986-4800
Nation's Restaurant News, 425 Park Ave., New York, N.Y. 10022 (212) 371-9400

Sandwich Shop

> *"I'm also in the construction business, where you don't get to spend much time with employees. Employees here are like a family. Also, this is good income for the hour a day I work at my sub shop."* – Bob Seneff, Sub-Station

Low Startup Investment: $40,000 (limited seating)

High Startup Investment: $120,000 (larger franchise)

Time Until Breakeven: Six months to one year

Annual Revenues: $100,000-$700,000

Annual Pre-tax Profits: $20,000-$150,000

Staffers Needed for Startup (including founder): Three

Just ask Fred DeLuca about the American Dream. In 1965, he was a high school senior worrying about how he'd pay for college. He mentioned the dilemma to Peter Buck, a nuclear physicist and family friend, hoping Peter would reach into his pocket. Instead, Peter remembered how good submarine sandwiches were when he was a kid, and offered to back Fred in a business venture. If Fred ran the shop well, the income would pay for his tuition.

A couple of decades later, Frederick A. DeLuca has his bachelor's in psychology, all right. He's also president of the largest sandwich chain in the country, with five thousand Subway Sandwiches & Salads franchises projected by 1994. If he hits his mark, Subway will generate $1.25 billion in sales that year, roughly equivalent to Kentucky Fried Chicken's 1986 domestic sales.

HERO WORSHIP

Right now, the entire sandwich industry isn't as big as what Fred Deluca has in mind. But he's not the only sandwich shop-keeper poised for growth. In addition to several franchises, independents are doing better than ever. The U.S. Department of Commerce says the old American stand-by is gaining ground, with 35 percent more sandwich shops in 1987 (an estimated 4,530) than the year before. And NPD Research, Park Ridge, Illinois, suspects sandwiches account for 4.3 percent of total restaurant industry sales.

Bob Seneff had a hunch hero sales were on the upswing. But market share was only part of the attraction when he opened the Sub-Station in the Milwaukee suburb of New Berlin, Wisconsin, in 1985. "I had no restaurant background whatever. And I figured this was a part of the restaurant business I could get into with the least amount of knowledge. Startup costs were a factor, too. Because I owned the building, I opened the doors for about $25,000." If you don't own valuable real estate you'll have to buy or rent, which will push entry costs higher. Figure on another $7,500 to $15,000 if you buy a franchise. Nevertheless, sandwich shops are to restaurants what garage sales are to Saks Fifth Avenue: cheap to start and easy to operate.

One reason startup costs are thinner than a cold cut is because you don't have to outfit an expensive kitchen. The Sub-Station heats up prepared chili and soups during the Wisconsin winter, and Subways bake their own bread from frozen loaves. You might want to throw in a microwave oven to create a hot roast beef. Otherwise, you don't have to know the first thing about cooking.

You also keep food inventory to a minimum. Subway prepares its salads with the same ingredients it uses to dress its sandwiches. Operators swear by freshness, however. Nothing discourages repeat business faster than stale bread.

Bob Seneff developed the Sub-Station menu with some detective work and willing test subjects. "I did a lot of snooping in the sandwich business," he recalls. He would eat late lunches at competitors' shops when employees weren't so busy. "I'd ask how they cut their onions, that sort of thing." Then he tapped a friend in the food distribution business for some free passes to food shows. "That gave me ideas of what products are on the market." Most important were the "scientific" taste tests with the help of employees of a construction company Bob owns with his father. "I brought lots of meats, cheeses, and breads and had the construction crew tell me which they liked best."

SANDWICHES PLUS

Bob says his product is superior—and also larger than anybody else's he knows. But he attributes most of his success to location. The Sub-Station is the only eatery within walking distance of eight hundred businesses in the industrial park his father owns. The site generated great weekday business, but weekends were slow with no residences or commerce in the area. The Sub-Station still closes on Sunday, but Saturday picked up with two new additions to the restaurant: video rentals and really great ice cream in thirty-two flavors that brings those who know off the highway. "I can't make a living on video alone, but it's nice extra money," says Bob. Also, video renters are likely to buy sandwiches to go with their movie.

The Sub-Station also added delivery service to the nearby industrial park during its second winter. "Maybe it's because we live in Wisconsin, where it gets really cold and snowstorms keep people indoors," says Bob. "But there was a fall-off in business during the first winter." If the customer won't come to you, is there any reason on earth you can't go to the customer? Bob delivers up to 10 percent of his winter sales.

An average one-thousand-square-foot Subway unit reports annual sales of $200,000. International Blimpie, which counts some high-traffic urban stores among its franchises, sees average sales of nearly double that figure. In its second year in business, Sub-Station garnered $30,000 in pre-tax profits on about $180,000 in sales. "I'm only here for an hour at lunch time," says Bob, who leaves running the store to a dozen employees during less busy periods. "It's not bad for an hour's work, don't you think?"

SOURCES

Industry Associations

National Restaurant Association, 311 First St. N.W., Washington, D.C., 20001 (800) 424-5156
Regional restaurant associations

Publications

Restaurant Business Magazine, 633 3rd Ave., New York, N.Y. 10017 (212) 986-4800
Nation's Restaurant News, 425 Park Ave., New York, N.Y. 10022 (212) 371-9400

Take-out Restaurant

"I love food. I have to pinch myself to know that what I have to do is also what I really want to do. Of course, considering how fattening my job is, I have to do an hour of aerobics every day of my life." – Suzanne Reifers, Suzanne's

---

Low Startup Investment: $50,000 (modest storefront, limited menu)

High Startup Investment: $150,000 (larger operation with major city address)

Time Until Breakeven: Six months to two years

Annual Revenues: $250,000-$1 million

Annual Pre-tax Profits: $10,000-$100,000

Staffers Needed for Startup (including founder): Three to ten

---

• Item: A National Restaurant Association (NRA) study asked how often Americans purchased take-out foods. Eight out of ten people said they purchased a take-out meal or snack at least once a year, and seven out of ten respondents from households where the female head worked full-time said they bought take-out more than twice a month.

• Item: The NRA found that 21 percent of adults purchased gourmet, ready-to-eat take-out foods in 1986, compared with just 18 percent the previous year. Pizza figures into a whole other category: 47 percent of adults called for home-delivered pizza in 1986, compared with just 40 percent in 1985. (For a separate look, see Pizza Parlor.)

• Item: A Louis Harris poll found Americans' leisure time declined by eight hours between 1973 and 1984. "Juggling careers and families means little time is left for leisure activities," observes an NRA publication. "Consequently, many consumers look for ways to 'expand' their time," with such tricks as buying prepared meals.

▪ Item: With the introduction of such fascinating toys as video-cassette recorders and compact discs, the home has evolved into the prime entertainment center of the 1990s. And many homes also have microwave ovens that heat up prepared foods in seconds. If you want to stay home but don't want to cook, one attractive alternative is to purchase delivered or take-out food.

SUZANNE'S

In 1979, Suzanne Reifers didn't consider those market indicators. "Instead of doing market research," says the former speech writer, "I did research on myself. I lived in this Washington, D.C., neighborhood near DuPont Circle, and there wasn't much there at that time. I wanted a place to buy cheeses and pâtés." Since Suzanne knew *she* would frequent a gourmet take-out shop, she figured other apartment dwellers would too.

Evidently she was right. The ground-floor take-out shop at Suzanne's, which also includes an upstairs restaurant and a catering operation, contributed $400,000 of 1986's $1.7 million in revenues. "The average ticket is low—around $5—because people pick up two cookies on their way home from work," says the proprietor. "But we do volume." In addition to home-made pastries and salads, Suzanne's boasts some justly renowned specialties: Torta Rusica, a double-crusted quiche-like pie stuffed with salmon, cheese, and herbs; and Indian Somosa, "which sounds yucky but is really delicious," according to Suzanne, who adds that the cream-cheese-stuffed pastry contains a vegetable purée topped by a yogurt-and-poppy-seed sauce.

Suzanne Reifers opened Suzanne's with "you're going to laugh—$130,000," when she came into a small inheritance. That is incredibly low considering the capital went for a sit-down restaurant as well as the take-out boutique. Suzanne says she kept costs down by doing her own massive renovations to turn a dilapidated, turn-of-the-century townhouse that housed a jewelry and watch-repair shop into an attractive restaurant and retail food shop.

A FOODSERVICE BARGAIN

Anything under $200,000 is indeed paltry for a restaurant. However, one major attraction a take-out operation holds for entrepreneurs is its relatively low opening cost. You can open a gourmet carry-home shop for $100,000, compared with a total startup cost of $500,000 to $1.5 million for a full-service restaurant. With no seating to worry about, you need just half the space of a typical restaurant—say one thousand square feet—to accommodate a take-out operation. A well-stocked display case full of mouth-watering delicacies serves as your best decoration. Kitchen and clean-up facilities are smaller. And, if you specialize in just one or two foods, startup costs are even lower.

A take-out operator also doesn't suffer the crazy hours that a restaurateur puts in. People who want to run a foodservice operation and still spend time with their families score this advantage high. Depending on your neighborhood, you might open in time to catch residents who buy a croissant and royal Dutch chocolate coffee on their way to work. But you surely dish out the last yellowtail tuna by 7 or 8 P.M., when the restaurant next door still has hours to go before taps.

Take-out counters need an abundance of help, because customers consider convenience of supreme importance and don't relish waiting on long lines. But you can pinpoint the heavy traffic crunches fairly easily: When workers stream home from work, or, if you're in a commercial area, at lunchtime. So part-timers can make up the bulk of your staff.

NOT WHO YOU ARE, BUT WHERE YOU ARE

Where you hang your take-out sign is probably even more important than what you serve, unless, of course, your customers expect delivery. If 75 percent of your gross comes from deliveries, opt for the lower-rent district. Suzanne's tacks on a $10 delivery charge, which admittedly is pretty steep for customers who spend just $8.99 to stock a picnic basket. But her intent is to accommodate those few customers who really want deliveries and encourage most people to stop by the shop.

Today, however, say "delivery" and most consumers still think pizza. That reputation stems in large part from Tom Monaghan, who, in 1961, traded in his Volkswagen for controlling interest in a Ypsilanti, Michigan, pizzeria. Since then, his creation, Domino's Pizza, has revolutionized the entire food delivery industry with its promise of hot pizza in thirty minutes. By 1986, Domino's had grown to more than four thousand corporate and franchise stores, with worldwide sales of nearly $2 billion.

According to David Smith, a Domino's vice-president, "The job of getting the product out in thirty minutes is accomplished in the store, not on the delivery route." A fairly open secret is Domino's insistence on a simple menu, consisting of several varieties of pizza and only one beverage. "That way," continues Dave, "we focus on one concept: Delivering our product within thirty minutes. We've got it down to sixty seconds from order to oven and we're always looking for ways to shave seconds off the process."

But if customers come to you rather than the other way around, look for accessibility. Take-out only works on a well-traveled street in a densely populated area, which rules out most smaller towns altogether. Also, make sure you have the right population within a few blocks of your store. Shoppers won't do you much good, since they need a place to sit in order to eat. On the other hand, a railroad station could be perfect as tired commuters pick up your Moo Goo Gai Pan on their way home. "My partner and I spent a lot of money getting a good lease in Georgetown," says Geoff Elliott, who opened Take Me Home in the affluent Washington neighborhood in 1981. "But our customers didn't match what we wanted to do. Georgetown is populated by tourists [who eat in restaurants rather than order take-out foods] and older residents [who are not from the eighteen-to-forty-four age group the NRA says is most likely to order take-out]." Thanks to a busy lunch-time trade from area office workers, the carry-out menu still contributes about 20 percent of Take Me Home's $375,000 in annual sales. But Geoff survives on the catering service he added when he realized the strategic location mistake he had made.

A COMBINATION PLATTER

Like Geoff Elliott and Suzanne Reifers, many entrepreneurs combine take-out with other types of foodservice. You can use a kitchen and chefs for dual purposes. Indeed, your kitchen can prepare take-out foods before the restaurant lunch or dinner crowd arrives. Suzanne's operations complement each other. "The retail shop goes gangbusters at Christmas when the restaurant is dead," she says.

Decide what statement you want to make with your food. Ethnic take-out operations like Mexigo in New York City have proved popular, as have fast-food deliverers. But if you're taking the gourmet route, suggests Suzanne Reifers, "you need a well-rounded place. You can't put in just a little bit of this and a little bit of that." In addition to the quiches and broccoli, red pepper, and corn salads she proffers, Suzanne sells shelves full of packaged specialty foods, like virgin olive oil.

Suzanne discovered another must is pastry. "When I began, I assumed people in these health-conscious days didn't want desserts," she recalls. "So I hired a chef who would spend half her time preparing desserts and half pâtés. The desserts were so popular we had to hire a full-time pastry chef, assistant pastry chef, and cookie baker." Now, 35 percent of all shop sales are sweets. "I guess when people decide to splurge on calories they'd rather get something really delicious than buy a Heath Bar," says Suzanne.

Gourmet take-out is still a city phenomenon, since smaller towns and suburbs lack the numbers to support carry-out services. Most suburbanites settle for supermarket-prepared take-outs and drive-through windows at fast-food chains. However, some operators say the gourmands and closet gourmets could get their shot in the future. Thanks to the success of operations like Domino's, more and more Americans consider buying somebody else's cooking to eat in their home as an accepted alternative. What's the next carry-out hotspot? "I might consider opening a gourmet take-out in Topeka," says one operator.

SOURCES

See *Pizza Parlor*

Healthcare
and Fitness

Aerobics/Exercise Instructor

> *"You become a stand-up comedian, a mother, father, a confessor. People look up to you and it makes you more confident."*
> *— Karen Shaffer, Jazzercize Center*

Low Startup Investment: $2,000 (to rent community facilities)

High Startup Investment: $60,000 (to open a studio)

Time Until Breakeven: One month to three years

Annual Revenues: $30,000-$400,000

Annual Pre-tax Profits: $10,000-$100,000

Staffers Needed for Startup (including founder): One

Karen Shaffer taught French by day in 1979, but her passion was the Jazzercise exercise classes she took several times a week. Deciding to combine her love of dance exercise with her love of teaching, she bought a Jazzercize franchise. "I began by teaching at an adult school, then rented church facilities," she recalls.

Like many aerobics students who make the leap to instructor, Karen Shaffer got hooked. "Each routine is a performance and I ham it up. I teach people to make the most of themselves." She points to a svelte woman who was once overweight. "Before class she talked about her new boyfriend. The students give such positive feedback."

A WAY OF LIFE

Although the national obsession with exercise began leveling off in the mid-1980s, Karen decided a steady core of exercisers would always want to flex and stretch and move to the music. So in 1986 she and another franchisee went into partnership; instead of continuing to scrounge around for sub-par YMCA and firehouse facilities to rent for their classes, they plowed $60,000 into opening their own Jazzercize salon in a Pennington, New Jersey, shopping center. (Karen talks with near-reverence about the custom floor they now possess.) Today, except for minimal salaries, they still pour every dime into making the business work, but Karen foresees a steady 5-percent growth every year; and she never contemplates returning to the less strenuous drills she once led conjugating French verbs in a classroom.

According to the National Sporting Goods Association, in 1986 22 million Americans participated in aerobics in health clubs and exercise salons, in programs run from community facilities, or by working up a sweat with a VCR tape like Jane Fonda's. To put that into perspective, over 10 percent of the U.S. population works out at least occasionally. True, the double-digit numbers of those who discovered aerobics each year in the 1970s may never again occur, but aerobics isn't losing adherents either. The difference now: Aerobics entrepreneurs can no longer be mere instructors. Today, it takes marketing acumen to keep those revenues in shape.

BREAKING IN

The International Dance Exercise Association (IDEA) estimates that nearly 60 percent of the aerobics industry's one hundred thousand instructors work part time. If you wonder whether you can make a living doing sit-ups and jumping jacks, why not hold on to your present job and moonlight?

Three avenues lead to exercise instruction:

▪ Independent contracts. Many instructors freelance at health clubs or studios which pay by the hour. You don't need to worry about marketing since somebody else rounds up students. Bare bones startup capital covers leotards and Reeboks, and possibly some tapes and a portable stereo if your club doesn't provide them. If you go the independent route, be sure to carry liability insurance if your employer doesn't.

▪ Satellite classes. Following Karen Shaffer's entry strategy, many instructors lease community facilities, such as a recreation center or school gymnasium. You probably can hold initial costs—for rent, tapes and a stereo system, clothing, and insurance—below $2,000. If you join a franchise, tack on another $500 or so. (Jazzercize, for example, sells franchisees video tapes with its routines and provides training and the use of its name. In return, the franchise takes 30 percent of revenues, after expenses.) Operating with a floating home base, as Karen explains, has it drawbacks—when basketball season begins for a school, or when the church expands Wednesday bingo to Thursdays the landlord grabs back the site. After scrambling to find a new place, invariably you lose members who won't travel with you.

▪ Opening a studio. *Club Industry Magazine* estimates converting a twenty-four-hundred-square-foot empty shell into an aerobics studio would cost $32,600 to $60,200, depending on how much you spend for a ceiling and floor, lights, sprinkler, mirrors, air conditioner, professional sound system, and fans. The publication assumes a studio hosting thirty classes weekly could attract a total attendance of six hundred. If you charge a fairly typical $3.50 per head and pay instructors $10 an hour, you'll net around $88,000 per year. From that, deduct overhead, advertising, and debt service.

DIVERSIFY

Of course, you can offer other money-makers beyond those thirty classes. "It's imperative to add things other than aerobics classes to survive," advises Barbara Fisher, who runs Bodies by Fisher in a Victorian brownstone in the Back Bay section of Boston. "You can only offer classes at the times when lots of people want to take them. During the other times, offer individual consultation, rent the space to dance groups, or offer skin care or nutritional counseling." And don't forget clothing and food and drink concessions.

Many studios expand their repertoires beyond challenging workouts. Lead classes for special groups like pregnant or overweight women or even children. You also can offer less stressful exercises, such as low-impact aerobics or, if you have access to a pool, aquatic routines.

The biggest untapped market is spelled M-E-N. The National Sporting Goods Association estimates that men make up only 14.2 percent of aerobics' participants, a stat ambitious entrepreneurs regard as an opportunity. And some observers see hopeful signs. Kathie Davis, executive director of IDEA, notes that some high school football teams now emulate the pros by including aerobics in their conditioning. Could be players will continue aerobics after their football glory days are gone. Kathie suggests aerobics instructors make slight changes to erase the effeminate stigma. For example, offer a sports conditioning class—basically aerobics with dance references deleted from routines. Instead of incorporating graceful flourishes into the routine, clench those fists.

GET OUT THERE AND SELL

"Try to tap all markets," Barbara Fisher advises. Many corporations pay dues as an employee benefit, so why not call on area employers and leave a notice on their bulletin boards. Once you book your own facilities to capacity, add outreach programs. Some schools that have cut back on physical education classes hire instructors to lead after-school aerobics in the gym as an extra-curricular activity. Ask the recreation director of a senior citizen condo whether residents might like aquatic aerobic instruction in the pool. Barbara sends instructors to hotels and corporations for on-site aerobics and goes through the convention bureau to find meeting organizers. "Propose health breaks instead of coffee breaks. Corporations provide yogurt and juice instead of coffee and donuts, and you lead fifteen minutes of stretching and breathing to break up the seminars. Low-impact aerobics won't leave them sweating."

While many aerobics instructors build a loyal following of students who stay with them for years, count on constantly replenishing your exercisers. As many as 6 million of those 24 million aerobics participants are debutantes, and a similar number of exercisers drop out each year. To replace the transients, budget for advertising: newspapers, direct mail and hand-out flyers, and even radio and TV in some markets. Studios can offer open-houses and guest passes, while freelance instructors can demonstrate at the local country fair. You can even offer a membership as a prize in a charity-related fund-raiser.

SOURCES

Industry Associations

International Dance Exercise Association, 2437 Morena Blvd., 2nd Floor, San Diego, Calif. 92110 (619) 275-2450

Aerobic & Fitness Association of America, 15250 Ventura Blvd., Suite 802, Sherman Oaks, Calif. 91420 (818) 905-0040

International Racquet Sports Association, 132 Brookline Ave., Boston, Mass, 02215 (617) 236-1500

National Sporting Goods Association, 1699 Wall St., Mount Prospect, Ill. 60056 (312) 439-4000

Publications

Dance Exercise Today, 2437 Morena Blvd., 2nd Floor, San Diego, Calif. 92110 (619) 275-2450

Club Industry Magazine, 1450 Beacon St., P.O. Box C9122, Boston, Mass. 02146 (617) 277-3823

Daycare for Seniors

> *"It's incredibly gratifying to see severely depressed people bloom again. We get strokes from the families—'I don't know what I'd do without you,' they say. 'We really look forward to seeing Mother or Dad in the evening now. We can be better to them than we could before.' "— Thelma Freeze, L.I.F.E. Center Inc.*

Low Startup Investment: $5,000 (operating from a community facility)

High Startup Investment: $50,000 (setting up your own center)

Time Until Breakeven: Six months to two years

Annual Revenues: $100,000-$400,000

Annual Pre-tax Profits: $15,000-$200,000

Staffers Needed for Startup (including founder): Three

After Martha died five years ago, Sam's son and daughter-in-law watched the once-vibrant salesman retreat from life. "Dad watched TV all day," says the son. "He complained that his arthritis hurt too much to shop or do housework, so we moved him in with us." The daughter-in-law quit her job when Sam became so frail they feared leaving him alone. The little boy complained that his grandfather always seemed angry, and the teenagers stopped bringing friends over for fear he would insult them. Stress mounted as the family considered a nursing home. Then Sam's physician suggested an alternative: daycare for senior citizens.

Within a month, the family's life returned to normal. Initially, Sam's son pushed him to mix with other seniors at the center. His daughter-in-law resumed her job and his grandchildren relaxed as tensions dissolved. But the biggest changes occurred in Sam. He began to look forward to his activities at the center and was inspired by his interaction with folks older than he; they managed tasks Sam previously thought he could no longer tackle. Little by little, Sam began to assume simple tasks he hadn't performed in years. Over dinner, the once silent old man now regales his grandchildren with his day's activities.

WE'RE GROWING OLDER

The National Institute on Adult Daycare estimates that just a dozen daycare centers for the elderly existed in 1970. A decade later, the count soared to six hundred, and by 1986, operators managed fourteen hundred daycare facilities for seniors. Only about 5 percent ran as for-profit ventures that year, but, in the same manner that charitable and for-profit hospitals coexist, participants predict substantial growth in both daycare segments. "We've seen the number of adult daycare centers double in North Carolina over the last year," says Thelma Freeze. In 1986, her own twelve-year-old center, L.I.F.E. (Living Interest for the Elderly) Center Inc., Concord, North Carolina, opened its first satellite to accommodate the overflow of applicants in a state that already had forty-three centers.

If you suspect there's a need to help our seniors now, just look at the predicted growth of the older population. The Census Bureau projects the sixty-five-and-older crowd will expand 23 percent from 28.5 million in 1985 to 35 million by the year 2000. Thanks primarily to better medical care, retirement-aged adults will comprise 13 percent of the U.S. population by the turn of the century.

According to the U.S. Government, 375,000 of the 1.45 million elderly in nursing homes in 1985 had no medical reason to live there—and most didn't want to be there. The alternative, however, was living alone or with middle-aged children who were ill-equipped to care for them. Adult daycare provides a third option.

Don't confuse daycare with nursing or convalescent homes. "We don't replace nursing homes, but we can delay or prevent institutionalized care in many cases," says Thelma Freeze. Daycare helps the elderly remain independent using two complementary approaches: The staff performs services the elderly find difficult to manage, such as preparing hot meals; and the centers motivate seniors with therapy and gentle peer pressure, which keeps them active enough to help themselves.

WE HAVE NO BEDS

"The staff's job is to constantly stimulate our clients," explains Arlene Snyder, executive director of Vintage Inc., Pittsburgh. "We have no beds because a daycare center is much more activity-driven than a nursing home." In addition to ceramic courses, card games, and sing-alongs, some centers offer dance and exercise classes. Elderly who remain at home "never get to expend their energy because they take catnaps all day in front of the TV," says Arlene. But once they join the active centers, "We promise the families Mom or Dad will sleep through the night."

Centers are not babysitting services, either. Many employ nurses equipped to handle emergencies and schedule physical, speech, and motivation therapy. On-call doctors visit for regularly scheduled checkups.

Directors design services with the special needs of the elderly in mind. Susan Cook Armstrong, who operates three Cook's Home Health Centers Inc. in conjunction with her Plymouth, Connecticut, nursing home, charges $5 on top of the daily $28.50 fee to bathe clients, set their hair, and manicure their nails. And Susan considers transportation a necessary adjunct. "Probably half couldn't come if we didn't have transportation." Cook's operates three cars and nine vans equipped to lift wheelchairs.

THE DOCTOR CONNECTION

Operators say their biggest challenge involves educating clients and their doctors about adult daycare. Physician referrals eventually provide most clients, but be warned: Until the concept is more widespread, expect a suspicious medical community. Deal with the suspicion by taking a professionally persistent stance. Call doctors both in private practice and in hospitals. Send them brochures and ask for appointments to explain your service. Emphasize your staff and expertise.

And once a physician refers a patient, "maintain your contacts by updating them regularly if anything happens," says Arlene Synder, whose company consults with entrepreneurs entering the adult day-care business. "If a patient's blood pressure rises, for instance, let the doctor make the call on what to do." In addition to being good medical practice, Arlene explains, alerting a patient's doctor also makes good business sense since M.D.s, like other businesspeople with their customers, "don't want to lose control over their patients."

Doctors may not immediately respond to your sales pitch, but if you've implanted the idea, they may make that first recommendation when the time is right. Arlene Synder recalls a doctor who was treating the wife of an Alzheimer's patient. "Her own blood pressure had risen to dangerous levels under the burden of constantly caring for her husband. The doctor mentioned Vintage for the husband as a way to give her part-time relief. At her checkup three months later, she told the doctor she felt wonderful. He's made seven referrals since then."

In addition to encouraging physicians to refer patients, Vintage establishes real partnerships with hospitals. The hospital provides free checkups for seniors, and in exchange Vintage helps the hospital find new patients, which has become a real concern during the 1980s. "If they receive free routine dental care, Vintagers [Arlene's name for her center's clients] will think of the hospital's dentists when they need more extensive work," explains Arlene. And hospitals often receive grants in exchange for community service.

WE CAN HELP YOUR MOTHER

While you may send the same brochure to both doctors and clients, your marketing focus is broader when you try to attract families. Susan Armstrong advertises through newspapers, does direct mail, and even buys a few television spots. She also speaks to civic groups like the Lion's Club.

Rather than gear your pitch to the senior citizens, aim consumer advertising toward the at-home caregiver, who is typically a fifty-five-year-old daughter or daughter-in-law. Arlene Snyder recommends deemphasizing the relief your center can provide families, since the children often feel as if they're "pawning off" the care of a loved one on someone else. Instead, stress the benefits that you can offer the senior, namely companionship, stimulation, and at least limited medical attention.

Arlene says families invariably enroll a parent just one or two days a week. "After two months, 99 percent ask for five days a week [which, incidentally, Vintage is too booked to offer except to those seniors with children who work full time]. The family becomes comfortable when they tell us 'Harry got up and dressed himself this morning and said he was ready to go to the club.' "

GUIDELINES

The fifteen states that license adult daycare regulate facilities rather than caregiver credentials. For example, Pennsylvania requires fifty-square-feet per patient. Some states specify the ratio of caregivers to elderly. The National Institute on Adult Daycare suggests at least one staff member care for every five to seven clients.

Arlene Snyder tells centers to figure an annual budget of $140,000 to pay for rent, salaries, meals, transportation, recreation, and other expenses. She suggests you can cover costs with tuition as low as $18 a day, although national tuition is nearly double that, which allows for profits. While some centers, particularly those attached to nursing homes, care for one hundred or more clients, the typical freestanding facility caters to nineteen people at any one time. Many centers encourage part-time attendance, where a client comes just a couple of days a week. Because the center alternates several seniors in one spot, this time-share arrangement not only fills otherwise vacant slots, it also spreads community consciousness.

Startup costs vary widely. You may be able to talk church officials into renting or donating facilities for weekday use. Assuming that the space is already equipped with ramps for wheelchairs and rails in the bathrooms, and that a kitchen and furniture are part of the bargain, your only costs may involve a one- or two-person staff, insurance, and advertising. Susan Armstrong financed a more expensive startup. A geriatric nurse, she opened her third daycare facility in Woodbury, Connecticut, in July 1986 on a $50,000 budget. That covered two months' rent, a used van, and furniture worth about $20,000, such as reclining chairs and sofas that can convert to beds should the need arise. Recreation equipment included a TV, VCR, and movie projector. Most activities, such as card playing and crafts, carry almost no initial investment. "We also bought a couple of wheelchairs and walkers and some emergency equipment, like oxygen tanks," she recalls. Woodbury trucks in its lunches from the Cook daycare facility in Plymouth, Connecticut, which is connected to the nursing home Susan also owns.

THE GOVERNMENT HELPS, A LITTLE

While grants go only to nonprofit groups, many families tap various government programs for tuition. Susan Armstrong opened Woodbury knowing the State Department of Mental Retardation had set aside $129,000 to cover tuition for twenty mentally retarded adults. In addition, some of the ten seniors served by the facility receive government funds to cover part or all of their fees. "We put the families in touch with the correct agencies, such as the Department of Human Resources," says Susan. If Medicare ever recognizes adult daycare, which the National Institute of Adult Daycare considers a strong possibility, the field should blossom.

Breakeven depends on how fast you line up clients. Because the state reserved twenty of her thirty slots on opening day, Susan says Woodbury made money almost immediately. Her three centers also benefit from bulk buying, a central kitchen, and shared resources. For example, she keeps at least one facility open on weekends and holidays. "A lot of people can't even cook for themselves," says Susan. "But mostly, it's just too lonely for them to be left home on a holiday." Since so few seniors come on Christmas or Thanksgiving, Cook's opens just one center and buses seniors from the other two. Even if you don't have additional sites, perhaps some facilities can be shared with another operator.

While Woodbury is too new to offer reliable figures, Susan says five-year-old Plymouth generated 1986 revenues of $200,000, with just $95,000 in overhead; Torrington, which was two years younger, was a little less profitable with revenues of $150,000 and costs of $100,000. Susan sees yet more opportunities in the senior market. In 1987, she built a fourth daycare center, as well as a condo retirement village and added beds to her nursing home that she reserved specifically for people who are normally daycare participants and occasionally require overnight care. As she explains it,

"Families who want to take a couple of weeks during the summer can't find vacancies in nursing homes." When it comes to providing care for the elderly, always keep the families' needs in mind.

ALZHEIMER'S

Costs also depend on the amount of care you provide. Some centers specialize in Alzheimer's patients or stroke victims. The more mental and physical therapy you provide, the greater your need for expensive specialists and equipment.

Also, design your facility with your particular clientele in mind. For example, Alzheimer's patients need lots of space to roam and release their energy. "The real tragedy of Alzheimer's is they're in pretty good physical shape, but their brain is dying," says Arlene Snyder. "Their energy turns into anger unless they can expend it." She also recommends limited points of entry and exit that caretakers can easily monitor so people don't wander out of the facility unnoticed.

While some centers must resort to waiting lists because their services are in such demand, others report a sluggish growth rate. Even some of the less successful entrepreneurs are gambling that the future will provide greater demands and are expanding. As the industry grows, observers predict that the government will step in with rules and regulations. However, reputable centers say such recognition, and a honing of industry-wide standards, will further legitimize the field. Susan Armstrong's attitude is exemplary here: "I believe we should all be required to have a nurse on board," she argues. "Our elderly are frail and at risk. It's time to start regulating."

SOURCES

Industry Association

National Institute on Adult Daycare, National Council on the Aging Inc., 600 Maryland Ave., S.W., Washington, D.C. 20024 (202) 479-1200

Consultant

Vintage Inc., 401 Highland Ave., Pittsburgh, Pa. 15206
(412) 361-5003

Diet Clinic

> *"I'm like an adolescent in love. I love the advertising, accounting, nutrition, public speaking, and counseling—everything that goes with this business. I've never had a day I wasn't roaring to get into work."* —Jeannie Geurink, Slender Center.

Low Startup Investment: $10,000 (small independent, limited advertising)

High Startup Investment: $50,000 (franchise in larger market)

Time Until Breakeven: Three months to one year

Annual Revenues: $60,000-$500,000

Annual Pre-tax Profits: $20,000-$200,000

Staffers Needed for Startup (including founder): One

Behind every successful weight-loss clinic is a former fat person. After years of unsuccessful dieting, the typical entrepreneur found the secret formula to losing fifty pounds . . . seventy-five pounds . . . one hundred pounds. . . . Once the dieter loses all that excess weight, the natural thing to do is to found a diet company or buy a franchise. In fact, knowing that previously overweight individuals understand the rules and can best empathize with their clientele, both Diet Center Inc., Rexburg, Idaho, and Fortunate Life Center, Charlottesville, Virginia, sell franchises only to individuals who have completed their programs.

Sybil Ferguson, who founded Diet Center in 1979 based on a strategy that helped her lop off fifty-eight pounds, offers some clues as to why about 70 million Americans are overweight: "Ten years ago, the average man burned thirty-five hundred calories a day; he now burns only twenty-eight hundred calories. Women ten years ago burned twenty-four hundred calories daily; today they burn only eighteen hundred. Based on these figures alone, a person could gain up to five pounds a month if his or her eating habits are basically the same as they were ten years ago."

"I THINK I CAN, I THINK I CAN"

While some diet clinics combine exercise with nutritional advice and others sell diet supplements, the majority stress behavior modification using individual diet counselors. The theory: "If you change your eating habits, you can become thin." Once they've provided hints on how to eat for health, the centers back up that message with loads of positive reinforcement and subtle peer pressure that comes with scheduled weigh-ins.

"We stress 'Breakthrough Thinking,' " explains Jeannie Geurink, who was a client with one hundred pounds to lose and then a franchisee before she bought the Slender Center parent company in Madison, Wisconsin, in 1982. A 256-page manual and individual counseling sessions lead Slender Center clients through FRIA, an acronym that stands for Focus (on how to change your eating behavior), Relaxation (you can't change your behavior if you're uptight), Imagery (imagining that you are thin motivates you to carrythrough), and Affirmation (think positive, you can do it!).

The dilemma weight-loss centers face is snaring clients who have heard it all before. The typical customer, a woman under age fifty, has been through numerous self-help diets in the past. None worked in the long haul, otherwise she wouldn't be twenty-five to thirty-five pounds too heavy, which is about average among Slender Center clients. Now you must convince her that your solution really will help her. "Our message tells people not to feel guilty about those times they tried and failed to lose weight," says Jeannie. "Don't feel guilty about asking for help. Then we offer a written guarantee that, as long as dieters make no deletions, additions, or substitutions to our diet, they can lose two to three pounds per week."

Plan on spending as much as 25 percent of gross on advertising and marketing when you're first establishing a reputation. Advertise in newspapers and the Yellow Pages, and possibly radio and TV in markets where rates are low or where you can share expenses with other centers. Once you are better known in the community you can downscale your ad budget to 7 to 10 percent of gross, since most clients come through referrals from skinny customers.

Missionary work helps, too. Set up booths in health fairs or ask the local radio or TV talk show host if you might do a spot on nutrition. Also, more corporations are investigating "wellness programs." You can offer a corporate discount to attract employees.

FIND US IF YOU CAN

One reason you have to advertise so heavily involves location. Many diet clinics look for an easily accessible—but not terribly visible—site. This advice could change in the future if the heavy crowd becomes less inhibited about walking through the doors of a diet clinic. But many clients today "don't want to meet their neighbors when they go into a diet clinic," says Jeannie Geurink. "They have a fear of failure until they're about twenty pounds down." Jeannie recommends a professional office setting near, but not in, a mall. "Even a back entrance or upstairs is okay," she says. Of course, the benefit of choosing a secondary rather than a prime location involves startup costs. Depending on what backup materials you offer, even franchisees likely can hold initial capital in the $20,000 ballpark.

Your staff-to-client ratio depends upon your market and the approach you take. Slender Centers usually begin with just the entrepreneur and a part-time counselor to handle the thirty to seventy-five clients that a startup clinic might schedule per week. The weigh-ins, which range from twice a week to daily, usually last about fifteen minutes, during which time the counselor discusses FRIA with the client, in conjunction with the particular weight loss and problems encountered. Slender Center's fees differ from location to location. But in the Madison company–owned center, a ten-week program with daily weigh-ins costs $585. Each client receives four weeks of stabilization counseling after the weight loss is achieved, and six months of maintenance supervision at no extra charge.

What type of person makes a good counselor? If you're joining one of at least fifteen franchise organizations, you can pick up a knowledge of nutrition and the basics of a particular program from them. Solo entrepreneurs can take nutrition courses at community colleges. Beyond that, "it helps to be outgoing," says Barbara Davies, who runs the Diet Center of Hunterdon in Flemington, New Jersey. Barbara admits she was introverted until she lost one hundred pounds in nine months with Diet Center before buying her franchise. "After losing all that weight, I really like myself—and others like me too," she says. "That gives a person confidence."

Diet clinics have no fear that they'll run out of clients. Despite the growing emphasis on health, more Americans are overweight than ever before. Particularly as the millions of baby boomers age, pounds increasingly become a problem. "I can see acceptance growing every year since I first started in 1981," observes Jeannie Geurink. "People still have reservations about joining a weight-loss program, but that reluctance is declining. By the late 1990s, I really believe it will be automatic for someone to join a weight-loss center anytime they need to lose five pounds."

Freestanding Medical Center

> "You meet important needs of patients with timely care, compared with a physician who has to set up an appointment for next week. That's the way any healthcare provider would like to attend to patients." –Jerry Hermanson, North Federal Management Group

---

Low Startup Investment: $250,000 (leasing a small facility)

High Startup Investment: $750,000 (buying a larger building)

Time Until Breakeven: One to two years

Annual Revenues: $500,000-$2 million (for a single center)

Annual Pre-tax Profits: $100,000-$500,000

Staffers Needed for Startup (including founder): Eight to ten

---

The healthcare industry is changing faster than you can say "freestanding emergency medical centers." On the one hand, modern medicine is increasingly able to cure all manner of deadly diseases, allowing us to live longer and healthier lives. On the other hand, we're paying for it. The Health Care Finance Administration says Americans spent $425 billion in 1985 to cover medical bills, in contrast to an amount almost half that—$240 billion in comparative dollars—a decade earlier.

As insurance companies and Medicare throw up their hands with cries of "We're not going to take it anymore," premiums increase and payments to patients fizzle. In response, the medical establishment is scurrying for ways to provide quality health care at more affordable rates. Instead of prescribing lengthy hospital stays, physicians recommend home healthcare. (See Home Healthcare.) Instead of treating heart disease when an attack necessitates surgery, employers are signing on for preventive care with health maintenance organizations.

DOC-IN-THE-BOX

In addition to home healthcare, observers report a trend toward ambulatory care centers—patients walk in without an appointment at any hour of the day or night. Because private walk-in centers operate without a hospital emergency room's high overhead, they can charge a small percentage of what a hospital might charge for the same procedure. For example, Jerry Hermanson, president of North Federal Management Group, says the four Minor Emergicenters that his group operates in Pompano Beach and Deerfield, Florida, charge $125 for administering to an arm injury that requires suturing and X-rays. "A hospital in my area would charge $225 for the same procedure," says Jerry, a hospital administrator before he opened the first Emergicenter in 1984.

Lured by less costly bills and shorter waits for treatment, patients turn to ambulatory centers in increasing numbers. With every treatment, they learn to trust the care they receive at the centers the media used to call "doc-in-the-boxes." The public's heightened awareness, along with increased visits, result in more centers opening to fulfill the demand. According to the National Association of Ambulatory Care, four thousand freestanding centers operated in 1987; the trade group predicts half again as many in 1988.

WHATEVER AILS YOU

The complexion of the centers is changing. The early clinics treated almost exclusively non-life-threatening emergencies like sore throats or sprained ankles, as reflected in such trade names as Minor Emergency Center or Urgent Care. In the future, many operators expect that primary-care facilities will provide the biggest boost to the new business. These facilities treat patients for all kinds of illnesses on an ongoing basis, just as general practitioners have always done. A separate trend is toward centers that specialize in such areas as birthing, X-rays, and opthalmology.

You can build a freestanding clinic for about twice the cost of setting up a general practitioner's office (which doesn't require a laboratory or X-ray equipment). While the initial cost is higher, you'll turn profits far faster: Seeing patients in volume means higher revenues. If you rent real estate and lease medical equipment, you can fund an emergency center that operates eighty hours a week for as little as $250,000. That assumes you're doing some advertising and paying only for two doctors, two nurses, two receptionists, and two X-ray technicians for the year or so before breakeven. If you buy your own building and equipment, or staff a larger center, plan on needing more capital. Some of the larger medical equipment companies can provide a list of equipment, pharmaceuticals, and incidentals you need to get started.

You can afford to pay your staff salaries similar to what they would make working in a hospital or doctor's office. Doctors, for the most part, are young and see working in a center as a way to increase their experience.

The medical community splits in about a dozen different directions on whether they like the walk-in centers. "Local primary-care physicians see us as direct competition," says Jerry Hermanson, who consults for hospitals and individuals wanting to set up ambulatory care centers. "Since we refer patients to specialists, the specialists don't object." Hospitals, already feeling the revenue pinch as insurance providers insist on shorter stays and fewer tests, recognize that the emergency centers are stealing their emergency room clientele. Their reaction: If you can't beat 'em, join 'em. As many as 75 percent of hospitals either set up their own freestanding centers, or are thinking of adding one, says a 1987 American Medical Association study. The hospitals either operate a center as a hospital adjunct, or as a joint venture in partnership with an entrepreneur.

MARRY A DOCTOR

As often as not, the operating partner isn't even a doctor. In fact, some centers are backed entirely with non-M.D. dollars, although, says consultant Arthur E. Auer of Auer & Associates, "I find centers don't work unless a physician has a billfold on the line. If you work with a partner who has medical expertise, the centers can represent good business opportunities."

They sure can. Once you break even on annual revenues of a half-million or so, you can probably keep 20 percent ($100,000) as pre-tax profits. Since you commit to low-cost, quality care in order to beat out hospitals, the key to profitability involves volume. Jerry Hermanson says a center needs to treat thirty patients a day at $50 each to break even. That would represent annual revenues in the $525,000 range. An even busier facility with two doctors on board at all times could bring in double or more the annual revenues.

A revolving door waiting room is just as important to the patient as to the medical center. After all, most patients don't worry too much about whether you are cheaper than the competition; they expect their insurance carrier to reimburse the cost of the visit. But who wants to wait all Saturday afternoon in a hospital to get that nasty burn treated when they'd rather return to the barbecue? "We look at a twenty-minute turnaround from the time the patients walk in the door until they leave," says Jerry. "It may take another five minutes if they need a test, or ten minutes for an X-ray. But if the visit takes longer than that, it's time to open another center."

Which is just what Jerry did. When the first Minor Emergicenter grew too busy in Pompano Beach, he and his three partners opened another one five miles away in Deerfield, Florida. Jerry wanted the second clinic near enough to benefit from shared advertising, but distant enough to avoid overtaxing the patient base.

WHERE YOU WANT TO BE

Location is as important to a walk-in clinic as it is to a retail store. In addition to considering what clinics are nearby, check out other medical competition, such as hospitals and primary-care physicians. Competition isn't always bad. If the emergency room in the only hospital in a five-mile radius is overburdened, your center may catch the overflow just by proximity. A dense population is important, but it should be the right kind of population. For example, Jerry Hermanson warns against locating in a retirement area. "The over-sixty-five population has already established a relationship with a doctor, so they are low utilizers of emergency centers."

Jerry also looks for a good industrial and residential mix, since Minor Emergicenter's employers refer 15 percent of its patients. "We have an active marketing campaign to get work-related patients," he explains. "We provide a group rate for pre-employment physicals, for example." While his company doesn't discount workers-compensation treatments, businesses often refer employees for minor injuries because the centers are convenient and swift. In a similar fashion, Minor Emergicenters also contact schools and camps to suggest students stop by for required physicals.

You might also lean toward a location that allows bold signs. If you're too discrete, patients who have passed your clinic a thousand times may not recall you exist as they drive the other direction to take care of that earache.

HEALTH FAIRS

Increasing chunks of health providers' budgets are going for advertising. Even hospitals dole out great gobs of money to bring in "customers" nowadays, and your walk-in service has to compete. Although Jerry Hermanson advertises in the Yellow Pages, the newspaper, and through direct mail, he says the best returns come through community involvement, such as participating in chambers of commerce health fairs.

Minor Emergicenters enjoy about 55-percent repeat business, meaning more than half of its patients have visited the centers before. That's a fairly high statistic, considering most consumers see walk-in clinics as emergency facilities. But Jerry says the staff physicians court the repeat business. "We make a point of following up visits with next-day phone calls," to see how an infection is healing, he explains. In the minds of entrepreneurs who are opening the ambulatory clinics at an increasing rate, patients are quickly accepting walk-in service as an alternative for on-going care as well as emergency treatments.

SOURCES

Industry Associations

National Association of Ambulatory Care, 5151 Belt Line Rd., Suite 1017, Dallas, Tex. 75240 (214) 788-2456

American Hospital Association, 840 N. Lake Shore Dr., Chicago, Ill. 60611 (312) 280-6236

Publications

Emergence, 5151 Belt Line Rd., Suite 1017, Dallas, Tex. 75240 (214) 788-2456

Emergency Medical Care Digest, 14545 Friar No. 106, Box 2160, Van Nuys, Calif. 91404 (213) 873-4399

Urgent Care Business Report, 4550 Montgomery Ave., Suite 700 N, Bethesda, Md. 20814 (301) 656-0450

Convenience Care Update, 67 Peachtree Park Dr., Atlanta, Ga. 30309 (404) 351-4523

Consultants

North Federal Management Group, 639 North Federal Highway, Pompano Beach, Fla. 33062 (305) 376-8788

Auer & Associates, 1268 Jackpine St., West Palm Beach, Fla. 33414 (305) 790-0100

Healthclub

> *"Everybody needs fitness. Health is the most important product in the world."* – Ron Shepherd, The Twin Falls Athletic Club

---

Low Startup Investment: $100,000 (small, single-purpose club with leased equipment)

High Startup Investment: $4 million (large facility)

Time Until Breakeven: One to five years

Annual Revenues: $200,000-$4 million

Annual Pre-tax Profits: $40,000-$500,000

Staffers Needed for Startup (including founder): Two to twenty

---

Falling out of a helicopter put a real fast end to Ron Shepherd's military career in the early 1970s. But when he joined a healthclub for rehabilitation, he found a new vocation. "Soon, I hired on to train members in weight lifting," Ron recalls. "Then I started selling memberships. Then I managed the club."

By 1983, Ron was overseeing a four-unit Colorado chain when a member approached him with a proposition. The member wanted to hire Ron to manage his small healthclub in his home town of Twin Falls, Idaho. Noting the potential in a twelve-thousand-square-foot club that had just two hundred members, Ron agreed to come on board—with three provisos: One, he would have a free hand in marketing; two, they would plow profits into expanding the facilities; and three, in addition to his $25,000 annual salary, Ron would get 50 percent ownership of The Twin Falls Athletic Club, vested over five years.

Within two months of moving to Idaho, Ron had doubled membership with an aggressive promotion campaign. Estimating a growing membership roster will bring revenues of $400,000 in 1987, Ron figures that "bills will eat up $156,000, and we'll reinvest half the rest for improvements." The remainder—or $122,000—goes into the owners' pockets.

THE BOTTOM LINE

John McCarthy, executive director of the International Racquet Sports Association (IRSA), says full-service mega-facilities, complete with exercise equipment, tennis or racquetball courts, swimming pools, and exercise classes, typically return 10 to 12 percent of their usually seven-figure revenues as profits. With fewer services to maintain and a smaller staff, compact clubs like The Athletic Center make even more. A snug—say ten-thousand-square-foot—facility (without sport courts and swimming pools) can realize up to 20-percent profits ($20,000 to $60,000) on revenues of $100,000 to $300,000 annually.

Some 20 million Americans belong to more than fifty-five thousand fitness facilities, healthclubs, country clubs, and YMCAs across the country, estimates John McCarthy. While expecting the industry to continue the 5- to 7-percent annual growth rate it has boasted since 1980, IRSA projects the steepest increase for the smaller fitness-studio segment, which houses exercise machines and classes but no sports such as racquetball.

POCKET CLUBS

John McCarthy estimates that full-service facilities cost about $100 a square foot to build and equip—or as much as $4 million for a large multipurpose club, depending on location and such accoutrements as saunas and whirlpools. But you can renovate a warehouse and lease exercise equipment for a small, bare-bones club with $100,000. You can plunk down a ten-thousand-square-foot Nautilus-and-aerobics facility in urban areas with lots of people and not much real estate. Although you do everything you can to keep patrons coming back for more, a club makes a profit by signing on more patrons than its facilities can accommodate. For every member who comes seven days a week, others attend sporadically, and many stop attending before their membership expires.

While you should make sure you don't plop down a club in an area of intense competition, finding the right spot may not be too hard. In fact, landlords may even court you; highrise apartment and office developers have been known to offer sweetheart terms since healthclubs attract tenants. You might even talk a municipality into a joint-venture project: The city provides real estate or a tax-free bond to build a club in an underdeveloped neighborhood. And pocket-sized fitness centers increasingly pop up in hotels, shopping malls, and even hospitals.

But don't overlook your customer base in your search for a generous landlord. Experts stress location—which means proximity to a great number of reasonably affluent, reasonably young customers— above most other considerations, like whether you want a sauna or whether your rent will be a few dollars less a month. If you're in the right location, you'll have your fair share of customers.

START SMALL, GROW FAST

Pocket clubs don't work everywhere. Unless you locate in a central city or other area with a captive customer base, you need to offer variety in order to attract a large membership. Although you can start small, operators prescribe growth as early as possible, particularly in suburbia where the population is not so concentrated. The strategy not only builds revenues, but keeps members reenlisting for a second term and beyond. "If you have just one element, the membership becomes disenchanted," warns Roger Ralph, who began the Bel Air Athletic club in the Baltimore bedroom community of the same name with flexibility in mind.

The entrepreneur, who has a Harvard business degree as well as a master's degree in Asian studies, spent $800,000 in 1980 in an attempt "to build a Cadillac on a Chevrolet budget." According to Roger, he "came up with an Oldsmobile." The original facilities, twenty-five thousand square feet with ten racquetball courts, twelve pieces of Nautilus, and leased aerobics and foodservice concessions, today encompasses thirty-five thousand square feet. "We took over the aerobics and foodservice ourselves, and converted two racquetball courts to free-weight facilities," adds Roger. Most important, as the popularity of racquetball faded, Bel Air added a swimming pool in 1986, the year the club grossed $1.5 million. IRSA data suggests that facilities with pools average 25 to 33 percent more members and have twice the bottom line of those clubs lacking swimming.

YOUR LOCKERS WILL LIMIT YOU

Plan for the good times. "Make sure you have space to expand either up or out when you sign your lease," advises Roger. And, because a small locker room inhibits growth, devote more space to showers and lockers than you initially need; the same applies to your parking lot.

Once presented with a budget and building size, many large equipment manufacturers will draw a detailed floorplan, including the type of equipment and layout best suited for your needs. For example, says Lynn Black, national sales and education director at Universal Gym Equipment Co., Cedar Rapids, Iowa, "Keep your child-care facilities in front so parents don't have to drag their kids through the club. And, if they have to pass through the shower room in order to get to wet areas like the swimming pool or hot tub, people will be more likely to shower."

Customers expect the same services throughout the term of their memberships, so study your community before opening your doors. For example, downtown clubs have little need for child-care facilities, but suburban facilities cater to families. And recognize that if you provide free babysitting the first day members will balk if you charge for it later. All those little services may be worth it— but they do add up. Before giving out free towels in the shower room, consider that Bel Air annually spends $10,000 to replace stolen towels.

Different owners have different philosophies about extras. Ron Shepherd feels the little things are essential. "Service begets obligation," he says. "Members feel they owe it to you if you service them." In addition to providing shampoo and towels in the bathrooms, The Twin Falls Athletic Club phones twenty members a day to ask if they have any complaints.

LURING MEMBERS ABOARD

Ron says he doubled The Twin Falls Athletic Club's membership to four hundred within two months of joining the club through such strategies as placing contest boxes in stores. For the cost of a few free memberships it gave away through a drawing, the club gained valuable exposure.

In addition to stuffing mailboxes with flyers and advertising for members in newspapers and radio, fitness operators pay particular attention to groups. For example, corporate memberships provide a way of signing up a whole parcel of people at a single swoop. To encourage corporate membership plans, club salespeople cite a study by Toronto-based Canada Life Assurance Company, which found a 2.7-percent increase in productivity and a 22-percent reduction in absenteeism among employees who followed a fitness program. Roger Ralph devises an "exercise prescription" (a workout routine) at a discount for health-maintenance-organization subscribers in his area. "It enables the HMO to give subscribers a benefit and gives us access to their seventy-six hundred members," he says. You might also join forces with a hospital to offer cardiovascular or rehabilitation programs.

Roger says his aggressive marketing to groups has given Bel Air 7-percent market penetration—or forty-two hundred members out of an area population of sixty thousand. That's an extraordinary figure to boast. IRSA says to expect no more than 1.5 percent of the population within a twelve-minute drive to join a club.

JOCKS SECOND

Successful operators are businesspeople first and jocks second. To run a club, you employ skills ranging from accounting and personnel management to equipment purchasing and marketing—and you might have to tackle such sidelines as foodservice. It doesn't hurt to know physical fitness, but you can hire people who know that. Estimating that a small club can get by with only half a dozen employees, experts advise recruiting physical education majors from local colleges. Many clubs employ part-time instructors. Bel Air's eighty-person staff, for example, includes only twelve full-timers. Although the industry remains unregulated, growing numbers of clubs and instructors take voluntary physical education certification courses given by industry associations.

Absentee management usually is a disaster. If you want to own a club, you'd better plan on spending a lot of time there—the majority of healthclubs operate seven days a week, sixteen to eighteen hours a day—and Ron Shepherd says you'll learn the business best by working at a club for a few months before opening your own. But consultants and some equipment manufacturers also train prospective club owners; Universal offers a $500, four-day program that covers such basics as how to weed out those applicants for membership who physically shouldn't participate, marketing, employee motivation, and designing a fitness program.

If healthclubs bewitch you because you're a jock, you can certainly preach what you practice. Continue to instruct members in the use of equipment or give exercise classes. Meantime, you stay in great physical shape. Ron Shepherd still puts in eight hours a week working out on exercise machines and with free weights.

"Providing fitness is absolutely exhilarating" says Roger Ralph. He has no doubt that healthclubs will continue to add members as an aging population grows more aware of the benefits of exercise in preventing heart disease and managing the aging process itself. Observes Roger: "It's been said that fitness is replacing sex as the topic of conversation in the 1980s and 1990s."

SOURCES

Industry Associations

Association of Physical Fitness, 600 Jefferson St., Suite 202, Rockville, Md. 20852 (301) 424-7744

International Racquet Sports Association, 132 Brookline Ave., Boston, Mass. 02215 (617) 236-1500

National Sporting Goods Association, 1699 Wall St., Mount Prospect, Ill. 60056 (312) 439-4000

Publications

Athletic Business Magazine, 1842 Hoffmann, No. 201, Madison, Wisc. 53704 (608) 249-0186

Club Industry Magazine, 1450 Beacon St., P.O. Box C9122, Boston, Mass. 02146 (617) 277-3823

Club Management Magazine, 408 Olive St., St. Louis, Mo. 63102 (314) 421-5445

Consultants

Universal Fitness Institute, 930 27th Ave. S.W., P.O. Box 1270, Cedar Rapids, Iowa 52406 (319) 365-7561

Club Marketing and Management Services, Box 1156, Helena, Mont. 59624 (406) 475-3438

Home Healthcare

> *"It's real exciting for the nurse in me to deliver services people need rather than just what the government says they're entitled to."* – Kay Hollers, Wellstream Health Services

Low Startup Investment: $60,000 (to provide nonmedical service, such as meal preparation for the infirm; operated from home with no marketing budget)

High Startup Investment: $300,000 (larger facility that provides skilled nursing and holds a license to accept Medicare patients)

Time Until Breakeven: Two to four years

Annual Revenues: $150,000-$4 million

Annual Pre-tax Profits: $10,000-$400,000

Staffers Needed for Startup (including founder): Eight to twenty-five

A number of major trends are converging to bolster the home healthcare business. As our population ages, more people need medical care, or just assistance in performing the daily routine. Capital-strapped hospitals discharge patients—regardless of age—quickly, often before they are ready to resume their day-to-day activities. And nursing homes hold little attraction for those seniors who want to remain independent. Meanwhile, the largest users of home healthcare—the elderly—have more money than ever before, enough to pay for their own well-being.

These trends promise a growth of home healthcare agencies, companies that bring to clients' homes everything from high-tech respirators and chemotherapy to aides who help bathe aged or ill patients. According to Biomedical Business International, a research firm, the home healthcare field will bulge from 1985's $10.3

billion a year to $19 billion by 1990. In 1987, the National Association for Home Care estimated about five thousand home health agencies, five thousand homemaker home health aide agencies (providing nonmedical services), and twelve hundred hospices cared for more than 2 million Americans.

PEOPLE WHO NEED PEOPLE

But those are just numbers. What really counts to typical entrepreneurs who enter the home health field is people. Consider
* Ninety-three-year-old Jesse. Although her son Frank cooks for her and cleans her house, a nursing home seemed imminent because neither felt comfortable sharing intimate tasks like bathing. A home aide visiting three times a week allowed the proud woman to remain at home.
* Stanley, whose active lifestyle screeched to a halt when he suffered a stroke at age sixty. Home therapists assisted his wife in returning him to independence.
* Tiny Mary, born prematurely with severe respiratory problems. Instead of months of hospitalization, Mary grew stronger in the warmth of her own home with the help of visiting nurses and a home respirator.

"Home healthcare is a badly needed service, especially for older people," states an emphatic Ruth Constant, who holds a Ph.D. in nursing and operates four agencies in Texas. "People ask why I stay in, when I might make more money elsewhere. But it gets under your skin."

YOU'RE BETTING ON THE FUTURE

Despite the obvious benefits of home care (the National Association for Home Care estimates even extensive home care can cost just one-quarter the bill for institutional care), the field still struggles. But nearly everybody sees home healthcare as a top money-maker of the future for those who can hang in until the federal government loosens Medicare pursestrings and insurance companies agree to reimburse more of the costs. "The industry will overcome the crisis because demographics will demand it," says Jennifer

Hirshan, a spokesperson for the National Association for Home Care. She also points to legislative action and lawsuits that she predicts will force the government to be more generous with home healthcare dollars. Already, some large hospital chains are starting home healthcare divisions or buying entrepreneurial companies as they bet on the field's potential.

This attention comes despite the fact that Medicare-based home health companies can barely meet costs—and making a profit on Medicare alone is out of the question. Until the industry's health improves, operators compensate by accepting only non-Medicare/ Medicaid patients, or by providing a balance of private-pay and government-reimbursed healthcare.

For example, Ruth Constant, who also does outside consulting with home-health startups, bids on state contracts to perform such social services as meal preparation for patients under a physician's care. "The primary- and family-care programs supplement what I lose in Medicare," she explains. When more than one agency competes for state-funded programs, the low bidder wins. "But hopefully you bid $10 to cover something that just costs you $9 to perform so you can make a profit." As a rule, companies providing primary care—meaning nonmedical functions, such as house cleaning for an infirm client—shoot for about 5-percent profits.

You can do a lot better—maybe 15- to 20-percent profits—in private care, or providing services paid for by the family- or private-insurance carrier. Much of the financial elbow room comes because you don't deal with the sheer bureaucracy of government programs. "I can provide the same services for 50 percent less when I don't have to deal with the Medicare red tape and restrictions," says Ruth Constant.

Private services also cost a lot less to set up. Kay and Jim Hollers invested less than $100,000 to launch Wellstream Health Services in Austin, Texas, in 1986. Most of the capital went to open a small office, secure licensing, and do marketing—which meant a Yellow Pages ad and brochures mailed to zip codes in areas where older and more affluent citizens live. "If you plan on government reimbursements, you can wait six months to a year to get paid—and even then you're not assured you'll get 100 percent," says Kay, who ran a chapter of the non-profit Visiting Nurses in Lansing, Michigan, before she and her husband decided to move back to their home town and start their own business. Kay and Jim also avoided governmental red tape: "Because we didn't go into Medicare, Jim and I could handle most of the records. We didn't need rooms full of clerks getting records together for the government." Wellstream's first year was slow. However, after signing on twenty patients (some requiring full-time care, others just four hours a week), the company realized "better than breakeven" on 1987 revenues of $200,000.

Kay blames Wellstream's difficult break from the starting gate on undercapitalization. "To grow faster, I would have liked $200,000 to market to bring in patients," she says. A larger marketing budget would have allowed a full-time staffer to call on physicians who in turn might refer patients to them. Also, Wellstream lacked a major source of referral: the government. Because the company shunned the Medicare license, it lost the beneficial side effect of Medicare patients who eventually improve and graduate to private care.

THE STARTUP CATCH-22

A home healthcare agency has three challenges the entrepreneur has to work on simultaneously: getting government approval to operate; hiring employees; and lining up patients. Like the song says, you can't have one without the other, or in this case the others.

Whether you go the government or private route, you still need licensing in about forty states. In addition, some states have certificate-of-need laws—you must demonstrate there is enough need before you set up a home care agency. (Research your state's requirements with your Department of Health.)

To get a license, some states require a limited track record before they'll even review your policies. Getting patients during that startup period without the state stamp of approval provides a frustrating Catch-22. To get past it, you might sign on with a franchise that already has similar branches afloat. The recognition factor pacifies both patients and regulators, because they know something about you from the start. The trade-off, of course, is paying the parent company an entry fee and a percentage of profits. Another shortcut to finding those first patients is hooking up with as many physicians as possible. In fact, the federal government requires that a home health agency list a physician and registered nurse on its professional advisory committee before it becomes eligible for Medicare.

Kay Hollers paid some courtesy calls on area doctors, but says most referrals came after proving Wellstream's reliability with a specific patient she shares with the physician. "We call about arranging for Mrs. Jones's appointment, for example." Then, next time a cataract patient needs transportation for an exam, the receptionist remembers Wellstream. Or the next time a surgery patient needs companion services after being released from the hospital, the doctor recalls the conscientious attention Wellstream provided in a similar situation.

The moment you open for business, you also need aides or nurses to provide care for your patients. Some states stipulate that aides have some hospital or nursing home experience, and a few require certification, which Medicare programs also demand. In addition, you might think about accreditation through the National HomeCaring Council. Even in states that don't require it, accreditation adds credibility.

While you can find employees through newspaper ads, unless you can keep them well supplied with jobs, you could lose them to other employers. To keep its employees busy, Wellstream supplements home healthcare by offering sick-child services. "We will care for a seriously ill child over a period of time, but ordinarily our children have chicken pox or the flu and can't go to school," says Kay Hollers. Wellstream lets daycare centers know of its service and advertises in the Yellow Pages. Key estimates sick-child care contributes just 15 percent of Wellstream's revenues, "but it fills in the gaps for workers who don't have other cases this week."

NOT JUST HEALTHCARE

Kay suspects Wellstream will offer even more varied services in the future. Currently, its aides perform primarily homemaking chores and personal grooming services for ill or elderly patients. "We get their meals, clean their homes, and help them dress and bathe," she explains. The company also runs errands, like food shopping, and provides transportation to doctors' offices. "We usually start with people who think they need nursing care, but really need maid services with a health-care base," explains Kay. Charges range from $7 to $9 an hour, depending on the types of services requested. However, Kay expects her clients will request nursing care as they age, which Wellstream is prepared to provide. "We will evolve to answer what our clients need." Those needs could extend beyond the medical arena. One possibility is providing legal services through attorneys who make house calls. "We constantly ask What is home care and how do we do it?" says the entrepreneur. "The fairly traditional answer is professional and paraprofessional healthcare. But there's no reason we have to stop with that."

Jennifer Hirshan of the National Association for Home Care points to other nonmedical services—such as banking and dog grooming—that agencies are placing on their home care menus. "We're moving in two directions," she says. "Especially as the population ages, we'll expand to more nonmedical care. On the other front, as technology grows, we can provide more medical procedures at home." She notes that in Sweden, considered a leader in the home care industry, even minor surgical procedures such as vasectomies are performed at home.

SOURCES

Industry Associations

National Association for Home Care, 519 C St., N.E., Stanton Park, Washington, D.C. 20002 (202) 547-7424

American Federation of Home Health Agencies Inc., 1320 Fenwick Lane, Silver Spring, Md. 20910 (301) 588-1454

American Hospital Association, div. of Ambulatory Care, 840 N. Lake Shore Dr., Chicago, Ill. 60611 (312) 280-6461

American Association for Continuity of Care, 1101 Connecticut Ave. N.W., Washington, D.C. 20036 (202) 857-1194

National HomeCaring Council, a division of the Foundation for Hospice and Homecare, 519 C St. N.E., Washington, D.C. 20002 (202) 547-6586

National HomeCaring Council, 235 Park Ave. S., New York, N.Y. 10003 (212) 674-4990

National Council on the Aging, 600 Maryland Ave. S.W., West Wing 100, Washington, D.C. 20024 (202) 479-1200

Publication

Homecare Magazine, 2048 Cotner Ave., Los Angeles, Calif. 90025
(213) 477-1033

Consultant

Ruth Constant & Associates, 1501 Mockingbird Lane, Suite 404,
Crossroads Plaza, Victoria, Tex. 77904

Household
Services

Alarm Systems

> *"Most of my subscribers are little old ladies. I've got honorary grandmothers who knit me scarves and send me fruitcakes for the holidays. One lady found out I have a ten-year-old daughter and sent her a hand-made doll."* – *Ken Miller, DKW Enterprises*

Low Startup Investment: $2,000 (using a family car to make service calls)

High Startup Investment: $20,000 (includes a franchise fee, buying a truck, some advertising)

Time Until Breakeven: Three weeks to two years

Annual Revenues: $25,000-$250,000

Annual Pre-tax Profits: $10,000-$100,000

Staffers Needed for Startup (including founder): One

An elderly Jenkintown, Pennsylvania, woman slowly lowered herself into her bathtub one evening in 1980, hoping the warm water would ease the pain of her arthritis. When she attempted to leave, she found herself helpless, unable to rise. Her screams for help went unheeded, and it was the next afternoon before someone rescued her. Terrified of being alone, she asked her son-in-law what might prevent such an occurrence. Three years later, Lifecall was born.

Lifecall Systems Inc., Camden, New Jersey, is a security monitoring franchise that specializes in medical alerts. Had the woman stranded in the bathtub subscribed to Lifecall, she would have pushed a button embedded in a pendant worn around her neck, which would have triggered a series of events: An electronic signal would have activated a unit attached to her telephone, which would have dialed a toll-free number in Ohio. If the victim was within fifty feet of the telephone, she could tell the monitoring center what was wrong. If she was unable to talk, the center's computer bank—armed with her name, medical history, directions to her house, and phone numbers of the nearest ambulance service, police, and her doctor—would automatically call for help.

Medical alert may be the fastest-growing segment of the alarm industry. Fewer than one in ten U.S. homes and just 28 percent of businesses contained any sort of fire or burglar alarm in 1985, according to the National Burglar & Fire Alarm Association, and no one even bothers to count the paltry—but growing—number of medical alert systems. That, according to a spokesperson, means "the potential for the alarms industry is tremendous compared with other products and services. The market is virtually untapped."

EVERYONE NEEDS SECURITY

Fear of crime permeates modern America. In the ten years between 1973 and 1982, the U.S. Department of Justice reported 73,308,000 household burglaries; during the course of these entries, burglars committed 2.8 million violent crimes, including rapes and assaults.

If crime isn't enough to scare you out of your home, consider accidents. The National Safety Council estimated 3 million Americans were disabled in home accidents in 1985.

While alarms may not prevent crime or accidents, alerting the proper authorities swiftly can mean the difference between a minor incident and a tragedy. The 12,800 alarm-installing companies that *Security Distributing & Marketing Magazine* counted in 1985 grew 16 percent in 1986, with another 13-percent hike anticipated for 1987. In dollars, the industry estimated its take at $5.3 billion in 1986 and $6 billion a year later. Those figures do nothing to suggest the possibilities, says Skip Gundlach, whose Better Bottom Lines consultancy helps entrepreneurs get into the alarm business. "There's more business than anybody's taken care of," he insists. "Nobody doesn't need security."

Critics growl that the industry is growing slowly. The industry has barely kept pace with new home starts, when the potential market is virtually all of America. They cite two reasons for this disappointing stat:

• Alarms of the past were expensive and unreliable.

• Even today, the public remains unaware that monitoring services exist.

Problem No. 1 may be a relic of the past. "Maturity is coming about in the industry," says the National Burglar & Fire Alarm Association spokesperson. "Manufacturers are making systems that don't cause false alarms, are aesthetically pleasing, and the costs are coming down. There should be considerable growth with a better product at a lower cost."

WAITING FOR THE PHONE

While alarm companies are making converts, signing on customers remains a concern. Skip Gundlach insists all you need do is market your services properly. "The industry is made up of individuals waiting for the phone to ring," he fumes. "It has done its dead-level best to starve itself." In Skip's book, Yellow Pages and newspapers don't pay. He advocates literally knocking on doors, especially commercial doors, to spread the gospel directly to the consumer.

Tod McQuaid, who operates TEMAC Inc., agrees, but adds that you should approach those doors with caution. Don't frighten merchants with a hard sell when you should be reassuring them that you've come to help. Tod had worked for a large alarm company for twelve years before relocating to Lewisburg, West Virginia, to start his own practice in 1983. "When I first came to the area, I dropped my business card with commercial establishments," he recalls. "I told them to call for an appointment." By letting customers come to him, Tod made friends instead of enemies and has since installed not only fire, burglar, and medical alarms, but also emergency lighting, fire extinguishers, and driveway- and fence-protection devices in banks, hospitals, and residences throughout the mountains of West Virginia.

KNOW YOUR CUSTOMERS

Study the psyche of your customers. Tod McQuaid says that, while cold calls targeted residentially may work elsewhere, they are taboo in the small Appalachian communities he serves. He recalls a competitor who tried door-to-door sales. "The sheriff caught him before he hit the third door."

Don't approach the sale of an alarm system the same way as you might sell a vacuum cleaner. "Security is both tangible and intangible," points out Skip Gundlach. Like Tod McQuaid, Ken Miller contends that people who employ fear tactics see more doors than contracts. His DKW Enterprises, Secane, Pennsylvania, operates a Lifecall medical alert franchise. "These people contacted you. They know they need the product. They've been beaten to death by salesmen for aluminum sidings and insurance. What they need from you is a sincere presentation of what your system can do to help them."

Some installers have success with stuffing mailboxes or buying mailing lists and sending flyers to a targeted audience, such as people over sixty-five or families likely to have valuables to protect. Ken Miller advertises on local radio and in pennysavers, which, he says, stay in the house longer then daily newspapers. "But it's a mistake to spend $5,000 for a radio ad until you are ready to service the business," he warns, noting that a radio campaign may generate seventy-five to one hundred leads. Although it takes just fifteen minutes to install a Lifecall system, Ken allocates three to four hours per sales call. That chunk of time accounts for driving, the pitch, and paperwork, which includes taking a complete medical history. Ken's customers don't mind the intrusion. "The little old ladies make you lunch," he says.

A PERPETUAL-MOTION MACHINE

Alarm business profits can be good—and long-term profits can be excellent. You can sum up the beauty of the security monitoring business in two words: recurring revenues. Once you sell a subscriber, you generate cash flow each month like a utility. Revenues build from a small base like an upside-down pyramid. Explains Skip Gundlach: "A one-person show would have a hard time installing $10,000 worth of systems a month. Those three to six systems would generate monitoring fees of $30 to $150 a month. But that's cumulative. Next month, you install another five systems—and get an additional $100 in recurring revenues."

After six months in business, "I now have $650 a month in residuals," in addition to installation fees of some $2,000 a week, calculates Ken Miller. In his case, the monthly income includes not only monitoring, but some leasing fees for the Lifecare systems he installs. His goal is to reach monthly residuals of $2,000 within a year. "Life will be a lot more comfortable," he said. "When I want to take a vacation, I know the money still comes in."

You break even on the sale of the $1,000 to $1,500 systems, making your profits on the recurring revenues. After the installation, responsibility becomes, for the most part, passive. In other words, monitoring centers wait for the equipment to trip an alarm before going into action. Action, you'll note, is no more costly than calling the local fire, police, or medical authorities.

Small and mid-sized operators turn that responsibility of responding to the alarm over to a monitoring station. For $6 or $7 per month per subscriber, a central monitoring service located thousands of miles away receives any alarms and notifies the local fire and police departments of emergencies; you keep the rest of the $20 to $30 monthly monitoring fee as profit. After you sign on several thousand accounts, you might consider spending the $75,000 or so to staff and equip a monitoring station with computers and phones. Until you catch eight or ten thousand subscribers, it doesn't make economic sense to operate a monitoring station.

Since consumers rarely change services once the system is installed, entrepreneurs who can build a base of subscribers see profits that mount steadily with each new customer. In general, companies that decide to sell can command anywhere from fifteen to fifty times their monthly recurring revenues. Even at those prices, Skip Gundlach tells newcomers who have the capital to buy existing businesses with accounts if they wish to build business quickly.

Installers either sell systems outright, or rent the hardware for monthly fees on top of the monitoring charge. The leasing arrangement brings in longer-term profits, unless the customer pulls the plug on your services. It's easy enough to discontinue the monitoring functions, but regaining possession of leased hardware can sometimes be sticky. Although the law grants court orders to retrieve your equipment, most installers don't bother since the cost to enforce a contract often exceeds the value of the contract. And operators say the problem is no greater for security firms than for other services doing business in private homes, such as servicing built-in vacuum cleaners or swimming pools.

ALL OVER THE LOT

An entrepreneur can still break into the alarm business for under $5,000. With a phone for making appointments and a car to cart the equipment to the installation site, all you really lack are tools to install the systems, sales brochures, and incorporation papers. Most distributors will sell you one or two systems as your orders come in, so you don't have to spend heavily for inventory.

The potential of the business varies, depending on how many alarms you install, the price of the service, and the amount of marketing hustle you employ. *Security Distributing & Marketing* estimates that nearly half of all installing firms in 1985 realized revenues of less than $100,000, although 11 percent raked in over $1 million.

A technician or salesperson heads the typical one- or two-person operation, although a growing number of regionals are amassing war chests to gobble up moms-and-pops, and several national chains are getting into the act. On one end of the spectrum, cable-TV installers and electricians moonlight by installing systems part time. Playing the same game with a quantum leap in advertising dollars, venture capitalists and even some major Japanese electronics behemoths reportedly are scrutinizing ways to pour millions into the security business.

The installation expertise necessary varies with the type of system. Ken Miller, who managed nightclubs before opening DKW, says installing a Lifecall unit is no more complicated than plugging an answering machine into a phone jack. But Tod McQuaid, who climbed an eight-year ladder of installing systems for other companies before starting TEMAC in 1983, warns that some of the microprocessor-based systems require a high degree of expertise. Some full-service companies install everything from sprinklers to closed-circuit TVs, each system needing custom design. Although some states have licensing requirements, Tod advocates stricter standards to eliminate the "occasional people" whom he blames for systems that trip too easily or not at all. Both the National Burglar & Fire Alarm Association and local burglar and fire alarm associations provide licensing information and courses.

As an installer, you're responsible for servicing what you sell, but little can go wrong with the simple alarms that most subscribers require. Should a Lifecall system malfunction, for example, Ken Miller unplugs the old unit and replaces it with a new one, supplied free of charge from the franchisor. Because the servicing is so minimal, Ken has installed systems as far away from his Pennsylvania base as Florida and Oregon.

LATCHKEY KIDS

Ken predicts a vast market well beyond the seniors who are the core of his business. Parents with babies prone to illness as well as households with latchkey children represent an untapped potential. In fact, Ken personally experienced the terror of a working parent when his daughter suffered a nasty cut while both he and his wife were working. "I immediately put a system in my house and told her to push the button if she ever had a problem again."

The one-person operations have mixed feelings about nationals. While they may cut into the potential pie, "their TV campaigns and mass marketing may awaken awareness," predicts Anne Armel, senior editor at *Security Distributing & Marketing Magazine.* "The industry is going to expand geometrically once the heavy bucks come in," says Skip Gundlach. Adds Ken Miller: "Particularly in the medical area, I don't have enough competition. Common knowledge isn't to the point yet where people know we exist."

SOURCES

Industry Associations

National Burglar & Fire Alarm Association, 1120 19th St. N.W., Suite LL20, Washington, D.C. 20036 (202) 296-9595
Security Equipment Industry Association, 2800 28th St., No. 124 Santa Monica, Calif. 90405 (213) 450-4141

Publication

Security Distributing & Marketing Magazine, 1350 E. Touhy Ave., Des Plaines, Ill. 60018 (312) 635-8800

Consultants

Skip Gundlach, Better Bottom Lines, Rt. 14 Box 548 A, Cumming, Ga. 30130 (404) 887-0397

Lee Jones, Support Services Group, 910 W. San Marcos Blvd., San Marcos, Calif. 92069 (619) 744-7444

Carpet Cleaner

> *"People don't just tell me once I do a great job, they tell me over and over. If I work through lunch, people offer me a sandwich and customers feed me Cokes all day long."* – Bobbie Carter, Carter's Carpet & Upholstery Cleaning Service

Low Startup Investment: $3,000 (professional carpet cleaning equipment)

High Startup Investment: $15,000 (including upholstery cleaning equipment, advertising, and a used van)

Time Until Breakeven: One month to one year

Annual Revenues: $20,000-$200,000 (two employees)

Annual Pre-tax Profits: $10,000-$70,000

Staffers Needed for Startup (including founder): One

When Bobbie Carter calls to estimate the fee for Carter's Carpet & Upholstery Cleaning Service, she has no guarantee she'll get the job. But she puts her equipment in her mini-van just in case. Nine times out of ten, the customer can't resist Bobbie's enthusiasm: She's sure her cleaning method beats anybody else's in the small town of Franklinton, Louisiana. She clinches the sale by pulling out before-and-after photographs illustrating the miracles she performs. The pitch ends with Bobbie suggesting she start with just one room. If all goes well, she ends by cleaning carpets throughout the entire house.

PARTY LINES

Carpet cleaners say the domino effect doesn't stop with doing multiple rooms in the same house. Joe Wasson, proprietor of Hoosier Carpet Care in Rushville, Indiana, figures "one job well done equals three other jobs because word-of-mouth advertising works so well in this business." Bobbie Carter furnishes an example: "One day I was doing an estimate that led to cleaning the woman's carpeting. The mother-in-law was visiting and had me come to her house after I finished. From there, I did such a great job they asked me to do the carpeting at the jewelry store the daughter owns."

Bobbie solicits good will by leaving a thank-you note with every job and calling back the next day to make sure the customer remains pleased with the job. "I always mention my work is guaranteed and if you have a problem I'll come back."

Recommendations only come if you do a superb job, of course. So make sure you buy equipment capable of results. Joe Wasson stresses the importance of walking through a home with the customer before attempting any cleaning. "Let them know which spots won't come out, and they won't be disappointed," he suggests.

Even though word-of-mouth is the strongest business builder in this or any other industry, carpet cleaners say you drum up business any way you can, and different methods of securing clients work best for different entrepreneurs. One Colorado cleaner did his first carpet at the bank that loaned him the money to buy his equipment.

Carpet cleaners are split on the value of advertising, although most do to some extent. Bobbie Carter, who launched her company in 1987, says her best inquiries come from simple three-line ads in the newspaper's classified section. "The ad costs just $26 dollars a week, so one job pays for the ad and that job usually leads to others," she calculates. Bobbie's vivacity makes her a natural salesperson, and she uses her personal contacts to develop customer leads.

In contrast, Joe Wasson's more subdued personality means he relies more on advertising to pull in customers. In 1987, Joe allotted fully 35 percent of his gross—which amounted to $40,000—to advertise anywhere and everywhere. "I use radio, newspaper, leave coupons door-to-door. I donate my services to raise money for charity."

Joe also pens a newsletter that he sends to customers every three to four months. "I tell what type of vacuum works best and how to take out certain stains by yourself. Getting my name to the customer periodically reinforces repeat business," he explains. He estimates that "60 percent of customers whose carpets I cleaned a year ago have already called me back to do them again."

Households are just one type of home for carpets. The more ambitious carpet cleaning services send letters and make cold calls on businesses. Commercial accounts offer several advantages. Carpets in an office complex are often much bigger jobs than a single house. Also, restaurants or retail establishments need their carpets cleaned often, and you may land a contract that promises repeat business in exchange for a slight discount. Finally, says Bobbie Carter, "The people who work in a business often hire you once they see what a great job you did on the business's carpet."

HOW YOU CHARGE

Just as carpet cleaners differ in how they approach advertising, they also support two schools of thought on pricing. You can price either by the room or by the square foot. Joe Wasson says he switched from square-foot pricing to room rates to simplify matters. "I was charging about 12 cents a square foot. But I found I often had to make two trips: one to estimate a job, and a second trip to do the job itself," he explains. "It was just too time-consuming." So he switched to a flat rate of $17 a room, which he says works out to around 9 cents a square foot. "I can offer the customer a better price and still make more money because I don't waste time," he explains. Also, room rates make advertising more effective because many people have no idea how many square feet their rooms contain.

Bobbie Carter disagrees vehemently with Joe's room-rate reasoning, however. She says most people hire her on the spot so she doesn't waste many trips on estimates. Besides, "Is it a nine-by-twelve-foot room, or twelve-by-twenty-four?" she asks. "People get mad if you quote them one price then try to charge more if their rooms are too big." Instead, she charges 15 cents a square foot when she doesn't move furniture, and 22 cents when she does. "I only weigh seventy-seven pounds," says Bobbie, who has to hire somebody to move the furniture if customers want rugs cleaned under the bed or behind the chest.

One attraction carpet cleaning offers is the relatively low entry cost. Since you work out of your home, you basically need equipment and a way to transport it. Usually the family car suffices in the beginning, so your budget will cover heavy-duty equipment, which can run several thousand dollars. "I arranged for a loan divided into forty-eight monthly payments of $107 each for $4,100 worth of equipment," says Bobbie. "But business was good enough in the first eight weeks that I made sixteen payments and still put some money in the bank."

In addition to equipment, you also need industrial-grade supplies. Of course, you can buy supplies as you go, paying for them from cash flow. Bobbie used an income tax refund to stock up on $600 worth of cleaning fluids in order to get a bulk discount from the Von Schrader Co., Racine, Wisconsin, which manufactures her equipment and supplies.

Von Schrader, which provides carpet cleaners who use its equipment with such backup materials as advertising and a toll-free number to answer any questions about carpet cleaning, says entrepreneurs average $30 an hour. Many carpet cleaners begin part-time, moonlighting on weekends or evenings until they build enough reputation to quit a day job. Therefore, if you clean carpets part-time—say ten hours a month—you could expect to add $15,000 to your income, minus cost of equipment and advertising. Full-timers who clean carpets forty hours a week can gross $62,400. Of course, that kind of hustle leaves little time for such necessities as marketing and travel to and from each job.

PIGGY-BACK

No law says you have to stop with carpet cleaning. Upholstery cleaning is one natural piggy-back service that offers better profit margins even than carpets. "I see carpet cleaning as a way to get in the door," says Joe Wasson, who also cleans upholstery, cars, and full houses.

Another way to increase income is to add employees. Joe recently invested $3,000 in a second set of equipment and hired an employee who has a car. "I make 10 to 20 percent on the jobs someone else does, and still pay them a good salary," he says.

Adds Bobbie Carter: "I expect to have six to eight trucks on the road eventually."

Closet Organizer

> *"Closets are something people never, ever show. Even if you sell your house, you beg the real estate agent, 'Please don't show my closets.' But people are proud of what I design and build for them."* – Marty Ginsberg, California Closet Co.

Low Startup Investment: $20,000 (home-based independent)

High Startup Investment: $100,000 (franchise with retail or warehouse space)

Time Until Breakeven: Three months to two years

Annual Revenues: $100,000-$2 million

Annual Pre-tax Profits: $6,000-$200,000

Staffers Needed for Startup (including founder): One

Entrepreneur magazine estimates that 344 million closets lurk in America's homes. Chances are, 343,999,000 of them are towers of doom, with tennis racquets poised to fall upon forgotten prom dresses, or circa-1940 suits rubbing shoulders with paisley bell-bottoms from 1968. Not to mention what's going on in the additional millions of attics, garages, kitchen pantries, etc.—all those storage places where we stuff our long-lost treasures.

MAKING A KILLING

Marty Ginsberg wondered aloud to a friend why somebody didn't make a killing designing a better closet, a closet that could hold a person's possessions in organized splendor rather than keep them in chaos. "I had never heard of California Closet Co. until the friend sent me a newspaper ad he ran across," says Marty, who was a trucking company vice president. "Two weeks later I was on a plane to check out the franchise. Two weeks after that, I quit my job."

Marty and his wife Ruth, who had raised three kids and managed an office for a group of psychologists, bought a California Closet company franchise in 1984. They hired a single employee and opened a two-thousand-square-foot combination warehouse, showroom, and workshop in Randolph, New Jersey. By 1987, they had hired fourteen salespeople and woodworkers. Considering the dire need for closet organizers and the growing public awareness of the field, "With work, you should be able to do $1 million in the business," says Marty.

INDEPENDENTS VS. FRANCHISES

The Ginsbergs laid out cash for a franchise and a business address, but independent woodwork designers can start from their homes. You need a van capable of lugging around material, and you might need to lease warehouse and workshop space if you don't have a good-sized home garage. Now, draw up a budget for inventory (most of which you can buy as you go along), tools, and advertising. Barbara Clevenger started Closet Tamers in Fort Wayne, Indiana, in 1985 by spending $300 to paint a logo on her van. Instead of bringing her clients by to see samples in a showroom, she visits their homes with a photo album containing before-and-after shots of her closets.

One advantage of buying a franchise involves the training the parent company provides. Marty Ginsberg had designed a couple of tables and cabinets from his workshop in his basement before opening his California Closet franchise, but "it was strictly a hobby," he says, "nothing on a commercial scale." By following the training guidelines provided by California Closets, Marty says he was able to earn while he learned.

California Closet can install a standard eight-foot closet for $475; extras like wire baskets or drawers increase the figure. Marty or a salesperson designs each closet separately, depending on the home-owner's needs and budget. Although some independents subcon-tract the construction, keeping the total job assures quality and also keeps the profits in-house.

Closet organizers advertise heavily in the home section of news-papers and pennysavers. Less traditional advertising works, too. Take a booth at a home show, for example, or prepare slide shows for social and civic clubs.

UNLIMITED VISTAS

Most organizers don't stop with closets, although closets usually provide the bulk of the business. California Closet Co. offers a line of accessories that range from hangers to safes to ski racks. "I can't buy as cheaply as Bradlees, so I make sure to carry a more sophisti-cated shoe box," says Marty Ginsberg. "It's something you wouldn't find except at the better stores."

Once you're comfortable with closets, you can expand into other storage areas—one West Coast organizer sells an oak veneer garage storage system for $12,000 or more. Let customers know you will install shelving, drawers, and other storage nooks wherever they need them.

Marty Ginsberg even offers a do-it-yourself kit. "We design the closet, and fabricate the pieces," he explains. "Then we give cus-tomers written and pictorial instructions to do it themselves."

Marty says he gets his share of high-end customers who can af-ford to spend $12,000 to redo all seventeen closets in the old homestead. But he also gets their less affluent neighbors. "Every-body has the same problem with storage, and the smaller the closets, the more help you need," he says. "When you're out of space, you're out of luck."

Not if you're Marty Ginsberg. Business is so good that he and

Ruth tripled the size of the facility within two years of startup. And recently, they moved to Fairfield, New Jersey, and doubled their California Closet square footage again.

Drycleaner

> "I've gotten to know wonderful people I wouldn't know otherwise. I enjoy educating my customers." – Marvel Zuercher

---

Low Startup Investment: $75,000 (small plant)

High Startup Investment: $150,000 (additional service, such as laundry)

Time Until Breakeven: Nine months to three years

Annual Revenues: $100,000-$400,000

Annual Pre-tax Profits: $8,000-$100,000

Staffers Needed for Startup (including founder): Two

The drycleaning business mirrors the mood of the country. In the late 1960s and early 1970s, as America donned mini-skirts and cut-off jeans, and as demonstrators took on political issues, drycleaning shriveled. People were not concerned with their appearance. Also, technology brought us polyester, the miracle synthetic that never sees the inside of a drycleaning plant.

Now shift to the button-down 1980s. Influenced by the "Dress for Success" ethic and the Hollywood presidency, Americans again long for creases in their trousers and blouses of real silk to offset their three-piece suits. The International Fabricare Institute (IFI) says drycleaning revenues more than doubled—from $1.55 billion to $4 billion—between 1975 and 1986.

What's to keep the pendulum from swinging away from drycleaners? Simple demographics. Explains Marvel Zuercher, who runs The Habit Cleaners in Berne, Indiana: "Working mothers don't have time to iron even cotton clothes that you can wash." But isn't drycleaning expensive, compared with throwing the sweaters on the gentle cycle? What happens when the country isn't feeling quite so flush? Several franchises hedge by specializing in discount cleaning. For example, Clean'n'Press Franchise Inc., Phoenix, cleans any garment for 99 cents. But even traditional cleaners don't worry much about economic slumps. "No business is depression proof, but this comes close," says Ken Faig, director of education for the IFI. "In bad times, people don't buy clothes and have to keep the old ones in good shape."

DO IT YOUR WAY

That bigger picture of drycleaning may have been in the back of Marvel Zuercher's mind when she bought The Habit in 1981, but really she wanted a job. "I had been a librarian and teacher when I quit to have a baby," she recalls. "When my son went to kindergarten, I wanted to go back, but jobs weren't available. This business came up for sale, so I grabbed it."

Marvel, with her sunny disposition and combative attitude toward such indignities as cooking grease on wool slacks, has a personality right on target for a drycleaning entrepreneur. "I'd always had some mechanical ability and an interest in selling, which fits in real well with what I do. I just about majored in home economics in college."

Running a drycleaner, she says, is almost an extension of the home: "I can keep my son near me. Brian has a corner of the office where he studies. Summers are slower, so I spend more time at home." True, drycleaners keep long hours, but the three trusted employees Marvel inherited when she bought The Habit pinch-hit when she wants an afternoon off, and she shuts down entirely between Christmas and New Year's and during a slow week in August.

If you don't know anything about drycleaning, don't despair. Franchises welcome newcomers with open arms. For independents, the IFI hosts a three-week intensive course, and regional trade groups sponsor seminars. For example, the nine-state Neighborhood Cleaner's Association, headquartered in New York City, spreads its eighty-hour curriculum over ten weeks. In the mid-

1980s, the organization began offering courses in Korean as well as English. "Nationally, probably 20 percent of the industry is Korean," estimates William Seitz, who heads Neighborhood Cleaner's. "A lot come to the industry because other Koreans recommend it. Also, they feel comfortable that they can learn the basics in a relatively short time and feel they can handle the amount of communication required."

AMBIANCE

There's no rule that drycleaning establishments have to be stark cubby-holes in run-down shopping centers. When The Habit's lease expired in 1985, Marvel Zuercher bought an eighty-four-year-old carriage house. Her designer not only turned it into a modern drycleaning plant, he also added such touches as flower boxes and French doors that open onto a drive-under balcony. The brown-and-white barnlike structure reflects the Swiss character of the little Indiana town (population, 3,500). An *American Drycleaner* article praising the eighteen-hundred-square-foot structure, which won "Top Ten" honors in the magazine's 1985 Plant Design contest, noted it's practical advantages: "Promoted subliminally are good looks, cleanliness, and the fact that people feel better when they know they look their best."

Modern equipment, which recycles the fumes and vapors, allows entrepreneurs to locate small drycleaners in previously unlikely settings, like shopping centers. The *American Drycleaner* magazine, which estimates a typical plant at two thousand square feet, tracks a trend to units less than half that size that require just one or two operators. Of course, you still need easy access to a parking lot because customers won't cotton to carrying their dirty laundry through a busy mall.

Such an environment costs extra, but you could lease and equip a modest location for $75,000. If you decide to launder shirts as well, budget another $20,000 for additional equipment. For operators who wish to have the expertise of a franchise outfit behind them, a few thousand dollars will give them an affiliation with a group such as Miami-based Dryclean-U.S.A., or One Hour Martinizing, which is headquartered in Cincinnati. To buy an existing business, figure on spending about one year's projected gross revenues.

The IFI says an average plant grosses $171,600 a year. Without taking a salary, figure a pre-tax profit of 30 percent, or $51,480—if you're average. Cash flow is good, since customers pay (in cash) when the work is done. You may have to bill if you line up large-volume jobs, such as cleaning uniform rentals, but your revenues will increase as well. Also, decide whether your particular community will support facilities to launder shirts or dryclean furs. If you're unsure in the beginning, you can always subcontract that add-on business with another professional.

HOW TO PULL THEM IN

Drycleaners don't budget much for advertising, unless they intend to lure customers from a competitor. But savvy operators increase business through education. Marvel Zuercher gives tours through her plant to civic and high school groups. "They see how we can clean better than they could at home," she explains. You could also give visiting lectures on topics such as "How to Care for Your Clothes."

Marvel says the most important marketing tool is to let customers know you care about their clothes. She often jots notes on The Habit stationery explaining how customers might treat similar stains in the future. Or she just tells them when they come to pick up their clothes. "We educate customers so they'll be happier with their investment in clothes," explains the former English teacher. "For example, don't rub a silk tie when you get something on it— just blot it to absorb the moisture. Then take it to your cleaner." She also tells customers when they can wash garments just as well at home. "If they trust me to give them the right information, I may lose a particular sale, but I gain a customer."

SOURCES

Industry Associations

International Fabricare Institute, 12251 Tech Rd., Silver Spring, Md. 20904 (301) 622-1900

Neighborhood Cleaners Association, 116 E. 27th St., New York, N.Y. 10016 (212) 684-0945

Publication

American Drycleaner, 500 N. Dearborn St., Chicago, Ill. 60610 (312) 337-7700

Consultants

New York School of Dry Cleaning, 116 E. 27th St., New York, N.Y. 10016 (212) 684-0945
International Fabricare, 12251 Tech Rd., Silver Spring, Md. 20904 (301) 622-1900

Grocery Shopper

> *"The potential is great. Think of all those people who make a lot of money and don't have a lot of time to waste doing chores." – Linda Baker, Washington Grocery Service*

Low Startup Investment: $2,000 (advertising costs)

High Startup Investment: $20,000 (includes a van)

Time Until Breakeven: Two weeks to one year

Annual Revenues: $15,000-$1 million (solo at low end, with employees at high end)

Annual Pre-tax Profits: $12,000-$500,000

Staffers Needed for Startup (including founder): One

"My partner and I were talking about businesses we could start," recalls Linda Baker, who, like Elizabeth Antinozzi, was tired of toiling in the middle management ranks for someone else. "We talked about how we live in America, how people work too much and need help with their lives. And we decided to base a business on that."

In 1984, the partners formed Washington Grocery Service to take at least one burden off the lists of working women. "In the District, demographics are with us," says Linda Baker. "We have a great concentration of upwardly mobile working women, who are the traditional providers of food."

FEEDING A NEED

Nobody has counted the number of grocery-shopping services that have responded to the frantic lifestyle of the modern career woman (and man, although patrons of a shopping service are predominantly women). The reason: The services vary so wildly. Some are attached to large supermarket chains; they are a division of the parent company or lease space as a concession. At the other extreme are homemakers who make an extra buck while doing his or her own shopping (and don't report the income).

But Linda Baker thinks entrepreneurial enterprises like Washington Grocery have stepped through the proverbial window of opportunity. She believes serious-minded shoppers can make a good living for the next dozen years or so, until supermarket chains catch on. If you're really ambitious, computerize your record keeping, and round up employees to fill several hundred orders a day, you can gross around $1 million. Add a warehouse and more employees and you'll do even better, although profits will probably fall from 80 percent of the take to 40 or 50 percent. But what happens when the supermarket chains catch on and decide to step up delivery efforts? Then, gambles Linda, "when the big boys see the potential, hopefully you'll have name recognition and you can merge or sell the business," at a very large profit, she adds.

In the meantime, Washington Grocery plans to make a name for itself by signing on as many customers as possible, shopping for up to two hundred a day. Since the charge for shopping and delivering groceries to a customer's door is $8 for orders under $50, $12 for orders of $75, $15 for orders of $100, $18 for orders up to $150, and 15 percent of orders above $150, that kind of volume could push annual revenues to a staggering $900,000. "The bottom line in this business is volume," Linda explains.

STARTING ON A FLYER AND A PRAYER

You can enter the wonderful world of grocery shopping for the cost of lining up your first patrons. Washington Grocery's partners invested a couple thousand dollars to print and mail about ten thousand flyers throughout more affluent neighborhoods within the capital's sixty-four-square-mile radius. That's a lot of territory for two people to cover, and you may want to limit your parameters. "Pick your area and flood it with advertising," Linda Baker advises. Look for neighborhoods of affluent families where both spouses work. (Singles won't frequent the service because they don't buy enough at one time to make it worth it.)

You can employ kids to take the flyers around or get reduced postal rates by bulk mailing to one zip code. Newspapers, especially pennysavers, or other neighborhood publications provide another advertising vehicle. You might also ask the manager of the supermarket you plan to frequent if you can post a notice on the bulletin board or distribute brochures in the parking lot. While a growing shopping business will always have to advertise, Linda Baker says attracting clients gets easier as word-of-mouth takes over: "Once you get the foot in the door, your patrons will start talking about you and their friends will start calling."

Since you can start from your kitchen table, the only other expense is a car, preferably a roomy station wagon or van. If you don't have one and startup cash is tight, lease one. Later on, you may add coolers to keep perishables on ice to lengthen your delivery route. Further down the road, you might even turn your basement into a warehouse (or rent a real one) and stock high-margin, bulky items like Pepsi and Pampers. The addition could improve your profit margins while cutting down on the time you have to spend in the stores.

MAKE A LIST AND CHECK IT TWICE

Some shopping services require customers to place an order each week, or ask them to check off items on a preprinted shopping list. Such an approach guarantees a sales floor and makes employee scheduling easier. But Washington Grocery decided to "make it as easy as possible to deal with us," says Linda Baker. Customers call in orders between nine and one for same-day delivery. While the average customer uses the service once every ten days, "some call us three times a week, others just if they're going to throw a big party," says Linda. Washington Grocery pays for the order, and collects a check when it delivers the groceries. "It's dangerous to carry around a lot of cash," explains Linda, who adds they haven't yet been stuck with a bad check.

Regardless of the approach you choose, creating a standardized shopping list, complete with brand names, eliminates confusion. Rank items alphabetically or by store layout. With a little ingenuity and a personal computer, you can shuffle an alphabetical list (best for order-taking) to an aisle-by-aisle printout (to speed shopping).

Linda says it pays to build a rapport with one supermarket. Not only do you instantly know where to find the instant pudding, but you also get to know the personnel. "We're Safeway's biggest customer," she says. "We're able to speak with the butchers and get good cuts of beef."

EXPRESS SHOPPING

Shopping pre-packaged goods is a piece of cake. Linda says she can fill a $100 cart in five to eight minutes if all she has to worry about is Kal-Kan and Birds-Eye. "But you have to inspect the produce or fish or meats. If there's no good zucchini in the produce section, you have to talk to the produce manager. You won't have clients long unless you provide them with good produce."

For clients that want items unavailable in the supermarket, like wine or take-out food, Washington Grocery stops by a liquor store or deli. The charge is the same as for groceries, but the more expensive price tags make it worthwhile to make the extra stops.

Once in the supermarket, the biggest challenge is keeping orders straight, since shoppers buy for several accounts at once. "Each shopper has two carts and hand-held baskets," explains Linda. "You can put the baskets in the bottom of the cart to create separations." Of course, cashiers must ring up each order independently to provide a separate receipt for each customer.

Sound confusing? Linda shrugs. "It's probably confusing to run General Motors, too."

Home Decorating Center

> *"I'm a people person. I really enjoy waiting on the customers." – Bill Elliot, Upstate Color Center*

Low Startup Investment: $60,000 (one-product-line shop)

High Startup Investment: $150,000 (multi-purpose center)

Time Until Breakeven: Two to four years

Annual Revenues: $100,000-$1 million

Annual Pre-tax Profits: $10,000-$100,000

Staffers Needed for Startup (including founder): Two

In 1984, Bill Elliot began laying the groundwork for his new life. He quit his job as a cable TV installer and went to work for the Benjamin Moore paint company. His friend and soon-to-be-partner Steve Huggins, a school teacher, had worked summers in a paint store. By 1985, they had completed enough on-the-job education to open Upstate Color Center. Since the paint line they wanted to carry was already assigned in their home town, they moved 185 miles to an untapped territory in Easley, South Carolina.

Upstate Color is one of a thousand or so home decorating centers that open each year. According to the National Decorating Products Association (NDPA), the industry rang up 1985 sales of $9.4

billion. Is now a good time to be in the business? "We've barely scratched the surface," says Bill Elliot.

CUSTOMERS COMING AND GOING

Decorating centers draw customers from two sources: homeowners and the building trade. During strong building cycles, you can sell contractors items such as paint and linoleum, and offer homeowners curtains or blinds for their new windows. When high interest rates slow home building, many individuals remodel their old abodes. "Existing housing—most of it over twenty years old—is prime for new exterior and interior design," says a recent issue of *Decorating Retailer*. "And the new residents of these houses . . . are profiled as vitally interested in fashionable home decorating."

The industry association says it takes about $100,000 to open a twenty-five-hundred-square-foot home-decorating store that expects to do at least $350,000 in annual sales by the end of its second year. Smaller stores, of course, cost less, as do shops specializing in one or two product lines, such as paint and wallcoverings. But here's what the NDPA says the average store (which counts 38 percent of its business in paint, 24 percent in wallcoverings, 12 percent in sundries such as drop cloths and paint brushes, 9 percent in floor coverings, 12 percent in window treatments, and 5 percent in "other," such as picture framing, bath boutique items, and art supplies) should set aside:

- $15,000 for fixtures (you might shop for used shelving in good shape)
- $39,000 for inventory (some dealers offer "buy now, pay later" plans)
- $31,000 for operating expenses during the first two years
- $15,000 for accounts receivable if you anticipate dealing with contractors or others who don't pay as they go.

Like most other retailing enterprises, a home decorating store takes several years to hit full stride. But NDPA found the typical dealer had 1.7 stores and $800,000 in 1985 sales. You need the volume, because pre-tax profits averaged between just 1.3 percent to 7.9 percent, or $10,400 to $63,200.

THE SUPPLIER CONNECTION

While you carry hundreds of different items, you can get them from just a handful of suppliers. Bill Elliot uses just five for the sixteen-hundred-square-foot Upstate Color Center: one paint company, two brush manufacturers, and two sundry distributors.

Choose suppliers with care, because manufacturers can be a particularly helpful lot when starting in the home decorating business. Some paint suppliers offer free dealer training courses and help with site selection. A few even help track down financing. However, experience can only come by working in a decorating center. *Decorating Retailer* advises, "If you have a difficult time finding an opening for yourself as a temporary and eager but ignorant deco center employee, contact major paint or wallcovering manufacturers and perhaps they can find a spot for you among the stores they supply."

Some suppliers also advise on store layouts. If you shoot for a homeowner customer base, you may want a pretty shop with model windows showing off the latest in woven verticals and a plethora of in-store displays. If your business comes from builders who buy in bulk, you might opt for a filled-to-the-rafters image. "Some people have a small display area and keep the majority of their paints in a back storeroom," says Bill Elliot, who estimates a fifty-fifty split between customers and contractors at Upstate Color. "We feel if a customer sees hundred of gallons of paint, it reaffirms we're in the business."

NOT MUCH WALK-IN TRADE

In areas where rents are high, many successful operators settle for an accessible, but not necessarily prime location. "We're a block off the main artery," says Bill. "If you have good products and good service, customers will find you."

Because home decorating products are not an impulse buy—and because profit margins are generally on the skinny side—many entrepreneurs restrict their conventional advertising to a Yellow Pages ad and sporadic eighth-of-a-page ads in the neighborhood pennysaver. If you advertise, be sure to inquire about co-op ad allowances from manufacturers. With their help, advertising may not be as expensive as you think.

Inexpensive marketing works well in the home decorating area. If you have a van, paint it with a bright logo for all the world to see. When the van isn't delivering valances and floor tiles, park where it's visible from a main drag. Contact area builders regularly to remind them you offer discounts for bulk buying. Bill Elliot also calls on local industry periodically. "They paint every year or two and we give discounts for large volume," he says.

SOURCES

Industry Association

National Decorating Products Association, 1050 N. Lindbergh Blvd., St. Louis, Mo. 63132 (314) 991-3470

Publication

Decorating Retailer, 1050 N. Lindbergh Blvd., St. Louis, Mo. 63132 (314) 991-3470

Household Management Service

> *"Customers never ask to place an order. They always say, 'Can you do me a favor?' People are so grateful that you take the hassle out of their lives."* – Laura Pelco, The Stepford Group

Low Startup Investment: $1,000 (home-based)

High Startup Investment: $7,000 (city storefront, with some advertising)

Time Until Breakeven: One to six months

Annual Revenues: $20,000-$500,000 (solo at low end, with up to ten employees at high end)

Annual Pre-tax Profits: $18,000-$100,000

Staffers Needed for Startup (including founder): One to ten

When Laura Pelco and Melissa Schwartz say The Stepford Group tackles every household management chore, they mean it. "We've got about forty different kinds of services we list, and still get surprised with new requests," says Melissa. The exotic and mundane accomplishments the twelve-person group performs include

- Window washing
- Party planning ("We pulled together a complete New Year's Eve party at the drop of a hat," recalls Laura. "We rented tents, tables, crystal, and arranged for the caterer, all on thirty-six hours notice.")
- Upholstery cleaning
- Grocery shopping on a weekly basis

- Visiting the motor vehicle bureau to get a license renewed
- Picking up and dropping off dry cleaning (or shoes for repair or clothes for alterations, etc.)
- Researching and buying big-ticket household appliances like washers and dryers
- Getting squirrels (or raccoons) out of attics (Although they prefer not to get involved with wild animals because of liability hazards, "After the raccoon appeared in a newspaper story, a real estate agent called and said she had a client with a raccoon in her attic, too," says Laura. "So we did it all over again.")
- House painting, repairs, and additions (Laura recalls the time they took bids for a deck from contractors then supervised the entire construction.)
- Supervising a complete house moving ("A customer called when he was transferred to Texas," says Laura. "His wife had just had a baby and he had to be there in two days. So they left every-thing—even dirty towels in the bathroom and the unmowed lawn. They gave us the number of the moving company and we super-vised everything." Adds Melissa: "That wasn't all. We took down the curtains, washed the dishes in the sink, and did loads of laun-dry.")

POTPOURRI CHORES

The Stepford Group operates out of Westport, Connecticut, the affluent community that was chosen as the film location for *The Stepford Wives,* the "horror" movie in which real women are re-placed with look-alike robotic—and perfect—housekeepers. "We did some primitive marketing before we started the service, asking friends about their pet peeves," says Laura Pelco, who had been an accountant and had worked for an importing firm before co-found-ing The Stepford Group in 1985. "It turned out that everything was a pet peeve, so we decided to do everything it takes to run a household." The sole exception is child care, which the partners don't offer because they see it as a separate service altogether, with its own personnel and insurance needs.

Any woman who works a salaried job knows exactly why The Stepford Group can employ a dozen full-time staffers and contract with any number of outsiders less than two years after startup. The days are long gone when the husband earned the bread and the wife baked it—or at least trudged to the store to buy it. When they can afford to, many women simply reject the "superwoman" syndrome of juggling career, family, and household duties. And husbands who participate in all these chores find it difficult to handle too. Indeed, some firms who haven't learned the terminology of the equal-partner household include the nomer "wife" in their corporate title, as in "Wife-for-Hire," or "Rent-a-Wife." Household management firms ease the pressure by taking on chores that full-time housewives once did. "Something has to happen in society to make the family work," observes Laura Pelco. "This is going to be a great industry."

TRAIL BLAZERS

Household management is truly an infant industry, with numerous variations on the theme popping up daily. Not all services strive to be all things to all people. Some specialize in grocery shopping or house cleaning (see Grocery Shopper and Maid Service), while others act as employment agencies for household help. One New England service, for example, bills itself as "a multipurpose home services agency," and offers "child care, meal preparation, chauffering, gift and grocery shopping, companionship and nursing for the elderly, and plant and pet care on a full-time, part-time, one-time, or temporary basis." The entrepreneur charges employers $750 to place a full-time worker. For part-time help, she splits a $12-per-hour minimum fee down the middle with the employee. "I operate like a registry and I'm licensed with the state as an employment agency," says the founder, whose 1986 $50,000 salary far surpassed what she had made two years earlier as a secretary.

Prices differ significantly even on errands done by the same agency. "We try to charge an hourly rate based on the kinds of skills necessary to perform a function," explains Melissa Schwartz. "We can hire students who need time to do their homework to wait for a repairman to fix a washing machine and pay them less than someone who has more responsibility. Supervising a move is more complex since you must make decisions. For that person we might charge $15 to $20 an hour."

In truth, some household managers don't last long, possibly because they see themselves as part-timers and don't devote energy and capital to rounding up clientele. You can distribute flyers suggesting your services either through direct mail or as hand-outs at the grocery store or commuter station. While display ads in big-city newspapers may be cost-prohibitive, you can easily budget ads in pennysavers.

You can court visibility in other ways as well. Paint your logo on your car to create a moving billboard. In addition to their office in Westport, Laura Pelco and Melissa Schwartz maintain a drop-off counter at the train station where commuters catch the train for New York City. The site serves two important functions: "People drop off things like grocery lists and ask questions about party services," says Laura. Because of the location, every commuter in town knows about The Stepford Group.

Deciding which customer group to target is tough. To be sure, lower-income families can't afford to farm out tasks, and the very affluent support live-in help. So decide if your area has enough middle- to upper-income households in which both husband and wife work. Beyond that, according to the managers, just about everybody who holds a job is a potential customer. "We work for bachelors and bachelorettes, young professionals, and couples with children," says Laura Pelco.

More good news: Most clients are repeaters. "Some have us run their whole lives; others just send us for the dry cleaning," says Laura. "But once they start using us, every time those customers go to the grocery store, they ask themselves 'Why am I doing this when I know someone else will do it for me?'"

Kitchen and Bath Design

> *"Occasionally I get a $40,000 to $60,000 design job that's a lot of fun. I remember one kitchen where we put in stainless steel sinks, marble countertops, commercial pot racks, granite floors. We installed an antique phone booth and an eighteen-foot-long island. The creative jobs make it all worthwhile."* — Ann Patterson, City Design

Low Startup Investment: $80,000 (modest showroom with three sample rooms)

High Startup Investment: $200,000 (larger showroom in a metropolitan area, with five to eight sample rooms)

Time Until Breakeven: Two to five years

Annual Revenues: $250,000-$5 million

Annual Pre-tax Profits: $15,000-$1.25 million

Staffers Needed for Startup (including founder): Four to eight

"You rarely see a bathroom without a Jacuzzi any more," says Ann Patterson, who launched City Design in West Des Moines, Iowa, in 1984, along with her husband Rick Martinez. "Sometimes you see one Jacuzzi for the parents and another for the kids. I did one $40,000 bath that we turned into a sunroom with skylights and curved glass walls. It had a sunken Jacuzzi, of course. And a fireplace."

OUT OF THE WATER CLOSET

A fireplace in the *bathroom?* And not in Beverly Hills, but in *Iowa?* Needless to say, Americans have brought their bathrooms out of the water closet. And as for kitchens, well, we're putting in labor-saving devices like microwave ovens meant to get us out of the kitchen. Then we turn our kitchens into entertainment and creativity centers by stocking them with televisions and rangetops that grill. If you want to do your Julia Child number, you can prepare anything from shish kebab to sashimi on professional-quality equipment. But thirty-foot-long kitchens aren't just for cooking.

"Something's happened to the way we view kitchens and bathrooms," agrees Russell Platek, a certified kitchen designer and director of education for the National Kitchen & Bath Association (NKBA). As business booms for kitchen and bath designers, more people are setting up shop. "Last year alone our association membership grew by 15 percent," says Russell.

You can enter the kitchen and bath business as a retailer, designer, installer, or all three. In 1980, after Ronald Robinson had managed someone else's store for fifteen years, he and his wife Ida set up Top Notch Kitchen & Bath Boutique in Mount Vernon, Illinois, primarily as a showcase of kitchen and bath equipment. "We do some installing, but an installation takes Ronnie three days to complete," says Ida. "That cuts into the time Ronnie has to sell on the floor." Product sales command a higher profit margin than design or installation because sales is less labor intensive. You can realize as much as 30 percent of revenues as profit. As a result, Top Notch typically designs a kitchen or bath, measures and orders the equipment, and lets someone else worry about installation.

Using another approach, City Design relies as much on design and installation as product. You might have to drop profit margins by as much as 5 percent to pay for the time it takes to install a kitchen or bath, but your overall fees can be higher because you charge for construction as well as products. Another source of income comes through designer fees: homeowners, architects, or contractors ask you to draw the plan, but not to build it. On sales of $5 million, a large shop with several designers in a metropolitan area could see profits of $1.25 million.

OFF (BUT NOT TOO FAR OFF) THE BEATEN TRACK

In either case, you must get the customer through your door. Instead of a slot in a high-rent mall, look for visibility with the kinds of customers you need to attract. City Design is one street away from the antique district, an area with stores and restaurants where "people in the income bracket we serve go to play and shop," says Ann Patterson. These potential customers have seen City Design, but don't drop in to browse because it's not on the main drag. "I cannot afford walk-in traffic," says Ann. "I figure to pay for my overhead, I need to average sales of $40 an hour. If I spend half of every day chatting with people who are not interested in buying, I can't pay that overhead."

Even though your average customer only buys once or twice from your shop, their purchase is a big one. Ann Patterson's kitchens average $15,000, and her typical baths cost $5,000. In a major urban area, the averages can be even higher. To make sure the people who put in a custom bath buy from you, it pays to advertise. Francis Jones, executive director of the NKBA believes in marketing that encourages people to dream up dream rooms in the first place. "Our competitors do not come from our industry," he says. "They come from the auto, vacation, and investment industries," other businesses geared to high-income dreamers who eventually carry out their fantasies.

The NKBA's Russ Platek suggests that a mature design firm spend 3 to 5 percent of its gross on advertising, and a brand new firm allot up to 15 percent to get the name out. In addition to advertising in such places as symphony and theater brochures, City Design rides its manufacturer's cooperative plan to advertise on television. Ann Patterson also keeps close ties with architects who refer clients to her since few architects tackle her two specialties.

A WHIFF OF POSSIBILITIES

Because each design is customized to fit a particular home's configuration and a particular homeowner's taste, "we sell a product that's not even conceptualized until we do the work," says Ann. Therefore, your showroom permits a customer to sense the possibilities of a truly interesting kitchen or bath. The NKBA says a minimum-sized showroom would need twelve hundred square feet, although Top Notch utilizes sixty-eight hundred square feet to accommodate its five lines. With just two manufacturers, City Design operates with under two thousand square feet. Neither store warehouses items. Instead, they avoid high inventory costs by waiting for a customer down payment before placing an order.

A couple of tips on the showroom designs: If you plan to design and install, look for higher-end merchandise and ask for exclusive rights in your area from the manufacturer. "When you have to pay for design time out of the cabinet margins, there's no room for bidding wars," says Ann Patterson. Also, before putting in a sample room, ask the vendor how long till obsolescence: you can only hope for two years before models change. Stocking new appliances every year is common as manufacturers constantly update, but you can sell the floor samples. Cabinets are a different story since they must be custom fitted to exact measurements.

PROFESSIONALS

Salespeople need to be experienced estimators. Most customers have no earthly idea what converting their dreary linoleum scullery into a cheerful dream kitchen will cost. There's no need to give firm figures at this stage, but you must be able to estimate based on the size and age of a customer's kitchen, the appliances they need, and the cabinetry they like. Even in new houses, Top Notch will estimate off a blueprint, "but we won't order until we can measure a job," says Ida Robinson. "Contractors have a way of moving a wall a couple of inches and that's enough to destroy the measurements."

Before going the extra steps of measuring and designing a kitchen, Ann Patterson asks for a $250 to $500 retainer, although she applies that fee to the final cost if customers buy cabinets from her. "I figure for every hour I spend with the client, it takes two to three hours of pricing, paperwork, and drawing," she explains.

To arrive at a close appraisal, the installer accompanies Ann to estimate his time as well as the time for such subcontractors as electricians and plumbers. After the installer determines labor and equipment charges, the customer receives a standard NKBA contract that outlines down to each electrical outlet what City Design will do.

City Design asks for 25 percent of its fee when the contract is signed, 50 percent more when construction begins, 15 percent when the kitchen is in working order, and sets aside the last 10 percent for contingencies. "Maybe a special-order tile didn't come in, or one cabinet came in damaged," Ann explains. "By asking for our fee in stages, the client can't hold more than 10 percent if something goes wrong."

No licenses are required to either install or design kitchens and baths. But you'll need some training. Auburn University in Auburn, Alabama, offers a bachelor degree in the kitchen and bath field, which includes a minor in business administration. If you're not interested in a four-year program and already have a carpentry, engineering, or art background, check out the NKBA's home study and regional traveling courses for both designers and installers. The association even offers a certification in kitchen design.

SOURCES

Industry Association

National Kitchen & Bath Association, 124 Main St., Hackettstown, N.J. 07840 (201) 852-0033

Publications

Kitchen & Bath Business, 1515 Broadway, New York, N.Y. 10036 (212) 869-1300
Kitchen & Bath Concepts, 20 E. Jackson Blvd., Chicago, Ill. 60604 (312) 922-5402

Consultant

Joe Boarman, 1625 Oliver Ave., Indianapolis, Ind. 46221 (317) 635-8979

Landscaper

> *"You do something aesthetically pleasing that contributes to the ecology. When you plant a tree, you think of it as something that might outlast you on the earth."* – *James Douglas Davis, White Oak Landscape Co. Inc.*

Low Startup Investment: $4,000 (tools for a garage operation)

High Startup Investment: $50,000 (small business location)

Time Until Breakeven: Two months to two years

Annual Revenues: $25,000-$3 million

Annual Pre-tax Profits: $10,000-$300,000

Staffers Needed for Startup (including founder): One

Landscapers thank Lady Bird Johnson for awakening interest in exterior decorating. In the 1960s, the First Lady's "Beautify America" program prompted average citizens to plant trees and trim hedges as never before. The 1970s followed with a more serious concern with our environment; government programs encouraged landscaping to combat pollution and prevent erosion. The latest boom, however, comes from upwardly mobile, two-income families who allot 10 percent of the purchase price of their new homes to sow bluegrass and plant dogwoods. As their country cousins struggle to hold onto their farms, landscapers say they've never had it so good.

And, there's still room to grow. "We're way behind the Europeans," says William Doerler, who operates Doerler Landscapes Inc., in Lawrence Township, New Jersey, next door to wealthy Princeton. "The Europeans have planted annuals for hundreds of years. Now the U.S. has discovered petunias and marigolds. Jazzy landscapes are the hottest thing."

Some landscapers employ landscape architects to design layouts; some also sell rhododendrons or birches on a retail basis. But most characterize themselves as service businesses—entrepreneurs who maintain and install plants. "We visit your new house, find your needs, likes, and dislikes, and create a look," explains William Doerler. "We're similar to an interior decorator for the outside of your house."

SHOESTRINGS

While you don't need a degree in ornamental horticulture to run a landscaping business, it doesn't hurt; after all, you will be called upon to install irrigation systems and grade slopes. If you don't want to go for the whole four-year program, you can audit some classes at land grant colleges and agricultural schools, or work for an established landscaper.

You can locate your business on a couple of acres twenty minutes out of town where the rent is cheapest: Landscapers just don't get off-the-street business. Also, since you are not a retailer, you don't need a visible presence. Many landscapers even begin from their garages, often performing maintenance (mowing, pruning, and the like) rather than planting. Take the case of James Douglas Davis, who operates White Oak Landscape Co. Inc. from the Atlanta suburb of Kennesaw, Georgia. "I began on a shoestring in 1977," says Doug, who has a degree in ornamental horticulture from the University of Georgia. "My initial capital was maybe $3,000 for a mower, blower, and a used van. I did strictly maintenance in the beginning—cutting grass, pruning, mostly residentials and some condos and banks. You need to build a client base so you can get referrals to do installation."

Within a year and a half, Doug Davis began acquiring equipment, including a one-ton dump truck; he also began stocking plants as his installation business began to grow. "The county zoning commission got after me for working out of my house, so I rented a small lot. In 1980, I needed more space, so I bought two and a half acres. By 1986, I had twelve and a half acres." White Oak has grown to one of the top fifty landscapers in the country, with $2.5 million in 1986 sales and between forty and eighty employees (during the fall and spring planting seasons Doug doubles his staff).

Since installations provide large doses of capital, many landscapers strive to develop this side of their businesses. White Oak has charged up to $100,000 for landscaping some ritzy residences, and between $50,000 and $200,000 for commercial installations; of that the company nets profits in the 10-percent range. William Doerler adds that, in addition to setting off new homes to best advantage, his company "designs lots of swimming pools and hot tubs into the environment."

But installations swing up and down, following construction cycles. Also, they are one-time deals, unless you convert installations into maintenance contracts. With those drawbacks in mind, most landscapers retain at least some upkeep jobs. "Once you get a maintenance contract, unless you screw up, that's revenue from here on in," points out Doug Davis. Large corporate accounts, of course, are the most lucrative. Some landscapers in the frostbelt provide snow-removal services to carry them through the slow winter months.

KEEP THE BUSINESS GROWING

In addition to cold calls to condominium groups and corporations, you can generate business through contacts made at civic organizations. Follow leads from architects, builders, and real estate agents. Label your trucks prominently, and post a sign at each installation project to generate customer awareness of your business.

Your biggest residential customers are those homeowners who can afford your high prices: people who don't cut the grass themselves or hire the teenager down the street. "Our carriage trade is the crowd in their fifties and sixties who don't want to do it themselves, but want a showcase home," says William Doerler. He calls them "The Mercedes group."

SOURCES

Industry Associations

American Association of Nurserymen, 1250 I St., N.W., Suite 500, Washington, D.C. 20005 (202) 789-2900

American Society of Landscape Architects, 1733 Connecticut Ave.,
N.W., Washington, D.C. 20009 (202) 466-7730

Publications

American Nurseryman, 111 N. Canal St., Chicago, Ill. 60606
(312) 782-5505
Garden Supply Retailer, P.O. Box 2400, Minneapolis, Minn. 55343
(612) 931-0211
Nursery Business, Northwood Plaza Station, Clearwater, Fla. 33519
(813) 796-3877

Consultant

Ian Baldwin, P.O. Box 896, Elkgrove, Calif. 95624
(916) 689-11968

Laundromat-Plus

> *"There's very little stress in what I do. I walk away from the business when I go home. Once you get a laundromat running, it's a vending business. You work in a host or hostess capacity."* — Jim Bogen, Duds 'N Suds franchisee

Low Startup Investment: $100,000 (small storefront with limited amenities)

High Startup Investment: $250,000 (elaborate franchise)

Time Until Breakeven: One to three years

Annual Revenues: $100,000-$250,000

Annual Pre-tax Profits: $25,000-$75,000

Staffers Needed for Startup (including founder): Two

After four and a half years as an industrial sales representative on straight commission, Jim Bogen had had it. "I was putting on sixty thousand miles a year, and I was tired. I had started a family and I wanted something less stressful—I didn't care what it was."

A friend suggested laundromats. "I wanted not so much the income, but the life style. I saw basically a self-serve business that wasn't real management intensive." In 1986 Jim Bogen opened a Duds 'N Suds franchise in Bozeman, Montana, where he now works just twenty hours a week. His work often consists of mingling with customers waiting for their rinse cycle to finish. "The atmosphere of my store is that of a living room with a lounge area and lots of plants and posters on the wall. It's conducive to talking with people. If you take the time to visit, you find everybody has their own stories to tell."

Jim's venture brought him the life style he craved—and apparently decent income as well. He doesn't like specific talk about profits, but, just eighteen months after startup, Jim was using his free time to launch a second business next door—a self-serve car wash. "Traditionally car washes and laundries are good business partners. They serve the same demographics and can trade off customers."

START WITH AN OPEN MIND

Indeed, some entrepreneurs combine the two facilities under one banner. The Coin Laundry Association says the number of laundromats remains fairly constant—between forty and fifty thousand. But the industry is in the middle of revolutionary change as imaginative entrepreneurs supplant the laundries of the past with new ones. The dingy, depressing laundry outlets of the past are fast disappearing. Springing up in their stead are comfortable facilities like Jim Bogen's that combine other services or profit centers under one roof.

"The newer facilities are better designed, prettier. They offer more amenities," says Ben Russell, editor of *American Coin-Op*. Jim Bogen's Duds 'N Suds has a pool table, television, and snack bar that serves soft drinks and packaged Frito-Lay products. Ben says you can add just about anything you want to a laundry service. But the addition typically either lets customers get rid of a second chore while they're doing their wash, or makes a boring task fun by adding a social element. He lists the following typical laundry partners: convenience store grocery sales; electronic games; sun tan parlors; dry cleaning; beer, coffee, sandwiches, or other refreshments. The list goes on and on.

WHAT'S YOUR POINT?

Before deciding what amenities to offer along with wash and dry, consider your customers and whether you want another income producer or just a way to increase laundry traffic. Jim Bogen says even though he devotes just one-third of his shop's thirty-three hundred square feet to his sixty-eight washers and dryers, 90 percent of his revenues still comes from his laundry facilities. But he believes those revenues are higher than the old wall-to-wall machine shops could generate. Duds 'N Suds attractiveness invites customers in and brings them back. "We're a freestanding brick-and-cedar building with a split-shake roof. I really think we're the nicest-looking building in town," says Jim.

Some additional services can be real money makers, however. Some singles-bar-*cum*-laundromats make better margins on $2.50 Daiquiries than 50-cent dryers. The capital to open and staff a bar only pays off if you serve lots of singles, of course. If you open near a trailer park populated with young families, you might be more successful cordoning off a children's play area. If you cater to working-couple condominium owners, perhaps they'd appreciate the convenience of dry cleaning or wash-and-fold services.

DO IT FOR A SONG

All additions are not equally expensive. To entice senior citizens in on slow afternoons, Richard Torp, communications director for the Coin Laundry Association, suggests hiring speakers who aim their talks at retirees. "Help them see it as a social outlet, a chance to get out of the house," he counsels. "You might have free cake and coffee on certain afternoons, or a little entertainment. Create a reason why people should gather."

Jim Bogen spends about 5 percent of his revenues to advertise through direct mail, newspaper, college papers, and door hangers. But, recognizing that people won't drive miles out of their way to do their laundry, he emphasizes the importance of the right location. "Look for university communities and multiple-family housing in lower-income areas," where people are unlikely to have their own washers and dryers. "The most common users of laundromats are young singles and people living in crowded conditions, like city dwellers," adds Ben Russell.

LOTS OF HELP FOR A SELF-SERVE BUSINESS

To help him over the startup hurdles, Jim opted for the franchise route, becoming the twenty-fifth franchisee of Ames, Iowa–based Duds 'N Suds. He says the parent company helped him bypass some startup glitches, and its group-buying plan eased startup costs a bit. Machine distributors represent a deep well of startup help for the independents who dominate the coin-operated laundry industry. "They install the machines and will help develop a location and lay out a store," says Ben. "Some even build stores from scratch." In addition, distributors service the machines either on a contractual basis, or when the need arises.

Startup costs in large part depend on the amenities you offer. Washing machines can run from $500 for a small top loader to $4,000 for a thirty-pound front loader; dryers average $1,200 to $1,500. Some manufacturers also lease their machines. Main-street locations (and rents) usually are unnecessary. But you may have to add plumbing to accommodate the machines and comply with local codes. "In some communities, the sewer system tap fee can run $1,000 per machine," warns Richard Torp. "If you have thirty machines, that runs into money."

Most operators learn the basics of repair and call in $35-an-hour specialists only for the big jobs. *American Coin-Op* editor Ben Russell, who also operates The Village Laundry in Elmwood Park, Illinois, says repair costs are minimal: "My laundry averages about $3 per machine per month in service charges."

Because laundromats remain basically self-serve, labor costs remain low. Jim Bogen keeps two staffers on board for thirty hours a week. A solo attendant handles the balance of the week. "We start at minimum wage, so labor doesn't cost any more than utilities," he says. In fact, some facilities operate staffless for days on end. Some manufacturers promise machines that will accept credit cards instead of coins in the near future, which could reduce employee needs even further. More likely, because they won't have to worry about handling cash, employees will be free to tend to other chores, such as operating a drop-off service.

Richard Torp figures about 15 percent of all laundries currently offer something more than just machines. But now that the public has experienced the benefits of laundries with pluses, he has no doubt the percentage will increase. Adds Jim Bogen: "Traditionally, customers felt nobody took the effort or time to make the environment more attractive than a bus depot." Now that they've tasted laundry luxury, why in the world would they ever go back to yesterday's unrelieved drudgery?

SOURCES

Industry Association

Coin Laundry Association, 1315 Butterfield Rd., Suite 212, Downers Grove, Ill. 60515 (312) 963-5547

Publication

American Coin-Op, 500 N. Dearborn St., Chicago, Ill. (312) 337-7700

Maid Service

> *"I dream big. I'm thirty-four now and intend to be a millionaire by the time I'm forty."* – Ruby Burgis, Personal Home Care

Low Startup Investment: $150 (liability insurance; classified ads or flyers)

High Startup Investment: $1,000 (putting together a four-employee team)

Time Until Breakeven: One week to three months

Annual Revenues: $15,000-$500,000 (solo at low end; twenty full-time maids at high end)

Annual Pre-tax Profits: $13,000-$200,000

Staffers Needed for Startup (including founder): One

With 45 million working women in this country, is there any wonder that maid services are booming?

If you don't mind housework, there's lots to be said for running a cleaning service. "Getting started was so simple," admits Ruby Burgis, who left a personnel management position at Aetna Insurance to launch Personal Home Care in the Atlanta suburb of Norcross, Georgia, in 1986. Her entry vehicle was an ad in the Gwinett County newspaper's classified section, which landed her "a tremendous response. There's such a need for domestic help," says Ruby.

And the potential? Solo practitioners can't shoot too high, probably no more than $20,000 to $30,000 a year. But add a few employees and let their brooms do the sweeping. If you spend your time managing others and rounding up jobs, you can keep 40 to 50 percent of the take yourself—as profits. The only overhead you need worry about is advertising to collect both employees and clients, relatively simple bookkeeping, a few supplies, and insurance.

There are three aspects to running a maid service. In reverse order of importance, consider:

NEXT TO GODLINESS

Cleaning. "Just because you know how to clean house doesn't mean you know a thing about the housecleaning business," warns a Chicago entrepreneur. "You have to know so much about managing—managing people, managing your time." The importance of delivering a clean house to clients can't be overemphasized, but polishing a house to a shine is the easy part. If you're diligent and pay attention to detail, you can accomplish almost any housekeeping chore.

The key to the cleaning business is organization. To clean efficiently, set and stick to a cleaning routine. Ruby Burgis devised a training program for her maids that begins with a session in her office. There, each maid receives a manual Ruby wrote that walks them through the basics of dusting, vacuuming, glass polishing, and bathroom and kitchen scrubbing. Then she accompanies them on their first job to teach by example. Admitting "I hate housecleaning," Ruby cleans right along with employees on their first house or two to show them her own methods. She provides a checklist for clients who want such extras as laundry or window washing, and tacks on extra charges.

Most operators swear by the team system. Two to four maids visit the same houses every week, so they become familiar with the customers' needs. The team divides the chores, rotating tasks among the members from house to house to reduce monotony. Ruby Burgis disagrees with the buddy system, however. "I want people to have their own personal housekeeper who would be in the house for several hours." A good maid can develop a following.

You can either furnish equipment and supplies or ask to use the customer's. Stocking your own cleaning arsenal insures you have the best ammunition to clean with, and, except for a vacuum, which can cost several hundred dollars, supplies are inexpensive. However, an urban service that relies on public transportation might request that customers provide the equipment so maids won't have to drag mops on buses.

GENERATING LEADS

Finding clientele. You don't need sixty-second spots on prime-time television—inexpensive advertising works just fine in the maid business. You can target specific audiences with flyers stuffed in mailboxes or mailed via zip code. Leave your number on the supermarket bulletin board. One-inch ads in the classified sections of neighborhood or pennysaver newspapers often provide the best leads. If you provide company cars, mark them with your telephone number and logo.

Maids, while no longer only for the rich, aren't for the lower-income brackets either. Target advertising to professional neighborhoods whose households earn $40,000 or more. Families need more help than do singles.

Follow up those leads promptly and at the customer's convenience. You may need to visit people on evenings or weekends to accommodate working people. Some entrepreneurs guess the price for the first visit in order to avoid the nuisance of an estimate trip, but "how can you quote standard fees when a three-bedroom, two-bath house can be eighteen hundred square feet or four thousand?" asks Ruby Burgis. Also, touring the house with the customer allows you to sell extras like carpet cleaning.

To price a job, have in mind an hourly fee per employee (Ruby bases her fees on $12.50 an hour) and guess how long a cleaning will take. Households with children or pets or collections of knick-knacks require more time than homes of professional couples who like sleek, modern furniture and who travel constantly on business. Also, you can offer lower prices for weekly cleanings than monthly marathons, since the house had a thorough scrubbing just the week before.

Carry liability insurance to pay for any breakage. The larger maid services also are bonded to cover theft. Although she spends about $150 a month to blanket six employees with both kinds of insurance, Ruby Burgis says customers rarely ask whether she's covered. "You need the liability, but smaller services can usually just give references in lieu of getting bonded," she says.

While the bulk of your revenues will come from steady residential clients, you can also discover other sources of dirt to clean. For instance, unless you are very busy, don't turn down one-time cleanings for people who are preparing for the holidays; you can charge more for one-shot deals, and they sometimes blossom into regular arrangements once clients see how their houses sparkle. Be creative in your advertising: One service suggests gift certificates as presents for new mothers. Ruby Burgis does some offices for entrepreneurs whose houses she cleans; but she warns that heavy janitorial work requires contracts and a complicated bidding procedure (see Janitorial Service). Also, network with people who have lots of houses to clean, like real estate agents who might recommend you to clean houses before or after a sale. Or check with apartment contractors who need post-construction cleaning.

THE MAIDS

Employees—getting them and keeping them. Don't underestimate the frustrations here. Getting good, reliable people is tough, and you must constantly refill your employee ranks since turnover is notoriously high in this industry. Ruby Burgis uses the same newspapers to advertise for employees and attract customers. In addition, she asks workers to recommend friends who might want jobs. She also lets the state employment service know when she needs maids.

If you think hiring employees is tough, getting them to stay committed for a long time is tougher. "When a maid doesn't show up, I take the job," groans Ruby Burgis. "In a pinch, I've used friends, boyfriends—whoever can help me out." Turnover is a fact of the cleaning entrepreneur's life. But some tricks of the trade make life a little easier.

First, make employees realize their importance. Some franchises issue uniforms to create a professional team spirit.

Second, don't be greedy. Remember, the housekeepers do the hard work, so pay them well. You can outpay most jobs that hire unskilled labor by offering a respectable $6 to $7 an hour and still keep an equal amount to cover overhead and profits. Since your maids likely subcontract as independent operators, you don't pay for benefits like health insurance. Hint: Properly trained employees complete jobs more efficiently, which allows them to squeeze more houses into their cleaning schedule. Since you pay by the job, they make more money and therefore stay on board longer.

Third, offer flexibility. The maids with families particularly like part-time work. If you need more employees to work Friday afternoons, pay them a bonus.

THE MATCHMAKER APPROACH

Ruby Burgis, who started Personal Home Care as a typical maid service, changed her focus in 1987 to deal with the constant employee turnover issue. Now, instead of taking responsibility herself for maids who clean clients' homes, she matches maids and households. It works this way: After an individual answers her ad, Ruby trains the maid in specific houses that contract with her for services. After a two- or three-week training stint, during which time the maid gets a salary, the maid buys the rights to clean that house, as well as others that Ruby lines up. If a homeowner decides within fourteen days that the housekeeper is not up to par, Ruby finds a replacement. "A contract is based on the amount of monthly income it will bring," she explains. "If it's a weekly house that pays $50 for each cleaning, I charge $200 for that contract. If the maid does five houses a week, the fee would be $1,000."

As a result of the new approach, Ruby still has to attract maids to train and customers to clean for, but she doesn't worry about a maid quitting after six weeks.

Meanwhile, Ruby points out a side benefit of her business. Since she hates housework, she knows exactly who to call when she wants her *own* house cleaned.

SOURCES

Industry Associations

Cleaning Management Institute, 1550-D Rockfield Blvd., Irvine, Calif. 92718 (714) 770-5008

National Maintenance Management Association, P.O. Box 3916, Texas City, Tex. 77592 (713) 871-8236

Self-storage Center

> *"As income-producing properties offering positive cash flow, self-storage centers can be financially rewarding." – Michael Knuppe, AAAAA Rent-A-Space*

Low Startup Investment: $750,000 (suburban locale)

High Startup Investment: $2.5 million (urban center)

Time Until Breakeven: Three to five years

Annual Revenues: $100,000-$125,000

Annual Pre-tax Profits: $10,000-$125,000

Staffers Needed for Startup (including founder): One

Michael Knuppe, who operates eleven AAAAA Rent-A-Space centers from San Leandro, California, holds up an industry survey that reveals just one out of ten Americans even knows what a self-storage facility is. "Think of the untapped potential!" he exclaims. The potential he refers to extends beyond the kind of customers with whom the industry was pioneered: individuals who leased space to store out-of-season water skis in self-storage facilities. Mike believes other markets are thirsting to be tapped—whether they know it or not. "Retailers can store excess inventory with us. Doctors and lawyers can keep files. I haven't yet figured out what group can't use us!"

The eighteen thousand or so self-storage facilities across the country are, simply put, big closets that rent by the month. The 88-percent majority of Americans who don't include the phrase "self-storage facility" in their lexicon might recognize the misnomer "mini-warehouse." But unlike a warehouse tenant, self-storage customers don't share the key with other renters and the landlord assumes no responsibility for the property stored inside. Also, self-storage facilities take myriad sizes and shapes. Storage is not a type of building but a use of real estate.

The mini-storage business began in the late 1960s in the fast-growing South and Southwest, where storage space was at a premium. The climate in those regions didn't require enclosed garages, and new houses springing up often lacked basements. Recognizing the need for storage space, some enterprising individuals divided old sheds into surrogate garages for overcrowded homeowners, and the industry took off. Mike Knuppe, a developer who entered the business in 1971 when he decided running self-storage centers beat building apartment houses and condominiums, suspects the more lucrative areas of the late 1980s and early 1990s will be in "northeastern and southeastern suburbs with populations of one hundred thousand. Then the opportunities could swing back to the West."

REAL ESTATE

Mike Knuppe isn't the only real estate investor who bolted to the self-storage industry. Contractors relate to the tenant-landlord relationship inherent in renting storage facilities, and positively gloat over the relative advantages of renting space to boxes and furniture rather than to people. "You don't have to do call-backs on leaky toilets," Mike explains. "Also, we used to build properties and try to sell before the interest rates ate us up. Self-storage facilities produce income from the first tenant."

Contractors also understand why the cost of building storage centers often surpass seven figures. "The average-size facility among our association members runs about forty-seven thousand square feet," says Gail Pohl, executive director for the Self-Service Storage Association. In contrast to the few mom-and-pop holdovers who launched the industry with five- to ten-unit garage spaces, today's entrepreneurs need at least thirty thousand square feet of property to build on. Unless you reach the three hundred customers to fill all that air, you won't be able to afford a site in a well-trafficked section of town. Those couple of requirements mean the real estate alone could run you $1 million in a pricey suburb.

Then there's the facility itself. "We used to build sheds with doors for $5 a square foot," says Mike Knuppe. Now, such elaborate extras as double-paneled bronze doors, indoor-outdoor carpeting, and computerized alarm systems push building costs to $30 to $50 a square foot. Some multi-story facilities in cities require elevators and climate control.

Okay, but is it worth it? A lot of heavy investors think so, including some franchises and conglomerates that, rather than assume debt, raise money to build units through stock market public offerings. "The typical return without debt service runs 20 to 25 percent of revenues," says Mike Knuppe, whose operations cover a total of 1.25 million square feet spread out over the San Francisco Bay area. Using his figures, a typical thirty-thousand-square-foot warehouse brings in revenues of about $200,000 a year. Once you pay off your construction loan, you keep at least $40,000, assuming you hire a manager to oversee the property. If you operate the facility yourself, keep another $15,000 to $20,000 as salary. The Self-Service Storage Association says facilities larger than thirty-five thousand square feet usually justify a manager living on the premises. So if you operate a larger center, you get an apartment in the bargain, worth maybe $6,000 a year.

TAKE IT EASY

Frankly, a single self-storage facility is pretty easy to oversee, say the experts. In fact, many small-town centers combine storage with other services, such as truck leasing. Basic duties include three functions:

- Maintaining the outside of buildings (most facilities are concrete, steel, or other easy-to-care-for material)
- Collecting monthly rents
- Signing on new customers

The industry is still grappling with the question of whom to hire to manage the facilities. Originally, most on-site managers were retired couples who saw in the opportunity a way to supplement their incomes that would put relatively few demands on them. When the period between startup and full occupancy lengthened in the early 1980s (figure on a couple of years to fill all your cubicles), "the management companies hired individuals with sales expertise." So recalls Mike Knuppe, who cuts an eighty-three-person payroll for his eleven facilities. However, the higher salaries that the sales breed demanded—which often included a percentage of the gross—was not justified by the speedier occupancy. Owners who do not manage the facilities themselves now are experimenting with a third approach. "I'm hiring retired couples from the military or with police backgrounds who are not quite as old," says Mike. He offers them the same percentage cut he gave salespeople, but keeps base salaries lower.

The sales effort should include consumer marketing and a more concerted effort to attract business users, remembering that a whole sea of potential users don't even know you're out there. "Definitely plan on 5 percent of your gross for advertising," Mike counsels. In addition to Yellow Pages and direct marketing, companies increasingly add radio and even television in reasonably priced markets.

Once a customer calls, Mike says you run an 85-percent chance of closing a sale right on the phone—if you drop everything to hold the caller's hand. "People call a storage center during traumatic times in their lives. There's a death or divorce, or they're getting ready to move, and they need to store items. It sounds corny, but you need to be their knight in shining armor, their salvation in a crisis."

The other sales approach involves calling directly on big potential users, namely businesses. Sell them on the fact that they can free up floor space and stock more top selling items by stashing slow movers or out-of-season items with you. Once you land a business customer, life indeed becomes easier. "They're longer-term clients than consumers who just use us to store items while they're moving," says Mike Knuppe. On top of that, businesses more likely pay on time.

WHAT'S IN THOSE BOXES?

While the delinquency problem may sound scary, industry insiders say only 1 to 2 percent of all customers refuse to pay their bills. And, to make life easier, about three-quarters of all states spell out specific procedures to gain possession of the goods in the event of nonpayment, detailing circumstances in which a self-service center can auction off a tenant's property.

"Unfortunately," admits Mike, "I don't know of a mini-storage facility that hasn't been caught" accepting illegal items, including drugs and arms. AAAAA virtually eliminated this danger by working closely with the Drug Enforcement Bureau. "They even train their dogs on our facilities." Also, when the manager announces that AAAAA photographs each customer, most unsavory suspects scoot without a word.

As the industry discovers competition, "you need to create a strategic differential." Mike's strategy: "To close the gap on the moving experience, I rent trucks and sell padlocks and generally make life easier for those who are moving." Service and flexibility are increasingly important as well. AAAAA offers forty sizes of rental units, ranging from $12 to $185 a month, "so price is never the reason not to rent with us," says Mike. And some enterprising souls have surpassed merely giving advice; they offer to take over the real headaches. For example, one service delivers modules to a customer's backyard. The customer packs items inside, and the storage company picks up the module to cart it back to the lot. How's that for pick up and delivery?

SOURCES

Industry Association

Self-Service Storage Association, P.O. Box 110, Eureka Springs, Ark. 72632 (501) 253-7701

Publications

Self-Service Storage, P.O. Box 110, Eureka Springs, Ark. 72632 (501) 253-7701

The Mini Messenger, 2531 W. Dunlap Ave., Suite 201, Phoenix, Ariz. 85021 (800) 824-6864

Water Conditioning Company

> "I left a $55,000-a-year job—in 1978 dollars, mind you —to start this water conditioning business. That was the smartest move I ever made. I wouldn't sell my company now for less than a half million." – Harold Posey, Posey Fresh Water

---

Low Startup Investment: $20,000 (garage-based operation; truck, minimum inventory)

High Startup Investment: $50,000 (warehouse and a small sales and installation staff)

Time Until Breakeven: Three months to one year

Annual Revenues: $250,000-$5 million

Annual Pre-tax Profits: $35,000-$1 million

Staffers Needed for Startup (including founder): One to three

---

American drinking water has been called *the* political time-bomb of the 1990s. In a Federal Environmental Protection Agency survey of 3,012 adults, 84 percent saw water pollution as a major national problem. In a Harris Poll, two out of three respondents called the condition of our water "a very serious problem." A General Accounting Office study cited one-fifth of the country's sixty-five thousand community water systems as falling below minimum safety standards.

Okay, Americans voice outrage that the H_2O flowing so freely from our taps may be poisoning us. But are we doing anything about it? According to the Water Quality Association's latest figures, we spent $3 billion in 1985 to treat water. But industry observers say we ain't seen nothing yet. RainSoft Water Conditioning Co., which franchises from Elk Grove Village, Illinois, estimates that just 7 percent of the market for home water treatment devices has been sated. That, say dealers, gives them a huge market as the country becomes more and more aware of the problem. More than nine out of ten households remain to respond to their promises of pure water. "Not every home is a potential sale," says Harold Posey, who operates Posey Fresh Water from Houston. "But nearly every home is."

IT'S A LARGE NEIGHBORHOOD

To show how much faith he has in the growth of his industry, Harold Posey invites competitors to move in next door, saying there's more than enough business to go around. Harold has installed at least seven thousand water treatment units in Houston since 1978, and insists his own market remains less than 10 percent tapped. In 1987, he reported sales of $3.5 million and says he does better than 15 percent pre-tax profits.

Harold Posey knew he was on to a good thing when he first discovered the water conditioning industry as a vice president at ITT Financial in Denver a decade ago. He was a banker back then, and, "when customers applied for financing, I would get a finance statement on their business. I reviewed finances for water conditioning companies each year, and started noticing how fast these dealers were accumulating wealth. I began to compare them with other industries. The more I looked, the more intrigued I became."

Unable to withstand the lure any longer, Harold bought a Rain-Soft franchise in Houston where he had once lived. "I remembered how bad the water was—and how dynamic the city." Those two elements convinced him to invest $50,000 to set up shop, which primarily involved marketing.

Even today, Harold budgets 12 percent of gross for advertising and lead development, on top of what he spends on the sales staff's salaries. He builds sales through two approaches: telemarketing to generate leads, followed by direct door-to-door sales to nail down those leads. He turns a battery of six full-time and six part-time telephone operators loose to cold-call potential customers, such as upper-income households or businesses like restaurants or dry cleaners that need especially good water. Only after an operator gets a nibble does the eighteen-person sales force go into action. "That approach keeps the salespeople in front of qualified buyers," says Harold. "I don't send them to a house on stilts with chickens in the front yard because they won't buy the systems." An average Posey Fresh Water sale hovers around $2,500, which includes a system to soften the water, a drinking-water unit under the kitchen sink, installation, and a four-year supply of soap to keep the tap water clean.

Unlike most products, you must customize each water treatment package to a particular client's needs. That means you have to test each tap, since additives differ by water district and household. But, thanks to training available from vendors and the Water Quality Association, you don't have to be a chemical engineer to test the waters or a mechanical genius to install the units.

You target two basic customers with water treatment equipment: residential and commercial. Most sales so far involve units to soften water and make it taste better. More expensive units can remove contaminants in drinking water as well. "Most water supplied by municipalities in this country is potable—meaning safe," says Harold Posey. "But it's not palatable—meaning it tastes *baaad.*"

Whether you approach a residential or a commercial customer, and whether that customer is interested in water treatment or water conditioning, you have three basic ways to make money:

- Sales
- Leases
- Maintenance

SALES

To maximize your cash flow, try to sell products outright. Particularly in the early days, a rush of cash from a $750 reverse-osmosis unit feels real good going into the pocket. If you work it right, you don't even have to pay for the inventory until a customer places an order. If you sport a healthy credit rating, many dealers waive their fees as long as you stock equipment in a bonded warehouse. Of course, once it leaves the warehouse on its way to a customer, you'll have to cover the cost of the item.

Large industrial companies and businesses generally prefer to buy equipment rather than rent it. Buyers, they reason, claim depreciation as an expense and spend less in the long haul. In addition to contacting hotels and hospitals directly, you can call on contractors and engineers putting up new sites. Businesses are particularly good customers for a couple of reasons. Sometimes fees top $100,000 on a single, large installation. One system to purify water for a hospital's kidney dialysis machine costs about $30,000, and a hospital usually buys more than a solo unit. Also, a business lead often means repeat business. A contractor who likes your water in a fast food operation might ask you to outfit a white-tablecloth restaurant as well.

LEASES

"Renting is like prostitution: You sell it and still own it," grins Harold Posey. It works like this: You front the $400 to $500 equipment costs and charge customers $20 a month to use your unit. Within two years you've collected your entire investment. And, since those $20 payments come in indefinitely, everything else is gravy. "Leasing is going to be my retirement," says Harold, who hopes to increase his lease business from 10 percent of sales to 30 percent in the next year or two.

Homeowners in particular like leasing since the $20 monthly fees don't sting the way a $700 purchase does. Now that operators are selling more water treatment systems to middle-income Americans instead of just the wealthy, observers predict that leasing represents the wave of the future.

SERVICE

One more way to build residual income involves service contracts. One out of every five Posey Fresh Water customers spends $10.50 a month on a preventive maintenance contract. Once a month, Harold's service department delivers salt, which is used to clean the unit's filters, right to the customer's door. Posey Fresh Water also dispatches technicians to fix anything that might go wrong.

Harold warns startups not to promise service until you have the volume to support technicians. He also warns that maintenance headaches throb until you learn proper installation. Once you pass through the learning curve, though, service calls likely will diminish. "I have a lot fewer problems today than I did in the beginning, even though I have seven thousand accounts out there now," says Harold.

Water-softening units have, until recently, been the staple of the industry. Now, dealers sense an increasing willingness to invest in drinking-water systems as well. That's good news for treatment companies who can make bigger sales by offering both options.

SOURCE

Industry Association

Water Quality Association, 4151 Naperville Rd., Lisle, Ill. 60532
(312) 369-1600

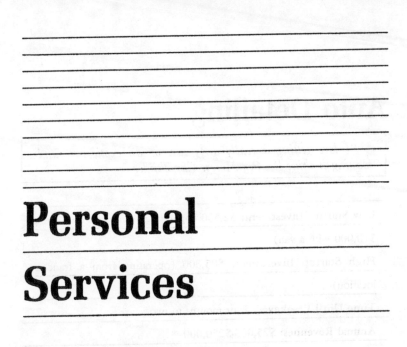

Personal
Services

Auto Detailing

"I love getting a really dirty car, or an exotic car, and making it shine." – Peg Mosey, Car Tender

---

Low Startup Investment: $2,500 (operating from your own garage; $10,000 with a van)

High Startup Investment: $85,000 (operating from a franchised location)

Time Until Breakeven: Four months to two years

Annual Revenues: $25,000-$250,000

Annual Pre-tax Profits: $15,000-$100,000

Staffers Needed for Startup (including founder): One

During slack times when Peg Mosey sold Fords in Fort Wayne, Indiana, she wandered into the cleanup area to watch the staff polishing and vacuuming cars before putting them in the showroom. "I used to spend two to three hours a week cleaning my own car and I thought, if you use professional products, this is not hard work. It's just time-consuming."

In the summer of 1985, Peg borrowed $5,000, using a certificate of deposit as collateral. She paid $400 for supplies, and bought a buffer and a wet-dry vac. Then she plopped down rent money for the building that was to house her new auto detailing business. With what was left over, Peg bought signs for her own spotlessly clean 1980 Grand Prix that displayed her phone number and address. Voilà! Car Tender was in business.

THE OLD JALOPIES NEVER LOOKED SO GOOD

According to the Automotive Vehicle Manufacturers Association (AVMA), the typical passenger car on the road today is 7.5 years old, up from 5.5 years in 1970. That's the oldest average since the Korean War. People hang on to their cars because new ones are so expensive these days. And, whether new or old, the cars are being better taken care of. For example, the International Carwash Association estimated carwash revenues at $8 billion in 1986, up a half-billion from the year before as volume climbed.

But it costs hundreds of thousands of dollars to build a conveyor or brush carwash plant, and it can take years to recover your investment. Entrepreneurs like Peg Mosey have found an inexpensive way to enter the auto appearance field, and are cleaning up. Instead of counting on high volume to bring in the bucks, they charge handsomely for doing an extraordinary cleaning job, one car at a time, by hand. Called detailing, the work they do would make a dress sergeant proud. "I shampoo seats, do the dash with Q-tips, the chrome with steel wool," Peg rattles off. "I completely dress the engine, treat all the rubber." Her twenty-nine-step process takes up to five hours per car, and runs $125.

It's tricky, but you can also ride into the business by way of the executive parking lot. Some detailers outfit vans with the equipment they need and round up BMW and Caddy owners as they leave their cars on the way to board meetings. To set up a mobile shop, you need access to running water and permission from the municipality as well as the company whose lot you camp out in.

If you don't want to go it alone, you have the option of franchising. Boca Raton, Florida–based Tidy Car figures a new franchisee needs $75,000 to $85,000 to open its average fifteen-hundred to two-thousand-square-foot shops. That capital covers the $20,000 Tidy Car licensing fee and $15,000 for a store-opening media blitz, as well as equipment, inventory, leasehold improvements, and payments on a courtesy van to shuffle customers in and out. Since Tidy Car gives you four weeks of training, you don't need to know the first detail about detailing before signing on. The parent company also teaches you related skills, such as how to install sunroofs.

FROM VOLKSWAGENS TO JAGS

Independent detailers cater to several groups: luxury car owners and corporations, car dealers, or limousine operators to whom image is everything. Peg Mosey has rubbed sparkles onto everything from a '67 Corvette show car where she spent days removing every last speck of dust from the engine (the owner won top points in the cleanliness category), to a twenty-three-foot travel trailer. "That was like cleaning someone's apartment. It took six hours."

Peg recommends passenger cars go through the complete treatment twice a year and offers discounts to customers like the Mercedes owner who has her wash his car once a month. But "car dealers are my cushion," because they provide steadier work than the individual owners of Porsches and BMWs. Peg spends a little less time detailing a dealer's used car, but charges just $65. "They can usually get a couple of hundred dollars more at auction for repossessions if the cars are really clean," says Peg.

In addition to the luxury and car-dealer market, Tidy Car considers all of the 140 million or so passenger cars on the road its potential customers—as well as the 35 million pickup trucks and vans. To entice such volume, it charges a little less than most independents and advertises a lot more heavily. Its franchise material also notes this: "There are many nonretail areas where significant revenues can be generated, such as insurance companies (i.e., flood-damaged interiors), commercial fleet accounts, institutional and government accounts, body shops, car rental companies, and new-car dealers who may purchase Tidy Car services at wholesale prices for resale to new-car buyers as part of their option package."

Gary Goranson, then a regional sales manager for Magnavox of Canada, began Tidy Car in 1975. He originally sold his car-polishing and detailing services from a van parked on the street. Tidy Car's more than four hundred locations still offer those services, along with such extras as window tinting, rust proofing, and sunroof installations. Gary's theory: Once you get customers in the door, why stop with just cleaning their cars?

TRAFFIC

Even if you start from your own garage, you might consider leasing a visible location as soon as feasible. How will the drive-in traffic find you if you're tucked away in suburbia? Tidy Car is partial to retail auto malls, but also approves freestanding sites close to major retail shopping areas in an "upscale environment." Other major inducements include a speed limit of forty-five m.p.h. or less (so drivers have time to see the prominent sign as they pass) and a daily traffic count of twenty thousand vehicles.

Although it buys the old saw about location, location, location being the three most crucial aspects of success, Tidy Car says "the next three factors, in order of importance, are advertising, advertising, and advertising." Marketing is even more important if you can't afford a prime Main Street address. Peg Mosey uses flyers, newspapers, magazines, and TV, and gave away a detailing job as a promotion in a radio station tie-in. Tidy Car insists new franchisees set aside $15,000 for a splashy opening ad campaign, and follow that up by budgeting 5 to 10 percent of revenues for advertising on a regular basis. Don't be afraid to call car dealers and other potential corporate clients and offer them package rates. The worst they can say is "No thanks."

In her first year in business, Peg Mosey hired an employee to buff the cars and still netted $15,000. She is bullish on the future, noting "the consumer market hasn't been tapped." While the government won't let Tidy Car talk about profitability since each franchisee differs, a spokesperson allows this: "Most of the [older] dealers are remodeling and building new Tidy Car buildings—and buying new cars and boats for their families."

SOURCES

Industry Association

International Carwash Association, 1 Imperial Place, 1 E. 22nd St., Suite 400, Lombard, Ill. 60148 (312) 495-0100

Automotive Tune-up Center

> *"The business is growing and changing so dramatically; I feel I'm on the edge. My goal is to make us the experts in our market."* — Susan Gerber, Precision Tune franchisee

---

Low Startup Investment: $100,000 (leasing a center)

High Startup Investment: $350,000 (building a center on prime real estate)

Time Until Breakeven: Six months to one year

Annual Revenues: $235,000-$500,000

Annual Pre-tax Profits: $35,000-$110,000

Staffers Needed for Startup (including founder): Three to six

---

In 1979, following a stint as head nurse at the University of Iowa hospital, Susan Gerber moved with her family to Spokane, Washington. With two small children, she decided she wanted the flexibility of being her own boss. "I explored restaurants (the classic business people want to start) and a children's clothing store (I'd bought enough children's clothing, so I felt I should know something about the field)." But nothing seemed right until she stumbled upon the automobile tune-up business. Her husband Hank, a neurosurgeon, races sports cars as a hobby. "The whole family goes to the races," Susan explains. "So the tune-up business attracted me."

Susan Gerber readily admits her initial reservations: "I knew how to change tires and not much else about cars." But a trip to Precision Tune's Beaumont, Texas, headquarters reassured her that she could manage the business. "They showed us the men who were signing on as franchisees who didn't have an auto background either." To this day, Susan Gerber—who now operates four of her own Precision Tune sites and oversees two others in the capacity of subfranchisor—has never tuned a car. But she's plenty busy managing the books and staff, placing advertising, and handling customer relations. Meanwhile, "our best center did over $400,000 in revenues last year and we did way over $1 million total. Our returns were *very* healthy on that."

OPEC FALL-OUT

Tune-up centers and other automotive aftermarket businesses gained momentum following OPEC's oil embargo in the 1970s. *The Wall Street Journal* estimates one hundred thousand full-service filling stations and three thousand auto dealerships left the repair business in the past decade. Many operators responded to what Stan Stephenson, publisher of *Chilton's Motor Age Magazine,* calls "the gas-and-go syndrome." Self-service pumps replaced service stations that checked under the hood and operated mechanic bays. "Periodic car maintenance plummeted precipitously," says Stan.

That's not to say that drivers don't need their cars repaired. In fact, new computerized auto technology makes do-it-yourself repairs less likely. And busy working couples would rather drive to a quick tune-up center than leave their cars overnight at the repair shop. In addition, people keep their increasingly expensive cars longer—an average of 7.5 years, according to the Automotive Vehicle Manufacturing Association. And today's smaller, four-cylinder cars achieve 11 to 15 percent better gas mileage following a tune-up, according to Precision Tune literature.

In place of full-service repair shops, America has embraced auto specialists: transmission businesses, lube shops, brake stations, tune-up centers, and more. *The Wall Street Journal* estimates that twenty-six hundred Jiffy Lube, Midas Muffler, and other auto service franchises operated in 1987.

By concentrating on one specialty, you cut startup costs dramatically because you don't need sophisticated equipment to diagnose and treat every car ailment under the hood. "Realistically, you'd need $1.5 million to equip and operate a full-service repair center today," says Stan Stephenson. But you can launch a tune-up service for under $120,000. You also don't need a Ph.D. in auto repair if you concentrate on one area. That's a good thing, because "training is getting longer and longer because the technology increasingly is more complex," says Stan. Even technicians who specialize need elaborate training to understand today's complex cars. Precision Tune requires mechanics to complete a four-week certification course, followed periodically by in-person or video-taped refresher classes.

FRANCHISE ROUTE

Most newcomers to the automotive aftermarket join franchises or build multiple centers to establish a presence in a market. "It's the pizzazz that separates the franchises from individual operators," says Edward L. Kaufman, an industry consultant. "It's tougher to do business without big company resources for advertising, promotion, signage, training, and a warranty on merchandise." Still, he cites opportunities for individuals with "a serious, professional attitude about fixing a car," and doesn't discourage independents who know their stuff.

But for individuals like Susan Gerber who lack an automotive background, observers recommend hooking up with a franchise. "If you follow their plans, you cannot help but make money," says Stan Stephenson. Industry pre-tax profits often hit 16 to 22 percent on revenues of $200,000 to $500,000.

Precision Tune recommends franchisees put aside $101,000 to $120,000 in addition to real estate costs to start a tune-up center. That capital covers the franchise fee and equipment for a three- or four-bay facility. Depending on the location, expect to spend another $1,500 to $5,000 monthly to rent an eighteen-thousand-square-foot site—or $84,000 to $108,000 to construct your own. Whether your specialty is tune-ups, mufflers, or transmissions, you'll want a visible location with heavy traffic, since much of your business comes from drivers who notice your shop as they chug to work each morning.

In addition, plan on heavy promotion. Precision Tune franchisees commit 9 percent of gross sales to advertising. In markets where air time is inexpensive, or where multiple franchisees band together to share costs, television is the most popular medium, followed by radio, newspaper, and direct-mail coupons.

"There are two kinds of ads," explains Susan Gerber. "We emphasize price through coupons in direct mail or in print." The parent company estimates that the Precision Tune tune-up, averaging $32 to $49 depending on the area of the country, costs "as much as 50 to 100 percent less than competition."

Susan says another important draw along with price is expertise. "We're qualified to take care of the technical problems of today's cars. We talk about the extensive training of our technicians." Precision Tune ads also point out that their franchisees tune a car in about forty minutes—far faster than repair shops that ask customers to leave their transportation for hours or days.

ALL THINGS TO ALL PEOPLE

Susan says the very meaning of the phrase "tune-up" is changing. "People tend to think of replacing the spark plugs and cap and rotor," she says. "But carburetors have given way to fuel injection; new cars don't even have points and condensors. We've made the equipment and training changes necessary to address the different car we tune today."

Precision Tune responded to the modern car by expanding its services. In addition to the tune-ups and oil changes the company always offered, its mechanics now replace distributors and perform fuel-injection repairs. Other auto franchises have broadened their menus as well. For example, some lube shops also repair car air conditioning.

The approach expands the revenue base as it attracts customers for multiple jobs. "Just as with McDonald's, which now has a salad bar and a fish sandwich, a one-product-line marketing effort is not feasible for automotive shops in the long run," says Stan Stephenson. The balancing act of the future will involve offering just enough services: too many will require the very expertise and startup costs that pushed general-repair stations out of the business.

SOURCES

Industry Association

Independent Automotive Service Association, 1901 Airport Freeway, Bedford, Tex. 76021 (817) 283-6205

Publications

Chilton's Motor Age Magazine, 201 King of Prussia Rd., Radnor, Pa. 19089 (215) 964-4229

Automotive Marketing, Chilton Way, Radnor, Pa. 19089 (215) 964-4394

Service Station Management, 950 Lee St., Des Plaines, Ill. 60016 (312) 296-0770

Consultants

Lindsey-Kaufman Co., 53 Hamilton Place, Tenafly, N.J. 07670 (201) 567-6158

National Institute for Automotive Service Excellence, 1920 Association Dr., Reston, Va. 22091 (703) 648-3838

Beauty Salon

> *"We're not magicians or doctors, but the beauty business is part of the healing industry. Making someone look good makes them more confident. There's great satisfaction in knowing I made a difference in someone's life."*—Erika Zimmerman, Erika's Hair-Um Inc.

Low Startup Investment: $2,000 (to outfit a room at home with used equipment)

High Startup Investment: $150,000 (for a large, multipurpose salon)

Time Until Breakeven: Two months to four years

Annual Revenues: $20,000-$250,000

Annual Pre-tax Profits: $15,000-$75,000 (tips can add $5,000 to $10,000)

Staffers Needed for Startup (including founder): One to four

"I remember a woman who had horrible eyebrows," shudders Erika Zimmerman, proprietor of Erika's Hair-Um Inc., in the Chicago suburb of Darien. "The arch made her look so stern, so I asked if she found it easy to make friends. She was distant with me, too, but she admitted she'd always had a hard time with people.

"Well, I told her there was nothing wrong with her face," continues Erika, lacing positive reinforcement along with recommendations that she reshape the woman's eyebrows. "I said her face was classic, but her eyebrows gave her a domineering look. You know that woman was so grateful! She said, 'I've had to go through my whole life without someone pointing out what a simple change in appearance could mean!' "

ONE-STOP BEAUTY SHOPPING

Observers suspect beauty shops of the future will fall into two camps: franchises that offer low-cost haircuts and deal in volume; and full-service salons like Erika Zimmerman's that provide, along with cuts and perms and coloring, such specialties as eyebrow arching, skin care, manicures, body massages, and even fitness facilities. According to a 1986 survey conducted by *Modern Salon* magazine, the average salon still pulls 42 percent of its gross from haircuts, 32 percent from perms, and 12 percent from hair coloring. That leaves just 14 percent from other areas, including nail care, retail sales, and skin care. (In addition, many of the country's 152,339 hair-care salons that do not offer additional services themselves rent space to concessionaires.

But the dependence on hair care alone appears to be changing. For example, *Modern Salon* says 54 percent of those salons that offered manicures increased their nail-care business between 1985 and 1986. Of course, you can still start with just hair care and grow. But you should have a good idea of which path you want to pursue, since growth will depend on one of two approaches: Either you must pull in lots of customers for hair care, or you can sell more services to fewer customers. Your pricing, your advertising, your equipment purchases, even whether you chose to start as an independent or a franchise may all depend on which star you shoot for.

Erika Zimmerman gambled on the supermarket over the fast-food approach when she spent $100,000 to create Erika's Hair-Um in a former residential site in 1980. In addition to equipment purchases for six hair stations and a skin-care and steam-and-massage room, the cash went for visual effects. Erika gutted the entire house, knocking out the attic to create a cathedral ceiling and skylights. She also landscaped the outside with pine and apple trees. The entrepreneur felt that establishing a special ambiance would alert customers that she was more than the traditional beauty parlor. "When I opened, there was no such thing as a total concept salon under one roof," Erika says. "Still many beauticians haven't visualized the upgrading of the industry." Has the gamble worked? Evidently. Erika estimates half of 1987's $157,000 gross came from skin and nail care.

WHERE THE CASH COMES FROM

Your first expense goes not for your own beauty boutique, but for your training. The national license requires fifteen hundred hours of schooling, which you can get part time or in about six months of full-time study at numerous schools throughout the country. Expect tuition to run around $3,000.

Most freshman beauticians sign on with an existing shop both to gain experience and build clientele who will follow when they open their own boutique. While you're working in someone else's establishment, polish skills and learn other elements of your trade, such as skin care and makeup.

A well-run shop can cover rent, utilities, and miscellaneous costs (such as advertising and bookkeeping) through retail sales. Many salons neglect the natural add-on business of selling shampoo, makeup, and even accessories such as jewelry and scarves. Margins are high, the items take little space, and carefully selected products appeal to customers who are already predisposed to look stylish. The sales pitch can be subtle. You can easily afford to give 10 to 20 percent of the retail price as commissions to stylists who recommend the superior products you stock.

After you cover overhead, your only other expense is the talent you employ. Most salons pay commissions, splitting the price of each haircut, makeup, or manicure fifty-fifty with the employee. (In addition, good beauticians often pull a third of their salary in tips.) Some beauty shops even charge stylists for supplies. Another approach is to contract with stylists who rent space from you and charge their own rates.

Depending on your salary arrangements with employees—and whether you count your own paycheck as an expense—expect to keep between one-third to one-half of the fees you collect as profits.

SELLING BEAUTY

Beauty parlors typically advertise in newspapers and the Yellow Pages, or hand out flyers announcing specials. But letting the services sell themselves is your most effective marketing tool. You can do this in three ways:

■ Make each element of your boutique visible. "A customer having her hair permed will see another who's having a body massage and realize how relaxing that looks," observes Erika Zimmerman. "It's contagious. She asks for a massage too." Ask stylists to recommend manicures while they're coloring a client's hair; throw in a bonus to the employee who generates the most nail business of the month.

■ Build steady clientele. For example, instead of selling a facial here and there, package treatments. Erika offers a five-treatment skin-care special for $155 and points out to customers that, if paid for separately, it's a $260 value.

Also, you can call on groups such as nursing homes and offer to do their hair at a discount during slow morning hours. And don't neglect your contacts. Erika sells gift certificates to a plastic surgeon and a cosmetic dentist. "When they're finished with patients, they send them to us for a complementary treatment," she explains.

■ Involve your customers as salespeople. Some promotions are apparent to the customer. You can give away a free manicure with every three friends a customer brings in. Your other marketing partnership with a customer is less conspicious—but more effective than any advertising you'll ever buy. Namely, get your customers to recommend your establishment. Hair-Um's skin-care business boomed when Erika packaged treatments not only because of the perceived value, but also because results are much more obvious with weekly skin care than with sporadic treatments. Customers sign on for repeat packages and act as walking billboards. Their friends remark on the glow, and clients recommend Erika.

Knowing the value of word of mouth, Erika and her five stylists take pains to teach clients how to care for their new hair-dos or show them how to perform at-home skin-care techniques. The longer customers look good, the longer their friends will ask for recommendations.

SOURCES

Industry Associations

National Hairdressers and Cosmetologist Association, 3510 Olive St., St. Louis, Mo. 63103 (314) 534-7980

Associated Master Barbers and Beauticians of America, 219 Greenwich Rd., Charlotte, N.C. 28211 (704) 366-5177

Intercoiffure America, 540 Robert E. Lee, New Orleans, La. 70124 (504) 282-4907

National Beauty Culturists' League, 25 Logan Circle, N.W., Washington, D.C. 20005 (202) 332-2695

Publications

American Salon, 747 3rd Ave., New York, N.Y. 10017 (212) 418-4100

Modern Salon Magazine, 400 Knightsbridge Parkway, Lincolnshire, Ill. 60069 (312) 634-2600

Consultant

National Association of Accredited Cosmetology Schools, 1990 M St., N.W., Washington, D.C. 20036 (202) 775-0311

Clothing Alteration Shop

> *"I've found an idea that I can leverage: First I get one or two stores to work, then show somebody else how to do it, then one hundred somebodies. I can grow to be the Baron of Alterations."*–Paul Malham, ASAP Alterations & Monograms

---

Low Startup Investment: $65,000 (small strip-center site)

High Startup Investment: $120,000 (franchise in regional mall)

Time Until Breakeven: Six months to two years

Annual Revenues: $25,000-$250,000

Annual Pre-tax Profits: $20,000-$60,000

Staffers Needed for Startup (including founder): Two to seven

---

Traditional tailors are literally a dying breed. The sixty-year-old tailors who apprenticed for years in Europe before opening single-room, ill-lit studios in urban lofts find few successors as they retire. Basically, the profession no longer can compete with mass manufacturers of suits.

A STITCH IN TIME

While corner tailors may be a vestige of former times, their evolutionary offspring—spiffy alteration shops in high-traffic shopping malls—have found their niche and are thriving in it. Customers drop by to have the seams let out on their favorite (but just-too-snug) suits. The best sources of business, however, are the retailers in the mall who send customers for alterations on brand new clothing. "The last thing retailers want to be involved in is alterations," says Paul Malham, who operates ASAP Alterations & Monograms with his wife, Beverly. Also, "The woman who used to stay home and sew works today." Even if she knows a back stitch from a square knot, she's not about to spend evenings hemming skirts.

ASAP is a success story, all right: The Malhams operate two company-owned stores in Atlanta malls and franchise units in Huntsville, Alabama, and San Antonio, Texas, with another ten franchises on the way. But, as do most businesses, ASAP required careful construction—and a little bit of luck. Paul, a New Jersey insurance broker, and Beverly, proprietor of an Atlanta housewares shop, met as Hunger Project volunteers. When they decided to get married in 1983, "it was easier for me to move," recalls Paul. While he was slowly building an insurance-customer base in his new home town, Kitty Evans, another Hunger Project alumni, asked Paul to help expand her alterations business. "Kitty fit flight attendants for the airlines and wanted to contract with department stores to do their alterations," says Paul.

Kitty and Paul visited a nearby regional mall to test her idea: "We would pick up garments to be altered in a van, bring them to Kitty's facilities, and return them at the end of every week," Paul explains. But the stores saw even that much alteration involvement as too much of a hassle. "Each store we called on said they wanted nothing to do with alterations, period. But each one said they would be happy to refer business our way."

References wouldn't help, however, because Kitty's workroom was eight miles down the highway near the airport, too far for retail customers to travel. "But after hearing the same spiel from different retailers for the tenth time," says Paul, "it dawned on me that we should open a store in the mall." The next day, Kitty and Paul visited a different mall with an altered proposition: If they opened a service within the mall, would retailers send them business? "They all loved the idea," says Paul.

UPSCALE CONTEMPORARY

That same day, they visited the mall manager. "We were concerned about the image the alteration business has. We knew we needed a higher-end look," says Paul. "The mall manager suggested we offer monogramming, too, and invited us to open shop." That monogramming suggestion not only created a more upscale identity for the alteration shop, it also proved profitable. Corporate and retail monogramming now accounts for about 40 percent of ASAP's business.

Four months after speaking with the mall manager, in April 1984, Paul, Beverly, and Kitty opened the first ASAP Alterations & Monograms. Two months later, they opened a second shop. Soon, the Malhams bought out their friend and Beverly sold her housewares boutique to begin fine-tuning the alteration concept with visions of franchising.

Image was all-important in order to bring in clients, attract personnel, and secure a prime lease. "The stores have a contemporary feel, with a gray-and-red color scheme and stripes on the walls," Paul Malham says. "We use modular store fixtures, counters, fitting rooms, and fitting stands all in gray-and-red formica. The sewing area is behind a barrier, so you don't see the fabric scraps on the floor, but you still get a feel of action. The monogram machine is up front because people like to watch it at work."

An ASAP franchisee requires about $115,000 to open a large mall store, including a $15,000 franchise fee, machinery and equipment (such as a dry-cleaner-like conveyor belt to hold garments), and working capital of $40,000. But you could open an independent shop in a strip-center for half the price. A busy mall alterations center with regular department store clients might generate pre-tax profits of $60,000 a year on revenues of $300,000. A compact strip-center site might squeak by with $20,000 profits on revenues of $80,000. While numerous entrepreneurs sew part time from home, you probably won't accumulate more than pocket-change going that route. If you're an accomplished tailor or seamster, however, you could gain enough experience through a home test to decide if a retail alteration business fits your personality.

SIMPLIFY, SIMPLIFY

ASAP never made suits, but in the beginning it tackled just about any other tailoring job, such as relining jackets. The Malhams soon decided that they "needed to build a reputation on speed and quality," says Paul, so they started referring time-consuming jobs to other tailors. Soon they were offering "while-you-shop" $6 pants hems in one to two hours and everything else in two to five days.

For a 25-percent express charge, they hurry along a $9 dress hem or $8 waist alteration.

Such simplification takes care of 90 percent of the customer's needs and also makes it easier to find employees. While not everyone knows how to sew, you'll probably have your pick of those who do. People who would never consent to hunching over a sewing machine in a department store backroom jump at the chance to perform similar services in a cheerful retail environment. "We've brought excitement to an obscure industry," says Paul Malham.

If you locate in the right place, your best promotion will come from your neighboring retailers. Ask dress shop owners if you can leave business cards at their check-outs. Stop by department stores to introduce your service to the clerks. ASAP discounts alterations for those stores that keep the fitting in-house but send the actual alterations to the Malhams.

But what if you don't sew? It doesn't matter: Just hire people who do. It turns out that Paul and Beverly Malham are sewing up business opportunities—and neither of them sews a stitch.

Dating Service

> *"I help people with the most important aspect of their lives: finding their mates. We average one wedding a month."*—Susan Hendrickson, Georgetown Connection.

Low Startup Investment: $10,000 (modest office in mid-sized town)

High Startup Investment: $200,000 (lavish setting in major city)

Time Until Breakeven: Six months to three years

Annual Revenues: $100,000-$500,000

Annual Pre-tax Profits: $40,000-$200,000

Staffers Needed for Startup (including founder): One

More than 50 million single adults live in the United States. Because of the rising divorce rate and the increasing age of the average bride and groom (we postpone nuptial bliss until our mid-twenties), the Census Bureau reports that by 1990 one out of every two households will be headed by a single person.

There are two kinds of singles in the world: men and woman who already cuddle with a steady, and people looking for Mr. or Ms. Right. Today's business community is falling all over itself to bring the sexes together. In addition to computer- and video-dating services, restaurants, adult schools, and for-profit hobby associations have all gotten into matchmaking. (A restaurant might promote a gourmet night where participants change tables at every course, for example. A class on "Meeting Your Perfect Match" provides dating tips for the outside world, but students have been known to exchange phone numbers before the bell rings. However, businesses designed specifically for matchmaking also achieve fame and fortune. Many fine-tune their appeal to a particular group. Cities big enough to boast specialty dating companies match blacks, classical music lovers, even the overweight. "People are tired of singles bars," says Susan Hendrickson, who operates the more general-interest Georgetown Connection dating service in Washington. "They don't want to pick out men and women the same way they go to a supermarket to pick out apples and oranges."

Susan's partner, and the founder of Georgetown Connection, is her mother, Joan Hendrickson. Like many entrepreneurs who start dating services, Joan learned from experience just how dreadful the singles scene can be. After spending twenty-three years of marriage raising three daughters, in 1976 Joan found herself divorced. "She had never worked before and had no skills," recalls Susan. "The only job she could find was as an interviewer at a video-dating service."

Serendipity! Joan's natural warmth and curiosity made her a good interviewer. Her tapes brought out clients' personalities and she genuinely liked what she was doing. When the business folded a year later, she scraped together enough savings to buy out the previous owners.

NO PH.D. REQUIRED

Joan was no video technician. She didn't have to be. The technical aspects of filming a dating interview are simple, compared with, say, taping a drama or even a training film that calls for following swift-moving action and creative dissolves and fade-outs. Most video dating companies don't splice or edit the interviews. (If you're looking for a creative challenge, see Videographer.) Likewise, you don't have to be a computer programmer to start a computer dating service. But it doesn't hurt to take a course or two at a community college to polish your skills.

A good video interview ignores the vital statistics that Jack is five feet eleven inches tall or Jill is a chiropractor. Your clients read that sort of information in a short bio you furnish with each tape. Instead, the tape should capture personality. Most dating services say a three-minute interview allows a viewer plenty of time to decide whether a meeting would be worthwhile. "We chat for about fifteen minutes, but the camera's only on for three minutes," says Susan Hendrickson. "I begin by talking about the weather or myself—I say 'My seven-month-old didn't let me sleep last night.' It relaxes the client. Most people don't know when they're being taped. An interview works best when it is spontaneous."

Susan always asks, "What is your most special quality?" You could also ask about hobbies or faults. What kind of vacation sounds perfect? Who is the ideal date?

KEEP OUT THE BAD APPLES

A dating service's several-hundred-dollar registration fee generally deters kooks. But many services ask new clients to fill out extensive application forms and show a couple of forms of identification so they can verify claims made by suspicious characters. Some services suggest dating partners meet in a public place the first time. What you're really selling at a dating service is your reputation for putting the right people together, so you try to minimize the chances for bad experiences.

The registration fee also marks you as attracting fairly affluent clients. People who can afford you know their prospective dates also have financial wherewithal, "All the video-dating people I interviewed felt it was crucial to have a prestigious location to impress potential clients," wrote Charlene Canape in *How to Capitalize on the Video Revolution* (Holt, Rinehart and Winston, New York, $16.95, 1984). "A tastefully furnished office in a convenient part of town was viewed as important." She points to a New York startup that spent $50,000 on video equipment but more than double that on its offices.

Joan Hendrickson decorated Georgetown Connection with Colonial furniture from her Reston, Virginia, home. "People are nervous walking into a dating service," remarks Susan. "The stock phrase is 'I've never done this kind of thing before.' Our office relaxes them. The studio looks like a den, with an Ethan Allen couch and a shag rug—except it's got some lights and a video camera in the corner."

You can create ambiance with other touches as well. Many services provide coffee or wine, and Georgetown Connection tries to know members by name. "If you know their eccentricities and what they like and don't like, it's easier to steer members to dates they get along with," says Susan. One of her clients, Mary, is a busy attorney who doesn't have a lot of free time to view tapes. "If John picks Mary's tape, I call and describe him. She trusts me enough to say 'Sure,' and I give out their phone numbers at that point. If I have any questions, I recommend she come in and view his tape."

A New York City service, Video Chemistry Inc., goes a step further for its harried clients. Each month it mails out a magazine which profiles members. Clients choose tapes from that list, which Video Chemistry mails so they can watch on the VCR at home. For busy new members, the company will tape an interview at their home or office.

DO YOU HAVE ENOUGH ELIGIBLES?

The pivotal question to ask regarding site selection: Do enough singles live in your area? If you charge $500 a year to join your service, figure you need one hundred members to gross $50,000. From that you must pay for equipment, advertising, rent, utilities, and salaries (including your own). You may need three or four or ten times that many members or a higher membership fee to meet your expectations. The Census Bureau can tell you how many singles live in your area and local newspapers may also have figures. Check to see what dating alternatives exist. Is there enough business to split between two dating services? How can you be different?

To attract your first applicants, you may have to provide incentives, such as special introductory offers or a get acquainted wine-and-cheese party. Budget plenty for advertising, as marketing will continue to be important throughout the life of your business. Just as a retailer keeps shelves stocked with merchandise, you must keep a plump portfolio of eligible singles. *How to Capitalize on the Video Revolution* notes that "if you are successful at what you do, you have to expect some of your members will no longer need your services. Therefore, you must constantly be replenishing your supply."

In addition to city magazines and newspapers, some markets offer cost-effective radio and cable-television spots. You can also buy direct-mail lists that segregate the marrieds from the officially unattached. If you specialize in a particular type of date—senior citizens, for example—you may advertise in publications geared specifically to your audience.

Joan Hendrickson courts free publicity. She's been on "The Phil

Donahue Show" and the front page of the *Wall Street Journal*. Local credits include the Washington "PM Magazine" TV show and the Washington *Post*: "We've lost track of how many times we've been in the *Post*," says Susan. Each appearance adds ten or fifteen members. "Dating services have no credibility," explains Susan. "This type of publicity erases the stigma."

Will there always be enough singles to support dating services? Of course some areas become saturated with too many services. In such locales, you may set yourself apart by catering to specific populations. But, as a rule, modern society provides a ready supply of singles. Susan Hendrickson points to the member who married a video date shortly after Georgetown Connection opened and recently rejoined after that marriage ended in divorce.

SOURCES

Publications

Local singles and city magazines

Consultant

Joan Hendrickson, Georgetown Connection, 1656 33rd St., N.W., Washington, D.C. 20007 (202) 333-6460

Financial Planner

> *"I remember a client who brought in a pile of documents. We uncovered $100,000 worth of stock he didn't know he had. You get vicarious satisfaction from helping people realize their financial goals."*–Glenda Kemple, Carter Financial Management

Low Startup Investment: $10,000 (teaming up with an existing office)

High Startup Investment: $50,000 (setting up a lavish shop from scratch)

Time Until Breakeven: One to nine months

Annual Revenues: $30,000-$3 million

Annual Pre-tax Profits: $15,000-$1.5 million

Staffers Needed for Startup (including founder): One

Case study: Between two professional incomes, David and Samantha earn about $200,000 a year. They have a lovely Colonial on 1.5 acres—and a high thirty-year mortgage that won't go away. They have a seventy-foot yacht, a seventeen-year-old with her eye on Princeton, and a fifteen-year-old who wants to take flying lessons. An ex-spouse collects monthly checks, and aging parents may need financial help in the future. And, because David's a pediatrician and Samantha's a sole proprietor who refurbishes art work, neither can count on retirement benefits to gild their golden years. Even the wealthy need financial planning.

Not everybody who sells investment products is a financial planner. Unlike a broker who recommends only stocks, a planner chooses from all sorts of investments: bonds, real estate, venture-capital opportunities, whatever. And, instead of just advising on investments, a financial planner takes a client's entire financial life into consideration, including income from all sources and all financial commitments and goals.

BOUTIQUES

Applying a loose definition of financial planners as individuals who sell specific products such as stocks, as many as two hundred fifty thousand financial planners exist. But the Institute of Certified Financial Planners puts the figure of true financial planners at about twenty-five thousand. Regardless of the industry size today, observers believe financial planners may outnumber stockbrokers before the century is over. "Expect a tremendous influx into the profession," predicts Glenda Kemple, a CFP (Certified Financial Planner) as well as a CPA (Certified Public Accountant).

Why the increase in planners? Classic supply-and-demand. As the tax bite continues to sting, and investment vehicles become ever more complicated, even the middle class is seeking out financial consultants. "I expect employers soon will offer affordable financial planning from banks as a cafeteria benefit along with health insurance," says Glenda Kemple, who operates out of Carter Financial Management in Dallas. It's becoming easier to get in the game as insurance companies, banks, and brokerage firms all test the financial planning waters, creating salaried positions in an industry that, until now, has been a boutique field. A few universities now bestow MBAs and even bachelor's degrees in financial planning as well as courses to prepare would-be CFPs for the necessary certification test.

DO THE TWO-STEP

Financial planning has two stages: devising the financial plan over a period of a few weeks, and keeping the plan on track over a period of years through ongoing surveillance. Assume you're Samantha and David's financial advisor. To write their plan, first you compile all their assets and liabilities, and match them to the family's goals. If the couple has neglected wills or insurance, you help get those in place. If you just happen to be an attorney, you can even draw up the will, although more likely you would just recommend a lawyer.

More planners, however, earn licenses to sell insurance. After David and Samantha's financial house is in order, you outline a budget that allots money for investments as well as every other obligation, such as mortgage and tuition payments. "Financial planners typically work with people who have money to save and invest," explains Glenda Kemple. "If a client is in financial trouble, we refer them to a credit counselor."

Up to this point, you'd have dealt with the science of numbers. Now comes the "art" of planning. You take that analytical data and match it to Samantha and David's goals and their tolerance for risk. Now you make specific investment recommendations. "I try to blend my suggestions with existing investments and make sure the entire portfolio is diversified between such areas as stocks, bonds, real estate, etc.," says Glenda. Samantha and David's plan calls for both near-term liquidity to pay for their children's educations, and investments that won't mature for twenty years to shelter retirement income. Since both are adventurous and can afford to gamble, you suggest they stash 10 percent of their investments in more volatile commodities or even to back that new technology David ran across in his medical research.

For the written plan, you charge a flat fee that ranges from a minimum of $300 or so for a simple plan, to the $30,000 stratosphere for really complicated plans that involve millions of dollars of income coming from various sources that must be divided between dozens of investments and obligations. "Clients feel organized and content when the plan's complete," says Glenda Kemple. "The challenge is to keep them on course." Glenda visits with each of her fifty clients three times a year, and talks with them monthly. On top of that one-time fee, some financial planners charge annual retainers. Some charge by the hour—anywhere from $50 to $200. Other planners take a percentage of income. Some take commissions on the sale of stocks, bonds, insurance, or other products recommended to implement the plan.

Those fees add up swiftly. "Successful, established planners earn in the six-figure range," says Glenda, who doubled or tripled her CPA salary after becoming a CFP. If you hire associates, your firm's revenues can move into seven figures.

PLANNING TO BE A PLANNER

Most planners have at least a bachelor's degree in some financially related field, such as accounting or economics. But dentists, attorneys, psychologists, and teachers also have become financial planners. Currently, no state or federal laws define financial planner qualifications, although you need licenses to sell specific products, such as stock, insurance, or real estate. You may need to register with the Securities and Exchange Commission to become a Registered Investment Advisor.

If you decide you want the credibility (and probably the higher fee) of a Certified Financial Planner, expect to devote a year or two to intensive study. Glenda Kemple completed the eighty-hour course work as a correspondence course from the College for Financial Planning while still on her accounting job. Other planners earn certification while practicing, similar to the way in which many accountants achieve CPA designations while working. You have to pass exams in six areas to become a CFP: tax management, investments, insurance, employee benefits, retirement, and estate planning. And it's not over yet: To keep that CFP status, you have to complete forty-five hours of continuing education every year.

SETTING UP SHOP

Unlike consultants who work out of clients' offices, financial planners invite the customers in for a visit. Asking a client to have a seat in your living room may be relaxing, but where their future is concerned, clients expect professionalism—so you really do need an office. In addition to secretarial help, busy planners hire "paraplanners" to do some of the grunt work, and you'll need a PC to juggle all the figures. After setting aside a little money for marketing, a solo practitioner might spend $20,000 to hang a shingle. You can cut overhead in half, however, by teaming up with other financial planners, much like lawyers or doctors form group practices and share rent, some personnel, and library facilities.

If you know how to plan finances, you're only halfway home: Who're you going to plan for? To attract clients and gain credibility, you might give seminars or write a newspaper column on particular aspects of personal finance. Or send out newsletters to clients and potential clients. Offer an hour of free consultation—provided new clients bring in recent tax returns, balance sheets, and a list of financial goals. This will eliminate "tire-kickers."

Glenda Kemple exchanges referrals with people she calls "strong centers of influence"—bankers, attorneys, accountants, and other professionals who monied people rub shoulders with. In addition, she cold-calls on prospects, asking to plan their finances. Glenda is particularly fond of lawyers, who make up about 25 percent of her practice, saying she understands the type of investments that appeal to them. "A lot of planners specialize in just doctors or small business owners," she adds. Others take on a particular age bracket, or just people above (or below) a certain income level.

Whatever the specialty, Glenda Kemple says financial planners meet the most interesting people. People with money, people with influence. But people who, despite their successes, need help with their finances.

SOURCES

Industry Associations

The Institute of Certified Financial Planners, 2 Denver Highlands, 10065 E. Harvard Ave., Suite 320, Denver, Colo. 80231 (303) 751-7600

International Association for Financial Planning, 2 Concourse Parkway, Suite 800, Atlanta, Ga. 30328 (404) 395-1605

Consultant

College for Financial Planning, 9725 E. Hampden Ave., Denver, Colo. (303) 755-7101

Image Consultant

> *"I have the knowledge and talent to change someone's body
> language or hair style. Their new confidence makes them do so
> much better on the job and in their personal lives."*–Brenda
> York, York & Associates

Low Startup Investment: $0 (starting through word-of-mouth from
home)

High Startup Investment: $20,000 (an office plus advertising)

Time Until Breakeven: Immediate to six months

Annual Revenues: $20,000-$200,000

Annual Pre-tax Profits: $15,000-$150,000

Staffers Needed for Startup (including founder): One

You've seen The Makeover on "Donahue" and in all the magazines. You've read about the importance of looking "right" in *Dress
for Success* and *Color Me Beautiful.* It appears that we Americans (1)
don't like the way we look and (2) are willing to spend money to
turn ourselves into vice-presidential material.

Brenda York, who heads the Association of Fashion and Image
Consultants in the Washington suburb of McLean, Virginia, estimates the total field, including speech/public appearance and
dress/color consultants, employs five thousand individuals. And she
says we ain't seen nothing yet. With so few practitioners and so
many people desperately in need of an improved image—especially
professionals looking for an edge on the job—she predicts the size
of the field will quadruple over the next decade. "People are just
now hearing about personal image consulting. When you start from
ground zero, you grow quickly."

FROM FAD TO BUSINESS TOOL

The industry began in the 1970s as a service to wealthy women "who sat around their country clubs talking about their consultant," says Brenda, who founded York & Associates in 1976. Today's clients more likely are bound for business success than the putting green and have no time to shop. And now we're talking both male and female clients. "So many women entered the work force and looked great that men felt they had to dress better as well," says Marilyn Ciccolini, who founded Wardrobe Images Inc., in Tenafly, New Jersey, in 1986 to specialize in male makeovers.

As a personal image consultant, you help clients look the part of an executive in their chosen industries. (Wall Streeters don a more sober uniform than do Madison Avenue ad executives.) The tasks of image consultants vary, depending on their expertise. For example, they might

- Analyze clients' coloring and advise on makeup, hair style, and coloring
- Shuffle through a client's existing wardrobe, discarding pieces and coordinating what survives
- Shop for new clothing
- Comment on ineffective body language and mannerisms
- Coach clients on speech techniques

For these services, image consultants charge a flat $300 to $600 fee, or $35 to $85 an hour. Some corporations even place personal image consultants on retainer to makeover entire legions of sales people, vice presidents, and other reflectors of the corporate image.

CAPITAL AND CONFIDENCE

But you don't have to do all those things at once—or ever. Some personal image consultants concentrate on one specialty, say shopping, while others branch out in even more directions, such as producing fashion shows. And speech consulting is a major specialty unto itself. Unless you have a lot of capital and self-assurance, Brenda York recommends startup consultants moonlight part time while holding another job. "Work nights and weekends—that's when clients want you anyway," she says. "If your apartment is inadequate, meet them in a hotel or restaurant or in their home." She also advises tackling one specialty at a time. "First learn color, then makeup, then wardrobe, then men."

Marilyn Ciccolini had the money—about $20,000, which is at the highest end of a personal image startup scale—and the confidence to plunge in with real commitment. Her background seemed tailor-made for an image consultant. She has degrees in buying and merchandising from the Fashion Institute of Technology in New York, and is a psychiatric nurse to boot. Credentials included stints as a manager for the Stern's department store chain and as an account executive for Liz Claiborne. Before setting up shop, Marilyn spent a year researching the industry. She read numerous books on personal image consulting, and talked with competitors listed in the $25 *Directory of Personal Image Consultants,* which had three hundred sixty-four entries in the 1986-87 edition, including specialties, fees charged, and background. She also took Brenda York's two-week, $2,500 "How to Start Your Own Fashion & Image Consulting Business" course.

To avoid competition in the New York City area, and to follow her own inclinations, Marilyn decided to consult exclusively for men. "I love men's clothing. It's better made than women's. Also," she adds, "men are more receptive than women who have been raised with fashion and have definite ideas about what they like."

From the beginning, Marilyn tailored means to ends. "I'm selling a package," she reasoned, and it was essential to "package myself well." She custom designed stationery and business cards and printed brochures and back-up information to distribute in seminars. She incorporated in New York and New Jersey and outfitted an office attached to her home. She also hired a press agent to get publicity and invitations to do seminars.

GETTING CLIENTS

"When I first started, I ran an ad," Marilyn recalls. "I attracted more people who wanted to work for me than I did clients." When you're selling your services as a consultant of any sort, clients want assurances that you are truly expert in your field. They ask for recommendations rather than check out the Yellow Pages. "Advertising just doesn't work," says Brenda York.

Instead, network. Discount services for colleagues and acquaintances in order to build a referral base. People will ask who your clients are, and you should get permission to use clients' names. Says Brenda York, "Everybody is a potential client, because everybody is interested in looking better."

Get your name out to a wider audience by speaking to social and civic groups. Those speeches are freebies, but you leave business cards and brochures with members of the audience who may contact you later. You can charge for speaking to business groups. Brenda checks the *Washington Post* business calendar, which lists upcoming trade-association meetings each Monday. In addition, "I call people who are planning meetings to tell them I'm available to speak on 'Polishing Your Professional Image.' "

Marilyn Ciccolini sells to both corporate sponsors and individuals by calling cold, explaining her services, and asking for an appointment. "The best-selling tool I have is explaining you can look great year-round and only spend four hours doing it." Those four hours include an initial two-hour interview in which Marilyn and the client talk about budget, measurements, and the proper image to project. Marilyn likes to meet in the client's office so she can see how his peers dress. She spends another hour at the client's home going through his wardrobe. Marilyn discards what doesn't work, and catalogs what does so the client knows which shirt and tie match which suits. The final hour is spent at the store where Marilyn awaits with a tailor and a number of suits from which to choose. Although the client has put in just four hours buying maybe $1,000 worth of clothes, Marilyn has spent up to ten hours, for which she charges $60 an hour.

Because of her proximity to New York, Marilyn has no shortage of potential clients. Personal image consulting works best with a ready pool of executives close by. In rural areas you might offer variations on the theme. For example, Linda Hunt consults from her Greenburg, Vermont, dress shop, Linda's. In-shop advice is free, but she charges a fee for visiting clients' homes to check out their existing wardrobes.

ADD-ON SERVICES

You won't get rich in image consulting because you're limited to hourly fees that average $50 (more in urban areas). But many personal image consultants push their income well into six figures by developing business boosters, such as conducting seminars. "Figure you do wardrobes twice a year—for spring/summer and fall/winter," reminds Brenda York. "Color analysis is a one-shot situation. You have to figure out what to do the rest of the year." York & Associates sells makeup it custom blends for clients in a makeover at 100- to 150-percent markups. Scarves, books, even clothing present other possibilities.

Some beauty salons and retailers pay consultants 10- to 15-percent commissions for sending along clients. But Brenda warns against buying everything from one store. "Then clients don't need you. Next time they just go to the store's shopper."

Also, don't let commissions sway you into recommending items the client doesn't need. If your goal involves bringing clients back every season, get the most value for the budget they've set. "If a recent college grad can only spend $350, I say let's get a nice suit," says Marilyn Ciccolini. If you dress your client well—and if the client has the talent and drive to go along with the new image you've created—next season you'll have a bigger budget to work with when the client returns with a raise and a new title.

SOURCES

Industry Associations

Association of Fashion & Image Consultants, 7655 Old Springhouse Rd., Suite 211, McLean, Va. (703) 848-2664

The Professional Image Consultants' Association International, 4 Forest Laneway, Suite 509, Willowdale, Toronto, Canada M2N 5X8 (416) 229-4077

Publications

Directory of Personal Image consultants, 10 Bay St. Landing, Suite 7K, St. George, Staten Island, N.Y. 10301 (718) 273-3229

Fashion News & Views, 7804 Foxhound Rd., McLean, Va. 22101 (703) 442-0183

Acropolis Books Ltd. (publishes a library of personal image books), 2400 17th St., N.W., Washington, D.C. 20009 (202) 387-6805

Consultants

Academy of Fashion & Image, 7655 Old Springhouse Rd., Suite 212, McLean, Va. (703) 442-9411

Emily Cho, New Image, 14 E. 90th St., New York, N.Y. 10128 (212) 289-7897

Dominique Isbecque, New York Image Institute, 235 W. 75th St., Suite 2Z, New York, N.Y. 10023 (212) 580-4786

Mediator

> *"I love problem solving. I love coming up with the third alternative in a high-conflict situation."*—John Haynes, The Haynes Mediation Training Institute

---

Low Startup Investment: $0 (as an add-on to an existing practice)

High Startup Investment: $10,000 (setting up an office)

Time Until Breakeven: Immediate to six months

Annual Revenues: $50,000-$300,000

Annual Pre-tax Profits: $35,000-$150,000

Staffers Needed for Startup (including founder): One

Susan and Jim handled the first four years of their divorce with relative harmony. They share joint custody of Kimberly, who alternates weeks with Mom in town and Dad in the suburbs. But Kim enters first grade in September. Susan argues that the magnet school in town provides an exciting, challenging curriculum, while Jim wants Kim to attend the suburban school, with its fresh, open-air setting. Kimberly will live with whichever side wins, since she can't shuttle between schools.

"It's fascinating that neither thought of the third school district that lay between them," says John Haynes, who practices family and business mediation and also teaches courses in the subject at The Haynes Mediation Training Institute. Both of Kimberly's parents agreed to move into the central district—Susan on the north side closest to the city, and Jim on the west edge, within walking distance of his previous home. While both adults compromised, each kept what they really wanted: joint custody of Kimberly.

GROWING DISPUTES, GROWING SOLUTIONS

According to the National Center for Health Statistics, after three years of decline, divorces increased from 1,155,000 in 1984 to 1,187,000 in 1985, the most recent year it tracked. With the breakup of each marriage comes conflict: not only the personal animosity, but also the practical decisions of what happens to the children, the house, alimony, and joint property. About half the states in the country, as well as local jurisdictions in other states, require couples to seek mediation before they file for separation or divorce.

Business disputes are no less cumbersome. Thanks to clogged courts, the average civil suit takes forty-two months—nearly four years—before litigants get their day in court. "And you can't get to court with less than $5,000 or $10,000 paid by each side in legal fees," says John Haynes. Mediation is not yet mandatory in business or interpersonal conflicts; but, as the debt crisis threatens more farmers, Minnesota and Iowa both require mediation in disputes between bankers and farmers. Several other states recommend the process even though they don't require it.

Mediation began in America as a tool in labor-management disputes. The practice is much more widespread in some European countries, such as Norway, where it is perceived as an alternative way to settle many forms of disagreement. While everyone agrees no U.S. mediators practiced full-time until the late 1970s, nobody knows how many hang shingles today. John Haynes, author of *Divorce Mediation* (Springer, New York, $17.95), estimates that ten thousand divorce mediators practice, but says those figures are meaningless because the field is growing so rapidly. "Expect a dramatic increase as more states require mediation and more people see it as an alternative. People are disenchanted with the cost of litigation and want more control over their lives."

DEFUSING

Mediation offers a route to solving conflicts outside the legal arena. The step defuses volatile situations before angry litigants waste time

—and money—in court. No judge decides who's right and who's wrong; instead, the enemies themselves devise solutions to problems. Unlike a lawyer who pledges allegiance to one side or the other, the mediator acts as a referee, helping to resolve the conflict in the interest of both sides. Business people who would rather not air their trade secrets appreciate mediation because it occurs behind closed doors rather than in the open courtroom.

Those states that require mediation offer two alternatives: either court-appointed mediators who practice out of courthouses; or private practitioners. As of this writing, no state licenses mediators. However, the Academy of Family Mediators accredits only lawyers and members of such helping professions as social work and psychiatry as divorce mediators, and many courts use Academy standards to define whose mediation is acceptable. In addition to lawyers, many ex-business people practice business mediation.

HOW IT WORKS

Mediators charge $20 to $100 an hour, per side. The average divorce mediation runs twelve hours over the course of six weeks. A business issue might be solved in two hours if the issues are clearcut and unemotional. A complicated environmental case involving the public as well as private and government groups could take years. Typically, the first one-hour session orients both sides to the process. In divorce situations, the mediator gives both husband and wife forms to fill out, asking what each expects future incomes and expenses to be. From there, the parties return for two-hour sessions until both sides agree to the issues at stake: parenting responsibilities and how to divide the marital assets, for example. At that point, the mediator writes a document in plain English that the couple takes to an attorney, who turns it into a legal separation or divorce agreement—a step which makes the decision binding. "Lawyers we use in New York charge $350 to do the filing," says John Haynes. "That compares with retainers of $2,500 both the husband and wife would pay if a lawyer did the whole procedure."

YOU CAN WHOLESALE

John Haynes estimates a mediator in a metropolitan setting seeing clients twenty hours a week, forty-eight weeks a year grosses $75,000, which accounts for cancellations due to bad weather or illnesses. You can do better if you include bigger corporations as clients because they don't balk at stiffer hourly fees. "Figure a New York rent and telephone costs $20,000 a year; $55,000 isn't bad for twenty hours work a week." John advises sharing offices with other mediators, lawyers, or therapists to cut overhead. "You can also move from wholesaling to retailing." By that he means hiring other mediators to work on an hourly basis. As manager of the practice, you keep $60 out of the $100 fee. Haynes Mediation operates two full-time offices as well as two that it rents one day a week. Revenues in 1986 amounted to $250,000.

Breaking into the business part time is also an option. Professionals, such as social workers, attorneys, or consultants, can continue practicing until they build a clientele. Individuals can sign on with groups like the American Arbitration Association or the Center for Dispute Resolution, which offer business mediation. Approach existing mediation practitioners and courts that might want to use your services. Ask other professionals for referrals. "Don't go to family lawyers since this would take away their divorce business," advises John Haynes. "Instead, talk with tax or corporate lawyers. They'll be overjoyed to give you the business and keep their clients for wills and other things." Also, make the rounds of PTAs, local mental health agencies, and civic and business clubs. Haynes Mediation also advertises in local law journals.

John Haynes, who once worked as a labor-management negotiator, says his greatest satisfaction comes from helping families through all sorts of rough situations. He recalls the case of the daughters who couldn't agree on what to do with their ailing mother. "Two daughters wanted Mother to stay home, but the third argued she really needed the attention of a nursing home. We finally agreed Mother should go to the nursing home, but we developed a calendar of visitation. One daughter visited Mother each week to insure she kept contact with her family. Again, we found the third alternative between the two extremes."

SOURCES

Industry Associations

American Arbitration Association, 140 W. 51st St., New York, N.Y. 10020 (212) 484-4000

Academy of Family Mediators, P.O. Box 4686, Greenwich, Conn. 06830 (203) 629-8049

Publication

Mediation Quarterly, 433 California St., San Francisco, Calif. 94104 (415) 433-1740

Consultants

Center for Dispute Resolution, 1900 Wazzee St., Denver, Colo. 80202 (303) 295-2244

The Haynes Mediation Training Institute, 156 5th Ave., Suite 720, New York, N.Y. 10010 (212) 645-1494

Laury Adams, Alece Egan, 1200 Blalock, Suite 204, Houston, Tex. (713) 465-2347

Divorce and Marital Stress Clinic, 1925 N. Lynn St., Suite 810, Arlington, VA. 22209 (703) 528-3900

Erickson Mediation Institute, 4570 W. 77th St., Suite 223, Minneapolis, Minn. 55435 (612) 893-0501

Personal Fiduciary

> *"One of my wards is a nine-year-old kid who was born without arms or legs. I stood my ground when his father wanted to put his money in some really off-the-wall investments and insisted on another approach. I was right, too, because the company whose stock the father wanted to buy just declared Chapter XI. I got my fee, but what really paid my bill was the chocolate bar that nine-year-old gave me the last time we left the judge's chambers."*—Sal LaGreca, fiduciary accounting and taxation

---

Low Startup Investment: $0 (home-based startup)

High Startup Investment: $$5,000 (modest office, some marketing)

Time Until Breakeven: Immediate to six months

Annual Revenues: $20,000-$200,000 (high-end figure assumes either a partner or execution of a large estate)

Annual Pre-tax Profits: $17,000-$125,000

Staffers Needed for Startup (including founder): One

For someone who deals with figures all day long, Sal LaGreca has a million stories. Consider the one about Elaine Freedman. Sal had been executor for her husband's estate and was managing the widow's assets when he got a phone call from the police that seventy-year-old Elaine had been in a car accident. No, she wasn't hurt, but her car was blocking two lanes of traffic. And she was scared. "She refused to get out of the car until I arrived," says Sal, who got in his car and sped twenty miles to the scene of the accident.

"My business card says I do fiduciary accounting and taxation," continues the Edison, New Jersey–based entrepreneur. "That means I do for individuals and law firms what bank trust departments do: manage assets, act as power of attorney, prepare income tax returns, do accounting for settlements of estates, offer investment advice." But where bankers strive to keep a strictly business relationship, personal fiduciaries often get involved in their client's well-being. Since he has access to checkbooks belonging to people not always able to look out for themselves, Sal gets personal: "I make sure my client at the nursing home has enough sweaters or another client's house gets cleaned regularly. In another situation, I arrange to have a woman taken to church every Sunday."

WHERE THE MONEY COMES FROM

Not to get mercenary, but fiduciaries do get paid for their missionary work because they charge an hourly fee. It's crucial to keep accurate time sheets where you record everything. Sal LaGreca, for example, gets $50 an hour whether he's preparing a client's income tax report or depositing someone's jewelry in the bank.

But income is not restricted by how many hours you can squeeze in between dawn and midnight. As a fiduciary you also are paid when you act as executor of estates. In New Jersey, executor fees amount to 5 percent of an estate's first $200,000 (or $10,000), and 3.5 percent on the excess. For a $400,000 estate, an executor might spend fifty hours preparing an accounting that answers such questions as What assets did the deceased have? How did the executor distribute the assets? Did the executor pay all taxes? Where any investments made for the estate? What problems arose and how were they handled? The executor receives $15,000 for the work that went into that typical forty-page accounting.

If you want to tackle personal bookkeeping or tax preparation, take specialized courses. Investment advisors can register for courses leading toward financial planning certification (see Financial Planner). But a fiduciary incorporates snippets of all those fields into one job. Experience in estate administration or taxes—such as you might garner with banking or legal training—probably provides the best fiduciary background.

Once you have the know-how, setting up shop is as easy—or as tough—as getting clients. Sal LaGreca was working as a trust officer for a large New Jersey bank in 1984 when he began thinking about going on his own. "I'd always paid for vacations or the kids' tuitions by doing tax work for individuals on the side," says Sal. But then he and his wife Joan decided they'd like to buy a house. So, Sal mentioned to a couple of attorneys he knew through the bank that he was willing to handle their clients' taxes. "Joan and I worked all day long at the bank, and spent nights doing the outside work," says Sal, who worked on tax preparation while Joan, who was also a bank officer, typed his correspondence. The bottom line: "We had the down payment for our house in three to four months."

It took just one other piece of evidence to convince Sal to leave a $36,000-a-year-job and such perks as a company car and a big entertainment allowance, which he spent to bring in bank customers. "Banks expect you to bring in so many wills or investment accounts," he explains. "In April 1985, right after I'd worked myself to death during tax season, I brought in business from another bank. They were paying $25,000 just for us—which really meant me—to do the tax work." Recognizing that he might as easily pitch that $25,000 account for himself rather than for the bank, Sal decided he was through hustling for an employer.

CLIENT TYPES

Fiduciaries service three types of clients, each responding to a different sales pitch:

- Banks (usually smaller institutions), which don't have the in-house personnel to fully meet their depositors' needs
- Attorneys who come in contact with tax and estate work, but would rather concentrate on the legal rather than the accounting headaches
- Individuals who have a tax or estate problem, usually referred by one of the first two sources or another individual. Once they sign on as tax clients, you can ask if they need someone to act as power of attorney or executor of their estate.

With ammunition in hand, Sal LaGreca approached his employer as his first account. "I saw that a CPA firm had charged $8,000 to do the accounting on one particular estate we'd farmed out. I looked at the records and figured I could have done it for $2,000." The discrepancy, he explains, involves overhead. If you start from a desk in your basement, as Sal did, and employ a part-time typist who works out of her or his home, you can keep nearly all of your

$50 per hour fee. In contrast, a large accounting firm with marble walls and on-line computers and a back-up librarian might count $25 of a $75 fee as profit.

Somewhat to Sal's surprise, the bank agreed to send accounts his way. Instead of a competitor, they saw an unofficial, outside partner who could help them service accounts that no one on staff was equipped to handle.

Sal sent out formal business announcements and made the same pitch to other banks and attorneys. To gain visibility with potential clients, he became a trustee for the state's Estate Planning Council, made up of lawyers, accountants, and bankers; he also spent $1,000 to host a hospitality suite at the annual meeting of the New Jersey Bankers Association Trust Division. "It's hard to say how much work I got from that party, because business tends to dribble in as banks need you," says Sal. "But, because they had been to my hospitality suite, the bankers remembered me when I called on them to solicit business."

Sal's first goal was to make $30,000 during the last six months of 1985. "We surpassed that," says the entrepreneur. "Then we said let's make $50,000 in 1986. We broke $72,000. I figured on the same income for 1987. We broke $72,000 in our first six months."

Now that Sal is contemplating hiring a part-time fiduciary to help with the overflow, he hesitates to put a figure on future goals. "Never in my wildest dreams did I think the business would take off like this," he says.

Private Post Office

> *"It's a cattle drive for customers trying to mail a package at Christmas [through traditional channels]. I prefer to treat customers the way they should be treated when they want to spend money with you."—James Mooney, Mail Room*

Low Startup Investment: $20,000 (bare-bones)

High Startup Investment: $60,000 (for a franchise)

Time Until Breakeven: Six months to three years

Annual Revenues: $40,000-$1 million

Annual Pre-tax Profits: $15,000-$300,000

Staffers Needed for Startup (including founder): One

It was nearly impossible to rent a post office box in parts of Southern California in the late 1970s. Recognizing that an indifferent government wasn't bothering to keep up with demand, a number of enterprising citizens stepped into the breach. Just as package and overnight delivery services had seen room to compete with the U.S. Post Office, these individuals carved out private mail box sites. For maybe $10 a month, you could rent a P.O. box with a private mail receiving agency for the first time.

SPARRING WITH UNCLE SAM

Providing mail boxes is just one area where entrepreneurs now compete with the government. So-called "privatization" now touches fields as diverse as fire protection, prisons, schools, mass transit, libraries, sanitation, air traffic control, and even space travel. The private sector seems to be chanting: "Anything the government can do, I can do better!" By operating with a tighter balance sheet and leaner bureaucracy, and sometimes by undercutting government wages, individuals can often offer better and cheaper services—and still make a profit.

Many of the early mail receivers just sat back and watched the cash roll in. At $10 rent a month per box, they raked in $60,000 a year on five hundred boxes. Deducting costs of perhaps $6,000 in rent and about the same for a part-time employee left profits of $35,000 or $45,000 a year—for approximately as much work as watching the clouds drift by.

Unfortunately for entrepreneurs, the government decided to fight back. "The Post Office reacted by installing literally millions of additional mail boxes," says James Baer, president of the Association of Commercial Mail Receiving Agencies. "That completely changed the complexion of the industry."

A 7-11 OF POST OFFICES

Today only about 5 percent of the revenues in the country's four thousand or so private mail receivers comes from mail boxes. Most operate as United Parcel Service drop-offs and many are Western Union agents. Some offer secretarial services, and one out of three provides facsimile (fax) transfer. Others wrap gifts and parcels, sell stamps, laminate, copy, and offer a slew of other services. "The reason we exist is convenience," says James Baer. "We're a one-stop service center for people in the vicinity. If you're willing to travel, wait in line, and put up with problems, you can probably obtain our services elsewhere at less cost."

The first new menu item most added was parcel shipping, which now accounts for about one-third of most mail box companies' business. Mail box companies contract with UPS (and often other delivery services—including the U.S. Postal Service) for bulk prices. UPS agrees to make daily stops to pick up parcels consumers have left, and bills the mail box company weekly. "Most UPS centers locate in out-of-the-way industrial parks," explains James Baer. "If you wanted to drive there, you could save the typical $2 drop-off charge. To have a UPS truck come to your door typically costs $3.25."

James Mooney, a former UPS manager who opened Mail Room

in Orange, Connecticut, in 1986, says parcel shipping is "a good draw, but the profit margins aren't great." With most mail transactions under $10, the trick is to offer a variety of services to bring in lots of customers. Some services sport higher profit margins than others.

HERE WE ARE!

Before you can sell all that variety, customers need to know you exist. James Baer recommends budgeting $5,000 for advertising during a new mail room's first six months. Many business and residential consumers still don't know what a mail receiving business offers—particularly since no uniform services exist from company to company. But once customers drop in to buy stamps they notice, for example, that you also print business cards. Jim Mooney says the newspaper advertising he tried was not as effective as direct mail. "I printed some flyers just listing the twenty or thirty services I provide, and got names from the phone book of people in the area."

On more specialized services, you can target potential users. For example, Jim Mooney contacted travel agencies and offered to cut $2 off the price of passport photos if their customers mentioned the name of the travel agency.

Tailor services to your customers and your own strengths. If you locate in a city, offer more business services, such as Telex, than you would in suburbia, where gift wrapping might attract more residents. Because Carol Mooney, Jim's wife and partner, is an executive secretary, they don't hire an outside typist for secretarial services. Therefore, even though Mail Room charges just $4 a page (compared with the ongoing rate of $5.50), Jim sees secretarial services as a lucrative specialty.

MAKE IT EASY

In addition to letting people know just how diversified you really are, you also need a really convenient address—"and the farther away from UPS, the better," says Jim Mooney. Customers won't trudge through a mall with heavy packages, so you need access to a parking lot.

While you no longer can get into the business for the price of one hundred mail boxes, you can still hold entry costs to $20,000 if you're on a shoestring, although the industry association recommends $35,000 to open and cover your first month's rent and a security deposit. Franchises are more expansive. Find one thousand square feet of retail space in a decent part of town. Stock it with one hundred to one hundred fifty mail boxes, an electronic scale, a typewriter or word processor (depending on how serious you are about secretarial services), a supply of stamps and wrapping materials, and whatever other equipment you decide will return your investment. "Nothing by itself is expensive since you're not heavily into equipment," points out Jim Baer, although it all adds up quickly enough. One of the frequent add-on purchases these days is a fax machine, which runs about $2,000.

What are you going to get for your investment? Jim Baer says to expect pre-tax profits of 20 percent of sales, or maybe $15,000 by your second year in business. "But we have people who net $50,000 to $100,000 on sales of a half a million. They offer a service that happens to be unusually well received in a community —fax or Telex, for example."

Seven months into business, Jim Mooney has yet to break even on monthly sales of $3,000. The turning point will come, he believes, when enough customers know the Mail Room exists, and recognize how many services he offers. Then, watch out, world. Since he intends to surpass the industry averages, Jim says, "The potential of my store is literally $2,000 to $3,000 a day—without working up a sweat. I believe the profit potential is almost half that."

SOURCES

Industry Association

Association of Commercial Mail Receiving Agencies, 10131 Coors Rd., N.W., Albuquerque, N.M. 87114 (505) 892-3331

Publication

ACMRA News, 10131 Coors Rd., N.W., Albuquerque, N.M. 87114 (505) 892-3331

Skin-care Aesthetician

> *"It's a glamour world. It gives me the opportunity to dress and look my best."–Judy Davidson, D'Lair Facials & Cosmetics*

Low Startup Investment: $5,000 (renting space in a beauty parlor)

High Startup Investment: $25,000 (opening a stand-alone shop)

Time Until Breakeven: Two to nine months

Annual Revenues: $35,000-$5 million (multiple salons)

Annual Pre-tax Profits: $15,000-$2 million

Staffers Needed for Startup (including founder): One

In 1987, the first baby boomers turned the dreaded age of forty. In addition to worrying about the paunch, they're now seriously scrutinizing their wrinkles. "I predict skin care will become bigger than the hair business," asserts Ron Renee, chairman of the Aesthetician International Association.

With fewer than twenty-five thousand licensed skin aestheticians (skin-care specialists) operating in 1987, compared with many times that number of cosmetologists (hairdressers), Ron sees great opportunity ahead. "We're a changing society," he says. "By the turn of the century, 30.6 million Americans will be over fifty years of age. The majority of those will be women—the most frequent skin-care salon visitors." Many of those women work and not only want to look their best on the job, but have the income to afford facials, which averaged $25 apiece in 1987. In addition, many aestheticians act as makeup artists, sell custom-blended skin-care and beauty products, treat acne, and offer leg and bikini waxing and body wraps.

PICKING UP THE KNOW-HOW

With just a few exceptions, each state requires licensing for aestheticians. But requirements vary drastically and, according to skin-care specialists, don't cover all you need to know. Many states expect an aesthetician to be a cosmetologist (see Beauty Salon). Training for cosmetology can last anywhere from three hundred hours during an eight-week crash course to fifteen hundred hours over nine months, but most programs devote only a class or two to skin care. Professional aestheticians are more comfortable with states that require degrees specifically in skin care; some states require both cosmetology and aesthetics degrees. In the past few years, a few schools have opened specifically for aesthetics.

Hairdressers, the first to the skin-care starting line, already possessed the degree (if not the expertise) to break into the business. Some doctors, particularly dermatologists, soon added facials to their practices, sometimes hiring aestheticians to provide the actual skin care. Nurses caught on and got their own aesthetics licenses.

I'LL SCRATCH YOUR BACK

You need relatively little capital to hang a skin-care shingle because you can ride the coattails of other professionals, like hairdressers. Although such giants as Christine Valmy and Georgette Klinger operate very successful stand-alone salons, the Aesthetician International Association recommends that entrepreneurs lease space in a beauty shop or other establishment that offers traffic and complementary services. Judy Davidson, who operates D'Lair Facials and Cosmetics in Hair Panache, Flossmoor, Illinois, praises the symbiosis of the services. "The clients' hair is trashed when I get through with them. They just walk over to the sink for their shampoo." She swaps referrals with hairdressers and manicurists. Some aestheticians build relationships with dermatologists or family doctors who send clients their way. "And a recommendation is everything in this business," emphasizes Judy. "Would you trust your face to a newspaper ad?"

Unless you are going with a multiple employee operation, you need no more than an eight-by-ten-foot space to house your treatment table or bed as well as your equipment—steamers, magnifying mirrors, lighting, cabinetry, and a sink. If you're renting space from another establishment, you can keep startup costs under $10,000. Just set partitions around your area for privacy. Judy Davidson, who has been both a hairdresser and a public relations entrepreneur, picked up a lot of used equipment, particularly such small items as apothecary jars, gowns, and towels, when she started D'Lair in 1984. But be careful where you cut corners. "You need a good, comfortable bed," recommends Ron Renee. "Use music and light therapy. The secret is to put the client to sleep while you're giving the facial. If someone spends ninety minutes in discomfort, they won't want that experience again." As with any personal service, your business is built on repeat customers.

CONCESSIONS

Although most beauty shops balk at the complications of actually running a skin-care operation, they often are happy to lease aestheticians space at reasonable rates since skin-care offers clients another reason to frequent a particular shop. "I stock five manufacturers in makeup and three in skin care and custom blend everything," says Judy Davidson. "Beauty shops don't want to keep track of the inventory, ordering, bookkeeping. Also, beauty salons pay their employees commissions, and I don't think I could make a living on commissions alone. I need the markups on products I sell to survive. Maybe 70 percent of my revenues come from selling products."

Judy makes those product sales to clients who come in for regular facials, acne treatments, or makeup consultations. She suggests that aestheticians in locations such as her suburban Chicago site could expect $40,000 in revenues the first year, keeping $15,000 as pretax profit. As you built a steady customer base, revenues should increase and profits should jump even faster, since such costs as rent remain fixed. At some point, you may want to add another treatment room or two.

ONLY YOUR AESTHETICIAN KNOWS FOR SURE

Unlike a hairdresser, who can assume an avant-garde look and bouncy attitude, an aesthetician should project a professional demeanor. Much of what skin-care specialists do involves consulting: Use this moisturizer to treat your skin, try that face pack to fight acne, or try this blush to enhance your coloring. Clients are paying for your expertise. For example, to custom blend a foundation, Judy Davidson mixes matte and oils in proportions suited to the client's skin type. Then she adds tints and color developers to match the skin color. "The foundation may only run me $3, but the client pays $22.50 for my expertise."

While some aestheticians emphasize makeup, Judy takes the European attitude that "if you have just $100 to spend, take care of your skin first." As products and techniques continually improve, the rewards for both her clients and herself escalate. "People come in saying, 'My face is so raw it hurts,' then return a week after I've given a facial and they've followed my home care suggestions. It's so satisfying when they say, 'I can't believe it's improved so much!'"

SOURCES

Industry Association

International Association of Aestheticians, 3606 Prescott, Suite D, Dallas, Tex. 75219 (214) 526-0760

Publications

Modern Salon, 400 Knightsbridge Parkway, Lincolnshire, Ill. 60069 (312) 634-2600

Dermascope Magazine, 3606 Prescott, Suite D, Dallas, Tex. 75219 (214) 526-0760

Consultants

Advanced Esthetics Training Institute, 11927 Olive St., St. Louis, Mo. 63141 (314) 997-6110

Prima Facie Skincare Academy, 850 Stanton Rd., Burlingame, Calif. 94010 (415) 697-6112

American Institute of Esthetics, 5482 Oceanus, Suite F, Huntington Beach, Calif. 92649 (800) 222-7016

Vocational School

> *"I like making winners out of losers. Even with El Paso's 11.7-percent unemployment rate, we place 85 to 95 percent of our students."—Donald Beardsworth, International Business College*

Low Startup Investment: $50,000 (to start a small cosmetology school)

High Startup Investment: $400,000 (to buy a large technical school)

Time Until Breakeven: Six months to four years

Annual Revenues: $50,000-$1 million (per branch)

Annual Pre-tax Profits: $5,000-$100,000

Staffers Needed for Startup (including founder): Two to five

Donald Beardsworth likes to say the secretarial students he attracts at the International Business College in El Paso, Texas, and its six Southwestern branches "qualify for everything but the IRS." About 80 percent pay for 100 percent of their tuition through government loans and grants; many students are on welfare and some lack high school diplomas. A few have college degrees but can't find a job. "My philosophy is to give them six to nine months of training, period. If they don't have a high school diploma, we give them a GED (general education diploma) prep course and take them to the testing center so they get their equivalent. We get them off the welfare rolls and onto the tax rolls."

EDUCATING THE PUBLIC PRIVATELY

Like Don Beardsworth, most presidents of vocational and trade schools are pragmatic sorts. But you don't have to scratch too deep under that touch exterior to find caring educators who provide the computer repair or truck driving education a public school doesn't. Proprietary schools supply two-thirds of the post-secondary vocational education in this country, according to the Association of Independent Colleges and Schools, an accrediting body. As high schools move further to basics (reading, writing, and arithmetic), their curriculums have even less room for typing, bookkeeping, auto repair, or electronics.

Meanwhile, businesses in the service and information age need skilled labor—and workers need skills. Workers' desire for a fast education is tantamount to a hunger: the recognition being, to put food on the table, the breadwinner needs to acquire new skills. Displaced assembly-line workers learn to repair robots. Former steel workers learn to retrieve information from data bases.

TO START OR BUY

Despite the need for private-sector education, starting a school isn't easy when you factor in paying rent, recruiting teachers and students, buying equipment, and winning accreditation. (The exception may be small cosmetology schools that take just a handful of students at a time. Startup costs are minimal, and the school receives income from cutting customers' hair as well as from tuition. The drawback? Cosmetology schools operate in a highly competitive field.)

For the most part, "it's easier to start by purchasing a school," says Joseph Thompson, president of Antonelli Institute of Photography and Art, a Plymouth Meeting, Pennsylvania, school that offers two-year associate degrees in photography, art, and interior design. He explains that the accrediting groups will not consider a school until two to three years after startup. And even then a school must prove it is financially stable to get a stamp of approval. Why is accreditation so critical? "Students cannot get government funding unless the school is accredited," Joe explains, noting about 40 percent of his students receive grants or loans. "And if you attract affluent students whose parents pay the tuition, they look for accreditation to make sure you're giving a good education and getting jobs for the students."

Joe, a former photo-lab operator who bought the Antonelli Institute in 1977, says to check the *Wall Street Journal* ads and business brokers to see what schools are on the block. Costs vary, depending on whether the school has a campus and how much equipment it owns. A school that teaches medical technicians, for example, pays more for teaching tools than a school for models. But, as a rule-of-thumb, expect to spend $1,000 per student to buy an accredited institution. In addition to students, your purchase price also buys such assets as instruments or equipment, a library, instructors, curriculum, and sometimes real estate, so you'll want to check on the conditions of each.

Don Beardsworth spent just $75,000 for the then seventy-five-year-old International Business College in 1973. "When I took over, it had a hundred and fifty-four students," says Don, a former banker who worked in admissions departments for two midwestern vocational schools. "Now we've got nineteen hundred students and seven locations. I wouldn't take $3 million for the school today." In 1986, the school made 8-percent pre-tax profits, or about $480,000, on $6 million in tuition revenues.

THIS IS THE WAY WE GO TO SCHOOL

Because you offer fast education, those students you inherit when you purchase a school won't be with you for long. Don Beardsworth starts new classes every three weeks and must replace his entire student body every six to nine months. Therefore, advertising and recruiting are crucial. "The main school has six hundred students and five admission specialists," he explains. "They go to high schools to give demonstrations and explain financial aid. They invite students to come for aptitude tests." (About 5 to 7 percent don't pass.)

Schools with high class turnover usually budget 10 percent or more of revenues for advertising: newspapers, radio, direct mail, even TV. Afternoon television soap operas could be renamed "trade school traumas" considering all the vocational-school advertising breaks.

Above all, recruiters sell students a new life after school—a new job and a new career. "You'll be out of business real fast if you don't place your graduates," warns Don Beardsworth. International Business School has at least one job developer on each campus who constantly calls on employers to line up interviews. Placement is why people pay $10,00 for a two-year education at Antonelli, instead of about $4,000 at a community college, adds Joe Thompson. "We tell students we teach more, faster. We use the latest techniques. Our graduates go out and start their own photography studios or get good jobs."

To keep that competitive edge, a school needs two things: good instructors and up-to-date equipment. Trade schools generally offer instructors and administrators at least competitive salaries and benefits. Since trade schools are more involved with recruiting and placement than their public-sector cousins, you may need one administrator for every instructor on board.

KEEPING CURRENT

Look at your market frequently to see what changes are taking place and change your curriculum accordingly. For example, many Southern California schools give business courses in Asian languages. All executive or medical secretaries who graduate from International Business College can operate word processors and input data. An adequate response to the business environment requires having the latest teaching equipment. You don't have to buy it, however, since many manufacturers offer lease packages. Don Beardsworth says he spends about $150,000 to outfit each new fifty-student branch school. As long as you keep the same curriculum and student-teacher ratio, branches automatically receive accreditation if the parent school has passed muster.

What about the future of trade and technical schools? Proprietary schools receive much of their tuition indirectly through government funds to students, and no one knows from year to year what Washington has in mind for students. But increasingly, older Americans are switching careers after their first choice fails them in some way. More and more, they look to private education to help them make that switch.

SOURCES

Industry Associations

National Association of Trade and Technical Schools, 2251 Wisconsin Ave., N.W., Washington, D.C. 20007 (202) 333-1021
Association of Independent Colleges & Schools, Suite 350, #1 DuPont Circle, Washington, D.C. 20006 (202) 659-2460

Real

Estate

Home Inspector

> *"Inspectors working for me have heads as big as watermelons. Their satisfaction comes from the praise their clients are always sending their way. No one is in the home buyer's corner except the inspector, so clients are really grateful to inspectors who help protect their investment."—Ronald Passaro, Res-I-Tec Inc.*

Low Startup Investment: $15,000

High Startup Investment: $50,000

Time Until Breakeven: Six to eighteen months

Annual Revenues: $75,000-$1 million

Annual Pre-tax Profits: $7,000-$300,000

Staffers Needed for Startup (including founder): Two

The consumer movements of the early 1970s dug the foundations of the home inspection industry as house buyers rebelled against the *caveat emptor* creed. The framework went up as housing prices soared in mid-decade. "People don't give real estate away. Buyers can't afford to come up with another $2,000 or $10,000 if they find their roof leaks," says Ronald Passaro, spokesperson for the American Society of Home Inspectors. When he started Res-I-Tec Inc., a Redding, Connecticut–based home inspection service in 1970, "only myself and one other guy were doing inspections in Connecticut. Now there must be forty or sixty companies."

Lending institutions contributed the bricks and mortar to the home inspection industry in the 1980s as they began requiring house inspections before they would grant mortgages. Simultaneously, states began enacting laws requiring sellers to disclose what was wrong with their properties, so sellers began calling on inspectors, too. "Inspector reports became a negotiating tool on the price of housing," says Kenneth Austin, president of HouseMaster of

America, a Bound Brook, New Jersey, franchisor of home inspection services. If an inspection indicated that the heat pump was gasping its last, the seller might be persuaded to knock off a few thousand.

BOOM TIMES—FOR A FEW

Despite the growing demand, by 1987, the American Society of Home Inspectors identified just twenty-five hundred inspectors across the country, although many times that number of engineers, architects, termite exterminators, and contractors occasionally inspect a house. "If you go by the names of new inspectors in the phone books, the industry doubles each year," says Ron Passaro. "But a lot of part-timers drop out when they realize inspectors are liable if they make a mistake." Regardless of the swinging door syndrome, he sees a 20- to 25-percent real annual increase in home inspectors continuing for at least ten more years. While inspections are a standard part of any real estate deal in some parts of the country, other areas are just now catching on. And the potential is huge: some 4 million homes change hands each year.

Just as the potential liability holds down startups (be sure to factor insurance into your startup costs), so does know-how. Several universities have designed courses with the guidance of the American Society of Home Inspectors. But most inspectors have taught themselves. And they need to know everything from how to evaluate a home's structural soundness to how to identify strengths and weaknesses of swimming pools and kitchen appliances. A working knowledge of plumbing and electrical wiring is fundamental. Ron Passaro hires only registered architects, engineers, or people with a building background, as inspectors. Even then, Res-I-Tec puts them through a thirteen-week formal course before letting them tackle solo inspections.

HouseMaster of America has similar requirements before accepting inspectors into its fifty-four-hour course. But you don't have to know a HVAC from a min-vac to spend an average $20,000 for a HouseMaster franchise. "We really prefer a marketing background—someone who can sell the service," says Ken Austin, noting you can hire and train qualified inspectors to check out plumbing and evaluate septic systems. Because the inspector you hire keeps only about 25 percent of an average $200 inspection, an owner who also sells the service should net at least that much after paying for overhead on a modest office.

HOME-BASED OFFICES

Many inspectors hold startup costs down by beginning either from home offices, or as divisions of established companies connected with home repairs. (However, the American Society for Home Inspectors frowns on inspectors who make repairs, saying an inspector who benefits from a report could face conflicts of interest.) If you opt for an office, you don't have to spend much on decor or location. "This isn't a walk-in business," says Ken Austin. "Home inspections are ordered over the phone so no fancy office is required."

Even in the beginning, unless you and your partner or spouse plan to handle all the tasks, you'd better allot some startup cash as salary for at least one other person. HouseMaster recommends three bodies: one to sell, one to inspect, and one to manage the paperwork back at the office (each inspection requires a professionally typed report).

Real growth comes as you add employees. You can only perform a home inspection during daylight hours. And, since each inspection takes two to three hours—not counting travel time—even a high-energy individual can't inspect more than three houses a day. If you can line up enough jobs, a solo practitioner can bring home $70,000 or so, leaving some time to market services.

To outgrow that home office, you'll need to drum up business, which is where a marketing background comes in handy. A few inspectors advertise directly to the public on cable TV and in newspapers. But that's an expensive, scattershot way to peddle to the small audience who plans to buy a home. Instead, most inspectors build relationships with real estate professionals. Call on realtors, corporate relocation departments, attorneys, and lenders. "Let them know you're there," says Ron Passaro. Some inspectors graduate to commercial properties as well.

Expect some big changes in home inspections during the next decade. "Several states are looking at licensing," says Ron. "If they give anyone a license who sends in $1, that could destroy the industry." He points out the potential room for abuses by incompetent or unscrupulous inspectors. A slipshod inspection is little better than no inspection at all. "But if licenses require education and set ethical standards, it could enhance the industry," by winnowing out the unfit and enticing more home buyers to spring for an inspection.

SOURCES

Industry Association

American Society of Home Inspectors, 1010 Wisconsin Ave., N.W., Washington, D.C. 20007 (202) 842-3096

Publications

Real Estate Today, 430 N. Michigan Ave., Chicago, Ill. 60611 (312) 329-8200

Real Estate Business, Commercial Investment Real Estate Council, 430 N. Michigan, Suite 500, Chicago, Ill. 60611 (800) 621-7035

Manufactured Housing Contractor

> *"As a custom builder, I would quote the customer a price and watch the subcontractors constantly ask for more than we agreed upon. In a modular house, prices are fixed and the work is done in a timely manner. I get great satisfaction from offering affordable housing and watching the company grow."* — Bob Brann, Shoreline Modular Homes Inc.

Low Startup Investment: $10,000 (to print brochures and advertise for custom design homes built on contract)

High Startup Investment: $250,000 (two model homes)

Time Until Breakeven: Six weeks to two years

Annual Revenues: $300,000-$10 million

Annual Pre-tax Profits: $30,000-$1 million

Staffers Needed for Startup (including founder): One

People tell the story of hairdresser Harold and his brother Ronald, a computer programmer, who inherited two acres of undeveloped land in mid-1986. Rather than sell the parcel for a fast buck, they decided to develop it themselves.

Neither brother had a construction background, but Harold had bought a modular home the previous year. He had watched his dealer truck in the two segments, and lift each by crane onto the foundation he had hired a subcontractor to build. The dealer's crew had joined the sections together and waterproofed the roof, all before the sun went down. "I saw no reason we couldn't do the same thing—buy factory-built modules and hire experts to add the

10 percent of essentials that don't come from the factory, like the foundations, plumbing, and electrical work," says Harold. The fifth bank the brothers approached agreed, giving them 75 percent financing, collateralized by the valuable land, on the $500,000 construction loan. By the end of 1986, the ten townhouses they ordered from a New Hampshire factory had each sold at around $100,000. The brothers figure they pocketed $200,000 above the price they were offered just for the land. "We used the money to buy more land in the next county, where we're doing it all over again," says Harold, now president of H & R Bros. Homes Inc.

The modular concept that is making the brothers' fortunes are fully constructed sections of houses, complete down to the wallpaper and light fixtures. Leo J. Shapiro & Associates, a Chicago research firm, says modular production rose 19 percent in 1986 over the previous year to ninety-two thousand units nationwide. In New Jersey, where modulars have caught on with a vengeance, sales tripled between 1985 and 1986 to forty-five hundred units. "Crystal ballers say one-third of the building industry will be modular by the turn of the century," estimates James R. Birdsong, executive director of the Home Manufacturing Council.

WHY BUILDERS LIKE MODULARS

Sales of modular housing spurted ahead in the Northeast when interest rates began falling in 1984. "When the market sprang back, contractors discovered that anybody who could tape a dry wall had gone to Houston to work," says Shepard Robinson, publisher of *Manufactured Housing Newsletter.* "With no skilled labor to be found, developers turned to factory work."

Modular housing appeals to both the building community and consumers. "Contractors don't have to buy $10,000 in lumber with no home buyer in the wings. You can wait until you have a customer," explains Shep Robinson. Factories that construct modulars in the quality-controlled atmosphere of a manufacturing plant also eliminate traditional building problems like on-site vandalism and weather delays. For the most part, factory labor is less expensive than construction crews, so employee costs are lower.

You can build on speculation, like the Fields, or you can operate as a dealer. Speculating requires a higher initial capital investment since you must purchase the land and modules and subcontract site-work. Dealers invest less—maybe $50,000 to $150,000 in a model home or two to show customers what they are buying. But if you are lucky enough to line up a buyer on the basis of brochures, you can start in the business with just enough cash to hire a crane crew to put the module in place and a finishing crew to join the modules together.

Here's how dealers work: "We take a $2,000 to $3,000 deposit from a customer and give the whole thing to the factory," explains Bob Brann, president of Shoreline Modular Homes Inc. in Madison, Connecticut. Shoreline pays the factory in full when it ships the home four to eight weeks after the order is placed. The dealer either employs or subcontracts with a crew that lifts the house onto the foundation supplied by Shoreline. Another crew spends a few hours joining the modules. At that point, the customer's mortgage kicks in, and Shoreline receives its cash immediately. "It's almost a cash business," says Bob.

WHY HOMEOWNERS BUY MODULARS

Customers like modular homes because they arrive months faster than a home built to order and because "brick for brick, a modular home costs 25 percent less than traditional construction," says Bob Brann. A typical modular sells in the $40,000 range; transportation costs, site preparation, finishing fees, and land costs might bring the homeowner's ultimate cost to $90,000. In 1987, the New York *Times* reported an average site-built home cost $116,000.

Modular home sales do not swing as wildly as do traditional home starts. "When interest rates reach 20 percent, sales drop, but not as fast as the rest of the home building industry," says Bob Brann. "People who would buy site-built homes save 25 percent on construction by coming to us, so they can afford a home by going modular. We get a larger share of the market, and they buy bigger houses."

Shoreline sells "every kind of home, up to three, four thousand square feet," continues Bob. "Contemporary, traditional." Highway laws allow transportation of modules up to fourteen feet wide and sixty feet long. Bob figures a two-story Colonial might cost $35 a square foot, or a total price of $81,000 (plus foundation and land costs).

CATHEDRAL CEILINGS AND GREENHOUSES

Today's modulars are indistinguishable from a site-built version. Deluxe Homes of Berwyck, Pennsylvania, Shoreline's supplier, offers a dozen pages of options on its single-family homes, ranging from whirlpool tubs to cathedral ceilings with skylights. "To satisfy a real custom market, we'll add a $3,000 greenhouse available locally," says Bob. "We just tell the factory where to put the opening and we add it on-site."

Bob Brann sells about a third of Shoreline's two hundred modular homes each year to developers, who buy for speculation. One customer specializes in whole developments containing twenty to fifty modular homes. The developers deal through Shoreline rather than directly with the factory to avoid the headaches of erecting the modules. However, most manufacturers will either subcontract an erection crew or recommend a local crane operator. "Builder markups are whatever the market will bear," says Bob. "We've sold houses for $100,000 that the developer turns around and sells for $200,000 or $300,000 after they add the lot. Most look for a 10-percent return."

Shoreline, which collected pre-tax profits of around $500,000 on revenues of $10 million in 1986, scatters its houses from Delaware to Rhode Island, although its six model-home sites are all in Connecticut. Bob Brann says the only constraint is the lot size and configuration, and Shoreline has gone to interesting lengths to accommodate location. "Modules are heavy," says Bob, "so we've reinforced some bridges to bring them across. Once we lifted a module over an existing apartment building." He recalls a customer who was quoted $500,000 to build the home he wanted on Block Island, R.I. "He spent about $100,000 on our package, plus another $3,800 to rent a barge for a house that's probably worth a half-million in that market," says Bob.

If you're selling a completely erected modular home, advertise the same way you would for a traditionally built model: in the classifieds and through real estate brokers. It's a little trickier if you're lining up buyers for homes still at the factory. Shoreline spends $4,000 every year (not counting the cost of the home) to put up an entire house at the New Haven Home Show. "It's expensive PR, but we get a lot of sales over the course of the year," says Bob Brann. When the four-day show ends, Shoreline dismantles and reassembles the house elsewhere either as a model or as a completed home with a for-sale sign in its front yard.

Modules offer applications in the commercial market as well as in the residential. Northeastern cities have purchased modulars as low-income housing projects. And Salt Lake City built a gymnasium and surrounded it with a dozen sixty-foot-long modules and called it a school. "Modules built the school in half the time," says James Birdsong of the Home Manufacturing Council. "Also, if the population shifts, they can transport the school to a new site."

In addition to single-family homes, Shoreline offers duplexes, townhouses, and apartment flats that can be stacked in all sorts of configurations. "You could join together four hundred units, or a dozen here, then add a space, and join another dozen," says Bob Brann, who lives in half of a manufactured duplex and rents out the other half. "People are just starting to see the potential for modulars."

SOURCES

Industry Associations

Home Manufacturing Council of the National Association of Home Builders, 15th and M Sts., N.W., Washington, D.C. 20005 (202) 822-0576

Industrialized Housing Manufacturers Association, 3236 Ridgeway Rd., Harrisburg, Pa. (717) 652-2395

Publications

Automation in Housing & Manufactured Home Dealer, P.O. Box 120, Carpinteria, Calif. 93013 (805) 684-7659

Manufactured Housing Newsletter, P.O. Box 1307, Barrington, Ill. 60010 (312) 381-4312

Real Estate Agent

> *"The business provides a lot of freedom. If you like people, you get the chance to meet a lot of them."* — John Major, Broker

---

Low Startup Investment: $1,000 (to become licensed)

High Startup Investment: $30,000 (to open a brokerage firm)

Time Until Breakeven: One month to two years

Annual Revenues: $300,000-$10 million

Annual Pre-tax Profits: $18,000-$300,000

Staffers Needed for Startup (including founder): One

When you bought that Colonial last year, one of two thoughts undoubtedly crossed your mind. Either "I'm sure glad that's over!" or "That was an exciting experience. . . . It might be interesting to be a real estate agent."

You're not alone in wanting to enter an industry so tied to the American dream of owning one's own home. In 1986, the National Association of Realtors counted 1.2 million real estate agents—more than double the number of practitioners during the housing industry slump of the early 1980s. In 1986, 4.7 million homes changed hands—and real estate agents sold 82 percent of them. While observers expect sales of commercial properties to suffer during the next few years because of tax law changes, the realtors expect home sales to remain strong. Regardless of what interest rates do, "we still see a strong demand for housing," says Elizabeth Johnson, director of media relations at the National Association of Realtors. "Households are still being formed and they need a place to live."

A TWO-YEAR RUNWAY

Because real estate is a regulated industry, the entry path is well marked. Although exact requirements differ depending on the state where you practice, you must follow three steps to open your own brokerage firm:

▪ Licensing. Community colleges and universities offer night or evening courses to prepare you in several weeks or months to take your state's test, which leads to a license.

▪ Apprenticeship. After you get a license, you sign on as a salesperson with an established broker for two years or so, a step most states require. During your training, you learn what the schools don't even attempt to teach you, so choose your mentor carefully. Not only should you look for an agency with abundant listings so you can make a living while you learn the ropes, you should also ask about benefits such as in-house training programs. "Most agents are independent contractors who set their own hours and are their own bosses—under a broker's guidance," explains John Major, a Coeur d'Alene, Idaho, broker. Agents get paid on commission, so put aside some money for groceries, rent, and so on, to tide you over until your first sale. While commissions differ depending on the sale price of the house and the amount of advertising the client requests, residential commissions average 6 percent.

▪ Brokerage. Many agents never take this step, but if you want your own office, you'll probably be ready to become a real estate broker after a couple of years of apprenticeship. The state licensing board looks at your performance record—the number of listings you've handled and the sales you've closed—and may set requirements for continuing education. Now you can hang your own shingle and hire other sales agents if you wish. You can opt for a simple, one-person office, or a computerized, multi-person franchise. (In 1987, about 15 percent of all agencies were franchised.)

If you want to offer elaborate enticements to bring in buyers, such as video-listings and limousine tours, factor those costs into the startup budget. You also may want to set aside money to advertise your own agency as well as the houses you sell. Many brokers routinely distribute newsletters or flyers to homes in their territory in hopes of someday picking up the sale when the owners decide to move.

People make fortunes by building large real estate brokerages. But, according to the National Association of Realtors, the median income for a broker in the depressed year of 1983 (the latest statistic it had available) was $30,000. A sales associate made just $18,000. According to those who generate salaries way above the norm, the best brokers have three things going for them: product knowledge, a willingness to hustle, and an inborn sales ability.

KNOW YOUR BUSINESS

Product knowledge boils down to understanding your market, the particular ranch or split-level you represent, and, perhaps most important, the financing climate.

The albatross hanging around the neck of every real estate agent is interest rates. Even when money is plentiful and consumers can borrow at reasonable rates, today's real estate agent must understand the thousand-and-one financing techniques available. Those who don't, risk attracting homebuyers who can't find the money to buy a home. But if you're savvy, you may be able to steer buyers into financing packages that will let them buy even in difficult times. For example, you might explain the benefits of seller financing to a couple who could afford to accept monthly installments on the sale of their home.

"Agents don't just talk the financial lingo, but actually act as a go-between between the lender and buyer," says Elizabeth Johnson, of the National Association of Realtors. "The agent has to understand the implications of a mortgage. Would a couple be better off with a fifteen-year mortgage that they can pay off faster with a lower interest rate? Or would lower payments over thirty years be better?" Bone up on current financing by talking with area bankers and even take courses if necessary. Most large franchisors provide continuing classes in financing techniques.

"A smart real estate agent may not know every financial structure available," admits John Major, "but knows where to look to find financing." He says good agents in his small Idaho town keep in touch with up to ten lending institutions. "I've seen agents fail because they make only one phone call to a banker who won't lend to the customer. Then they just give up without calling more banks. There are lots of reasons why banks won't loan money, so you have to know everything about the bank and about your client." For example, some banks shy away from commercial loans, and the client may want to turn that quaint Victorian into a restaurant. Or possibly the client forgot to mention he is unemployed, so meeting the monthly mortgage may be iffy.

Lenders will jump at the opportunity to talk with you, either in their offices or in yours. "After all," says John Major, "the bank is in the business of lending money." A chat every six months suffices in stable periods, but you'll have to gauge the current financing climate. "In the early 1980s, radical financial changes happened on a weekly or monthly basis," recalls John.

HUSTLING

Next comes a willingness to devote time and energy to your practice. You must not only unload your current listings in the least time possible, but also line up a steady stream of new clients. You must be visible: An attractive office on Main Street will draw more buyers and sellers than a dilapidated back-alley storefront. Check with the local government to see the ratio of realty offices to houses before setting your sights on a particular site.

Once you're established, don't wait for clients to sniff you out. Call and write area homeowners to offer free appraisals. Send post cards to everyone within a six-block radius when you get a listing. Even if they're not in the market to sell this month, that family with the Cape Cod may remember you when the time comes.

EMPATHY

Finally, those who succeed in the real estate business display a natural affinity for buyers and sellers. If you have sold cars or insurance or dresses, you have a leg-up in the real estate business. Although a home is the biggest purchase most consumers ever make, "sales is sales," insists John Major.

In addition to uncertainties about the flow of credit, a few other outside forces rock the real estate business from time to time, so an even disposition and a supply of Rolaids make life easier. Notably, even in the best of times, the industry is seasonal. "We do a tremendous business in the spring and summer when everything's beautiful," says John Major. "But we only sell to skiers in the winter."

The best agents make the most of drawbacks, planning winter vacations or using slack times to take—or give—courses in various real estate activities. For example, some states require a different license to sell industrial or commercial property as a major part of your business.

While anyone in realty decries the notoriously cyclical nature of housing, John insists the business isn't much worse than others. "Housing fluctuates to the economic pitch of the nation. When everything else is down, so is housing. But there's always a market, even in economic downturns.

"Consider the supply-demand factor," he continues. "There will never be any more land created than what we have now. But everyday, more babies are born. New families are created. They all need housing."

SOURCES

Industry Associations

National Association of Realtors, 430 N. Michigan Ave., Chicago, Ill. 60611 (312) 329-8200

National Association of Real Estate License Law Officials, P.O. Box 129, Centerville, Utah 84014 (801) 531-8202

National Association of Real Estate Brokers, 1101 14th St., N.W., Suite 900, Washington, D.C. 20005 (202) 289-6655

Publications

Real Estate Today, 430 N. Michigan Ave., Chicago, Ill. 60611 (312) 329-8200

Real Estate Business, Commercial Investment Real Estate Council, 430 N. Michigan, Suite 500, Chicago, Ill. 60611 (800) 621-7035

Real Estate Appraiser

> *"Every property has a different scenario, so appraisal never gets stale. The number and types of people I meet are just amazing."* – *Robert F. Heffernan, Professional Appraisal Associates*

Low Startup Investment: $3,000 (for a word processor and camera, using the family car)

High Startup Investment: $10,000 (includes an office, car lease, and some advertising)

Time Until Breakeven: Two months to one year

Annual Revenues: $70,000-$3 million (one person at low end; supervising a staff of appraisers at high end)

Annual Pre-tax Profits: $60,000-$500,000

Staffers Needed for Startup (including founder): One

"We're really real estate detectives," says Robert F. Heffernan, founder of Professional Appraisal Associates, in explaining what an appraiser does for a living. "We use our knowledge of the market to determine what a particular piece of property is worth."

Bob Heffernan's list of customer types runs the gamut. For example, properties must be assessed for

• Banks, every time they grant a mortgage or foreclose on a home loan

• Lawyers, when they distribute an estate or represent clients in a marriage or business partnership break-up where the couple must divide real estate

• Individuals, who want an uninterested party to tell them the true value of a home before they buy or sell, or before they contest real estate taxes

- The government, each time it condemns property or reassesses taxes
- Insurance carriers, before they agree to property-damage settlements

"Some appraisers specialize in one segment, or take just residential or commercial properties," says Bob Heffernan, who started his appraising company in 1980. "But we wanted a large base to cover the market fluctuations that occur in real estate. Residential may slow down while commercial sales are still strong. Or banks that don't grant as many mortgages when interest rates go up may foreclose on more properties." Bob's strategy works. By 1987, Professional Appraisal Associates had grown to one of the largest services in the Northeast with twenty-five appraisers and seven secretaries.

THE ART AND THE SCIENCE

There's a whole method to the madness of pricing real estate that goes way beyond looking up prices in the classifieds. The two professional societies that represent the industry, the Society of Real Estate Appraisers and the American Institute of Real Estate Appraisers, both require their members to follow three approaches:

1. The Cost Approach (or, count all those nickels and dimes). First you count all the individual components of a property, including what was originally paid for the land as well as the sticks and the bricks. You don't have to be an engineer since you don't inspect for construction flaws (to learn more about inspection, see Home Inspection). But you do need a rudimentary knowledge of construction prices. Next, assume what it would cost to build today. Then you subtract the depreciation since the land was bought and the building was constructed. Voilà—the cost of the property.

2. The Market Data Approach (a/k/a checking out the Joneses). Look for sales within the community that compare with the real estate under scrutiny. Of course, you must add any appreciation or depreciation that has taken place since the comparison property sold. Then you adjust for differences in size, quality of construction, and location within the community. (An ice cream stand on the

corner of Main and Second streets would go for more than one in the middle of the block.)

3. The Income Approach (or, how much cash can this cow generate?). This approach assumes the owner might want to rent out. You find what similar houses or storefronts lease for, as well as what improvements other landlords make to attract renters. That guideline suggests what your client might make as net income prior to mortgage payments.

Of course, if no income-producing properties exist in the area, appraisers don't bother with this last approach. Otherwise, they are expected to use all three techniques to arrive at a fair market value.

Since every deed is recorded at the courthouse, all you have to do is find a property roughly equivalent to the three-bedroom, two-bath townhouse you're assessing. Then you assume your client's property is worth about the same, right? Wrong. "Identifying sales is easy," says Bob Heffernan. "Determining the reasons why a property sold for what it did is the difficult part." For example, sellers who allow buyers to space out payments on installment plans likely ask for more than sellers who make a lump-sum sale. Or, say negotiations for an industrial plant stretched over two years; the deed may read December 1987, when the purchase price was actually agreed upon two years earlier.

The only way to dig up such clues is through detective work—typically talking to the buyer and seller or the attorneys and real estate brokers involved in the sale. "People wonder why we get our fees," says Bob Heffernan. "They pay for our judgment and ability to track down meaningful numbers."

LEVERAGE

Once you pin down an assessment, you can use the figures to help you assess other, similar properties—within a reasonable time period. Most lenders require residential property comparisons no older than six months, although commercial figures stay current for as long as a couple of years. But if you have to assess two homes roughly equivalent in size and value, you need do the homework only once. Such an economy-of-scale assessment of many similar properties can cut down on how much time you spend following paper trails.

Bob Heffernan says Professional Appraisal Associates takes between four and eight hours to assess an average residence. If he's doing the assessment for a bank that supplies much of the back-up information and provides a fill-in-the-blank type form, he charges between $150 and $300, depending on the difficulty of the assessment; a homeowner who wants a written narrative likely pays $400 to $450.

Appraisals for commercial real estate can take much longer than those for residences, depending on the size of the property and the number of tenants. "A typical Northeastern commercial property would run $2,000 to $5,000," says Bob, "but I've seen them up to $40,000."

Although few appraisers charge strictly by the hour, most figure a top-of-the-profession appraiser makes $100 to $125 an hour, while a less experienced junior staffer commands $50 or so.

Generally, the most successful practices fall into two categories: solo appraisers with no overhead, and large (fifteen to thirty people) firms. It's those in-between firms that have the most difficulty meeting expenses, because they have overhead but no economy of scale. "A three-person operation needs as much data as a one-hundred-person firm," says Bob Heffernan. "It is inefficient to run."

Let's look first at a one-person startup. You can easily operate from a spare bedroom equipped with a telephone. You'll need a tape measure to count off feet and a camera to record the general look of a property. The family car can provide transportation. If you type your reports, buy a typewriter or preferably a word processor; an alternative is to contract with a part-time typist. A Yellow Pages listing catches the eyes of individuals who need appraisals. Also, you may advertise with tasteful announcements in professional bank and legal journals. With such low overhead, approximately 75 percent of your gross—which might reach $70,000 annually—equals profits.

WHEN IT'S TIME TO GROW

Once you add a partner or a second appraiser, you'll probably need office space and a full-time secretary. "We figure half of the fees we charge goes to salaries, both secretaries and appraisers," says Bob Heffernan. "Overhead—cars, insurance, supplies, rent—leaves profits anywhere from nothing to 25 percent." Grow as fast as you can, because the smaller firms may have to struggle at the lower profit ranges until they can add enough associates to achieve those economies. Marketing becomes a crucial part of your strategy, as you need to attract more clients if you are to add appraisers.

Also: You need to hone your detective techniques. For example, instead of wading through court documents to find comparison properties, establish contact with real estate agents who will let you peruse their files. Many outfits join county real estate organizations which often provide regularly updated sale prices and descriptions of properties.

Some appraisers migrate into real estate brokering, although others consider this a conflict of interest. But nothing says you can't put some of your profits into real estate investment and even development of properties. After all, considering the homework you've done, who knows a community's real estate needs better than you?

SOURCES

Industry Associations

American Institute of Real Estate Appraisers, 430 N. Michigan Ave., Chicago, Ill. 60611 (312) 329-8559

Society of Real Estate Appraisers, 645 N. Michigan Ave., Chicago, Ill. 60611 (312) 346-7422

American Association of Certified Appraisers, 7 E. Swin Dr., Cincinnati, Ohio 45218 (513) 825-1603

Real Estate Auctioneer

> *"A good auctioneer would rather go to somebody else's auction than to a movie, just to drink in the atmosphere. There's electricity to an auction, intrigue, enthusiasm." – Dick Dewees, Missouri Auction School*

Low Startup Investment: $0 (to hold an on-site auction)

High Startup Investment: $5,000 (to market auctions and hire an auctioneer)

Time Until Breakeven: Immediate to six months

Annual Revenues (in commissions): $100,000-$25 million

Annual Pre-tax Profits: $90,000-$7.5 million

Staffers Needed for Startup (including founder): One

In 1977, Larry Latham's construction business was being suffocated by 20-percent interest rates. He was a couple hundred thousand dollars in debt when he heard a stranger talking about how he made $300,000 in a single day, auctioning off dock property for the City of New Orleans.

The banks were in as much trouble as Larry. They'd foreclosed on home mortgages and were stuck with property they couldn't sell. So Larry, who had kept his broker's license and knew the real estate business as well as anybody, figured he had some potential partners to launch him into the real estate auction business, whether they knew it or not. He approached the very banks that held his six-figure IOUs. "I said, 'I know you've got real estate you'd like to sell. I can sell it for you real fast. All you have to do up front is give me $1,000 per house for advertising.'

"I guess the banks wanted to give me a chance to get out of debt so I could pay them back," Larry muses. Anyway, they turned the advertising money over and authorized him to show the houses. Sure enough, during the next year, Larry auctioned off twenty-eight houses that the banks had been unable to unload. He received a 10-percent commission on each house, which ranged in price from $12,000 to $60,000.

Armed with his new track record, Larry graduated from knocking on the doors of bankers he knew, to doors of unfamiliar financial institutions. Then he let the government know he could get rid of the property it had collected in lieu of taxes. "That first year, I sold a half-million dollars worth of houses," says the entrepreneur. A decade later, Larry Latham Auctioneers still operates from tiny Moulton, Alabama—as well as fourteen branch offices scattered from Washington, D.C., to Los Angeles. Annual listings in 1987 amounted to a quarter-billion dollars. Of that, Larry Latham Auctioneers lands commissions of between 6 and 10 percent (about $15 million), compared with average commissions of 6 to 7 percent that real estate brokers command. The auction industry gets higher fees because they sell property faster.

LOW OVERHEAD—HIGH POTENTIAL

Unlike art or antique auctioneering that requires a facility where you can store and display your inventory, real estate auctioneering demands little overhead—unless you grow to Larry Latham's scale. (For a look at auction houses, which sell everything from comic strip illustrations to the Duchess of Windsor's jewelry, see Auction House.) You won't accumulate as much as a two-by-four in inventory. Somebody else fronts the advertising costs, and you can start as a part-time, solo auctioneer operating out of your own home and car.

Is it lucrative? Because you often auction estates (as well as the house itself), which consists of a person's entire worldly possessions, says Dick Dewees, who runs the Missouri Auction School in Kansas City, "you can get a percentage of the average person's life savings in a day or a week. Next week you can sell another estate. You can make as much as an average person saves in a lifetime in a year."

All an auctioneer has to do is bring in the sellers and let them fight each other like bargain hunters at a going-out-of-business sale.

"Americans are the most competitive people in the world," says Larry Latham. "All you do is create a market by telling the public you're going to sell to the highest bidder."

Auctioneers admit that some real estate goes for less than the owners would like. But they also insist other properties command premiums. Individuals decide to auction their houses because it's fast—and they gamble it might be more profitable. Auctions are to traditional real estate listings what Seattle Slew is to the old gray mare: fast. "Auctions create an urgency," says Larry. "Sometimes people won't buy a house on the market, hoping the price will go down. But once it's on the auction block, somebody else will buy it if you don't." While a real estate broker may advertise a home every week and still not sell it for months, an auction company advertises it once or twice, holds an auction, and somebody walks off with the deed.

While just 2 percent of all real estate sold in 1986 went under the auctioneer's gavel, the concept is spreading fast. The business publication *Barron's* predicts one out of every four houses sold in the late 1990s will be auctioned. Larry Latham scoffs at the notion of competition: "Business will grow at 100 percent a year for the next five to ten years," he says. "We honestly cannot keep up with the demand—we turn down three out of five properties. The smaller guys pick up some of them, but they get too busy to handle the overflow."

Real estate auctions, whether for a $10,000 vacant lot or $10 million estate, follow the same basic eight steps. You

- Round up some real estate
- Advertise
- Show the property at the set time
- Legitimize the property (verify the facts)
- Arrange financing (optional)
- Host the big day
- Close on each sale
- Get your commission

STEP 1: FINDING THE MERCHANDISE

If you're selling the Taj Mahal, you'll generate enough interest and commission to base the entire auction around that single piece of property. Otherwise, plan to bundle anywhere from a handful to a few hundred smaller sales together. Contact banks and other property holders who have houses, farms, or commercial or industrial property to sell. You can even go to real estate brokers and offer them a listing fee for turning a house over to you. Larry Latham signs four-year contracts with groups like the Department of Housing and Urban Development to auction blocks of houses monthly in different sections of the country.

Almost all real estate auctioneers operate on consignment, meaning you sell somebody else's property without ever taking title. However, occasionally an auctioneer willing to tie up a few dollars for a few days can gamble. "I've seen guys buy a plant the board of directors was afraid to auction," says Dick Dewees. "They pay $1.2 million and the auction company sells the plant and the equipment in pieces for $1.5 million."

Unless you state that an auction is "absolute," the sale is at the owner's reserve, meaning the owner can refuse the winning bid as too low. "Any decent auctioneer wants everything sold at absolute auction, and asks for that," says Dick, who calls minimums "pure foolishness. Properties bring 10 to 15 percent less if bidders know the owner can refuse their bid." He says serious bidders will not invest the time to really scout out properties—for example, bring in an engineer to inspect a house ahead of time—if they know it might not sell at the price they're willing to pay. Therefore they bid low, guessing they may have to invest more in after-purchase improvements.

STEP 2: FINDING THE BIDDERS

In order to push prices high, you must create a critical mass of buyers, all anxious to outbid each other. Instead of placing a one-inch ad buried in Sunday's paper, you "blast with a big ad," says Dick Dewees. In that ad, you list your properties, their addresses, the open-house times for prospective buyers, and the time and place of the auction. You also explain extra information, such as whether financing is available (and from whom), and what buyers must do to qualify.

Some auctioneers also advertise on radio and TV, or with direct mail and telemarketing. If Larry Latham thinks a property is ripe for development, he sends brochures to lists of real estate investors. For residential properties, he mails to people already living in the area. "We figure they know friends or family they'd like to locate in the same neighborhood," he explains. For the most part, the sellers pay for the advertising up front.

STEP 3: SHOWING OFF

If the property is unoccupied, the auction company usually shows it at the advertised open house. If the seller still lives in the house, the owner hosts potential bidders. Many auctioneers print brochures describing each home (3 bedroom, 1 1/2 bath, 2-car garage on 1/2 acre. Special features: skylights and Jacuzzi). Bidders use the open house to assess what they think the property is worth, and often visit several listings.

STEP 4: TYING LOOSE ENDS

This step is where that intangible—expertise—comes in. If you sell real estate, you must be familiar with the market in general as well as that particular home. In the period between taking the listing and the auction, you also check out titles to assure the house is truly free to be sold. Your reputation depends on verifying the facts. If you advertise a factory at 108,742 square feet, it had better be 108,742 square feet and zoned for industrial usage, or you can be sued for misrepresentation.

Larry Latham has enough business to be choosy. He refuses auctions in deeply depressed real estate markets, for example. While the dips may not be as treacherous as in traditional real estate sales, auctions still suffer the cyclical peaks and valleys other real estate experiences. "Also, if you take a property built over a toxic waste site, it reflects on you. I wouldn't touch it, even if the seller is willing to take 50 cents on the dollar. They should be negotiating the problems in a private sale, whereas we would advertise those problems to the public and ruin the market."

STEP 5: FINANCING

Lining up financing is an optional step, but Larry Latham says it pays off. You get commissions faster if banks are eager to participate, and buyers don't renege if they drop a down payment at the time of the auction. Larry calls on banks or savings and loans and tells them of the blocks of houses he auctions on a particular day. His ads and brochures specify which institutions will finance, and at what rate. Larry's auctions require anyone attending to bring a cashier's check. This tactic assures that the auctions will be full of bidders rather than the merely curious.

STEP 6: THE AUCTION

Depending on how many bidders you expect, you rent a hall, which could be a hotel room, convention site, or the municipal auditorium. Auctions of large estates are held on the property. When Larry Latham expects one thousand bidders to bid on one hundred properties, he might employ three or four auctioneers and ten "ringmen," or individuals walking the floor to catch bids. In addition, a dozen people working the desk register bidders, making sure each has a cashier's check.

To auction real estate, you must be a licensed broker (see Real Estate Agent for how to become a broker). Some states also require an auctioneer's license (see *Auction House*). If you don't call the auction yourself, you can hire auctioneers who either receive a flat fee, or a percent of each sale.

STEP 7: WRAPPING IT UP

After the auction is over, Larry Latham leaves a skeleton crew of three or four people to work with the buyers' lawyers to close each sale. This step may stretch over six weeks as buyers and lenders get together. Except to sign papers, the seller never has to appear.

STEP 8: MONEY

As soon as the buyer takes title, you get your commission check from the seller. Commissions vary depending on
- The local real estate market (you usually do a point or two better than brokers in a given area)
- The price of the property (a $10 million ranch sale often carries a lower percentage—but higher absolute fee—than a $50,000 house
- Deals you make with the seller (for example, Larry Latham takes a smaller commission to auction three hundred houses for a single client than he does for selling one hundred houses)

From that commission, you reimburse yourself for the cost of renting the auction hall and personnel salaries. For small auctions that you call yourself on the premises being sold, overhead may be zilch. "If I didn't have the overhead of forty employees and fourteen offices," says Larry, "I'd try to sell seven houses a week. If they average $50,000, I've made $35,000 at the end of that week."

Instead, Larry Latham Auctioneers concentrates on volume. Dick Dewees recalls a Phoenix auction he and his son, also a certified auctioneer, called for one hundred twelve of Larry's houses. "A thousand people showed up and the fire marshall wouldn't let anybody else in the municipal auditorium, so another two thousand people stood outside on the steps. These were the same houses that brokers had listed for two, three years, mind you."

Dick zeros in on a particular Phoenix property: "I remember one house we auctioned for $120,000. The developer who originally built it a few years before couldn't believe it, because he was selling brand new ones with identical floorplans and new microwaves and air conditioners for $117,000. He wanted to know who made the runner-up bid of $119,000 so he could sell a new house to that person."

Dick says timing is crucial in an auction, because you need as many bidders as possible to create competition. "If you sell residential property, you want a weekend or evening sale so both the husband and wife come. If it's a commercial sale, you auction during the week because business people go to the lake on the weekend. Mondays aren't good, though, because business people want to go through the weekend mail and get the crew started. If you think an investor might buy a property, you sell on Wednesday or Thursday. That's the doctor's day off, and doctors have more disposable income than any other group." Finally, says Dick, "in the State of Oklahoma, the cardinal rule is you never ever have a Saturday afternoon auction during football season."

What happens if it rains? "That's great," says Dick. "Farm bidders can't get into the field to plow. The guys who usually go to the lake would just as soon be indoors."

Real estate auctioneers say almost any property that two or more people want to buy makes good auction material. Half of Larry Latham's sales are residential, 20 percent are farms and ranches, and the rest are commercial properties. "We do $10,000 houses and $200,000 houses," says Larry. But the splashiest auctions are the really big multi-million-dollar deals. Take, for example, the Big Sky Movie Ranch in Simi Valley, California.

Backed with a $420,000 advertising budget provided by the Getty estate which owned the ranch, Larry Latham Auctioneers began marketing the seven-thousand-acre ranch, primarily to foreign investors, four months before the June 13, 1987, auction. The Los Angeles *Times*, *USA Today*, and *The Wall Street Journal* all carried front-page stories on the sale of the Movie Ranch, which hosted filming of such television shows as "Gunsmoke" and "Little House on the Prairie." In May, three thousand people paid $5 a head to attend a barbecue there, proceeds going to the YMCA. The publicity created excitement, and didn't hurt Larry Latham's reputation as an auctioneer *extraordinaire*, either.

Come the big day, two dozen people bid on the ranch, which was divided into four parcels. When the final gavel sounded, the estate sold for $35 million. Larry Latham Auctioneers collected about 6%, or $2.1 million.

SOURCES:

See Auction Houses

Relocation Consultant

> *"Friends hear you're moving to New Jersey and say, 'Are you crazy?' All they've seen is the turnpike with the oil tanks near Newark Airport, so they think it's horrible. It's gratifying to alleviate their fears and to see their smiles when we show them what the state really has to offer."* – Terri Fisher, Fisher Hornor Associates

Low Startup Investment: $5,000 (to set up a solo office in mid-sized city)

High Startup Investment: $10,000 (for an office in a metro area with several employees)

Time Until Breakeven: Three months to one year

Annual Revenues: $40,000-$500,000

Annual Pre-tax Profits: $20,000-$100,000

Staffers Needed for Startup (including founder): One

Brad and Arlene, who both work for large corporations with branches across the country, always kidded about who would make vice president first. In their case, it was Brad, and both were thrilled with his promotion. There was just one drawback, and it was a stinker: Along with the higher salary and prestige came a transfer to his company's St. Louis office.

The couple visited St. Louis and liked the Midwest. Nevertheless, they aren't so sure they want to leave family, friends, and Arlene's good job for what amounts to a foreign country. Brad's company has been in this situation enough times to know it can lose a good employee faced with such choices. To ease the dilemma, Brad's boss says he'll be getting a call from a relocation consultant.

If Arlene wants, a career counselor will also help her find a new position in St. Louis. With such hand-holding, the couple decides to join the 17 percent of all households who move to new cities each year.

A GUIDE TO THE BRAVE NEW WORLD

" 'Relocation consulting' is a generic term that encompasses anything having to do with assisting transferred employees," says Anita Brienza, manager of public relations for the Employee Relocation Council. When she says "anything," she includes
- Finding a moving company
- Arranging for a pet's transportation
- Describing the types of neighborhoods in the new town, and possibly lining up real estate to choose from
- Suggesting schools, churches, hospitals, day care centers, and nursing homes—any support organization that a family might need
- Brokering and even buying the house in the old neighborhood
- Stress-counseling
- Spouse job-placement assistance.

Of course, you can mix and match among those responsibilities, or add your own services. Except for career counseling, which really counts as its own unique specialty (see Career Counselor), most relocation consultants concentrate on knowing their territory better than anyone else in the whole world. "I sell my knowledge of an area and of its real estate practices," explains Terri Fisher, of Fisher Hornor Associates, Westfield, New Jersey. Even though you don't actually sell homes, you need a real estate license to offer such counseling. However, you can pick that up in several months (see Real Estate Agent). "I've hired people without real estate background who had experience with being transferred themselves," Terri says. "They know from experience exactly what has to be done and have the empathy to help clients through the process."

Typically, relocation counseling works this way: The corporation calls the relocation consultant with the name and phone number of the employee on the transfer track. Then, the counselor contacts the employee for an initial telephone counseling session. "We determine how the employee and family feels about the move and discuss the housing and personal requirements," says Terri Fisher.

HOLDING THE BUYER'S HAND

For employees who want to buy, relocation consultants discuss the homebuying process and actually qualify them for a mortgage by asking about their income and debts and assets. Then comes the "art" part, as you ask about life style and what the couple wants in a community. "Clients might want schools with a certain curriculum, or an idyllic rural area," says Terri.

Any good relocation specialist worth the moniker knows which areas sound appropriate for the income level and life style the clients describe. Some consultants actually broker houses themselves, although Terri Fisher considers that practice a conflict of interest since some agents tend to favor their own properties. Instead, before the client comes to town for the house search, Terri lines up real estate agents who cover the areas Terri selects for her client. Then she describes exactly what her client's dream house should include. The real estate agents plan an itinerary of houses to tour. Terri accompanies the client on the first day's tour to make sure that she properly conveyed the client's preferences. "New Jersey's idea of rural might be different from that of someone from another part of the country," she explains.

Since she's done the homework ahead of time to identify which neighborhoods seem perfect, and has screened realtors for efficiency, Terri's typical client buys a house in only four days. "It always blows my mind, but then we've eliminated the wasted time that clients usually spend looking at inappropriate houses and communities," she says.

Most relocation consultants receive their commission from the real estate agent rather than the corporation, a practice which brings everybody knocking on the consultant's door. Corporations like you because they have employees who have found housing quickly and efficiently and can now concentrate on the new job. Realtors are happy to pass along anything from 25 percent of the broker's commission to 1 percent of the sale price of the house because you bring them interested, qualified buyers. Buyers like you because you act as an objective party who protects their position and speeds along the house-hunting process.

TAKING THE RENTAL ROUTE

If the employee wants to rent, you take a different approach. "We ask if they're interested in an apartment, house, or condo," says Terri Fisher. "We learn what size family they have and what commute time would be acceptable. We determine whether the family has pets and the length of the lease they're looking for. Some families want to rent for a short time until they're ready to buy, for example."

With all the particulars in hand, a day or two before the client comes to town you call landlords to see what units are available, and sketch an itinerary. Then you meet the clients at their hotel or the company and give the grand tour. On the way to each rental, point out schools, shopping centers, community amenities, etc. "By the end of the day, clients know what's available and they're usually ready to sign a lease," says Terri.

When you relocate renters, as opposed to homebuyers, corporations will pick up the tab for your time. You can expect anywhere from $500 to one-month's rent as your fee.

The better you know your area, the less time you spend on research. With more time, you can sign on more clients and boost your potential income. An efficient relocation consultant can expect annual fees in the $30,000 to $50,000 range. But you can leverage that fee in a couple of ways.

LEVERAGE

Most obviously, you can hire staff or subcontractors and increase the number of clients your firm relocates. You can also do a real volume business by targeting large accounts like a corporation that's moving a whole division to your area. Each one of those transferred employees needs to find a new home.

Terri Fisher says her firm relocated one such group from Manhattan to New Jersey over one year. "This move involved researching the new area for the corporation and gathering current information on schools, housing, day care, senior citizen facilities, places of worship, recreational activities, etc." Using that information, Terri pre-

sented an orientation program to give the transferees a visual introduction to the new area and its offerings. "A 'Relocation Center'
was set up at the company's Manhattan site, and each of the three
hundred employees whose jobs were affected was eligible for a
personal counseling session with one of our consultants," recalls
Terri. Homebuyers were referred to real estate agents while Fisher
Hornor Associates found rentals for those who wanted to rent. For
such a comprehensive service on this scale, a relocation firm could
gross several hundred thousand dollars.

You can also offer other services, such as lining up moving vans
and storage. Terri Fisher goes beyond furniture rental to lease everything a renter needs to set up house—pots, pans, linens, and all
the odds-and-ends every household needs. "If the move is permanent, the client is better off to buy," explains Terri. "But for the
short-term moves, we'll stock an apartment with everything necessary. We even put the dishes away and make the beds so all the
client has to do is come in and unpack the clothes from the suit-
cases." In addition to serving corporations bringing in executives
for short-term assignments, Terri's household-linens rental service
gathers leads from real estate agents, furniture rental companies,
and even other relocation companies.

Terri stresses the importance of developing contacts with corporations and real estate agents and says not to be afraid to tackle even
the most finicky clients or difficult cases. She remembers one lead
she received from another relocation company that only handled
mass moves. The assignment had its difficulties. "The family was
looking for short-term rental, and landlords don't like to give leases
for less than a year. They also had a dog, so on the surface the
assignment was not appealing."

But Terri found the family a furnished house, and saw rewards
beyond that one-time fee. "In talking with them, I found the husband was going to be president of a health care facility and was
going to bring in people to work for him. They were only renting
because they planned to buy a house in the near future. So I got
additional business in the long run. That other firm did me a real
service by not listening to him."

SOURCES

Industry Association

Employee Relocation Council, 1720 N St., N.W., Washington, D.C. 20036 (202) 857-0857

Publication

Mobility, 1720 N St., N.W., Washington, D.C. 20036 (202) 857-0857

Retailing

Athletic Shoe Store

> *"I'm an athlete and I sell a product I relate to." – Matt Zale, U.S. Athletics*

Low Startup Investment: $110,000 (small independent)

High Startup Investment: $220,000 (large franchise with clothing as well as shoes)

Time Until Breakeven: One to three years

Annual Revenues: $225,000-$1 million

Annual Pre-tax Profits: $20,000-$200,000

Staffers Needed for Startup (including founder): Three

If you haven't given much thought to your feet, you probably aren't an athlete. Runners spend many happy hours ruminating on Nikes vs. New Balances. Aerobics participants argue Adidas vs. Avias ad nauseam. Forget the good old days of $20 sneakers; today's athletic footwear can cost as much as supersaver cross-country airfare. Tennis buffs who spend $100 for a pair of shoes gravitate to shops catering to their special needs. In fact, they often don't even know what those needs are until a salesperson explains them. Consider that some manufacturers stuff shoe boxes with "owner's manuals," and you'll understand why the bewildered athlete turns to athletic-shoe shops for guidance.

ENOUGH ATHLETIC SUPPORTERS?

But can America, whose obsession with physical fitness seems to be waning, support more shops in the dizzying $4 billion brand-name athletic footwear market? Matt Zale, who headquarters his thirty-six-store U.S. Athletics shoe store chain in Long Island City, New

York, sees enough shoe buyers to double 1986 sales of $10 million to $20 million within just a few years. "There aren't as many joggers as there used to be, but those left are more serious. They buy more shoes," says Matt, who entered athletic footwear in 1977 as a twenty-four-year-old by buying the right to franchise Athlete's Foot stores in Manhattan.

And, like other athletic shoe shops, U.S. Athletics isn't restricted to marathoners. "You have to think where the new sports will be," says Matt, who broke away from the franchise and went independent in 1987. "When I started, tennis was big, then running, then for a short while raquetball, then aerobics. Now it's general fitness for people who work out with weights and in gyms. Next will come walking, especially as a way for older people to get involved with fitness. After that, who knows?"

In fact, the first Urban Hiker opened on Manhattan's Upper West Side in 1986 to cater specifically to walkers with seventy varieties of walking shoes. Business is good enough to lead founder George Pakradoonian Jr. to talk of ten more Urban Hikers nationwide by 1988.

Matt Zale says the opportunities are still there. You only have to do three things right in the athletic shoe business?

- Sell the right merchandise
- Hire the right staff
- Find the right location

FOOT TRAFFIC

The vast majority of people in our country at least occasionally steps into sport shoes. An athletic-shoe customer profile covers both sexes, every ethnic and age group, and city, suburban, and rural dwellers. But an athletic-shoe merchant must be there when they want you. "An art gallery needs the right kind of traffic," says Matt Zale. "An athletic-shoe store just needs *high* traffic." Because athletic-shoe customers respond to spur-of-the-moment impulses rather than advertising, nobody's going to travel miles from a daily routine to find you tucked away in a back alley. Instead, athletic-shoe shops need bright-light visibility, the kind that comes with expensive regional shopping malls or gentrified city neighborhoods.

Of course, you also must consider the competition before choosing a spot. No mall wants two athletic-shoe boutiques. And if you think Reebok will ship you shoes if you park around the corner from its best account, forget it.

Rent in shopping malls or other visible locations is expensive, which explains why you'll spend at least $100,000 to open an athletic-shoe shop. The National Sporting Goods Association figures an operator needs $20 a square foot to set up fixtures, and most franchisors recommend another $50,000 in inventory from a dozen shoe vendors to open a thousand-square-foot store. If you carry clothing as well, you'll need both more space and more vendors.

However, if you choose the right spot, you don't need much space to do big numbers in athletic shoes. U.S. Athletics shops, each about a thousand square feet, average an astounding $900 a square foot in sales—and one of its Manhattan stores runs away with sales of $2,000 a square foot. Because price isn't usually a big factor for your customers, you don't need constant price reductions; margins remain higher than in most retailing. If you hit a home run with a store that generates annual revenues of $1 million, you can keep pre-tax profits of $200,000 or more.

Hint: If you do decide to run sales, check with your vendors. Chances are they offer generous co-op advertising plans because, even if *you* don't have to advertise, they do. All the footwear manufacturers are trying to yank business away from one another.

SALES SAVVY

Once you find the right location, next comes staffing with the right people. Matt Zale estimates his employees generate $300 to $700 in sales a day. "Using my formula, if you figure on doing $1,000 a day, you'll need two or three people." Since they sell an athletic product, make sure your salespeople look the part: robust and energetic.

Because new employees might not know everything there is to know about insteps and toe-boxes before coming into the store, plan on spending a few weeks teaching them about shoes. Build a relationship with your manufacturers, who will be happy to explain the merits of their various lines. Remember, customers come to an athletic-shoe store for only two reasons: advice and variety.

SHOES AND MORE SHOES

U.S. Athletics carries about two hundred styles and sizes of shoes, which account for 80 percent of its sales. The rest comes from socks and accessories—"jock clothing, strictly impulse buys," says Matt Zale. His chain's stores are located on city streets in Manhattan, Dallas, and Phoenix, where competition from department stores in clothing is too severe to go deeper into it.

Clothing margins are good, though. So if you're in an area where department and general sporting goods stores don't have the athletic-clothing business wrapped up, and if you can afford to devote space to jogging suits and leotards, go for it. But clothing turnover may be less, so remember why it is that customers come to you in the first place: for shoes. Don't neglect your strength.

You may have to fiddle with the inventory mix until you get a true reading of your market's feet. Observes Matt Zale: "New York is one of the better running markets and it's easy to see why: Running doesn't require space like tennis courts. Dallas loves its football, and tennis is big in Phoenix where it's sunny every day of the year." Okay, that makes sense. But here's an interesting "foottistic" from Matt: Did you know that feet are narrower in Dallas and longer in Phoenix?

SOURCES

Industry Association

National Sporting Goods Association, 1699 Wall St., Mount Prospect, Ill. 60056 (312) 439-4000

Publications

Sports Trend, 180 Allen Rd., N.E., Suite 300 S., Atlanta, Ga. 30328 (404) 252-8831

Sporting Goods Business, 1515 Broadway, New York, N.Y. 10036 (212) 869-1300

Sporting Goods Dealer, 1212 N. Lindbergh Blvd., St. Louis, Mo. 63132 (314) 997-7111

Children's Clothing Boutique

> *"I love children. I love having them in my store. I keep baskets of toys for them to play with while their mothers shop. I keep a carousel horse they ride." – Dorothy McNish, Elecia Michelle Inc.*

Low Startup Investment: $50,000 (modest boutique)

High Startup Investment: $200,000 (larger urban shop)

Time Until Breakeven: Two to five years

Annual Revenues: $100,000-$1 million (for a large metropolitan-area shop)

Annual Pre-tax Profits: $2,000-$200,000

Staffers Needed for Startup (including founder): Two to four

Today's upscale children's retail market is a shopkeeper's fantasy come true. As discounters clothe the masses and department stores scrape margins on mid-price points, children's boutiques flourish by offering $150 Giorgio Armani blazers in size toddler 2 or $650 Krizia sequined "cocktail" dresses for the under-six set. And 200-percent markups on $900 christening gowns can cloak a lot of mistakes.

Demographers and social scientists say the American baby boom generation is bringing up its own babies with panache. With mother working, modern parents possess the money (and perhaps the guilt) to buy their kids the best, including the best clothes. Two sets of statistics suggest that the population of children is growing, and that an increasing number of parents can afford to clothe their darlings with the help of Ralph Lauren and Liz Claiborne:

▪ The increasing pre-teen population. In 1985, the Census Bureau counted 44.7 million children under age thirteen. Whether or not the birth rate continues to climb, existing kids need a fresh closet-full of clothes every year to grow into. According to the children's clothing trade magazine *Earnshaw's Review,* the total children's wear market in 1984 amounted to $14 billion, a 40-percent increase over the $10 billion spent on kiddies five years earlier.

▪ Affluence. In 1984, the IRS tells us that 11 million households (13 percent of the U.S. population) had incomes of $50,000 or more. By 1985, 25 percent more families had crowded into the bracket. In the words of Texas oilman H. L. Hunt, "A billion dollars ain't what it used to be." But in 1985, the government counted 10,800 individuals with annual incomes of $1 million or more— more than twice the 5,286 people who made $1 million in 1980.

KIDDIE CACHET

"I cater to—I hate to say it—Yuppies," admits Dorothy McNish, who named her Little Rock, Arkansas, boutique after granddaughter Elecia Michelle. "People want top quality for their children— something everyone else doesn't have. These women waited longer to have children. They've been in the work force and have money to spend. They don't think twice about spending on their children. When they see what they want, they buy it."

Indeed. Dorothy does carry a line of Philippine smocked dresses in the $32 retail ballpark. But best sellers include $80 to $350 French and Italian matching sets and "little dresses" for up to $800. In 1987, three years after startup, Elecia Michelle was grossing nearly $20,000 a month and Dorothy was close enough to profitability to taste it.

Doris Cerutti, the grande dame among pricey children's clothing shopkeepers, allows that Cerutti's "used to be practically alone. Now there must be twenty children's shops in a twenty-block radius." But for Cerutti, on the upper-crust, Upper East Side of Manhattan, competition has been healthy as business has continued to grow. In her case, a shop on every corner merely legitimizes the trend; parents accept a $120 price tag on a pint-sized Burberry raincoat without blinking. Meanwhile, numerous affluent areas still lack a glitzy kids boutique, forcing moms (and grandmoms) to make semi-annual pilgrimages to Madison Avenue or Rodeo Drive.

Discounting the hordes of wealthy, middle-aged matrons who decide it would be "fun" to open a "sweet little shop," one consultant claims some successful shopkeepers live better than heads of large department store chains. "If you're an astute merchant and religious about working, retailers can live like barons," he insists.

IMAGE: YOU ARE WHAT YOU WEAR

Because you must locate in affluent areas to be near your clientele, rent may be on the high side. Your most expensive element in startup, however, will be inventory. A very small boutique can go easy on the decor and squeeze in for $50,000 or so. But opening a bigger store with adequate stock in an urban high-rent district may cost $200,000 or more.

If you want to operate an exclusive children's clothing store, you must look the part. The most important aspect of image is simply the merchandise on the floor. "Make a statement with your clothing," insists Doris Cerutti. If you intend to sell top-of-the-line clothing, "don't reach out for the masses," echoes Dorothy McNish, who worked in ladies' and children's stores before opening her own boutique. That's not to say you shouldn't stock basics like overalls and jeans, but make them unique since no boutique can compete with K mart on prices. "We're not a museum," says Maggie Chafen, who carries $24 Esprit short sets as well as $300 Joan Calabrese dresses at her Dottie Doolittle boutique. "San Francisco residents are not kings and queens. Real people don't send their children to school in $200 dresses, but they want one for parties."

Like other apparel retailers, children's merchants spend a lot of time scouting out new merchandise. Maggie Chafen, who opened Dottie Doolittle fresh out of business school in 1976, estimates she spends $150,000 annually to stock her two-thousand-square-foot store by shopping Europe twice a year as well as New York. Dorothy McNish not only filled her store, but also decorated it on a $62,000 shoestring. Acknowledging it's vital to keep a full stock, she and her husband Bill "do" New York markets four times a year, and Dallas, home of another major merchandise mart, once.

They hit the local boutiques as well as the apparel shows to see what competitors sell.

Doris Cerutti advises new shops to "get attached" to a buying office. For a stiff fee, these professional clothing buyers, most located in New York, will help determine the number of items you need in each size, the amount of inventory—all manner of things.

Vendors also court the boutiques, making client rounds once a season. Dorothy McNish credits designers with providing helpful hints and putting her on the track of other sources of merchandise. It won't hurt to ask for exclusive rights to a line within your trading zone. You might even get them.

IMAGE: WE'VE GOT THE LOOK

The other component of image is the shop's decor. Rugs and mirrors create enough of a look for some retailers, but exclusive boutiques need a one-of-a-kind look that would impress an interior designer. Dorothy McNish has thought out the twelve hundred square feet of Elecia Michelle, complete with "pale gray carpeting and pale, pale, pale pink walls," in minute detail. Take just the window display, for example: "We're in an old bank building with windows from the roof to the ground. A banister identifies the display area and keeps children out of the window. We lay merchandise on an easel and a white bench. Stuffed animals sway on a little swing when the air conditioner blows. I always keep ferns or fresh flowers or decorated baskets in the windows."

However, remember that children (and their parents) are your customers and strive for a comfortable, safe setting. "I hire people who like kids," says Maggie Chafen. "I don't want a tense atmosphere." You surely want toys for the kids to play with, and to strive for subtle childproofing: Hang rather than fold merchandise for easier maintenance; dangle those charming mobiles high from the ceiling where kids can see but not touch them.

WE DO IT ALL FOR YOU

Upscale clothing stores for all sizes exude an almost snobbish pride in their service. Create a personal relationship with customers through such touches as alterations, gift wrapping, delivery, and maybe even special ordering. "In department stores, you find your clothes and bring it to one of fourteen cash registers," says Doris Cerutti. "We're the opposite. We have one register and fourteen sales people. Our customers feel it's important to have someone help outfit their child in thirteen minutes so they can get back to their apartment or country house." Steady Cerutti customers buy from their own salesperson, who is familiar with their children's sizes and tastes.

Even smaller shops like Elecia Michelle, which Dorothy McNish runs with just two saleswomen, see one-on-one attention as crucial. "When we get a shipment, we call a customer to say we have such-and-such. 'Would you like to come in?' Then we put that merchandise aside. People spend $600 to $1,000 a trip. I couldn't survive without the call list."

Doris Cerutti goes one step further: Her sales staff delivers samples for customers who like to shop at home.

The question remains: Will today's affluent moms and dads abandon upscale children's boutiques and designer clothes from Betsey Johnson in favor of J.C. Penney and Oshkosh? The editor of *Kids Fashion* doubts children's clothing will ever be the same: "Women learned to dress when manufacturers first began mass production of clothes. Men caught on in the fifties when they got beyond black suits and white shirts. The only thing left was kids—and Europe has been way ahead of us for years.

"Whether the boom will continue, no one knows," he says. "But the trend is here to stay."

SOURCES

Fashion Markets

International Kids Fashion Show, 71 W. 35th St., Suite 1600, New York, N.Y. 10001 (212) 594-0880

Dallas Apparel Mart, 2300 Stemmons Freeway, Dallas, Tex. 75258 (214) 637-2171

Atlanta Apparel Mart, 250 Spring St., Atlanta, Ga. 30303 (404) 681-1222

Chicago Apparel Center, 350 North Orleans, Chicago, Ill. 60654
(312) 527-4141
Los Angeles Apparel Mart, 112 W. 9th St., Los Angeles, Calif.
90015 (213) 624-5992
Bayside Merchandise Mart, 150-160 Mount Vernon St.,
Dorchester, Mass. 02125 (617) 825-4040

Publications

Kids Fashion, 210 Boylston St., Chestnut Hill, Mass. 02167
(617) 964-5100
Earnshaw's Review, 393 Seventh Ave., New York, N.Y. 10001
(212) 563-2742
Children's Business, 7 E. 12 St., New York. N.Y. 10003
(212) 741-4039

Consultant

Edward M. Sachs Associates Inc., 31 Brewster St., P.O. Box 392,
Glen Cove, N.Y. 11542 (516) 671-5865

Florist

> *"Assembly-line workers never get to develop a sense of pride in their work. A florist controls the entire process from the raw product through the arrangement and gets to see the customers' reactions when you present them with a beautiful product."* – Ken Royer, Royer's Flowers Inc.

Low Startup Investment: $40,000 (neighborhood boutique)

High Startup Investment: $250,000 (urban shop)

Time Until Breakeven: One to three years

Annual Revenues: $100,000-$5 million (for a multi-unit operation)

Annual Pre-tax Profits: $5,000-$800,000

Staffers Needed for Startup (including founder): Two to four

When a florist thinks of heaven, Holland comes to mind. "You imagine bicyclists carrying a loaf of bread and a bunch of flowers," says Marcia Schaaf, proprietor of Schaaf Floral in Minneapolis.

In fantasizing what could be, consider that the average European spends $50 on flowers every year, compared to just $20 spent in the U.S. But there is hope: the U.S. Commerce Department reports that posies are much more popular than they used to be. In 1972, U.S. flower shops generated sales of $1.6 billion; by 1986 sales roared ahead to $7 billion—and industry experts project $9 billion in sales by 1990.

Season by season—or rather petal by petal—Americans are developing a love of flowers. Tradition continues to dictate floral displays at holidays and such festive and somber events as weddings, proms, and funerals. But the real sales increase comes from Americans' increasing fondness for occasional arrangements gracing dining room tables for no particular reason at all. Citing the ad campaign launched by the Society of American Florists, Drew Gruenburg, SAF director of communications, says Americans today are more likely to "Give Flowers to Someone Special: Yourself."

ARTISTS BEWARE

While the future of the flower business does sound rosy, florists averaged 1986 revenues of only $135,000. After overhead, a typical flower shop owner has about $11,000 left. Of course, some florists can tap larger markets. C. S. Cosentino's single, supermarket-sized shop, Cosentino's Florists in Auburn, New York, brings in more than $500,000 annually. Ken Royer's Flowers Inc., with eleven units throughout Pennsylvania Dutch country, generated $6 million in 1986. "The margins are there," says Ken. "All you have to do is get enough volume."

C. S. Cosentino, who also consults, warns would-be florists that "if you're an artiste—if you love flowers—stay away. If you're a business person who enjoys flowers, you have a chance." You must first and foremost recognize that you're in business to make money —not flower arrangements. Strive for volume through advertising and location and trim costs through business savvy.

Unlike other retail establishments, flower shops create on the premises. "Flower shops are not Liza Doolittle selling flowers from a stand," explains an FTD spokesperson. "You have to take the raw product, flowers, and manufacture a product—a bouquet or other arrangement—on the spot." Thanks to the florist's skill, a couple of nosegays and a few sprigs of baby's breath become a special anniversary gift.

Because of such variables as labor talent and product perishability, it's hard to control markup. Ken Royer's solution to the problem is an assembly-line approach that has earned him the moniker "the McDonald's of the Flower Industry." During holiday periods, Ken employs forty people to create designs in a central location. He posts a "menu" of arrangements at each store, and then advertises specific items such as a Daisy & Mini (carnation) Basket. This way he (1) cuts labor costs, (2) saves money by buying in volume, and (3) passes the savings on to his customers by selling many flowers with price tags well below the usual $18 or $20 minimums set by competitors. For example, Ken's chain sold fourteen hundred

Candelight Centerpieces for $12.50 each during Christmas 1986. While a single store can't match his volume, it can adopt a modified version of Ken's assembly line. Offer fewer arrangements, but promote those so you sell baskets and baskets of each item.

SHAKING OUT THE COBWEBS

Until recently, the traditional florist aimed at reducing overhead rather than building business. Take advertising. While the 3.5 percent of sales that Ken Royer devotes to direct mail, newspapers, and cable TV isn't overly generous by other retail standards, it's about 2.5 percent more than most florists set aside. And florists generally ignored the rule of thumb that location holds the key to success. In fact, since customers traditionally ordered most items over the phone for delivery to a hospital, the practice was to pick the least expensive site available.

Bucking the old traditions, modern florists are trading up to the high-profile, high-rent districts, which is pushing the cost of entry higher. You can still outfit a small, neighborhood shop for $40,000. But really elaborate urban sites can run to $250,000. In addition to scouting out the clientele in your prospective location, consider the other businesses in the area that will attract customers. For example, C. S. Cosentino reports that a successful Florida florist placed most of his thirty shops within a quarter mile of a McDonald's. "They already did the site selection for him," he explains. That florist basks in walk-in traffic.

The industry also is polishing its interiors. "The florist has a beautiful product to sell, and we're finally putting it where the public can see it," says Drew Gruenburg of SAF. Ken Royer hopes to rent franchisees a $225,000 prototype shop he developed under the name Flower Link. Compared to the dark cubby-holes associated with flower shops of the past, this store is astounding: a brick building with an atrium entrance, exposed wood ceiling, mezzanine, and drive-through window, all of which is splashed throughout with the colors of hundreds of flowers, of course.

The flower industry offers more startup help than most small-business fields. Consultants, colleges, and trade schools offer both design and business courses, and numerous publications publicize the latest industry developments. FTD and Telefloral, the two largest wire services, offer management as well as creative advice through hundreds of seminars. (Wire services aid shops in fulfilling the 15 percent of business that comes from out-of-towners. The customer simply contacts a local florist, who calls the head office of the wire service he or she subscribes to. The wire service relays the order to a member in the distant town, and a clearinghouse settles accounts between the parties once a month.)

THE BASICS OF JUGGLING

Entrepreneurs point to five different areas in which you need to develop skills to successfully run a flower shop.

- Selection and care of your product. "Trial and error is expensive when you deal with perishables," warns C. S. Cosentino. "You must know how to handle flowers—how to cut them underwater, which preservatives to store them in, a myriad of things." If you're big enough, you can order flowers directly from importers, local greenhouses, and growers in the California and Colorado "flowerbaskets." However, most small- and medium-sized firms secure their lilacs and birds-of-paradise through wholesalers.

- Flower arrangement. Although both art and science combine to create a centerpiece, ironically, design skills may be the easiest to learn. Scores of community colleges and even some four-year colleges offer courses.

- Customer relations. While all retailers deal with customers, florists encounter people at such emotional times as weddings and funerals. You must react sympathetically to a bereaved relative one moment, and hold the demanding hands of a parent of the bride the next.

- Delivery. In the beginning, you can sign on with a delivery pool or hire a part-timer with a station wagon. However, costs mount as volume grows. Marcia Schaaf, who owns five delivery vehicles, also subscribes to a pool whose driver drops orders outside her normal zone for a fee.

- Collections. Some florists honor just the major credit cards, but those with house cards say the paperwork and cost of collection is worth the trouble to build a loyal clientele. "We mailed out fifteen thousand of our own cards when we opened our last store," says Ken Royer. "It's an invitation to buy in the store."

Marcia Schaaf says 70 percent of her credit purchases are on her own card. Because in-house card holders represent a sort of inner circle of ready-made buyers, many florists direct advertising pieces to them. A computer that spews out address labels allows Marcia to send out periodic circulars to her four thousand or so card holders.

THE COMPETITION

New variations of the flower shop are appearing all around: supermarkets, stands at the entrances to subways, and mall-based kiosks. Instead of cutting into the floral pie, however, these retailers create consumer awareness of flowers for everyday and might even signal a need for a good florist shop in an area.

Despite the notion in the industry that competition is healthy, C. S. Cosentino recommends that new florists specialize. He points to a florist who advertises to the eight to ten thousand offices in Syracuse, New York. A bevy of weekly customers builds volume quickly. Marcia Schaaf likewise developed a "good corporate base" in Minneapolis and traces her best leads to her community involvement. Since she is on the board of the city's chamber of commerce, all the businesses know her.

Another lucrative specialty is parties. Approaching caterers to discuss your strengths doesn't hurt, although Marcia says a little reputation goes a long way in the party game. "Consider each wedding you decorate a showcase for your talents; do something unique that caterers will remember the next time they recommend a flower shop."

Like other retailers, florists work long hours and weekends. Nevertheless, says C. S. Cosentino, "because what we do is a craft, the hours don't seem as long."

SOURCES

Industry Association

Society of American Florists, 1601 Duke St., Alexandria, Va. 22314 (703) 836-8700

Publications

Flower News, 549 West Randolph St., Chicago, Ill. 60606
(312) 236-8648

Floral & Nursery Times, 328 Linden Ave., Wilmette, Ill. 60091
(312) 256-8777

Florists Review, Box 4368, 2231 Wanamaker, Topeka, Kans. 66614
(913) 273-1734

Consultants

C. S. Cosentino, Floral Business Services, 141 Dunning Ave., P.O.
Box 839, Auburn, N.Y. 13021 (315) 253-5316

Herb Mitchell, Herb Mitchell Associates, 234 E. 17th St., Suite
202, Costa Mesa, Calif. 92627 (714) 631-5551

Richard Milteer, Richmil Inc., 5514 Grate, Houston, Tex. 77096
(713) 669-0734

Wire Services

FTD, 29200 Northwestern Highway, Southfield, Mich. 48037
(313) 355-9300

Teleflora, 12233 W. Olympic Blvd., Suite 140, Los Angeles, Calif.
90064 (213) 826-5253

Florafax International, 4175 South Memorial Dr., Tulsa, Okla.
74145 (918) 622-8415

American Floral Services, P.O. Box 12309, Oklahoma City, Okla.
73157 (405) 947-3373

Garden Center

> "I love plants, and I love to introduce people to something unusual. I get excited when we head into spring planting season." – Bill Funkhouser, Funkhouser's Garden & Gift

Low Startup Investment: $30,000 (small suburban site)

High Startup Investment: $150,000 (shopping center location)

Time Until Breakeven: One to three years

Annual Revenues: $200,000-$500,000

Annual Pre-tax Profits: $20,000-$50,000

Staffers Needed for Startup (including founder): Two

In Atlanta, several massive garden center chains stock thousands of azaleas and tulip bulbs in their multi-acre lots, and they buy mulch by the dumptruck. But those people who want to buy exotic perennials like candytuft or other, even more unusual flowers make the trip to tiny Funkhouser's Garden & Gift, a fifteen-hundred-square-foot, closet-sized store with just two thousand square feet of outdoor selling space. Explains the proprietor Bill Funkhouser: "The mass markets carry the best sellers. They run full-page ads. We're not going to compete with them. So we carry the unusual." That approach earned Funkhouser's sales of $250,000 in 1986, its second year of business, and promises of its first profits in 1987 on sales of $350,000.

DO-IT-YOURSELF FLOWER POWER

Americans are dressing up their yards as never before. As baby boomers settle into their new houses, many allot 5 to 10 percent of the home's value to landscaping. The "flower power" generation has a couple of choices: Either hire a landscape contractor to plant the holly, or do it yourself. Both segments of the garden world are thriving. (See Landscaper.)

As Bill Funkhouser's situation illustrates, garden centers come in all sizes, with any number of specialties. You could open with $30,000 or $150,000, depending on your size, whether you locate in a high-rent shopping center or a suburban backroad, and the inventory you carry. "A lot of centers are almost equipment shops: power equipment, lawn mowers," explains J. D. Causey, who runs Causey's Garden Center in Wilmington, North Carolina. "We're 70 percent greengoods. We call ourselves a retail nursery center."

Many wholesale nurseries or equipment distributors will help sketch out a floorplan, depending on your specialty and the amount of cash you have to spend. Keep the needs of your local clientele and climate in mind. For example, Causey's Garden Center stocks large planters for decks and patios to cater to the outdoor-living orientation of its coastal region. A Tucson garden center carries Sonora cactuses that would not last a week in Milwaukee. Furthermore, mall sites lend themselves to portable merchandise, such as hanging baskets, while you need easy car access to sell fifty-pound bags of topsoil.

While the garden center business has never had more room for growth, it pays to differ from the K Marts and A & Ps that have started carrying Ficus trees and tomato seedlings. Since you probably can't match discount prices, customers come to you for just a handful of reasons:

- Your wide selection
- Your expert advice on what to buy or how to plant
- Unique merchandise they can't get elsewhere

SELLING KNOW-HOW

Bill Funkhouser has built his business on two of those criteria: His shop is known for its expertise and he specializes in the unusual. Bill, who has a degree in horticulture, teaches employee classes twice a week so the three-person staff understands what they sell. In addition, he is highly visible in the community, speaking to garden clubs and teaching free Saturday lectures in his office on such topics as "Perennial Gardening in Atlanta" and "Herbs for Shady Areas." As Bill puts it, "We sell information as much as product."

Funkhouser's sends customers to competitors for what Bill calls "the woodies," (trees and shrubs) and saves his precious space for items the gardeners can't get elsewhere, primarily perennials, wildflowers, and herbs, as well as some statuary and hanging baskets. "The books on perennials were written for the Northeast, so we do a lot of educating that contradicts the 'experts.' Most perennials do great here if you put them in the shade, but we especially look for heat-tolerant plants."

Garden center entrepreneurs usually find the consulting tasks more rewarding than bothersome. J. D. Causey says it adds a social element to business. "We deal with a lot of retirement couples who've just moved to the area and want to brighten their yard. We help them be creative and sort out problems like which plants like shade and sandy soil. We ask them about the architecture of their house so we can complement it with the plants we suggest. For example, formal shrubbery like boxwood is appropriate with Federal architecture, while Hollywood juniper would be best with ranches."

Location first attracts homeowners to your store; in addition, most garden centers set aside about 5 percent of revenues for advertising, primarily in newspapers with a smattering of direct mail and radio. Causey's even takes some television spots. "We're in a three TV-station area where rates are practical," says J.D. "You wouldn't do TV advertising in Philadelphia or Miami."

Bill Funkhouser sends newsletters to five thousand customers, mainly those who write checks over $20 and anybody requesting they be put on the list. The mailings sell a few pansies, but mainly they keep customers interested in gardening. "At Christmas, we say, 'Here are some plants that make nice gifts,' but the newsletter's main value is information, such as what diseases Black Eyed Susans suffer from, when they bloom, and the amount of water they need."

MONEY GROWS ON TREES

Although they are perishable, greengoods usually provide the best margins, as much as 80 percent. Less profitable books, chemicals, and tools may have margins about half as high.

Both hardgoods and plants have to be rounded up. J. D. Causey buys from some forty different sources, most of which he discovers at trade shows. "We get greengoods from five hundred, sometimes a thousand miles away," says J.D. "Nurseries call to say they're making deliveries in our area and ask what we need." The amount of stock varies with the season. Causey's may carry $30,000 worth of inventory in the winter, and double that in the spring and fall. J.D. tries to turn the inventory about eight times a year.

The best way to sell a showy garden product is to let it sell itself. Funkhouser's installed two tiny, two-by-fifteen-foot gardens to showcase its plants. The approach works so well that Bill is looking for a larger location so he can add more display gardens. "Take platycodon," he says. "It has beautiful blue flowers that bloom in profusion. In photographs, the blues come out pinkish purple. But there's no way we can get enough of them when people see how beautiful they really are."

SOURCES

Industry Association

American Association of Nurserymen, 1250 I St., N.W., Suite 500, Washington, D.C. 20005 (202) 789-2900

Publications

American Nurseryman, 111 N. Canal St., Chicago, Ill. 60606 (312) 782-5505

Garden Supply Retailer, P.O. Box 2400, Minneapolis, Minn. 55343 (612) 931-0211

Nursery Business, Northwood Plaza Station, Clearwater, Fla. 33519 (813) 796-3877

Consultants

Ian Baldwin, P.O. Box 896, Elkgrove, Calif. 95624
(916) 689-1968
Ernest Wertheim, Wertheim, van der Ploeg & Klemeyer, 2145
19th Ave., San Francisco, Calif. 94116 (415) 664-0832

Large-sized Apparel Shop

> *"Retailing is like show business. There's a certain excitement about selecting a bunch of merchandise and watching the customer blow you out by buying it all." – David C. Keller, Fashionfull*

Low Startup Investment: $50,000 (strip-center locale)

High Startup Investment: $100,000 (enclosed mall site)

Time Until Breakeven: Six months to three years

Annual Revenues: $200,000-$500,000

Annual Pre-tax Profits: $20,000-$100,000

Staffers Needed for Startup (including founder): Two to four

As America gets older, it gets heavier. In the late 1980s, one out of every five adults needs half-sized or extra-large clothing. Despite the bulging numbers of weight-reduction centers (See Diet Clinic), trend-watchers indicate we now accept a few extra pounds as an inevitable fact of life. Making the most of it, though, we'd like to toss out those polyester pant suits and look fashionable.

And, since we're willing to pay for it, capitalism is responding: Shops for both tall and heavy men and boutiques for full-figure women are proliferating. Designers who long ignored this market are creating chic dresses and slimming suits for it. Vendors are carrying not just larger versions of clothing initially cut for average sizes, but whole lines geared specifically to the needs of heavier individuals.

ROOM FOR GROWTH

"Eventually, stores for larger-sized women will have as much competition as everything else," says David C. Keller, former CEO of Wieboldt Stores Inc., the $200-million department store chain headquartered in Chicago. However, "Department stores will continue to appeal to regular sizes and discounters will be all over the lot. It will take years before the larger-size category becomes overstored."

David Keller and two partners opened the first Fashionfull in Buffalo Grove, Illinois, in 1987, citing a couple of enticements beyond scads of customers and a dearth of competition: Specialty stores achieve higher margins and have bigger tickets than do stores for a more general market. "Our customer can't go everywhere and find the merchandise that fits her, so she is not as concerned with price," says David, who was counting on 5- to 10-percent pre-tax profits—about double what department stores expect—on first-year sales of $250,000. Because the customers are willing to pay top dollar, "We don't have to run as many sales." One consultant to startup retailers adds, "If you're a size 42 and find a store with beautiful dresses you can wear, you'll buy three at a shot. You'll travel miles out of your way to get there. Large-size stores achieve better margins on a much higher average ticket. What's to lose?"

TURN, TURN, TURN

With higher tickets and fatter profits, breakeven comes faster. Also, since you can operate with a smaller store, you can create faster turns. That means you don't have to tie up as much cash in inventory. Fashionfull, at just fifteen hundred square feet, looks for six turns a year, compared with less than four at a department store. "We get new merchandise in weekly," says David Keller. Such volatility creates a retailing excitement that brings regular customers back often. "The store has a different look every week."

Because the store is small and because you turn inventory so fast, you can get into the business with a slender pocketbook. And, since customers arrive for the merchandise rather than the ambiance, don't plow too much cash into expensive fixtures. David Keller and partners opened Fashionfull on just $50,000. For this store—and the other five they plan for the Chicago area in the next two years—the trio chose a strip center rather than an enclosed mall. "Rent at enclosed malls in the Chicago area runs $25 to $30 a square foot, compared with $15 to $18 at a strip center," says David. "Strips don't provide as much traffic, but walk-in isn't where we get our business anyway. Advertising and word of mouth gets us our customers."

Fashionfull advertises freely in newspapers that cover the northwestern Chicago suburbs, and is experimenting with a twenty-thousand-piece direct-mail campaign. The names aren't sorted by size, David says, "but we expect those households who wear smaller sizes will have mothers or friends in our size range."

FLEXIBILITY IS YOUR STRONG SUIT

If you concentrate on selling just one category—apparel for women sized 16 and up—you get good at buying the right merchandise quickly. But David Keller says to have an open mind and a readiness to respond to customer suggestions. "We didn't realize we had so many working women in our area and weren't carrying suits at all," he says. "In the first few weeks we had quite a few calls, so now we carry suits." If you're located far from the major apparel marts—New York/Chicago/Dallas/California—you might not be able to react as quickly to customer demand for certain types of merchandise. But, at least in the early days, you might budget for a buying service in New York, or keep cash in reserve for fill-in buys to complement your opening stock.

Of course, try to know as much about your customers as possible before opening your doors. Shopping-center operators conduct demographic studies; ask your landlord what income, age, and population brackets live in your neighborhood. If you know customers have high incomes, for example, you might buy pricier merchandise.

YOU'RE SPECIAL

Many of the same rules apply to running an apparel shop for larger sizes that apply to operating any sort of specialty shop. For example, go heavy on service. Because you appeal to a relatively select group of people, chances are you won't have hundreds of customers in the shop at one time. Encourage your sales clerks to offer assistance and advice on accessories. Make an effort to know regular customers by name, and even call big spenders when you get in a shipment with merchandise just right for them. Your advantage over larger stores, besides the clothing itself, is the extra attention you lavish on customers.

However, clothing stores for the heavy set differ from other stores in a few key ways. "We hire saleswomen who are on the heavier side," says David Keller, saying they have greater understanding of the fashion needs of a customer who might resent a ninety-eight-pound clerk. His partner, Caroline Frowe, a former Wieboldt divisional merchandise manager, wears a mere size three. "I kid her to stay out of the store," says David.

You also have to tread gingerly about how you refer to customers who may be sensitive about their size. "Don't talk 'big' or 'fat,' although you imply it," advises David. "Be careful in naming your store. We advertise 'Size 16 and up,' rather than 'large sizes.' "

SOURCE

Publication

Big Beautiful Woman Magazine, 19611 Ventura Blvd., Tarzana, Calif. 91356 (818) 881-9229

Left-handers Store

> "I'm having a ball. When I show right-handers the advantages of a ruler made for left-handers, I love to watch their reaction." – Richard Keogh, Left-Handed Irishmen & Other Things

Low Startup Investment: $10,000 (low-rent district)

High Startup Investment: $50,000 (larger shop in urban setting)

Time Until Breakeven: Six months to two years

Annual Revenues: $100,000-$300,000

Annual Pre-tax Profits: $10,000-$50,000

Staffers Needed for Startup (including founder): One to three

"When I went for financing, the banker asked 'Aren't you limiting yourself by creating a store for left-handers?'" recalls Richard Keogh, who opened Left-Handed Irishmen & Other Things in Lake Mary, Florida, in 1984. "I answered that at least 11 percent of the population is left-handed, and the other 89 percent knows them and is going to keep me cleaned out."

DISCRIMINATION

Left-Handers International estimates more than 30 million Americans are left-handed. You would have to double the population of New England to equal the number of left-handers. Fewer golfers, gardeners, or goldfish owners exist than southpaws. Yet those comparatively esoteric consumers claim far more specialty products than do lefties. It appears the only left-handers who get any respect are pitchers who throw ninety-five-mile-per-hour fastballs.

But wait. Left-Handers International, which publishes *Left-Hander*, a bi-monthly magazine (bound on the right so it's easier for lefties to read) reports at least twenty-five shops across the country specialize in such items as scissors designed for lefties, ladles with the lip on the opposite side to help left-handers serve punch more naturally, and T-Shirts that proclaim "You Are Born Left-Handed; You Turn Right-Handed After You Commit Your First Sin." In addition to Richard Keogh's Left-Handed Irishmen, there's Left-Handed World in San Francisco, Lefty in Boston, and The Southpaw Shop in San Diego. *The Left-Hander's Catalog,* which Left-Handers International has mailed to about sixty-five thousand southpaws, lists one hundred thirty items for which a right-hander would have no use.

SMALL FISH IN BIG PONDS

As with other kinds of highly specialized shops, most left-hander boutiques land in fairly large cities. Since you expect to attract only a small percentage of the potential market, it pays to start with the biggest population of left-handers you can find. Also, retailers of any kind of limited item should "scout out your area to see if there isn't another similar place," advises Kim Kipers, executive assistant at Left-Handers International.

Richard Keogh, a retired banker, and his schoolteacher wife, Ettie Jane, knew the closest competition their Left-Handed Irishmen & Other Things faced was one thousand miles away in New York City. They also knew tiny Lake Mary (1987 population, around forty-two hundred) was next door to booming Orlando, which supplies most of their repeat customers. Because of the area's growth, Richard foresees a tenfold population increase in the Lake Mary area "in a couple of years." But they finally chose to locate in Lake Mary because it is home of their landlord and Ettie Jane's mother, Lena Gleason, who came in as the third partner. Both Ettie and Lena are lefties, although Richard favors his north hand.

"For years, we'd talked about when I retired I wanted to open a store for left-handers," says Richard. "We added Irish imports 'and other things' so we wouldn't be limited, but at least 75 percent of our sales are the left-handed items." Irish imports include etched water glasses and handkerchiefs, while other things include a tea-cart with such items as a tea bag rest and a lemon squeezer. But Richard says as he sells off stock, he may replace it strictly with left-handed novelties. Sometimes it pays to build a reputation with your specialty alone; don't water down your identity with unrelated items.

Like most really special shops, Left-Handed Irishmen is little—about four hundred square feet. Although the left-handed items carry 10- to 25-percent markups over traditional right-handed items, most still have low tickets. As a result, the specialty shop can't afford steep rents or a lot of inventory that doesn't turn. Richard Keogh estimates he stocks fewer than one hundred left-handed items, about twenty-five to fifty Irish units, and only odds and ends of other things. He gets most of his merchandise through Left-Handers International, and notes, "I can get resupplied real fast, so I don't tie up a lot of money in inventory." He also special orders items for customers.

BE PICKY

Because your space is at such a premium, choose your merchandise mix with care. "There's no need for left-handed ice-scraper mitts in warm parts of the country," says Kim Kipers. "And you can get away with a beach towel with a 'Southpaw' slogan in Florida, but there're no beaches in Kansas." Richard adds that he doesn't carry items like left-handed golf clubs that are readily found elsewhere, but he will special order such items upon request.

Richard says right-handers buying such gifts as a left-handed pen (already slanted to the left and containing non-smear ink) account for the majority of his sales.

Many older lefties have already learned to cope in a clockwise world. "My wife says left-handed shears throw her off about an eighth of an inch," he says. Although these old-hands have learned long ago to cope, Kim Kipers reports that parents buy items for their children. "Each year, the number of left-handers actually rises because people tend not to change the 'handedness' of their children anymore." Maybe someday, if enough children are allowed to develop their true inclinations, there'll be a need for a right-handers shop.

SOURCES

Industry Association

Left-Handers International, P.O. Box 8249, Topeka, Kans. 66608
(913) 234-2177

Publication

Left-Hander, P.O. Box 8249, Topeka, Kans. 66608
(913) 234-2177

Pet Store

"The animals are fun, but it's a great people business. I'd love to put 25-cent turnstiles in front of the stores and turn them into zoos. People love to look." — Jerry Pass, Pass Pets

---

Low Startup Investment: $70,000 (small strip-center site)

High Startup Investment: $200,000 (larger mall location)

Time Until Breakeven: Six months to three years

Annual Revenues: $175,000-$1 million

Annual Pre-tax Profits: $35,000-$200,000

Staffers Needed for Startup (including founder): Three to five

---

Jerry Pass says if you want to gauge a shopping center's customer draw, visit the pet store. "If the pet store isn't busy, you know the mall is dead." That's not to say pet stores outsell dress boutiques or book stores or ice cream stands—although typical pet store pre-tax profits of 20 percent beats most retailing returns by a long shot. But other than W. C. Fields, whom can you think of that could pass that doggie in the window without stopping to "ooh" and "ah"? Getting those customers into your store is easy: Just locate in a heavily trafficked area.

Apparently lots of those pet-store window shoppers also leave with a kitten or cockatoo. Almost 53 percent of U.S. households sheltered at least one pet in 1985, the year the pet-shop industry generated $1.65 billion in revenues—about 10 percent more than the year before, according to *Pet Supplies Marketing*. The 98 million dogs and cats in the U.S. represented a population greater than all but seven nations around the world.

SALES ALIVE

Pet stores offer warm and cuddly rewards you just don't get in other businesses. But loving animals doesn't qualify an entrepreneur to open a pet shop. "Many people get in as hobbyists—and 95 percent of those will fail," warns Jerry Pass, who says you need as much business sophistication to run a pet shop as for other forms of retailing. In fact, pet shops are far trickier in one significant aspect: You sell a living thing. That means somebody must visit the store to care for the animals seven days a week—even on Christmas and Thanksgiving when everybody else shutters their stores up tight. Also, you lose a certain amount of your stock to illness. "The public doesn't understand if a pet gets sick two days after they bought it," says Jerry Pass. If you buy one hamster carrying a deadly virus, you could lose your entire rodent stock. "You have to be a retailer, a merchandiser, and a vet, all rolled in one."

Pass Pets, which operates from a St. Louis, Missouri, base, largely solved the illness problem by putting a veterinarian on retainer at each of its thirty-one stores in six states. The vets make store calls twice a week, train the staff on which vitamins to dole out, and take any contagious critters to their clinics. Pass Pets also quarantines all new puppies for seven days before moving them in with other stock. Since addressing the illness question a couple of years ago, Jerry Pass says his pets have a 90 percent better health record.

TAKE AWAY THE BEASTS

Another way around the disease problem: Don't sell pets. "If you took the animals away, the pet business would be a piece of cake to operate," says Jerry. He laughs, but some retailers run pet supply stores that do a brisk business without a beast in sight. Take, for example, Lick Your Chops, a Westport, Connecticut, chain that calls itself "a complete department store for animal people." The decidedly upscale chain sells little sweaters and sequined collars and obedience-school graduation cards, but Lick Your Chops specializes in nutritious animal food (no additives or scraps) at about triple the price of supermarket brands.

The concept of a health food store for animals was born when Susan Goldstein's golden retriever, Leigh, quit responding to cortisone injections for his painful hip dysplasia and arthritis. Susan and her veterinarian husband Robert discussed putting Leigh to sleep or subjecting the seven-year-old dog to major surgery. Susan, who was studying nutrition and working for the Foundation for Alternative Cancer Therapies in New York, suggested a last-ditch campaign: She put Leigh on a diet of brown rice, fresh vegetables, meat, vitamins and minerals, and distilled water. Within six months, Leigh's symptoms disappeared and Susan began toying with the idea of Lick Your Chops. By 1987, when Leigh was still going strong at seventeen, the chain consisted of three company-owned and two franchise stores, a retail outlet in New York City's Bloomingdale's department store, a mail-order division, and a manufacturing subsidiary. Negotiations were under way for a pet nutrition talk show and video. A book contract was signed. In 1986, sales reached $800,000.

Pet-supply stores have one major drawback. They only work in the most populated areas with an affluent population. You can cut inventory and floor space and get rid of all those animal headaches —assuming you can do enough volume on supplies alone. Of course, animals are what attract most entrepreneurs to the business in the first place. So, if you want to keep the pets—but minimize your stock—open just a fish store, or buy a franchise that specializes in nothing but puppies instead of a full-service pet shop. While a specialty pet store still copes with living products, you deal with just one fish distributor, or only a handful of puppy breeders instead of a variety of sources.

While some operators look for ways to reduce their offerings, others are expanding. For example, *Pet Supplies Marketing* says 53.3 percent of retailers offered grooming services in 1985, compared with just 29.7 percent in 1983. Taking an average of just three hundred one square feet, grooming added $31,800 in revenues to the average store—and $15,690 in net profits. It also brought into the stores pet owners who often picked up a high-margin flea collar or pet bowl on the way out.

YOUR GRUBSTAKE

A two-thousand-square-foot store stocks about $35,000 worth of inventory (meaning pets and supplies). You buy that merchandise from various services: puppy and kitten breeders, bird importers, fish farmers, and a couple of dry-goods and accessory distributors. Mix and match inventory for awhile after startup to see whether local pet buyers are more partial to parakeets or Pekingeses. In addition, Jerry Pass says to put aside $200,000 if you want to open first class in a heavily trafficked mall. Part of this stake goes to adapt a location to handle your merchandise. For example, Pass Pets installs high-speed ventilation fans to eliminate odors. "What mall wants you as a tenant if you smell?" asks Jerry.

You can cut your opening budget nearly in half by opting for a decent strip center rather than a mall. But expect lower revenues. The highest-volume mall shops can sell $1 million worth of goldfish and their ilk a year, compared with about $200,000 for the average freestanding or strip-center boutique.

In some cities, those high-volume mall sites just aren't available. And even where they are, you need all the sales you can get to pay for the overhead. Increasingly, pet stores employ advertising to increase awareness. Many pet-food and accessory manufacturers offer co-operative advertising plans, so Hartz-Mountain might share your promotion expenses.

Two demographic trends hold bright promises for pet stores in the near future. The two most populous groups of pet owners tend to be youngsters and senior citizens. It just so happens that those two segments are growing faster than the rest of the population. "Polly want a parrot?"

SOURCES

Industry Association

Pet Industry Joint Advisory Council, 1710 Rhode Island Ave., N.W., Washington, D.C. 20036 (202) 452-1525

Publications

The Pet Dealer, 567 Morris Ave., Elizabeth, N.J. 07208 (201) 353-2373

Pet Supplies Marketing, 1 E. First St., Duluth, Minn. 55802 (218) 723-9303

Pet Business, 5400 N. 84th Ave., Miami, Fla. 33166 (305) 592-9313

Pro Athletic Shop

> *"Every day I deal with people interested in the same thing I've followed all my life. We talk sports all day long."* – Neil Spiegler, Pro Corner

Low Startup Investment: $50,000 (small, strip-center shop)

High Startup Investment: $250,000 (elaborate franchise)

Time Until Breakeven: Nine months to three years

Annual Revenues: $200,000-$15 million (multiple shops)

Annual Pre-tax Profits: $10,000-$1.5 million

Staffers Needed for Startup (including founder): Three to seven

When you were a kid, did you memorize the entire Dallas Cowboy playbook? Did you cheer when Billie Jean beat Bobby Riggs? Did you cry when the Dodgers left Brooklyn?

Have we got a business for you!

"Four years ago, I was teaching physical education at a New York City junior high school," says Neil Spiegler, who was wondering if he would be happy teaching the rest of his life when he heard about licensed athletic sportswear shops. "This kind of retailing was natural for me with my background. I relate to my customers and to my merchandise."

Neil sells all manner of licensed fanware: T-shirts, caps, pennants, jackets, buttons—you name it—all emblazoned with logos of professional sports teams and the best players. His Pro Corner, located in a Cherry Hill, New Jersey, mall on the outskirts of Philadelphia, carries gear from almost every team in the country, but best sellers derive from hometown professionals (The Phillies, Eagles, Flyers, and 76ers) and whichever team is on top. "Everybody loves a winner," says Neil.

Athlete's Locker is tiny—just six hundred square feet—which holds down rent but limits the amount of stock. Competitor Spectathlete, which does business in slightly larger locales as The Complete Athlete and Showcase stores, also sells college sports team regalia, as well as some hardgoods, such as team garbage pails and helmet telephones. According to Chief Executive Gary Adler, a onetime University of Georgia basketball player, the stores carry more than fifty thousand items, including all sizes and colors. Items from the National Football League make up 30 percent of sales; college merchandise, 25 percent; Major League Baseball, 20 percent; National Basketball Association, 15 percent; and National Hockey League, 10 percent.

THE JIMMY THE GREEK SCHOOL
OF MERCHANDISE BUYING

Knowing which sports to carry is easy—just make sure you're stocked to the rafters on opening day of any particular sport and keep lots of merchandise on hand during the playoffs. But knowing which teams to stock amounts to legalized gambling. You're betting on who will win and therefore who will enjoy the most popularity. "You have to go with your instincts and look at last year's standings" before placing this year's orders, explains Neil Spiegler.

If you've got room, all is not lost if you bet on the wrong teams. Instead of taking drastic markdowns like you would on most apparel, you simply store all those surplus Chicago jackets until the Bears mount another Superbowl season. Unlike clothing that goes out of fashion, "I can sell an Eagles' T-shirt for the next ten years," says Stan Shaker. Even when a team changes its uniform or a player retires, "sometimes collectors clean you out."

Pro Corner deals with about forty of the three hundred fifty–odd suppliers that sell licensed sports products, which sometimes makes ordering cumbersome. But a roster of second-string vendors also provides backups. "If one manufacturer has sold out caps of a popular team, I try another," says Neil.

THE PLAYOFFS

Licensed sports shops report a different seasonal schedule than other retailers. Christmas is big, of course, but so are five other times of year: the playoffs leading up to the World Series, the college bowls, the Superbowl, the Stanley Cup, and the NBA Championships. Revenues depend on who's hot. "In 1985, the St. Louis Cardinals and Kansas City Royals played in the World Series," says Neil. "That was probably great for Missouri retailers, but it didn't do a thing for us." On the other hand, some teams and players enjoy national attention. When the Dallas Cowboys or Wayne Gretzky have a good season, so do out-of-state fanware shops. Even in a mediocre year, you can probably count a pre-tax profit floor of $10,000 on revenues of $200,000. A larger store that attracts frenzied fans could easily double that figure. The Complete Athlete store in New York City's World Trade Center generates superstar sales of $1,000 per square foot. With thirty-four stores across the country in 1986, the Folcroft, Pennsylvania, chain generated sales of $12 million and started franchising in 1987.

PUT YOUR EAGLES IN THE WINDOW

Although most pro shops advertise in the sports sections of local papers and in publications geared to a hometown team's fans, pro shops generate mostly impulse sales. That means you need a prime mall or tourist location with heavy foot traffic. "If I put an Eagles shirt in the window, someone passing by remembers they're going to the game on Sunday and stops in to buy it," says Neil Spiegler.

Mall rents are expensive, but since the stores are small, you can buy inventory and create the locker-room look for $50,000 or so. Including a $25,000 franchise fee, opening the more elaborate Complete Athlete shops cost up to $206,500, depending on location and size. Those stores sport basketball flooring, batting cages on the ceilings, and ticket booths at store entrances.

In addition to selling to the general public, you can pay for that investment by dressing little league and school teams. The good news: such a tactic adds volume. The bad news: schools often take up to six months to pay. You can also sell tickets to local arena events. Showcase, which sells tickets to Philadelphia events, says its cut of ticket revenue is insignificant, but the service attracts customers to the stores.

Neil Spiegler acknowledges that fanware is a pretty narrow retailing niche, but he doesn't worry that fickle customers someday will turn to more serious apparel. "America's always been a sports-conscious country. Favorite teams will come and go. And Michael Jordan may take the place of Dr. J, but we will always have a future because America loves its sports."

SOURCES

Industry Association

National Sporting Goods Association, 1699 Wall St., Mount Prospect, Ill. 60056 (312) 439-4000

Publications

Sports Trend, 180 Allen Rd., N.E., Suite 300 S., Atlanta, Ga. 30328 (404) 252-8831

Sportstyle, 7 E. 12th St., New York, N.Y. 10003 (212) 741-4200

Professional Women's Clothing Shop

> *"The merchandising can be super creative. I love doing the window displays and having people compliment my clothes."* – Marilyn McNutt, Just Grand

Low Startup Investment: $200,000 (mid-sized town)

High Startup Investment: $400,000 (major metro area)

Time Until Breakeven: Two to five years

Annual Revenues: $200,000-$500,000

Annual Pre-tax Profits: $6,000-$25,000

Staffers Needed for Startup (including founder): Three

The story of Just Grand, a clothing store for professional women located on Grand Street in St. Paul started out, well, just grand. Then, its partners hit a too-fast expansion period that put them on speaking terms with Chapter XI. But the moral to the story—hang on and learn by one's mistakes—makes for a happy ending. "We can't expand now because we have so much debt to service from our previous attempt," says partner Marilyn McNutt. "But once we pay that off, we will grow. We know now where to avoid mistakes and we also know from the success of the remaining store that the concept is valid. We'll do lots better next time around."

Marilyn McNutt and her three partners can hardly be blamed for pursuing their concept so enthusiastically. Looking at the changing role of women, it seemed they couldn't lose. In 1986, the U.S.

Census Bureau reported 36 million American women worked full time outside the home. Increasing numbers of these women abandoned the "pink ghetto" of low-paid clerical jobs to enter the executive ranks. And the one piece of advice every business woman's magazine shouts to this day is Use your new-found income to dress the part.

Just Grand opened in 1980 intending to dress the executive woman with panache. "The professional woman doesn't want navy blue suits with white shirts and red ties," says Marilyn McNutt, who taught sales marketing before joining Just Grand. "She wants to look good without being too traditional. She wants something classy that she can wear for three or four years without tiring of it."

HOME SWEET HOME

Based on the reception working women gave to the pilot store, the partners decided to grow in 1984. Within nine months, they opened seven stores. The next year, only the original remained. "You always hear about the importance of location," says Marilyn. "But unless you experience a bad site, you can't believe how important location really is."

The concept of an executive clothing store for females has one drawback: Department store buyers also want to dress the professional woman. Recognizing that competition, you've got to locate smack dab in the middle of lots of professional women; know your merchandise and present it in a way that makes boutique shopping convenient; and offer superior service.

Just Grand's most serious expansion mistake involved locations. The entrepreneurs spent a lot of money getting what they thought were good locations in expensive shopping malls. But they found that not just *any* foot-traffic will do. Shopping malls in the suburbs may be great for a cruise-wear shop, and might stock some executive wear if the demographics are mixed, but malls that draw primarily from middle-class neighborhoods may not attract enough women who need $75 silk blouses. You may be better off in the financial district of at least a mid-sized town, but check your customer base carefully. Marilyn McNutt recommends camping out in a location before committing to a professional woman's boutique. Study the type of shopper and ask the landlord to produce demographic information, including the type of households and income levels in the area.

Malls are okay if your customer can get in and out easily and enough executives frequent the area. It may be a stereotype, but the traditional female executive isn't a shopper. She wants to get in, buy her wardrobe, and get out. So don't settle for a middle-of-the-mall spot that means she has to park six blocks away. This convenience is one of your prime draws over department stores.

Paying for the location that will make a professional women's clothing store work will admittedly make a dent in your purse. Your merchandise doesn't come cheaply, either. Plan on a startup ante of at least $200,000. And, like other clothing stores, margins are tight. The only way to get rich in retail clothing is to build a reputation or open several stores. While they are still paying off their debt service, Marilyn McNutt and her partners squeeze salaries in the $20,000 range, and haven't declared a profit. But if your debt-load is less, partners might figure on a $30,000 to $40,000 salary and profits of $6,000 to $25,000, depending on the size of your store. A solo owner might bump up the salary, although another salesperson will have to come aboard.

YOUR MERCHANDISE

Just as your customer hasn't the patience to discover a shop hidden in a less-than-prime location, she doesn't want to wade through racks of clothes to find a hidden treasure. Your clothing should portray an image. Display clothing already accessorized with a suede belt and pearls. Don't be mysterious. Know exactly what appeals to your customer and don't stock lots of superfluous items in an attempt to be all things to all people. After all, that's what department stores are for.

Just Grand has fine-tuned its merchandise mix since those early days. Separates (blouses, skirts, and jackets) make up 60 percent of the shop's sales; dresses account for 15 percent of the business; and the rest goes to accessories. "Our customer doesn't really buy suits," says Marilyn. "She wants the flexibility to mix-and-match, and she'd rather buy a skirt and jacket that go with other pieces of her wardrobe." Also, "our customer is older [typically in the twenty-six to forty-six age bracket] than shoppers in a junior's department. She is not necessarily the same size on the top as the bottom, so separates make more sense," adds Marilyn. Instead of sizes six and eight, Just Grand inventories more eights to twelves.

Any specialty store makes a mistake when it tries to compete with department stores which can better absorb price markdowns. So the eighteen-hundred-square-foot Just Grand attempts to carry different items than its competitors. "If a vendor tells me I'll love a particular dress because Dayton-Hudson just bought a slew of them, I say 'Thanks, but no thanks,'" says Marilyn. Just Grand also doesn't stock fifteen of the same blue worsted in different sizes. "We are a neighborhood store," Marilyn points out, meaning vice presidents don't fancy meeting their outfit in the elevator on the way to work.

MAKE YOUR STATEMENT

A specialty boutique spells its trump card: s-e-r-v-i-c-e. "Lots of people have a nice selection, but we're known for helping the customer decide what's right for her," says Marilyn. The ratio of sales help to customers is higher than a department store's because of the personal attention each customer requires. "You need a lot of sales help to mix-and-match the separates we stock. We don't let customers get out of the store without suggesting they might want a particular scarf for that new outfit." Not only do such suggestions build profitable add-on sales, they also prove to the customer that someone pays attention to their needs.

In addition, Just Grand offers free wardrobe counseling by appointment. (See Image Consultant for suggestions on how to master this specialty.) Partner Kadie DeMay outfits about thirty customers every season. When you realize each may spend $1,000 to $1,500 per wardrobe—each season—you'll understand why this is a profitable service worth the bother. Kadie keeps a file on what each client bought last season and encourages them to bring items from home for her to accessorize.

You also should consider offering alterations. This doesn't have to be a hassle. Just Grand pins hems and other minor alterations in-house and sends the garments for quickie alterations to a tailor. "We offer the service for free," says Marilyn. "After all, men's stores don't charge for tailoring, so why should we?"

Marilyn says Just Grand won't make the mistake of haphazard

expansion again. But she does see a chain of women's professional clothing stores in her future. Her reasoning: "We have a wonderful product. The concept works."

SOURCE

Industry Association

National Retail Merchants Association, 100 W. 31st., New York, N.Y. 10001 (212) 244-8780

Pushcarts

> *"I can't overstate the delight of selling a fun product directly to the public. People say, 'Oh look! Wouldn't Joe love this.' Customers get us high."* — *Karen Richards, Inkadinkado Inc.*

Low Startup Investment: $5,000 (low-price inventory and rent for a week)

High Startup Investment: $10,000 (more expensive inventory)

Time Until Breakeven: Three weeks to three months

Annual Revenues: $100,000-$400,000

Annual Pre-tax Profits: $35,000-$150,000

Staffers Needed for Startup (including founder): One

When the leasing manager approached Karen Richards about selling her decorative rubber stamps from a pushcart at Faneuil Hall Marketplace in Boston, she flatly refused. "I was selling the stamps along with batik ties at craftshows," Karen recalls. "I had no idea how to display or produce in volume. I didn't know the first thing about business matters like insurance and taxes. And I didn't *want* to know."

TRY IT FOR JUST TWO WEEKS

But Karen relented when the leasing manager gave her a two-week lease at $220 a week plus 10 percent of sales. Inkadinkado Inc. was born in 1978 with three hundred stamps on a pushcart. "Opening a retail operation is like going on the stage," Karen says. "You're all set for public humiliation. You're sure you're going to get booed—that nobody will buy."

Instead, Karen sold . . . and sold . . . and sold. "I began trying to talk people *out* of buying," she laughs. "I promised I'd ship them stamps free of charge. Anything to keep from running out of inventory. I had this two-week commitment and I was terrified I'd run out of stock."

The mall opened at 9 A.M. and didn't close until 9 P.M. "So all night I made stamps from a factory that let me use their tools, and all day I talked people out of buying," recalls Karen. Nowadays, she's more than happy to sell her stamps. Inkadinkado still operates the Faneuil Hall pushcart, but that's in addition to a manufacturing business, a wholesale operation, a mail-order catalog, and an importing subsidiary with thirty total employees and a gross of over $1 million a year.

THE PUSHCART RENAISSANCE

Pushcarts aren't what they used to be when rag peddlers and knife sharpeners roamed dingy city streets as mobile entrepreneurs. Observers generally credit Faneuil Hall Marketplace with reintroducing the pushcart theme—and sprucing it up to add color and excitement to shopping malls across the country. Today, pushcarts and kiosks purvey a range of fun products: They sell flowers and ceramic jewelry; teddy bears and Christmas tree ornaments; handmade leather belts and anything in the color purple.

If you're thinking of setting up a retail shop, consider some advantages of selling from a pushcart:

- Minimum investment. Rates have gone up from the days when Faneuil Hall first opened, but the average mall now leases a pushcart for about $1,000 a week plus 10 percent of weekly sales over $1,500. You need no fixtures and maintenance is minimal. You do need inventory. Inkadinkado recommends pushcarts selling its stamps start with a $5,000 wholesale batch of stamps, which will retail from $10,000 to $12,000, depending on how much markup you tack on. That stock could last anywhere from two weeks to a month, depending on how fast pushcarters sell.

- Cash flow. You shoot for volume sales, since most pushcart items sell in the $10 range. (As Karen puts it, "Who's going to buy a diamond bracelet from a pushcart?") But this arrangement means you get wads of cash in every day. If your startup budget is tight, use this month's cash to finance next month's inventory. In addition to your best sellers, you may want to stock a few larger, relatively expensive items as well. Not only will a $200 picnic basket, prominently displayed as your centerpiece, add a few substantial sales, it will also attract attention to your less costly wicker items. Most established pushcarters take credit cards to encourage high-ticket sales.

- The best location in the house. Malls usually place pushcarts and kiosks in first-floor sites that only a store with a well-known brand name as well as big bucks to cover first- and last-month rent deposits could afford.

- A short-term commitment. If you're a school teacher who wants to spend summers retailing those wonderful silk flowers you design, check out a pushcart.

- Intimate customer contact. "We now consider our pushcart a laboratory cart," says Karen Richards. "When we have twenty new unicorn designs, we see which ones sell before we ship them to our wholesale customers. Faneuil Hall says 1 million people a month go through the mall. The customers give you great feedback—'This stamp is too small, or can you make this one in orange?'" Indeed, a pushcart is a great place to test an entire concept before investing in a store. Sports Etc., a shop stocked with Boston sports team paraphernalia, began as a Faneuil Hall pushcart.

- Likewise, you can test a mall from a pushcart. Let's assume you want to open an earmuff store, but wonder whether a particular mall is right for you. Why not see what kind of sales you can eke out from the pushcart before signing a two-year lease?

AUDITIONS

Increasing numbers of malls lease pushcarts. Still, as competition among peddlers grows, you have to finesse to get a good cart in a good mall. Malls have no obligation to lease you space and expect two contributions from pushcarts: They should add an unusual or unique flavor to the shopping environment and generate profits for the mall. Some pointers on winning the pushcart lease:

▪ Unless you're wedded to the idea of selling pottery or leather, pick a more unusual product where competition is nil.

▪ If you're turned down for December (and can afford a slow month), apply for January. Once you prove you can sell under poor conditions, the mall will invite you back for the good times. Or, if your first-choice mall turns you down, apply to another. After a couple of months, take your profit record to your first choice again.

▪ Malls like track records and may ask what similar operations gross, so do as much homework as possible. Some pushcart vendors franchise, like the Purple Panache, which sells all sorts of purple clothing and knick-knacks. Inkadinkado offers "unfranchises." Explains Karen Richards: "We put dealers through a free, three-day training program on how to merchandise. They get a monthly newsletter and discount below the wholesale price for buying with us." Inkadinkado, which takes no fee for the service, asks that prospective dealers line up a location and buy $5,000 in starting inventory before attending its training.

▪ Check out the retail shops in the mall and don't compete. If a shopping center already has an art gallery, you won't get past the lease manager with a stand selling similar artwork. Many malls reject food kiosks for the same reason. Instead, display a complementary product. For example, assume a mall has no toy store, but a nearby retirement population. Your pushcart may offer a perfect solution for grandparents wanting to buy Christmas gifts.

▪ Present your case professionally. Before visiting with the mall's leasing manager, "sketch what the kiosk will look like and add some color," suggests Karen Richards.

EASY STREET

You can make a nice living selling from a pushcart. But, unless you have an incredibly hot product and locate in a very high-traffic area, a pushcart won't make you rich. Because mall hours are long, you probably will hire an assistant, whose salary cuts into your gross. Also, malls like to create excitement by changing pushcart vendors constantly; so you probably can't get a lease for more than six months a year—and probably not six consecutive months. You can, of course, work full-time by setting up your wares at a different (noncompeting) mall during off-seasons.

If a pushcart isn't the means to a more than comfortable financial end, you can build up experience and capital operating your pushcart and start a store. Or, like Karen Richards, you can branch out by pushing your cart items to other retailers. If selling to other retailers isn't successful, what's to rule out an empire of pushcarts— a franchise, perhaps, selling all manner of items from pushcarts all over the world?

Rental Center

> *"I love the diversity. One minute I'm dealing with a contractor on a piece of heavy equipment, then I'm talking to a hotel owner setting up a wedding, then a neighbor who wants to mow his lawn. There's nothing boring about the business."* – Lanny Anderson, Anderson Rent All

Low Startup Investment: $80,000 (small suburban store)

High Startup Investment: $300,000 (large urban center)

Time Until Breakeven: Three to seven years

Annual Revenues: $150,000-$1 million

Annual Pre-tax Profits: $10,000-$65,000

Staffers Needed for Startup (including founder): Two to four

At the close of World War II, thousands of soldiers received their discharge papers in California. Plans to vacation for a couple of weeks under the palm trees soon led them to settle down amid opportunity and sun. The California housing boom that followed catalyzed a new industry: rentals. Equipment-rental stores sprang up to supply new contractors with equipment to build houses for the transplants. Soon the new centers discovered that homeowners would rent roto tillers to dig their gardens and wheelbarrows to cart away the rocks, so they expanded their inventory to reach a wider audience.

FROM CONSTRUCTION EQUIPMENT
TO CHAMPAGNE GLASSES

A quarter-century later, the American Rental Association (ARA) estimates that approximately ten thousand rental companies scattered across the country carry everything from heavy construction equipment to champagne glasses. While the phenomenon has taken time to spread east, recent rental growth has been inspiring. ARA estimates that industry revenues climbed 20 percent between 1984 and 1986, when sales topped $7.5 billion. The association projects that, in the next few years, rental centers will surpass $10 billion in annual sales, lending out everything from baby carriages to sump pumps and construction cranes.

The rental boom stems from many sources, ranging from the mobility of American society to growth in the number of small homes and apartments with no room to store infrequently used items. And, with the cost of fix-it help today, Americans are more likely to tackle whatever's broken themselves than to hire a professional, and more and more, rental companies supply the tools.

Depending on your store's size and whether you choose an expensive urban setting or a less costly suburban locale, expect to spend $80,000 to $300,000 to set up shop. Most of that capital pays for inventory—the items you rent out. General-rental centers typically carry $300,000 to $500,000 worth of stock, using a rule of thumb that says that they should see $1 in rental fees for each dollar spent on inventory. In other words, if you spend $300 for a storage shed, expect it to bring in $300 in rental fees over a year's time. If you keep the shed for five years, renters pay for it five times over.

PAYING FOR THE GOODIES

Depending on your arrangement with the manufacturer, you don't have to shell out the full price of a $30,000 backhoe up front. If you're willing to pay their interest rates, many manufacturers of large equipment happily accept monthly payments. "We finance equipment just like you would a car," explains Jeanne McElroy, who runs Resource Rental Center Inc. of Council Bluffs, Iowa, with her husband, Jim. After the 35- to 40-percent down payment, you cover equipment costs with installments from rental income.

While you might not be able to round up enough cash to finance all the goods you eventually want to carry, you can start small and grow gradually, adding (and replacing) inventory as your cash flow allows. Lanny Anderson founded Anderson Rent All in Ithaca, New York, in 1968 with just $7,500. (He cautions that, if starting today, he would multiply startup costs by ten due to inflation.) That capital bought a skeleton inventory of rental items, which he added to as revenues grew. By 1986, after subtracting his own salary, Lanny saw $24,000 to $32,000 profits on revenues of $400,000. He forecasted a 15- to 20-percent sales increase for 1987.

The American Rental Association estimates the average general-rental store netted a pre-tax income of $34,700 in 1985. But you can do better in the right situation. The McElroys expect their community's growth to push their 1986 revenues of $400,000 (with net income of $64,000) to the half-million-dollar mark in 1987. "A lot of out-of-state contractors are bidding on a new shopping complex being built within a mile of us," explains Jeanne. "They don't bring their heavy equipment with them." Instead, they rent everything from earth movers to concrete pourers for hundreds of dollars a day.

INVENTORY FROM SOUP TO NUTS

Teaching skills serve rental entrepreneurs in good stead. You need product knowledge and the talent to explain to your customers the workings of up to one thousand pieces of equipment—from air compressors to typewriters. Be sure to ask the manufacturer's sales representative for full demonstrations when you take possession, and be patient when explaining items to renters. "If customers don't get expert instruction, they're either going to have difficulty with the equipment and be dissatisfied, or injure themselves," says Richard E. Detmer, author of *A Practical Guide to Working in an Equipment Rental Business* (available from the American Rental Association for $15.00). "Either way, they won't be back."

For inspiration on which items to stock, rental entrepreneurs shop equipment and hardware trade shows and talk to manufacturers' representatives. The best hints come from customers. When a half-dozen people request a wheelchair, for example, it may be time to investigate medical equipment. While someone in Jeanne McElroy's position might stock a lot of construction items for a construction boom, a center in a university town might rent out lots of typewriters around the end of the term.

Inventory mix does not always fall into place automatically, even for those who know the business, so be prepared for some trial and error. You might want to stock a limited number of products and wait to see which categories prove themselves. Jeanne McElroy, along with her sister, ran her parents' rental store in Omaha for several years. Even with that background, Jeanne had a few surprises when, in 1982, she and her husband took some cash and about $65,000 worth of equipment from the Omaha store, and qualified for a $100,000 Small Business Administration–backed loan to open their own shop. Instead of the homeowners she rented to in Omaha, she found a Cedar Bluffs customer base of light contractors—"groups of five guys who built apartments on speculation." Instead of $2 hedge trimmers and $10 snow blowers, she found herself renting giant backhoes for $160 a day, plus the trailers to haul them on for another $10.

To learn the needs of your community, read between the lines in local newspapers and check with the local chamber of commerce. Look for statistics on age, income levels, homeowners vs. apartment renters, and large building projects. Jeanne cautions that high-income homeowners tend to hire out their jobs. General rental stores tend to do better in middle-income areas with more do-it-yourselfers.

In contrast, if a lot of college kids live in the area, go heavy on party items. (For a separate look at stores that specialize solely in party items, see Party Rental Store.) Lanny Anderson's party business represents his fastest-growing source of revenues. Providing 25 percent of his total income, it already equals his construction business. The other half of his business comes from homeowners. In addition to supplying local fraternities and sororities, Lanny's party tents and punch bowls attend a lot of weddings. "A lot of people now have weddings at home or in the park," he says. "They do it themselves rather than go to the country club."

SOMEONE HAS TO BE MECHANICAL

You can break down the rental business into front-of-the-store functions, such as dealing with customers and manufacturers, and backroom responsibilities, which usually means maintenance. "Someone has to be mechanical, because equipment constantly needs repair," says Dick Detmer. A long fuse helps, too. "People will take a $700 chain saw meant for cutting firewood and try to cut tree roots out of the ground," Dick groans. "Do you know what that does to equipment?"

Customer use and abuse reduces a tool's life span. You have to assume a continual reinvestment. Some stores levy a refundable 5- to 10-percent deposit to cover damages or loss, which helps cover the costs. Jeanne McElroy simply assumes she must replace $20,000 pieces of construction machinery every three years or so, and homeowner tools like lawn mowers and chain saws annually. Knowing that, she prices rentals high enough to get her money's worth. Some competitors keep the equipment for five years, replacing just the motor when it blows. "But," says Jeanne, "we think the image of new equipment is worth the price. The industry has a reputation for being way too junky." Her tactic of establishing a quality image encourages repeat visits to Resource Rental Center.

Rather than absorbing the losses associated with the rapid turnover of equipment, Jeanne profits by selling used tools to customers who liked what they rented. "Some people say you'll lose your rental customers if they buy the equipment, but we sell them a service agreement to keep them coming back. You have to be flexible."

Rental stores thrive on repeat business; customers who catch on to the advantages of renting are loyal. Dick Detmer estimates the same consumers come back for either different equipment or the same item an average fifteen to twenty times a year; contractors, who comprise one out of every four of Lanny Anderson's clients, come in every day. Especially when you consider this type of repeat potential, it pays to keep customers satisfied. Working on community relationships pays, too. Dick says he invited gradeschool kids to the store he ran in upstate New York for field trips. They told their parents about the experience, and his business increased. He also recommends product demonstrations to local service clubs.

THE POTENTIAL

According to a Gallup poll commissioned by the American Rental Association in 1982, two-thirds of Americans never rent anything other than cars or real estate. While industry spokespeople see the statistic as a great opportunity, they feel the rental business needs to get its message across more clearly. "People are conditioned to think about buying," says Dick Detmer. "They just don't consider renting." Most rental-store owners are happy to recite the benefits of renting: Why buy a snow blower you drag out of the basement once each February? When visiting Grandma, wouldn't it be simpler to rent a carseat for the baby rather than lug yours on the airplane? In addition to a national marketing effort led by the ARA, many local entrepreneurs are increasing their advertising. Lanny Anderson puts aside 5 percent of his budget to advertise in the newspaper, Yellow Pages, and on the local radio stations, and to set up and staff displays in malls. The entrepreneurs say that, with a little effort on their part, America is bound to discover renting.

SOURCES

Industry Association

American Rental Association, 1900 19th St., Moline, Ill. 61255 (309) 764-2475

Publications

Rental Age, 1900 19th St., Moline, Ill. 60265 (309) 764-2475
Rental Equipment Register, 20048 Cotner Ave., Los Angeles, Calif. 90025 (213) 477-1033
Rental Products News, 36 S. 3rd West, Fort Atkinson, Wisc. 53538 (414) 563-6388

Other

Local chambers of commerce
Local newspapers

Specialty Bookstore

> *"Most children's books are upbeat and have happy endings. You meet wonderful people, the authors and illustrators. It's a very healthy world to be in." – Marilyn Hollinshead, Pinocchio Bookstore for Children*

Low Startup Investment: $75,000 (small shop, mid-sized town)

High Startup Investment: $125,000 (larger store in more expensive market)

Time Until Breakeven: One to three years

Annual Revenues: $200,000-$750,000

Annual Pre-tax Profits: $20,000-$100,000

Staffers Needed for Startup (including founder): Two

When you step into The Red Balloon bookshop in St. Paul, Minnesota, you step into a kind of privileged childhood. Brightly colored books line the natural wood shelves. Stuffed Babar elephants stand out against cream-colored walls. A funhouse mirror fronts the rounded red formica checkout counter, just the right height for three-foot-tall people. When the forty preschoolers leave the platform in the center of the store where co-owner Carol Erdahl has read to them during story hour, each receives a bright red balloon.

Marilyn Hollinshead, owner of Pinocchio Bookstore for Children in Pittsburgh and past president of the Association of Booksellers for Children, estimates that three hundred bookstores operated exclusively for children in 1987—compared with just fifteen or twenty a decade earlier. And children are not the only targeted audience among booksellers. Little shops have opened carrying only mysteries, or just science fiction; the occult has its own bookstores, as do cookbooks and biographies. As discounters increasingly take over the general bookstore realm, specialty stores attract readers hooked on one type of book. Aficionados know big discount bookstores carry only a handful of books they read, while the specialists line shelf after shelf of their favorite titles.

COZY

For the most part, specialty bookstores are small. Usually no bigger than one thousand square feet, these bookstores cram ten thousand titles into their small spaces. Marilyn Hollinshead, whose store at eighteen hundred square feet is bigger than most, estimates that she has thirty titles on dinosaurs alone. "You come to us if you need a book on rock collecting for children, or if you worry how your daughter will react to your divorce and want a fictional account."

Depending on the specialty, you might publish a mail-order catalog to offer your assortment to specialists all over the country. (See Mail-order Catalog.) However, most bookstores see themselves as retailers first and foremost, meaning they concentrate at least initially on local readers.

Since booksellers operate on tight margins and can't afford much advertising, most look for ways to generate free publicity. In addition to the typical author autograph sessions and visits from schools, Marilyn Hollinshead sponsors *Alice in Wonderland* reading marathons on Lewis Carroll's birthday (each under-age participant reads a chapter). These publicity stunts keep your store's name in the public eye, and the promotions "sure help boost sales," says Carol Erdahl.

THE PLACE TO GO FOR INFORMATION

Promotions establish your shop as *the* source in town of your specialty. As an expert, it pays to really understand what you're selling. "We hire former teachers, editors, and authors as our staff," says

Carol Erdahl, a former school librarian. "They all read every book that comes in. That way when parents come in and say 'I need a book for my seven-year-old,' you can recommend beyond the same old favorites."

Establish as much of a rapport as possible with your clientele. If your specialty is science fiction, for example, exhibit at the local Star Trek convention. A mystery bookshop might offer its facilities after hours for Sherlock Holmes clubs, or workshops on writing mysteries. Many specialty stores mail newsletters to customers in which they review new books and promote special events.

Children's bookstores court schools. Carol Erdahl says librarians might buy a few books from The Red Balloon, but the real reason to establish a relationship with schools is to let the kids know her bookstore exists. Many children's booksellers invite class tours where the owner explains how books are made and how a bookstore differs from a library. Pinocchio Bookstore sends books thirty to forty times a year to school bookfairs. According to Marilyn Hollinshead, after the school takes its 20-percent cut of proceeds and Pinocchio pays for the time it takes to select and package the books it sends, the store makes little money. But bookfairs generate an interest in books in general and Pinocchio Bookstore in particular, which pays off in the long run.

$100,000 BALLPARK

Because your store is smaller than a general bookstore, startup costs are proportionately lower. Depending on how many titles you stock and your rent district, expect to spend $100,000—give or take $25,000—to open your doors. In addition to furnishing, much of the cash pays for your first round of books. After you've established credit, most publishers allow anywhere from thirty days to six months for payment.

You might budget for a personal computer as well. Computers are great repositories for lists, the most important of which is inventory. Also, you can order electronically from some distributors and even publishers, a great time saver, especially on special orders. A specialty store generally does a brisk special-order business.

Keep your specialty in mind when designing your store. Many children's bookstores, for example, include play areas where the little ones frolic while Mom or Dad browses for books. The Red Balloon's shelves are further apart than racks in traditional bookstores to allow room for strollers.

As a rule, books carry a 40-percent markup, but freight costs subtract another 5 percent. Expect to pay for your overhead, including rent, salaries, and maintenance, from the remaining 35 percent. Many specialty bookstores carry a smattering of related items to complement their specialty and boost the margins. For example, many children's bookstores carry stuffed animals or educational toys.

STOCKING THOSE SHELVES

For hints on opening a bookstore, check with the American Booksellers Association (ABA). That group sponsors four-day courses for first-time booksellers in various cities in the spring and fall. You can get printouts of standard opening stock of various specialties from such distributors as Ingram Distributing Group in Nashville.

While you can order your entire inventory through distributors, you might get better discounts by going directly to the publishers. Carol Erdahl estimates the Red Balloon represents sixty to seventy different publishers, so getting them all working with you is no small task.

Request a list of publishers from the ABA, or peruse *Literary Market Place*, which lists all major U.S. publishers. Then write to each publisher for a catalog. Ask to open a credit account and have a sales representative contact you. "Reps can be helpful," says Marilyn Hollinshead. "Sometimes they'll provide bins for shelving. Also, they tell you what sells and what doesn't. When I opened in 1980, I didn't know what a pop-up book was. But a rep had put them in my order, so I had them when people asked for pop-ups." Another helpful tool is *Publishers Weekly* magazine, which will help keep you abreast of industry trends.

There's always the danger that your particular specialty will lose popularity and sales will fall. But, pointing out that a typical children's store caters through age fourteen at least, most children's booksellers don't suffer nightmares over loss of business. Other specialists figure they can always branch out with mail order. "We've created a market that wasn't here before," says Marilyn

Hollinshead. "People now understand specialty bookstores. Our customers won't ever want to go back to the fewer titles at general bookstores."

SOURCES

Industry Associations

Association of Booksellers for Children, 826 S. Aiken, Pittsburgh, Pa. 15232 (412) 621-1323

American Booksellers Assn., 122 E. 42nd St., New York, N.Y. 10168 (212) 867-9060

Children's Book Council, 67 Irving Place, New York, N.Y. 10003 (212) 254-2666

Publications

American Bookseller, 122 E. 42nd St., New York, N.Y. 10168 (212) 867-9060

Publishers Weekly, 205 E. 42nd St., New York, N.Y.

Children's Books in Print and *Subject Guide to Children's Books in Print*, Hilary House Publishers, 1033 Channel Dr., Hewlett, N.Y. 11557 (212) 916-1600

Sales
and Marketing

Auction House

> *"I never auction the same thing twice: I might get an airplane, a diamond ring, an elephant—who knows?"* – *Susan Stuke, Stuke Auctions*

Low Startup Investment: $5,000 (small structure for all-purpose auctions; limited promotion)

High Startup Investment: $40,000 (in-city site appropriate for art auctions; heavier marketing)

Time Until Breakeven: First auction to six months

Annual Revenues (in commissions): $75,000-$2 million

Annual Pre-tax Profits: $20,000-$500,000

Staffers Needed for Startup (including founder): One

In her third year as a business major at Washburn University, Susan Stuke faced up to her own particular reality: "My father ran his own business and I'd been raised to be real independent. I couldn't see myself working for somebody else the rest of my life. So I decided I'd have to start my own business."

But everything required money—which Susan just didn't have. "When my father suggested auctions, I was skeptical," she recalls. True, she had enjoyed attending auctions all her life, and she could open an auction house for the price of the first month's rent. A two-week course at the Missouri Auction School in Kansas City (which now runs $425) convinced her.

The enthusiasm of the instructors, all successful auctioneers in their own right, lit the bonfire. "The day I came home from school, in February, 1977, I rented a building," says Susan, who is now entitled to the honorary title of "Colonel," a holdover from colonels who auctioned off their mules at the end of the Civil War. Susan quit college, "which I didn't need anyway," and worked full time in a retail store. But she spent nights and weekends scouting for merchandise and rounding up audiences. That first year Stuke Auctions in Topeka, Kansas, auctioned off about $250,000 worth of everything from "trash to treasures." Susan soon devoted full time to the auction house. By 1987, business topped the $1 million mark, not counting what she made at on-site auctions or freelancing as an auctioneer for other auction concerns.

JUST A SALES TOOL

Experts trace auctions (the word comes from the Latin *auctio*, meaning gradual increase) through Greek literature, as far back as 450 B.C. Some categories—art, tobacco, horses—have sold at auction for years, causing many auctioneers downright amusement at the way auctions are turning the country upside down. Today, just about anything two or more people want to buy can be sold at auction. "Auctioneering is merely a method of selling," clarifies Dick Dewees, who runs the Missouri Auction School in Kansas City, and takes weekend auctioneering jobs. And a growing number of auctioneers who raffle off everything from $20,000 Persian carpets to $2 baseball cards agree. (For a look at real estate auctions, probably the hottest segment of the industry, see Real Estate Auctioneer.) In her regularly scheduled auctions twice a week, Susan Stucke says with pride she'll auction anything from cardboard boxes of garage-sale leftovers to tractors to estates. She also schedules specialty auctions: coins every Wednesday and once-a-month events devoted to antiques and restaurant equipment.

To set up an auction house, experts suggest five steps:

1. Learn what Dick Dewees refers to as "the auction method of selling" (including talking fast)
2. Establish an auction house
3. Gather merchandise
4. Attract bidders
5. Hold the auction

STEP 1: TALKING FAST

Several auction schools train auctioneers, and, if you want, you can receive certification from the Certified Auctioneers Institute. Dick Dewees's Missouri Auction school needs just two weeks to turn out auctioneers. "We take people who already know the product to be auctioned, so we don't teach you about your field of expertise," explains Dick. "We teach you the auction method of promoting." That basically means advertising—and how to talk fast.

It turns out you don't have to make Federal Express commercials in order to be a good auctioneer. Explains Dick: "I can say 'one-and-a-half'—that's four words. Or I can say 'one-naff' twice as fast. Crank that into a chant and raise and lower the voice with the help of a PA system, and you sound like you talk a lot faster than you really do." By the third night at school, Dick's students call a real auction. "They might not be good yet," he says, "but they get through it." After a few more sessions, the technique becomes second nature, he insists.

To be sure, you can't be a wallflower and call auctions. While being a bit of a showman helps, true loudmouths lose credibility. Auctioneers want to project a sense of fun and urgency, and their own confidence in the product. Auctioneers, like public-speaking instructors, say the basis of confidence is knowing your stuff. If you're auctioning pens, you'd better understand the difference between a Bic and a Cross. "You'd be amazed at how many just plain people get a microphone in hand and take charge," says Dick Dewees.

STEP 2: SETTING UP HOUSE

Unless you auction fine art or expensive antiques, you don't need a classy storefront. Instead, look for lots of traffic and easy access. "The better your location, the less you spend on advertising," points out Susan Stucke.

Your house needs a theater-like arena, as well as storage and display space for the merchandise. You also need office space and public restroom facilities. Susan recommends the optional restaurant or food stand. 'People can't bid when they're sitting down at McDonald's," she says. "Also, hot dogs and Cokes provide a little extra income." A small startup can squeak by with fifteen hundred square feet (plus parking and loading facilities), while large auction houses easily gobble up five times that space.

Check out competition and population draw from nearby communities to see how many auctions your particular region will support. Much depends on how often local residents frequent auctions. Topeka (population 120,000) supports numerous houses because consumers regularly buy and sell through auctions. Susan Stucke estimates three out of every four members of her typical audience are regular customers. Such loyalty lets her do two sales a week.

STEP 3: GETTING THE GOODS

"It's amazing where you can find merchandise," says Susan. Basically, general houses auction items from individuals (such as somebody who wants to sell an old car), dealers and collectors, and repeaters (such as bankers and attorneys who must dispose of estates or arrange distress sales). When Susan first began, she called newspaper want-ad numbers, suggesting that advertisers who failed to sell their television or washing machine through the ad bring it by Stucke's. She made the same pitch to people holding garage sales.

But those stray air conditioners and sofas require a lot of leg work. And often you can get stuck with junk. (Susan solves the junk problem by taking 30- to 50-percent commissions on items that auction for under a certain price.) Your time might be better spent in establishing long-term high-volume relationships. For example, banks and lawyers might hesitate to assign large estates to a new auction house, but they may send one or two pieces your way. Later on, they can become prime sources of merchandise, and even whole estates. Susan also contacts mini-warehouses and moving companies which repossess property that owners don't claim. Other sources include retailers who take bicycle or lawn mower trade-ins, and even car dealerships.

If you're successful, sellers will start knocking on your door, so the merchandise canvas gets easier. "As soon as I get booked up for the Wednesday auction, I tell sellers to come back again in time for the Saturday auction," says Susan. "When I come in on Thursday morning, I have eight or ten pickups full of stuff in the lot so they'll be first in line for Saturday." The seller is responsible for getting the merchandise to your door, and the buyer pays to cart it away.

Some auctioneers actually buy large lots of merchandise from close-out sources or overseas contacts. Then they refurbish the individual pieces and auction each item separately. While you tie up capital for the month or so it takes between buying and selling the goods, 100- or 200-percent returns aren't uncommon.

More typically, however, auctioneers accept goods on consignment. While fees to the seller average 15 percent, commissions range anywhere from 5 percent on really large estates to 50 percent on low-end items. Art auctioneers traditionally take 10-percent commissions from both the buyer and seller. In some cases, sellers ask for estimates of what their Remington (painting or typewriter) will bring. If you're qualified, you can eyeball the merchandise yourself; otherwise call for an expert appraisal and pass along the cost to the seller.

4. BRINGING IN BIDDERS

"Getting an audience is the least of your problems," insists Susan. "Everybody has auction fever now. I just have to let people know I'm having an auction—I don't even tell them what I'm selling. They'll come out of curiosity."

In areas of the Midwest where auctions are a way of life, radio stations and newspapers regularly devote an advertising section to auctions. If you're hawking expensive items that might draw national attention, consider advertising in specialty publications like *Antiques Magazine* or *Art & Auction*. Many houses use direct mail, either to the general public or to a list of regular bidders.

If you're selling items that attract a middle income audience, just let the folks know the theme of the auction. For example, you might sell general household goods, or antiques in the $100 to $1,000 range. But to attract heavy bidders to a collector's sale, you'll need to detail your inventory piece by piece. For example, Leslie Hindman Auctioneers in Chicago sends glossy, illustrated catalogs to regular bidders of art or estates. Each item is described and carries an estimate of what the appraiser expects it to bring. Prices usually fall somewhere between wholesale and retail.

Whether you're dealing with Louis XIV antiques or circa-1960 refrigerators, buyers like to inspect the merchandise. You have to invite all those prospective buyers to your premises beforehand so they can examine the goods. Dick Dewees emphasizes the importance of merchandising: "If you pile pieces of jewelry in a heap they won't bring as much as if you lay the better ones on black velvet."

5. THE EVENT

Until this point, a very busy entrepreneur could handle all these tasks—from renting the auction hall to bringing in buyers and sellers—alone. Now you need support: typically two or three "ring" people to display merchandise and take bids while you auction; a cashier to take the money; and a clerk to record transactions and settle accounts with the sellers. For really big auctions, or specialty events requiring expertise, you need a second—or third—auctioneer. The good news is you don't need a bloated payroll. Just subcontract with all these people as freelancers.

Most auctions sell sixty to one hundred items an hour, and most last no more than five hours. The audience (not to mention the auctioneer) simply tires if you go any longer. If you land a really big estate, stretch the auction over several days.

Different auctioneers use different techniques to keep the audience's attention. Susan Stucke alternates one large, expensive item with a lesser item at her general auctions. In large estate auctions, Leslie Hindman's catalogs note the order items go on the block, so buyers interested in a particular sapphire don't have to sit through the Chippendale antique segment of the auction.

WHERE DO YOU GO FROM HERE?

You can make a good living from an auction house, but most auctioneers don't stop with the business their auction houses generate, no matter how robust it grows. Unless you specialize in a particular category—autographs or fine wines, for example—shoot for the big, single-estate sales. You can hold those at your facility or on location. "Outside sales have so much more potential because you don't have overhead," explains Susan. On top of the regular commission fee, many auctioneers charge advertising fees to bring the bidders to the site.

With the proliferation of auctions, many medium-sized houses have more business than they can handle. When you're not auctioning your own account, chances are you can sign on with somebody else. For example, Susan Stucke receives expenses plus $300 to $1,000 a day to call business liquidation auctions for an Atlanta firm. She has so much fun calling auctions she even does some for free. "I call charity benefits like the Muscular Dystrophy Foundation," Susan says. "I donate my time, but I get to travel, all expenses paid, to the really fabulous resorts of the world."

SOURCES

Industry Association

National Auctioneers Association, 8880 Ballentine, Overland Park, Kans. 66214 (913) 541-8084

Publications

Auctioneer, 8880 Ballentine, Overland Park, Kans. 66214 (913) 541-8084

Auction & Surplus, 6730 San Fernando Rd., Glendale, Calif. 91201 (818) 240-5522

Art & Auction Magazine, 250 W. 57th. St., New York, N.Y. 10107 (212) 582-5633

Consultant

Missouri Auction School, Top Floor Livestock Exchange Bldg., 1600 Genesee, Kansas City, Mo. 64102 (816) 421-7117

Consumer Show

> *"You start with an empty hall and see it fill with thousands of people. You know you've created something all these people benefit from." – Mike Hallal, Mitch Hall Associates*

Low Startup Investment: $10,000 (small show, limited mailings)

High Startup Investment: $40,000 (extensive marketing to attract exhibitors and consumers to larger show)

Time Until Breakeven: One to four years

Annual Revenues: $50,000-$5 million (high end for a large show held in multiple cites)

Annual Pre-tax Profits: $10,000-$1.2 million

Staffers Needed for Startup (including founder): Two to ten

"Mindy Odegard and I had planned our pregnancies together and had daughters six weeks apart," says Deborah Rothman, president of Baby and Family Fair, Santa Monica, California. "I had been practicing law and she was in retailing, and neither of us wanted to return to our professions. So, we started Baby Fair to fulfill the fantasy of finding all the baby products and information together in the same place where you could also change diapers and play with the babies."

Deborah Rothman is reminiscing about the 1984 launching of Baby Fair, which has now expanded to include products and seminars aimed at toddlers and preschoolers as well as infants. That first show attracted over one hundred exhibitors and fifteen thousand consumers to the Santa Monica Civic Center. Deborah continues: "That first show attracted a total media blitz because of the wall-to-wall bellies," since many browsers were more than a little bit pregnant. Other consumers came with their tiny families in tow. "That was also the weekend where the term 'stroller gridlock' was invented."

THRILLS, CHILLS, AND EXCITEMENT

Baby and Family Fair doesn't sound much like a hardware show, or a plumber's convention, or any other exhibition staged by a trade organization, does it? Trade shows (see Trade Show) increasingly are serious undertakings, meant to educate members of an industry and provide a forum from which to do business. Consumer shows, on the other hand, combine education and sales with a lot of fun. For example, Baby and Family Fair has story-time and play areas for the kids along with booths displaying Aprica strollers. Whether you run a boat show or a flower fair, you're as much a part of the entertainment world as the theater up the block. To make it fun, you might decide to offer extras, such as food or raffles. In fact, exhibitors may agree to donate prizes.

Of course, there are a host of similarities between consumer and trade shows. For example, both shows nail down exhibitors in much the same way: through direct mail and telemarketing to lists bought through trade publications and associations. But a consumer show can survive with fewer exhibitors since your audience likely is local and therefore the hall you rent may be smaller than the mammoth (and expensive) caverns trade shows need. Depending on the type of show you run, you also can call on local business; for example, food shows can ask local restaurants to participate along with national distributors. In addition to contacting national toy companies, Deborah Rothman asked her daughter's gym to exhibit.

Following the practice of trade conventions, consumer-show exhibitors buy booth space before the show, which allows you to pay for auditorium space, advertise to the public, and cover set-up costs with exhibitor's money rather than your own. "A convention center gives you empty space, and you do what you like with it," explains Mike Hallal, vice president of Mitch Hall Associates in Westwood, Massachusetts, which throws open its Macintosh computer shows to the public. Setting up a show could mean elaborate decorations, carpeting, and flowers, or it could mean just stark booths. You provide these amenities yourself or hire organizations that specialize in show set up.

THE GATE

Unlike a trade show, consumer expos get to charge admission. Mitch Hall's Mac shows attract thirty-thousand people at a shot, all willing to pay $15 to shop the booths—or a very hefty $40 to attend seminars. These fees, mind you, come on top of $2,000 booth fees for maybe six hundred booths. And they come twice a year since Mitch Hall stages the expo both in Boston and San Francisco.

Of course, Mitch Hall can command such fees because the shows deliver—they deliver consumers for the products and products for consumers. You probably can't get such prices from either exhibitors or the public on your first convention. But as the show's reputation grows among both segments, your prices rise. If a Jacuzzi manufacturer generates solid sales and leads from your home show, it will be easy to sign the firm up next year—or for extra stops on your five-city tour.

To deliver those customers, you have to advertise. Unlike a trade event, consumer shows spend huge sums to advertise in local papers, on the radio and television, and to hobbyists in specialty publications. Baby and Family Fair spends $50,000 to $75,000 to advertise in every city it visits. And don't neglect free publicity. Most city magazines and newspapers carry a calendar of events. Also, invite reporters to cover the show, which will help build your reputation for next year.

TAKE IT ON THE ROAD

Once you get the formula down, you can duplicate the show elsewhere. If your idea works in one place, it likely will fly in another as well (unless competition gets there before you do). Some of the groundwork is already done since exhibitors might agree to buy booths in different cities. After all, a whole new group of customers will view their wares in each city. In 1986, for example, Baby Fair toured seven cities. If your show is at all specialized, however, make sure you put down stakes in the right places. Mitch Hall chose the high-tech Boston and San Francisco markets for its computer show.

SOURCES

See *Trade Show*

Craft Wholesaler

> *"The first time I saw hand-painted silk I knew it was the most beautiful thing I'd ever seen. It takes strong feelings to make a commitment, and that sense of wonder hasn't worn off yet." — Jan Mayer, Kriska Painting on Silk*

Low Startup Investment: $0 (using inexpensive materials at home)

High Startup Investment: $5,000 (setting up a studio)

Time Until Breakeven: One to six months

Annual Revenues: $100,000-$1 million

Annual Pre-tax Profits: $40,000-$500,000

Staffers Needed for Startup (including founder): One

Faced with a recession that was depressing his kitchen remodeling business, Bill Campbell decided to register for an interior design course to pass the time and complement his business skills. One day Bill left the community college, he passed a class on how to make pottery. "I found myself handing over $10 to enroll. That class changed my life because it showed me something I really wanted to do badly."

Bill spent the next five years studying pottery at the university level. Then he plowed into an "irrelevant" job for four years in order to save enough money to practice his art full time. "The last week in 1979, my new wife and I moved to Cambridge Springs, Pennsylvania, with $3,000 and a mortgage on our house and a mortgage on the building where I was going to make pottery and Jane was going to make jewelry. Somehow, we got through that first year. I did some retail craft shows, and one wholesale show. They weren't terribly exciting, but I got some orders and I learned how to display my work and how to present myself with a business card and catalog."

The next year, Bill returned to the wholesale show where retailers from across the country shop for crafts to sell in their stores. By 3 P.M. he had $10,000 in orders for the functional, beautiful pottery he makes. "I was so excited that when I went to call my wife, first I forgot the phone number, then I couldn't remember her name."

Today, Bill Campbell's Factory Studios sells by wholesale somewhere between $500,000 and $1 million worth of pottery (he won't be more specific) to four hundred retail outlets up and down the East Coast. Like most craftspeople who have hit the big time, Bill skirts questions about how many potters work for him. "When you have more than one employee, artisans start accusing us of being a factory."

THE WHOLESALE CONNECTION

Bill is one of thousands of craftspeople who might have struggled below the poverty line a decade ago. Today department stores, catalogers, and galleries snatch up ceramic jewelry and hand-blown goblets to sell to "Americans fed up with the garbage that's been dumped on us," says Wendy Rosen, whose Wendy Rosen Agency Inc. stages the two largest wholesale-only tradeshows for craftspeople in the country. (See Trade Show.)

Until Wendy and a few other individuals dreamed up wholesale craftshows, artisans sold one brass bracelet or hand-carved buckle at a time from booths at crafts fairs. Alternatively, they knocked on retail doors, hoping to interest the local men's shop in twenty or thirty belts. But retailers who order quantities in the thousands changed all that. "When I first began my shows in 1981, exhibitors [artisans] averaged $30,000 to $50,000 in production a year," recalls Wendy. "Now $1 million isn't uncommon and $150,000 is average. Many clients have doubled and tripled volume."

Michael Scott, editor of the *Crafts Report,* which reports on business aspects of the artisan colony, estimates "at least one hundred thousand people make all or part of a living through crafts." Pointing to universities that teach jewelry and pottery making (a few have even added business courses in the art department), he notes, "The attitude toward making money in crafts has changed. Once starving was considered a part of the artistic experience. Now it's increasingly acceptable to make a very comfortable living as a craftsperson."

LIFE STYLE

While artisans work hard, they get to organize their business on their own terms. As an artist, you work when and where you please. "I'm a powder skier," says Jan Mayer, who located Kriska Painting on Silk in Salt Lake City for easy access to the Alta ski slopes. "I don't care if it's my busiest season; when the powder comes, I take a day."

Jan Mayer and partner Christine Boiral (Kriska, herself) make delicate hand-painted scarves whose vibrant colors and abstract designs remind him of the geography of Bryce Canyon. Jan acknowledges that he could probably make more than the $20,000 to $40,000 he keeps out of Kriska's $500,000 annual revenues—if he wanted to compromise his life style. "Most of my employees make as much as I do," he says, noting that Kriska's profit-sharing plan gives employees a pride in their work and a sense of responsibility that allows Jan to travel up to six months a year on business and pleasure. In fact, he often combines the two; he recalls a seminar week in Ixtapa, Mexico, where artisans spent days wind surfing and evenings organizing a crafts equivalent to the Good Housekeeping seal of approval.

CRASHING THE GATE

The best place to meet retailers who will turn your hobby into your profession is at a wholesale show, or the crafts section of a gifts show for wholesale buyers. Some craftspeople win acceptance the first year they apply to the shows, but you may have to build a reputation first. Show juries judge the worthiness of your work, and, depending how crowded your particular craft is, weed out competition. If you can't crash one of the premier shows your first year in business, don't despair. You can still make contacts and build a reputation through smaller shows. You can even take your windchimes or wall hangings directly to stores.

Booth fees run from $100 to $600, depending on the show. Bill Campbell and his wife, Jane, set aside another $1,000 for large multi-day shows to cover transportation, food, and lodging. In addition to a sampling of your wares, bring brochures and catalogs. Set aside several hundred dollars to design and print the material. Spell out prices and terms in black and white, and picture your quilts or jewelry in glossy four-color.

CAN YOU MAKE ONE HUNDRED JUST LIKE THAT ONE?

The most exquisite craftsmanship in North America won't entice retailers who doubt that you can deliver on time, in quantity, and with consistent quality. Buyers want assurance that you can reproduce the quality they see at the show. While your craft represents your creative side, the printed brochure gives them a sense of your professionalism.

Craftspeople steer "true artists" away from the wholesale route, warning that you must ask employees to replicate a single pattern many times. Artistry often takes a back seat to delegation, leading many high-volume craftspeople to characterize themselves as designers rather than artisans. Bill Campbell insists he lacks "an ethereal sense" about his pottery, which retails from $12 to $50. Instead of crafting museum pieces, "I try to create a feeling of celebration when people use my pottery," he explains. "I want you to smile when you reach for an incredible salad bowl. And you won't have to guess at the function of my pottery. It's onomatopoetic—a fish platter looks like it's meant to serve fish."

Sergio Lub, an Argentinian native who makes brass and copper bracelets in Walnut Creek, California, recalls the moment of insight that changed his show behavior. "I realized that to make money at the shows was not my main objective. My real goal was to meet retailers, get to know who they are so they would commit themselves to represent me." Instead of waiting anxiously in his booth for orders as exhibitors do at retail fairs, Sergio began walking the aisles to meet retail buyers. "If I open just one new account, the reorders cover the show costs and much more."

Most big-time craftspeople attend eight to twelve shows a year, including some traditional fairs for the public. Although wholesale orders account for 90 percent of the Factory Store's revenues, "fairs are where the market is tested," Bill Campbell says. "Listen to the public. They're a mean jury—'This handle's too big.' 'Have you got this in blue?' " Remember that, unlike the purist, you're designing for bulk sales, so you must respond to the public whim.

After you take the public's pulse, listen to the other craftspeople. More than in most other fields, artisans share secrets that work for them. "Shows are an opportunity to pick the brains of people next to me," says Jan Mayer. "Network. The most successful people in the country are at these shows."

Jan and his artisan contacts often trade lists of wholesale accounts so they can approach likely retailers after the shows are over. The most successful craftspeople are marketers. They send brochures and call on gallery owners or museum shop buyers on their own turf. Jan's three-person marketing division also holds the hands of about six hundred old friends—retailers who already carry Kriska scarves. "Retailers need help; they're very busy people," acknowledges Jan, who has a toll-free phone number to encourage orders.

ON APPROVAL

Sergio Lub, whose $15 to $40 bracelets sell in approximately six hundred museum shops and galleries, developed a way to entice new accounts aboard. Basically, he trusts them with credit by offering his bracelets "on approval." Traditional artisans, possibly because they lived on the poverty level, expected up-front payment for their wares. But many retailers shied away from contracting with craftspeople, fearing their reputation for unreliability.

Sergio's no-lose solution gives retailers a display case with $1,000 worth of bracelets for a month or two on a trial basis. If they don't sell, ship them back. If customers like the bracelets, a retailer knows within thirty or sixty days and pays at that point. Now, the only way Sergio Lub Inc. does business is on approval. Returns equal about 5 percent of sales, but the policy has significantly multiplied the accounts willing to try his wares. "It's better to sell one hundred pieces and lose two or three than to sell just ten and lose none," Sergio says.

On-approval policies have limits, however. Sergio draws the line at difficult-to-ship work, such as big pots and fragile glass items that must be packaged very carefully.

GROWTH-ORIENTED

Even as the crafts world evolves from its cottage-industry roots to the big time, most artisans never consider marketing. But both Sergio and his good friend Jan Mayer offer retailers co-op ad campaigns; they pay half the cost of any ad that features their products. "I have a $20,000 ad budget, which many consider unrealistic. If I wanted to cut back on advertising, I could double my salary. But," says Jan, "I'm growth oriented."

Apparently, promotion helps. Stores that advertise Sergio's bracelets see an average 30 percent increase in business. Ad costs eat about 10 percent of the extra income, which, Sergio points out, "gives us a return of almost ten to one." He also notes that craftspeople make good copy for newspapers interested in alternative life styles. Since an interesting story sells more items than an expensive ad, approach the press with how you weave baskets.

WE'RE DIFFERENT

Even as they move into the mainstream, craftspeople still differ from most business people. While all manufacturers worry about quality control, for example, artisans take it to the extreme. Sergio Lub includes a lifetime guarantee with every brass or copper bracelet, even the $8 children's line. If it breaks, return it for repair or replacement. And, while competition surely exists among artisans, it is more subtle than in other industries. Craftspeople talk about the family-like atmosphere of their field. Artisans also value traits like integrity. "Over the years, I've probably taken $50,000 worth of checks at the Columbia University Show, which is right next door to Harlem," says Jan Mayer. "I never got a bad check."

One continuing debate involves the very prosperity crafts now enjoy. To grow large, artisans must hire employees to duplicate their work. Some die-hard craftspeople argue against what they consider assembly-line tactics. Even business people like Bill Campbell admit that "part of our strength is the uniqueness of our crafts."

The question remains, how many times can a crafts maker duplicate an item before it loses its uniqueness? Some million-dollar shops are convinced they still have room to grow before compromising their artistry.

SOURCES

Industry Associations

American Craft Retailers Association, P.O. Box 653, Cockeysville, Md., 21030 (310) 889-2933

American Craft Council, 401 Park Ave. S., New York, N.Y. 10016 (212) 696-0710

Publications

The Crafts Report, 3632 Ashworth N., Seattle, Wash. 98103 (206) 547-7611

American Craft Magazine, 401 Park Ave. S., New York, N.Y. 10016 (212) 696-0710

Quality Crafts Market, 521 5th Ave., Suite 1700, New York, N.Y. 10017 (212) 575-0140

Wholesale Shows

The Buyers Market of American Crafts, Wendy Rosen Inc., Suite 300, Mill Centre 3000 Chestnut Ave., Baltimore, Md. 21211 (301) 889-2933

American Craft Enterprises, P.O. Box 10, New Paltz, N.Y. 12561 (914) 255-0039

Direct Sales Company

> *"Direct sales triggers an almost magical change in some individuals. You see shy, retiring, inarticulate introverts on July 1, standing on a stage making a rousing speech in September. It's almost a cliché, but the principal reward of my business is helping people change their personalities." – Robert King, Consumer Marketing Services Inc.*

Low Startup Investment: $5,000 (initial inventory, sales brochures)

High Startup Investment: $50,000 (additional inventory and warehouse, advertising for sales representatives, computer system)

Time Until Breakeven: Three months to two years

Annual Revenues: $100,000-$1 billion (small startup at low end; Avon-sized firm at high end)

Annual Pre-tax Profits: $30,000-$1 million

Staffers Needed for Startup (including founder): One

The pioneer ancestor of the Avon Lady was the Yankee peddler who brought goods from the East to the little houses scattered across the prairies. Modern day descendants of these traveling merchants had created an $8.4 billion industry by 1986, the last year the Direct Selling Association guessed at U.S. figures. That year, direct salespeople called on 75 percent of all households, selling half of all households items ranging from vacuum cleaners to vitamins.

GARAGE CLASSICS

Despite the move from covered wagon to station wagon, a great many things have *not* changed in the direct selling industry. Importantly, it remains a low-cost business to enter. "You don't need $2,000 a month to lease a retail store or capital for half a million pieces of direct mail," says Robert H. King, chairman of Consumer Marketing Services Inc., Hollywood, Florida. Since the sales staff receives commissions instead of salaries, you don't need to worry about payroll and withholding taxes and fringe benefits. After the initial inventory purchase, additional product can be purchased using income from sales. "No other retail approach allows you to bootstrap the way direct sales does," observes Bob King.

Indeed, Bob King, who left the chairmanship of the direct-mail encyclopedia firm World Book Inc. to start his own direct sales consulting firm in 1983, jokes that "my partner and I were discussing plans to start our own ladies undergarment direct sales business, when he said, 'We'd better buy a garage,' When I asked why, he said 'Because all the successful direct selling companies started in a garage.' " In 1987, Consumer Marketing's first year as a direct sales operation, Bob did not object to losing $37,000 on sales of $250,000 because by 1988, Bob plans to earn $250,000 on $1.5 million in revenues.

Bob can afford to wait eighteen months for profitability, and is investing in a computer system and warehouse with his eyes on explosive growth. But "direct sales has always been a distribution channel where you can exchange perspiration for startup capital," he says, pointing to all those success stories that start with a tiny nest egg.

For example, Rita Berro Kasdon started Concept Now Cosmetics in Santa Fe Springs, California, in 1971 by cashing in a $6,000 life insurance policy. Rita put aside $1,000 to support herself and her two children until cash started flowing, and spent the rest on cosmetic inventory. "I couldn't afford to have the lab [that formulated the cosmetics] apply the labels," she recalls, "so I stuck them on at the warehouse myself." Today, Concept Now supports six thousand sales reps in the U.S., Canada, Mexico and Southeast Asia. With

1988 global sales expected to reach $10 million, Rita talks of taking the company public before too long.

One element that makes direct mail profitable is that money isn't tied up in inventory or bad debts. From the beginning, Concept Now required its salespeople to include a money order or cashier's check when placing an order, and used that capital to buy from suppliers. "There are no accounts receivable in this business," Rita Berro Kasdon explains. "I've never borrowed because it isn't necessary."

WHAT SELLS?

Before plunging into the direct selling world, consider what you're selling. Experts suggest choosing between two categories of products:

■ Big-ticket items that have a unique feature which a trained salesperson explains directly to the consumer. For example, Bose Corporation sells stereo equipment door to door, which allows its sales crew to show how such a compact system can deliver superior sound. Some companies precede door-to-door sales with phone solicitations. Additionally, many relatively expensive items, like *Encyclopaedia Britannica*, are sold "over-the-counter" from temporary booths set up in shopping malls or county fairs. Many big-ticket companies expect customers to pay in installments. So if you chose to hawk computers, you may need more startup cash to buy inventory than a company that requires immediate payment.

■ Small-ticket items with high mark-ups, like costume jewelry, cosmetics, and health food products. What you lose in the price of the merchandise you make up in volume since customers buy these types of goodies repeatedly. Since a salesperson with minimal training can explain the less complicated benefits of these products, this segment of the industry relies on part-time representatives who typically sell to friends and co-workers, as well as door to door. Parties, where several consumers are invited to see a product at the home of a host or hostess, are another popular approach.

A CAST OF THOUSANDS

Success rests with encouraging a sales staff to knock on doors. "Incentives are important in any business, but extraordinarily important in direct sales," says Bob King. To keep a steady flow of salespeople pounding their beats, expect to sponsor contests, travel, and recognition programs.

When starting Concept Now, Rita Berro Kasdon decided that, to attract a sales force in the face of savage competition from other direct sales cosmetics firms, she would offer a "far more generous" compensation plan than competitors. "Therefore, I was willing to take very little out of the company in the beginning. I only drew $700 a month for the first year, while one of CNC's top sales people earned over $50,000 during her first year." Concept Now kept interest high with such promotional bonuses as gold Cadillacs, diamond and gold rings, diamond watches, and trips to Hawaii. Rita's strategy of practically giving away the store in an effort to develop a strong, loyal sales force worked! Concept Now recorded a $25,000 profit during its first year in business.

Look at it this way: Instead of spending a bundle to lease a store and advertise directly to the consumer, you give that money directly to the sales reps. You can recruit your first salespeople through newspaper advertising. Consumer Marketing even offered some minimum-income guarantees to encourage sales reps to sign on in its first year. But your best source of sales help soon becomes other salespeople.

No matter how motivated each individual representative is, you need increasing numbers of sales people to grow. Successful direct sales firms encourage representatives to view new sales reps as a source of opportunity rather than competition. In using incentives to recruit, beware of illegal pyramid schemes. Your sales crew must legitimately buy products, either for their own use or to sell to customers, before you can reward individuals who brought them into the ranks. This prohibition against doling out dollars dates to the 1970s, when the industry earned a sleazy reputation from companies who paid "salespeople" who didn't sell to enlist other "distributors" who didn't distribute. Instead, each new recruit bought a required initial storehouse of inventory, then, rather than sell products, rounded up new recruits. Their commissions came not from the sale of products rotting in the basement, but from inventory fees paid by the next batch of recruits. Like a chain letter, pyramids are illegal.

It is perfectly legal, however, to pay a recruiter a percentage of the recruitee's sales, and direct sales compensation packages can get pretty elaborate. Explains Rita Berro Kasdon: "If you're a friend of mine and talk me into distributing, Concept Now pays you 5 percent on everything I sell." Once retail volume exceeds $800 a month for twelve consecutive months, the salesperson takes home an extra 4 percent of her friend's sales. But income opportunities don't stop there. If a recruit sponsors additional salespeople, the initial sponsor gets a percentage of all the sales made by people her recruit enlists as well. And so on. Concept Now's literature assumes that a salesperson working just six hours a week can host eight parties a month. If customers buy an average $150 worth of cosmetics at each party, the rep earns $600 a month. An Executive Director who sponsors twenty salespeople earns $4,856 for the same twenty-four hours she puts in, since her income is leveraged by the work of other reps, also working an average of twenty-four hours a month.

PROFIT CHUNKS

Sales commissions and related recruiting and incentive fees eat up the greatest chunk of your margins, followed by product costs and administration costs. As you grow, you can add computers to track inventory, billing, and commissions, or you can farm out those chores to firms that specialize in direct sales time-sharing. Likewise, some entrepreneurs hire warehouses to distribute their goods, although others would rather sip snake venom than entrust their distribution to outsiders. "If the parent company doesn't deliver those goods to the sales representative quickly and in good order, they'll hear about it," nods Bob King. "A lot of companies set twenty-four or forty-eight-hour deadlines for the turnaround time after the receipt of the order."

In the end, most direct sales companies look for pre-tax profits in the 20-percent range, which beats the spangles off of a retail store's 3- to 5-percent profits. Since the commissions must be high enough

486 / DIRECT SALES COMPANY

to attract a sales staff, "you need a product that doesn't cost much relative to what you can sell it for," advises Rita Berro Kasdon. Bob King says a product that costs more than 40 percent of your sales just doesn't qualify as a direct sales item.

Women typically represent both the direct sales customer and the salesperson. As women increasingly enter the workplace, observers see some changes ahead for the industry. For one thing, instead of visiting homes, more representatives are selling in offices and factories. The Direct Selling Association estimates one out of every five Avon Product sales takes place in the workplace. In response to the changing marketplace, Tupperware developed a twenty-minute rush-hour office party.

In addition, direct sellers are adopting other approaches to supplement door-to-door sales. Some organizations mail catalogs to customers and potential customers. A few are adding retail locations but retaining the personal attention consumers can't get anymore in most stores.

But those are auxiliary approaches, meant only to increase the effectiveness of the lone sales representative. "Those additions can come later," says Bob King. "The field is still open to an entrepreneur with a product the marketplace genuinely needs."

SOURCES

Industry Associations

Direct Selling Association, 1776 K St., N.W., Suite 600, Washington, D.C. 20006 (202) 293-5760
World Federation of Direct Selling Associations, 1776 K St., N.W., Suite 600, Washington, D.C., 20006 (202) 293-5760

Consultants

Consumer Marketing Services Inc., Suite 320, 3440 Hollywood Blvd., Hollywood, Fla. 33021 (305) 985-2674
Rita Berro Kasdon, Concept Now Cosmetics, 14000 S. Anson Ave., Santa Fe Springs, Calif. 90670 (213) 921-0534
Ronald A. Bernstein & Associates Inc., Chicago Place, 310 W. Chicago Ave., Chicago, Ill. 60610 (312) 440-3700

Import Entrepreneur

> *"Unlike manufacturing or retailing, where overhead is high, if you can find the right product and have a market for it, importing offers inexpensive entry."* – Gene Milosh, president, American Association of Exporters and Importers

Low Startup Investment: $2,000 (importing an inexpensive product in small quantities and selling to an agent)

High Startup Investment: $200,000 (selling a costly product directly to retail or wholesale buyers)

Time Until Breakeven: Three months to three years

Annual Revenues: $200,000-$20 million

Annual Pre-tax Profits: $30,000-$3 million

Staffers Needed for Startup (including founder): One

Ever since Marco Polo ventured east, the import/export field has been making history. The business sections of newspapers report daily on which countries the U.S. government will favor with trade agreements—and which lobbying group vows to keep foreign products out. While *Fortune* 500 giants take out 80 percent of the U.S.'s exports, international moms and pops run the import side of the equation, according to Gene Milosh, president of the American Association of Exporters and Importers.

American import/export revenues exceed the GNP of many countries who are our trading partners. The U.S. Department of Commerce revealed that in 1986 we shipped $217.3 billion worth of blue jeans, computers, and all manner of goods made in America, with Canada gobbling up nearly 21 percent of the total, and Japan another 12.4 percent. That same year we received $387.1

billion worth of blue jeans, computers, etc. (Japan sent 22.1 percent of our imports; Canada, 17.9 percent). And the experts say we ain't seen nothing yet. "The world is becoming even more interdependent year by year," says Gene Milosh. "As world economies grow, so will our opportunities in exporting and importing."

KEEPING TRACK IN TWO LANGUAGES

Importing is not a business for the faint-hearted. Complications can arise overnight and often in two languages. The American Association of Exporters and Importers publishes newletters weekly and monthly just to keep up with the shuffling regulations of our own government. For example, the so-called General System of Preference instituted by Congress provides tariff and quota breaks for underdeveloped countries and particular products. The regulations can change without warning and often follow seemingly meaningless logic. Says Gene Milosh: "Quotas for men's shirts with short sleeves may differ from long-sleeve shirts, and the quota certainly differs with the country of origin."

But if you do you homework—and are lucky enough to find, say, the hottest undiscovered Italian designer—fortunes can be made in importing. Although transportation costs often eat up 10 percent of revenues, your labor costs will be low. And, if you choose your product wisely, no domestic competition will exist.

Examine your own background to decide what product to import. Individuals with ties to the apparel world might consider textiles, while engineers might be more at home with a technical product. If you don't have a brand new product to spring on the American consumer, consider what you might make cheaper or better overseas. You can save yourself some headaches by importing items that are easy to transport. Beware of items that are fragile and may break during transit, or products that are exceptionally heavy and are costly to move from place to place.

Once you determine which product to import, the experts say finding a foreign source is a piece of cake. Most governments, eager to expand their balance of trade, will provide a list of manufacturers without charge. In addition, the U.S. Foreign Commercial Service assigns individuals to each industry and will provide a free or inexpensive list of manufacturers by product and country.

"It's common to start part time until the business gets rolling," says Kenneth D. Weiss, author of *Building an Import/Export Business* (John Wiley & Sons, $12.95, 1987) and president of Treico International Services, a trade consulting group. Profits all depend on the merchandise you import and the deal you cut with your foreign supplier. Ken offers the following example, which assumes an important merchant has orders for $20,000 worth of international widgets per month:

THE BUDGET

Planned sales for month	$20,000
Less total cost of merchandise	−12,000*
	$ 8,000
Less sales commissions of 15 percent to domestic staff	−3,000
	$ 5,000
Less operating expenses of 10 percent	− 2,000
Profit (15 percent) before tax and owner's salary	$ 3,000

* Includes the cost of the merchandise from your foreign supplier, foreign inland freight and insurance, foreign freight forwarding, international shipping and insurance, U.S. customs brokerage and import duties, inland freight and insurance to your warehouse, and miscellaneous expenses.

Using those figures, annual revenues of $240,000 would provide $36,000 in pre-tax profits. You usually have to pay that $12,000 merchandise cost and the $2,000 in operating expenses before they see any product, so have your customers in the U.S. already committed before buying your first shipload of widgets.

GLOBAL-SUPPORT STAFF

You can take courses on import/export at community and four-year colleges, and the Government Printing Office even offers a library of hints. In addition, a cadre of support services—brokers, transportation companies, etc.—can help part the waters. "The question isn't whether you'll use them, but to what extent," says Ken Weiss. An import agent or broker will handle the foreign end of the business for a percentage fee. Customs brokers and freight forwarders will take the pressure off in those areas for another fee. Query transportation companies about routes—the least expensive and quickest route may not be the shortest distance between two points if a dock strike is in the works. You can find these specialists in the Yellow Pages of most large city directories, and many airports and seaports also supply lists.

"Be careful how you select your representatives, since you are ultimately responsible," cautions Gene Milosh. "Check their financial backgrounds with Dun & Bradstreet and decide how much of a specialist you need." For example, do you want a broker with an office in London or Beijing? Does your representative have the technical background to deal with titanium or Indonesian curry? Is your representative knowledgeable about the inspections and safety modifications that ball point pens or BMWs may require?

You can sell your goods to an agent in the U.S. who will find retail or wholesale buyers, or you can line up buyers yourself. If you choose to sell directly to wholesale and retail buyers, your up-front costs will be higher, of course. You'll need to bring on board a marketing staff to call on the buyers and attend trade shows relevant to your industry. However, assuming you find a pipeline of steady buyers, your profits will eventually be higher.

DOT ALL THE "I" 'S

Because you pay up front for the goods, and because your manufacturer is oceans away, and because you are dealing with the nuances of a foreign culture, make sure to ask the right questions and get everything in writing. Certain foreign governments side with their own nationals no matter what. "In certain instances, the American company may be prevented from modifying or terminating its relationship with a foreign agent, distributor, or representative, even for good cause, without incurring a substantial liability," warns Ken Weiss. Customs and trade attorneys earn their livings by trying to keep importers out of trouble.

But forewarned is forearmed. To avoid the risks of inflation, specify the currency of payment where possible (although some governments frown on payment in dollars). There's no question howitzer will raise more eyebrows at the custom barriers than garden hoses, so have your answers prepared. And, should Brazilian source offer you shoes at a price that sounds too good to be true, perhaps it is. "If you bring in something that is selling under the price manufacturers receive in their own land, a country is dumping," warns Gene Milosh. "U.S. customs will embargo the goods. A tariff may even be slapped on retroactively."

JACK BE QUICK

Because U.S. and foreign guidelines change so rapidly, importers "have to be nimble," says Gene Milosh. If the Department of Commerce whisks your exporting country off the General System of Preference list it publishes daily, you may want to hop the next plane to the Third World to line up a new supplier.

While you may stumble on the 1990s version of the Hula Hoop during your next vacation in Singapore, most products meant for the U.S. market have long since found their way across our borders. "But if you can't find something new and exciting," suggests Ken Weiss, "take an existing product and modify it" through design changes or packaging or promotion to make it new and exciting. For example, "A clock importer may tell its Taiwanese factory to make the numbers fancy so it will sell better in the hotel gift shops it deals with," says Gene Milosh. "Or if you just decrease the size of this metal component by one-eighth of an inch, the clock will suddenly become cost competitive."

SOURCES

Industry Associations

American Association of Exporters and Importers, 11 W. 42nd St., New York, N.Y. 10036 (212) 944-2230

Council for Export Trading Companies, 225 Connecticut Ave., #415, Washington, D.C. 20036 (202) 861-4705

Publications

Import/Export Business, 93 Willets Dr., Syosset, N.Y. 11791 (516) 496-8740

International Trade Alert and *International Trade Monthly,* 11 W. 42nd St., New York, N.Y. 10036 (212) 944-2230

The U.S. Dept. of Commerce & The U.S. Small Business Administration both have books available through the Superintendent of Documents, Government Printing Office, Washington, D.C. 20402 (202) 783-3238

The Exporter Advisor, 330 E. 71st St., New York, N.Y. 10021 (212) 734-3816

The International Executive, 401 N. Broad St., Philadelphia, Pa. 19108 (215) 238-5300

Consultant

Treico International Services, 93 Willets Dr., Syosset, N.Y. 11791 (516) 496-8740

Mail-order Catalog

> *"Quite a few people were involved in putting the catalog together, but the finished product is an indication of my personality. It's my child."* – Tony Clemendor, Tymely Ventures Inc.

Low Startup Investment: $50,000 (small mailing, with items drop-shipped by manufacturers)

High Startup Investment: $500,000 (several mailings, with items shipped from a company warehouse)

Time Until Breakeven: Two to four years

Annual Revenues: $50,000-$1.5 million

Annual Pre-tax Profits: $5,000-$450,000

Staffers Needed for Startup (including founder): One

In 1986, *Newsweek* magazine reported 10 billion mail-order catalogs clogged mailboxes across the country—that's more than fifty for each American of voting age, and twice the number that mail-order entrepreneurs posted eight years earlier. In 1986, catalogs rang up sales of $50 billion. Observers expect consumer mail-order sales will continue to grow 12 to 15 percent a year, and business-to-business books that sell everything from office supplies to medical supplies will realize twice that increase.

NO TIME TO BROWSE

Why this insatiable hunger for junk mail? In seven out of ten households, no adult can shop during the day. In addition, businesses that sell by catalog eliminate an expensive sales force and keep showroom and even warehouse space to a minimum. "The movement goes beyond retailing—just about every business will be affected," predicted futurist John Naisbitt in a 1986 *Trend Letter*. Addressing manufacturers, he writes: "Ask yourself: Can the services and products we provide be marketed and delivered by mail?"

Since catalogers sell everything from abalone to zithers, the trick is to set yourself apart. Find a niche—products that consumers can't find easily in stores. Next, since you can't afford to market to the entire world, zero in on a targeted audience, individuals who will buy your items sight unseen.

Tony Clemendor has the first two rules down pat. After completing his Harvard MBA in February 1985, he began preparing Tymely Ventures Inc., Los Angeles, to sell products created especially for the black community. He credits his mom with the inspiration: "She was making Christmas tree ornaments with black figures for friends when she started getting calls from buyers at department stores like Bloomingdale's," he says. "I realized if there was a market for her product, perhaps I could create a whole catalog of items for middle- and upper-income black households." Tony expects 5 million of the 20 million blacks in the country may eventually buy from Tymely Ventures.

With one item down and another seventy-four or so to go to fill a sixteen page catalog, Tony began making the rounds of stores, street fairs, and trade shows. He ran classified ads asking for black products in magazines catering to black readers and wrote to publishers inquiring about books for blacks. Less than a year later, Tony had accumulated such items as stoneware ceramic figures with black features: *The Nubian Baby Book*, which tells parents how to help their children maintain their ethnic identity; and Huggy Bean doll. In February 1987, Tony mailed his first recipients one hundred thousand copies. Within two months, recipients of 2 percent of those copies had placed orders—and Tony began planning his second catalog.

A typical sixteen-page color catalog mailed to one hundred thousand names might cost $100,000 or more, assuming you bought and warehoused most items. If you mail to thirty thousand households and pay for inventory from the manufacturer only as customer orders come in, you could get by with $50,000. But if you don't mind slow growth, consultants recommend a far less expensive test for your idea.

CLASSIFIED SALES

It works this way: Advertise your unique widget in the classified section of a publication with similar mail-order ads. For $5,000 to $10,000, you can incorporate, buy a minimum number of widgets which you store in your garage, pay for the ad (the smallest ad in *House Beautiful*'s Window Shopping section runs about $1,200), and buy wrapping paper, cartons, postage, and so forth. Use the cash the customers send with your first orders to buy more widgets and run another ad.

While you sell products and test the validity of your merchandise, you also collect names that form the basis for your catalog's first mailing list. Although this approach can be slow, some fabulous successes began in the classifieds. In 1978, Richard Thalheimer spent $500 to advertise a runner's watch in *Runner's World* magazine. He mailed his first catalog a year later. By 1986, his catalog, The Sharper Image was mailing 3 million catalogs monthly, had twenty-six retail stores, boasted corporate sales of $100 million, and was predicting a 30-percent growth rate for the next several years. Whew.

Those consultants who advise this route say you should collect ten or twelve thousand names to justify a catalog. But some ideas are just too hot to sit on the classified shelf. "Since I got the idea, two catalogs came out on black fashions," says Tony Clemendor. Fearing competition, he jumped straight into the market with a catalog.

THREE STEPS TO MAILING

The Direct Marketing Association and numerous universities offer catalog courses. Basically, a mail-order startup has three stages:

- Creation of the catalog. Consultants estimate a typical color catalog costs $1,000 per page. That includes fees to the designer, photographer, models, and copywriter. Assume a sixteen page catalog will cost $16,000 to $20,000.

Higher ticket items require a glossy presentation, so Rolex vendors may spend more on quality paper than sellers of Mickey

Mouse watches. Also, since they can't squeeze the merchandise, customers respond to in-depth descriptions, so hire a good copywriter. The Sharper Image spends a whole page, complete with eight paragraphs of explanation and seven photographs, to present its $99 leather attache with $69 matching saddlebags.

• Inventory. After you've done the legwork to find your merchandise, set aside bundles to pay for it. This cost, of course, depends on the items. Will you sell $1,000 diamond rings or $10 junk jewelry

Work backwards to arrive at the amount of money you need for inventory. Figure merchandise costs 33 to 50 percent of sales. Some canny catalogers bypass this expensive step by cutting deals where the manufacturer ships only after each order comes in the door. Beware, however: The Federal Trade Commission requires you to ship products within thirty days of an order. Drop-shipping only works with suppliers who are responsible and agreeable.

Now that America has accepted catalogs, "sales figures indicate that consumers no longer are wary of buying high-ticket items sight unseen," writes John Naisbitt. "The sky's the limit on price, quality, and variety in the mail-order market." Keeping this in mind, you may wish to shop for the unusual and go for the heights, if you can afford it. The Sharper Image, which reports an average purchase of $145, sells everything from a $49 Caddy Card (a calculator-like device to help golfers track their game from green to green) to a $2,300 computerized treadmill. Incidentally, treadmill buyers pay another $100 for shipping charges.

• Mailing. Postage, renting lists, and printing costs about $500 per one thousand catalogs. If you send out fifty thousand catalogs, allot $25,000 for this step.

Now sit back and wait for orders. The industry considers a 1-percent response rate average; 2 to 5 percent is astonishing. Therefore, expect just five hundred orders from that first fifty-thousand-name mailing. Assume your average order is $40, and you average 50-percent profit margins. That's $10,000. But you spent $45,000 to put out the catalog—not counting merchandise. Ouch. You make up the deficit on future catalogs that you mail to repeat customers. There you get 5-percent response; twenty-five hundred orders for each fifty-thousand catalogs. The process involves honing a dependable mailing list. The process, and therefore your breakeven, can take two to four years.

Okay, it takes awhile to build your audience. But once a mail-order business gets rolling, it can be much more lucrative than a retail store. You're not as labor or capital intensive as a retail store. After taxes, a good catalog should net 10 to 15 percent.

Catalogers can be precise about costs and know exactly which items sell best because the mail-order business is highly statistical. Just look at your orders. If item A sells well, reorder. If item B is a dog, yank it from your next catalog. Tony Clemendor began revamping his catalog for a second edition toward the end of his first month in business.

If you want to hold startup costs low, avoid computerizing and staffing up by signing on with a fulfillment center equipped to shuffle all those numbers in its computer. For a percentage fee on each order, the center receives orders by mail, or by phone if your catalog includes a toll-free number. An order-taker logs each purchase into a computer that tracks lists and inventory, and generates shipping and packaging labels. The fulfillment house also cashiers the checks before sending its bill along to the cataloger.

ELECTRONIC PUBLISHING

The catalog of the future may hardly resemble the book that made Mr. Roebuck famous. Some industry insiders classify interactive cable television and computerized shopping in the same "nonstore" marketing category as catalogs and predict many mail-order companies will operate in various media within five years. Also, computer and printing innovations may soon lead to customized catalogs. For example, your computer-driven printing technology can send a message on a particular page to a New Hampshire–based customer who bought cross-country ski-wear from last season's catalog. That message will differ from the material you reserve for downhill skiers in Colorado.

SOURCES

Industry Associations

Direct Marketing Association, 6 E. 43rd St., New York, N.Y. 10017 (212) 689-4977

National Mail Order Association, 5818 Venice Blvd., Los Angeles, Calif. 90019 (213) 934-7986

Regional associations (check with Direct Marketing Association, above, for a group in your area)

Publications

Direct Marketing Magazine, 224 7th St., Garden City, N.Y. 11530 (516) 746-6700

NonStore Marketing Report, The Catalog Marketer, The Business to Business Catalog Marketer, all at 731 N. Cascade Ave., Colorado Springs, Colo. 80903 (303) 633-5556

Direct Response, The Digest of Direct Marketing, 25550 Hawthorne Blvd., Suite 114 Torrence, Calif. 90505 (213) 373-9408

Consultants

Michaelson Direct Marketing, 307 E. Chapman Ave., Orange, Calif. 92666 (714) 538-2368

J. Schmid & Assoc. 3209 W. 68th St., Shawnee Mission, Kans. 66208 (913) 236-6699

Richard Siedlecki, 2674 E. Main St., Suite C170, Ventura, Calif. 93003 (805) 658-7000

Telemarketer

> *"I enjoy the volatility. There are times when it's calm, and times when we prepare fifteen programs a week. It's a turbulent, interesting mix."* – Sandy Pernick, The Direct Response Corporation

Low Startup Investment: $10,000 (bare-bones telephone equipment for five part-time employees)

High Startup Investment: $50,000 (more elaborate automated equipment for ten employees, advertising, and two word processors with number-crunching ability)

Time Until Breakeven: Three months to two years

Annual Revenues: $50,000-$2 million

Annual Pre-tax Profits: $10,000-$300,000

Staffers Needed for Startup (including founder): Five to ten

"The whole world talks about productivity, but business hasn't done much to make selling more productive," observes Lee Van Vechten, publisher of the *Van Vechten Report,* a newsletter for managers of corporate telemarketing groups. As you might guess, Lee offers a solution to the high cost of selling: telemarketing. If you make sales calls—or at least weed out prospects—over the phone rather than via an interstate highway, costs tumble. "McGraw-Hill said that field selling cost about $260 per presentation in 1986," says Lee. "The average cost of a business-to-business telemarketing presentation is about $18."

WHO DOES IT?

Telemarketers sell stationery to businesses or carpet cleaning to consumers. Operators make an appointment for a salesperson to call in person, or ask, for example, what you like or dislike about *Newsweek* magazine. Operators standing by at an 800 telephone number offer fix-it advice on your washing machine, or take orders for the genuine cultured pearls advertised on Channel 3. Lee Van Vechten's definition, however, covers just about everything: "Telemarketing is intensive use of the telephone in the business environment."

Telemarketing companies range from in-house, multi-floor departments at large corporations (J.C. Penney employs around four thousand telemarketing operators answering toll-free numbers) to individuals who make calls part time from the kitchen telephone. "The industry is less than ten years old and nobody's developed statistics on its size, partially because we're a moving target, we're growing so fast," says Sandy Pernick, who runs The Direct Response Corporation. However, telemarketing has yet to reach capacity. The industry is still inventing methods of operation. U.S. News & World Report predicts that by 2001, 8 million people will make their livelihood through telemarketing. Lee Van Vechten estimated in 1987 that just 2 million telemarketing operators made calls. "Expect geometric growth," he says.

NO MORE $250 STARTUPS

Sandy Pernick invested $250 in 1982 to launch The Direct Response from her Des Plaines, Illinois, home. She spent $100 for incorporation, printed some letterheads, and put three people on residential phones. Today, the company employs one hundred five and achieves revenues over $1 million.

Although occasional successes still start from home, the cottage industry is fast turning professional. The good news is the cost of telephone equipment, Wats lines, and long-distance charges are all skidding downwards. A well run company can easily keep 20 percent of revenues as profits. The bad news is corporate customers have been stung once too often by telemarketers who have disappeared overnight without a trace, leaving customers who call the 800 number to follow up on their order with the message: "This service has been disconnected." Sandy Pernick, who was a supervisor for another telemarketer before starting The Direct Response, recommends telemarketing only to entrepreneurs with a direct-marketing background. "Businesses look for a professional image, for stability," she says. For you, that means showing clients the permanence that comes with fancy equipment and employees rather than a card table in a basement.

YOUR FIRST TELEMARKETING CLIENT: YOURSELF

Of course, you can still start small by convincing local businesses to use your services. Locate customers the same way you will operate for them: through telemarketing. After you call prospective clients, many will request a brochure, so be sure to have professional-looking literature ready to mail.

Sandy Pernick asks clients for year-long contracts. "Educate clients to the fact that stopping and starting a program is counterproductive," she says. "If a program works, keep it on full time. Consider it part of your marketing plan." Such long-term contracts do wonders for her scheduling. If in January she knows she will have a minimum level of business in July, she can take on new projects so she doesn't have to lay off staff.

Except for the image issue, you can start a service that only makes outbound calls with just a phone or two. Or you can get fancy. Automatic dialers that call each number in sequence and play back a recorded message can run $6,000 each. Traditional equipment that also accepts incoming calls is less expensive—but you need more of it since you also need employees. Telemarketing is both an equipment-heavy and people-intensive industry. "The industry has a personnel turnover rate of 150 to 200 percent," Sandy warns. "Historically that's because we've been part-time employers and attracted transient workers like students." Her solution is to hire only full-time, permanent employees.

Others argue that turnover is so high because telemarketing leads to burnout. It's hard making one hundred phone calls a day. Norm Pensky, who runs Adds Telemarketing from South Pasadena, California, counters this problem by switching people to new assignments often and making sure people take coffee breaks.

BEFORE THE PHONE RINGS

Sandy Pernick insists the actual phone call is the least important aspect of a telemarketing campaign. "You have to plan what to say, decide who to say it to, establish what time to call, and afterwards you have to analyze what people said. That requires more than just subjective opinions. You need number-crunching and you'd better be able to produce an automated report."

Most clients have a good handle on what they want from a telemarketer, but it's up to you to execute their plans. Sandy charges a flat fee for a script (often written in conjunction with the client) and training of her personnel (the client gets involved to impart any technical expertise). Then she charges by the "communicator hour." The industry norm ranges anywhere from $35 to $75 per operator per hour, based on how involved the conversations, the area of the country, and the size of the contract.

Some clients provide lists of contacts, while in other cases the telemarketer finds the most appropriate list. A good way to find customers for your clients is to rent names from publications or associations. If you're calling current customers, completion rate of the questionnaire should be fairly high. But when you make cold calls, only 2 percent may be positives. But, adds Lee Van Vechten, "Most of those rejection calls last less that 1.5 minutes, so those ninety-eight calls who don't buy go quickly."

Lee offers some advice to keep from getting the phone slammed in your ear. "If the customer knows your company, identify yourself. But the consuming public doesn't like telemarketers from organizations they don't know. So, instead of saying, 'I'm with Hal's Meat Packing,' ease your way in. Say, 'Good evening, this is Lee Van Vechten. I'm curious, do you think freezers save you money on groceries?'"

Don't be afraid to change your script, but do so early on. Sandy Pernick does test runs with two to four callers, then makes any alterations. You won't get meaningful statistics if your approach is haphazard throughout the calling period.

THE LOOMING SHADOW

While everyone agrees that telemarketing has explosive growth in its future, observers also say government regulations will shape the industry. Bills pending state by state may limit the types of consumers that telemarketers can ring up. For example, so-called asterisk bills would prohibit telemarketers from calling those individuals who place an asterisk next to their names in the phone book. Other bills may restrict the hours you can call. Sandy Penick notes that most legislation is aimed toward out-bound consumer telemarketing: one reason she restricts her business to in-bound consumer calls or business-to-business telemarketing.

Buy others say government won't be able to stop the momentum. Telemarketing supporters say telephone selling works. In the future, more and more consumers will become comfortable with the concept, and more businesses will adopt telemarketing because it is inexpensive. With that in mind, experts expect telemarketers will work with legislators to create a good climate. Telemarketing may undergo subtle changes, they say, but the concept is here to stay.

SOURCES

Industry Association

American Telemarketing Association, 104 Wilmot Rd., Suite 201, Deerfield, Ill. 60015 (800) 441-3335

Publications

Teleprofessional Magazine, 1049J Camino del Mar, Box 123, Del Mar, Calif., 92014 (619) 755-6500

Telemarketing Magazine, 17 Park St., Norwalk, Conn. 06851 (203) 846-2029

The Van Vechten Report, 80 Scenic Dr., Suites 7 and 8, Freehold, N.J. 07731 (201) 780-7020

Trade Show

> *"When all goes well, running a trade show is like throwing a great party."* – David Cheifetz, Conference Management Corp., Norwalk, Connecticut

Low Startup Investment: $10,000 (hotel table-top show)	
High Startup Investment: $150,000 (major industry get-together, where many chores are subcontracted)	
Time Until Breakeven: Two to five years	
Annual Revenues: $20,000-$10 million (single show at low end; management of ten to fifteen shows annually at high end)	
Annual Pre-tax Profits: $10,000-$3 million	
Staffers Needed For Startup (including founder): One to ten	

David Cheifetz did not want this chapter written. Companies like his Conference Management Corp., Norwalk, Connecticut, which stages trade shows for industries as diverse as genetic research and fashion accessories, have been "one of the best-kept secrets around," he says. Like other service businesses, trade shows benefit from high cash flow and no inventory. But trade shows possess another advantage: Unlike most manufacturing, retailing, *or* service businesses, trade shows operate with no accounts receivables; all the money comes before you deliver a product. Whether David Cheifetz like it or not, competition is catching on. Between 1975 and 1985, the number of shows doubled to nine thousand, resulting in a $9-billion-a-year industry. *Tradeshow Week* projects an 8.2-percent annual growth to continue through 1995.

CASBAH

Trade shows are little more than elaborations on ancient Middle-Eastern bazaar themes: manufacturers displaying wares for browsing buyers. Modern operators refined the trade show into a twentieth-century selling tool aimed at corporate buyers who stock up en masse. According to the Trade Show Bureau, exposition booths churn out quality sales leads for about $106.89 each, compared to about twice that ($229.70) for a salesman to make an industrial sales call.

Trade associations and other nonprofit groups once dominated trade show management. Such an environment, says David Cheifetz, provided "remarkable business opportunities for astute business people, since the kinds of people attracted to nonprofit fields are not terribly aggressive promoters." Professional managers, including individual entrepreneurs, publishing groups, and ad agencies, now operate about 60 percent of the country's three thousand or so expos with more than ten thousand square feet of exhibit space—and nobody even knows how many "tabletop" shows are set up in hotel hallways and suites for small events. These professionals either manage a trade group's operation for a fee, or own shows outright.

UP-FRONT DOLLARS

You can stage a small tabletop show in a hotel for around $10,000. If you can guarantee a hotel enough rooms, sometimes you can negotiate free exhibit space. On a more ambitious tear, a multi-industry extravaganza staged in a major convention center could cost you around $30,000, assuming you handle all the details yourself. If you hire specialists to decorate a show, for example, add anywhere from $500 to $2,000 to your out-of-pocket expenses. A small show might charge $50 for an exhibit table, while the biggies can go for ten times that. Both kinds of shows return profits with margins of 20 to 50 percent.

You can start with little up-front capital because your customers —exhibitors—foot most of the bills. Explains Wendy Rosen, whose

Baltimore-based Wendy Rosen Agency Inc. throws two annual wholesale-only trade shows for artisans (see Craft Wholesaler), "Most businesses don't see the cash until a hundred and twenty days after they provide service when the wolf's at the door. But a trade show doesn't need up-front cash because exhibitors pay for their space ahead of time." Wendy staged The Buyers Market of American Crafts in 1982 on a $500 overdraft from her checking account. Some eighty-five exhibitors took booths in a suite she rented at the New York Hilton Hotel; five hundred merchants showed up, anxious to buy crafts to sell in their department and specialty stores. By 1987, nine hundred pottery makers, jewelry crafters, and woodworkers paid for booth space at her shows, as ten thousand attendees went through the gates. Wendy's two shows together bill about $1 million annually.

You don't need venture capital or even large bank loans to get into the business, but you do require time. Since popular convention centers like McCormick Place in Chicago and the Jacob Javitts Center in New York book space at least thirteen months before an event (and up to ten years for very large expositions during popular times of the year), you should start planning your show eighteen months to two years ahead of its due date. David Cheifetz reserves space for some shows through 1999.

STEPS

You follow five steps to launch a trade show, regardless of whether you invite two hundred people or the entire state of Rhode Island:

1. Before making any commitments, test the concept. A telephone and letter canvas asks prospective exhibitors if they would buy booths, and attendees if they would travel to such a show. While testing a first-time concept, many operators hold onto their jobs just in case the idea doesn't fly.

2. Assuming that a high percentage of contacts say they'd jump at the chance to be in your show, line up blocks of hotel rooms and convention-center space. Since a significant cut of their action is the tourist dollars conventioneers spend, popular convention centers managed by municipalities often shy away from brand new shows. You might have to hold your show in a second-tier city until you establish a reputation. Wendy Rosen says one sure way to get space

involves planning a show for an unpopular time. "Every convention center in the country wants business between December 24 and January 1. Tell a convention manger if you cut me a good deal or take care of my insurance, I'll bring you a convention that week."

3. Print a brochure explaining the "who, what, when, where, and why" of your event. You can buy mailing lists from trade organizations and publications to supply the names of potential exhibitors. Follow up with sales calls to nail down booth commitments.

Direct mail, telemarketing, and printing costs during these first two steps range anywhere from $2,000 to $15,000, which is money you need ahead of time. From here on out, however, exhibitors foot the show bills. David Cheifetz points out that exhibitors are far cheaper to round up than attendees because they represent a smaller universe.

4. As exhibitor fees trickle in, turn your attention to the people who will visit the booths. Create a program. A typical agenda involves lining up speakers, devising seminars, arranging special dinners and spousal events. Along with a list of exhibitors, use this program as the calling card to draw the gate.

5. Begin a marketing attack with trade journal and regional newspaper ads and mailings to prospective attendees. Pointing out that a small ad in *The Wall Street Journal* runs $7,500, David Cheifetz admonishes, "Use your money wisely."

Unlike consumer shows, most trade shows do not charge gate fees. (Compare Consumer Shows.) Revenues come from what's left over from booth fees and, sometimes, from selling services (such as seminars) to attendees. Additionally, successful shows sometimes sell lists of attendee names.

MORE ART THAN SCIENCE

Once you've lined up acceptances from exhibitors and attendees, organize every aspect of the show in minute detail, from when you'll need cleanup crews to the menu at the awards banquet. Running a trade show "is more art than science," insists Russell E. Flagg, whose New York City–based Flagg Management Inc. runs events ranging from French fashion to ultralight aviation. Russell, who started her own company in 1984 after working for two large exposition companies, says contingency plans are crucial. Know in advance what to do if the power fails; if the union assembling the booths strikes; if an unexpected snowstorm grounds transportation.

Exhibition managers emphasize that one disorganized or meagerly attended show kills a concept forever. Who will return next year if this show was a disaster? What organization will hire you to manage their one big event if another expo you ran fizzled? The moral of the story: Don't skimp or cut too many corners.

Organization is key to everything. Like a boy scout, a trade show manager has to be prepared.

Hint: If you opt to learn the ropes as an employee of an existing firm, realize that most shows happen just once a year. It pays to join a major organization that puts on dozens of annual expos. The largest operator, Cahner's Exposition Group, Stamford, Connecticut, staged two hundred thirty shows worldwide in 1987.

PARCELING OUT THE CHORES

Most large operators choose to mount the entire show, overseeing chores that range from direct-mail tests of the concept to providing tablecloths at the convention hall. However, you can buy every type of expertise for a fee. For example, for anywhere from 85 cents to $2 per person, you can hire an organization to sign-in registrants, equip them with printed badges, and provide a computerized list of attendees for next year. "A wonderful cadre of professionals will write brochures, oversee the mailing, put on conferences," says Russell Flagg. "They won't work on dreams, though. Instead of costing you $20,000, it might cost you $150,000 to run a show."

Unless you're shooting for a one-shot deal, expect to lose money on that first event (or two). Although a show's budget may eat up only half the revenues garnered from booth sales, you need the profits to start immediate preparation for next year. "Sink every cent into promoting the show," advises Wendy Rosen. "Exploit the momentum you built for next time."

After the industry accepts a show as an expected annual event, promotion becomes much easier—and profits skyrocket. "You don't have to reinvent the wheel each year," says David Cheifetz.

"A good show is like a Mercedes. The salesman doesn't have to tell you it's a fine car. But he still has to sell his product."

BUCKING THE ODDS

Trade show managers fall into two groups: Professionals who sight opportunities to throw parties, no matter what the field, and insiders in particular industries who organize a group of friends into a trade show. Wendy Rosen, for one, is proof that outsiders can achieve success. Equipped with a publishing and advertising background, she was designing business cards and order forms for artists when she dreamed up a forum where craftspeople could present their silk screens and brass bracelets to the retail world. Wendy's almost overnight success came through instinct and application of her talents, a sure-fire idea, and perhaps some luck. Most important, her show brought exhibitors tangible results. "When I first began my show six years ago, exhibitors averaged $30,000 to $50,000 in production a year. Now $1 million isn't uncommon and $150,000 is average," says Wendy. Because of ready access to a wholesale market, "Many clients doubled and tripled volume."

Probably any industry large enough to support a large expo already has one, but don't let that stop you. If David Cheifetz sees room for a better-managed show, or a second event in a different area of the country, he rises tactfully to the challenge: "We call the association and tell them we'll stay as far away chronologically and geographically as possible. We ask for their endorsement, but we go ahead if we don't get their cooperation."

Wendy Rosen suggests getting in on the ground floor with shows in growth industries. And, if you can't do it all, do what you can. "Call up the small associations and offer to handle the marketing, direct mail, or advertising for their meetings," says Wendy. "If an industry is building, you can build along with them."

By segmenting large markets into specific niches, Russell Flagg stages shows for such hard-to-reach audiences as New York lawyers hungry for computer software. "Both sides know the show is not for the general public, but targeted to their needs, so they come," explains Russell, whose dozen 1986 shows produced revenues of $1.2 million.

As travel grows increasingly expensive, observers forecast fewer massive blockbuster shows. Instead, expect greater numbers of smaller shows scattered across the country. Trade Show Bureau executive director Bill Mee points out that expos have already changed from out-of-town stag-club parties to serious business events. "It's expensive to go to shows, expensive to participate. Now you go for the purpose of doing business."

SOURCES

Industry Associations

Trade Show Bureau, P.O. Box 797, East Orleans, Mass. 02643 (617) 240-0177

National Association of Exposition Managers, 334 E. Garfield Rd., P.O. Box 377, Aurora, Ohio 44204 (216) 562-8255

International Exhibitors Association, 5103-B Backlick Rd., Annandale, Va. 22003 (703) 941-3725

Publications

Tradeshow Week, Suite 236, 12233 W. Olympic Blvd., Los Angeles, Calif. 90064 (213) 826-5696

Exhibitor Magazine, 745 Marquette Bank Blvd., Rochester, Minn. 55904 (507) 289-6556

Tradeshow, 275 Washington St., Newton, Mass. 02158 (617) 964-3030

Tradeshow & Exhibit Manager, 1640 5th St., Santa Monica, Calif. 90401 (800) 421-6543

Meetings & Conventions, 1 Park Ave., New York, N.Y. 10016 (212) 503-5700

Successful Meetings, 633 Third Ave., New York, N.Y. 10017 (212) 986-4800

Meeting News, 1515 Broadway, New York, N.Y. 10036 (212) 869-1300

Show & Sell Magazine, P.O. Box 212, Santa Claus, Ind. (812) 937-4464

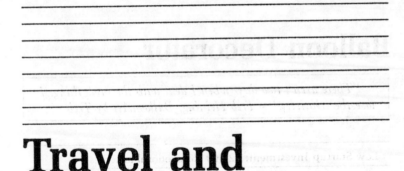

Travel and

Entertainment

Balloon Decorator

> *"There aren't two days when I deal with the same thing. I love the creativity,"* – Treb Heining, BalloonArt by Treb

---

Low Startup Investment: $2,000 (promotional materials)

High Startup Investment: $10,000 (includes a location and some props)

Time Until Breakeven: First event to six months

Annual Revenues: $25,000-$2 million

Annual Pre-tax Profits: $7,500-$600,000

Staffers Needed for Startup (including founder): One

Treb Heining got his first job at Disneyland at age fifteen, blowing up Mickey Mouse balloons. The balloon concessionaire taught him how to blow up three hundred balloons an hour, but brushed aside Treb's outrageous visions of how to decorate the park with balloons.

Treb (his father's name, spelled backwards) finally got his chance when, in 1985 he staged "the most spectacular effect I had ever created" at Disneyland's thirtieth anniversary celebration. Brightly colored balloons arched in a canopy over the Magic Kingdom's Main Street. At midnight, the park lights dimmed, turning attention to thirty seventy-five-foot-tall balloon candles lit from inside. Then, to the strains of "When You Wish Upon a Star," thousands of balloons floated skyward. The event was so memorable that, six months later, the city of Anaheim invited Treb back to honor Walt Disney. He topped his previous spectacular by releasing 1,121,448 balloons, tripling the previous Guinness world record set in Japan.

In addition to decorating birthday parties and bar mitzvahs with balloons, Treb Heining has created balloon masterpieces for the Los Angeles Summer Olympic Games and the New Orleans World

Fair. He's released hundreds of thousands of balloons for Las Vegas casinos and 1.5 million for the United Way. He's created a forty-foot-long Checker cab made from balloons for the TV series "Taxi" and decorated shopping malls with balloon arches and spiral balloon designs. In an average year, Los Angeles–based BalloonArt by Treb does $1 million in revenues—and much better in years when it lands an Olympics or other large contracts. But, "it's still hard to say I do balloon art for a living," Treb admits. "People always want to qualify—'You mean hot air balloons? Toy balloons?'"

A BALLOONING FIELD

Balloon decorating provides a living for thousands of people, although most practice on a more modest scale than does Treb Heining. Many balloon entrepreneurs get their start with balloon bouquets delivered along with a singing birthday wish. From there they graduate to decorations and sometimes to the kind of spectaculars Treb produces with his balloons. Acceptance by caterers and party planners has only come in the last few years. "In the beginning, when I'd tell people to expect a $300 to $500 balloon budget, they thought $50 was plenty," recalls Treb. "Now they expect columns and arches, and $1,000 for a party isn't out of line."

Treb entered balloon decorating in 1976 thanks to Wally Amos, a/k/a/ Famous Amos, the cookie mogul. Wally hired Treb as a counter helper, eventually promoting him to manager of Famous Amos's wholesale plant. One day Treb brought to work some balloons for a store opening, and amazed his boss by blowing up one every seven seconds. When Treb began arranging the balloons, Wally suggested he pitch his designs to caterers. Soon he was decorating Beverly Hills bashes for Elizabeth Taylor, Neil Simon, and Sylvester Stallone. After each party he decorated, four or five more calls came in. Treb now rents a two-thousand-square-foot warehouse for props, such as balloon release boxes and frames for birthday cakes made out of balloons.

IMAGE

But Treb Heining began with zero capital, operating out of his home, a course still possible for startup balloon artists. You can rent helium tanks and balloon blowers from balloon manufacturers and general rental companies, and pay for the relatively inexpensive balloons from the deposit on your first party. "But look professional," Treb advises. "What we do is 50-percent image and 50-percent follow-up."

By "look professional," he means present yourself to best advantage with brochures and professional-looking business cards and stationery. Treb says in the beginning he often threw in effects clients did not pay for just to take a picture to show at his next pitch.

Employees of BalloonArt by Treb follow a black pants and white shirt dress code. "We look like a team, not a bunch of gypsies," says Treb. "It's a lesson I learned from Disney, who stressed things like haircuts. It creates an image, and an organization you're proud to be part of."

By "follow-up," Treb means give clients all they pay for—and more. Balloons are cheap, so don't skimp.

CREATING A TEAM

BalloonArt by Treb's core staff consists of eight full-timers and twenty-five to thirty teachers, actors, and even executives whom he calls on for the extravaganzas. "I try to give part-timers three months notice of a project. They take vacation time to work on world-record or Olympic projects, because it's fun."

Treb says the most important thing a balloon artist can learn is how to tie a balloon. Some companies use clips, but Treb maintains they are really no quicker and let the air seep out faster. He puts new employees through rigorous training until the average crew member can tie one thousand balloons an hour.

Contrary to many in the business who charge per balloon, Treb charges according to the effect and the size of the area to be decorated. Even undercapitalized startups can usually afford the pennies it takes to buy a balloon; customers pay for is the skill and creativity involved, and Treb says he doesn't want to be limited by numbers of balloons. "We talk to a customer to find out what they want, then we do a rendering or sketch of the effect we envision."

While Treb says he thrives on the extravaganzas because they are "joyous experiences," he says the smaller, $500 parties are the bread-and-butter business. Corporate affairs and anniversary parties give him a chance to try new effects on a smaller scale before unleashing them at a $10,000 event.

Of the four or five events BalloonArt by Treb produces in a week, two or three may be small shopping mall openings or even just window displays for local merchants. "Look for new areas of business," Treb advises, pointing out that the balloon decorating field is relatively untapped. "Call on a shoe store and offer to decorate the store for Valentine's day. Print up a few sample balloons with their logo. Charity groups can actually save money by having a professional decorate. Balloons are fragile and react to sun and wind. Your skill is what they pay for."

SOURCES

Industry Association

National Association of Balloon Artists, P.O. Box 43472, Jacksonville, Fla. 32201 (904) 388-9060

Publications

Balloons Today, P.O. Box 43472, Jacksonville, Fla. 32201 (904) 388-9060
Special Events Magazine, 20048 Cotner Ave., Los Angeles, Calif. 90025 (213) 477-1033

Consultants

Balloon City, U.S.A., 1021 Market St., Harrisburg, Pa. (717) 939-1009

Red Balloon Co., 300 E. Pike St., Seattle, Wash. (206) 467-0318
Pioneer Balloon Co., 555 N. Woodlawn Ave., Witchita, Kans.
   67208 (316) 685-2266

Bed and Breakfast Inn

> *"I have a great excuse for living in a wonderful house with fresh flowers on the tables all the time . . . There are fifty nice restaurants in the area. Guests depend on us to tell them what's good, so we go to each once a year as a business expense."* – Joan Wells, The Queen Victoria

Low Startup Investment: $200,000 (small Eastern inn that "needs work")

High Startup Investment: $1.2 million (lavish West Coast inn)

Time Until Breakeven: Two to four years

Annual Revenues: $60,000-$300,000

Annual Pre-tax Profits: $1,000-$60,000 (plus lots of fringe-benefit living costs picked up by the inn)

Staffers Needed for Startup (including founder): One to four

Bed-and-breakfast scene No. 1: You and your spouse sip sherry with a fascinating parcel of guests around a cozy fireplace. The conversation leaps from nuclear disarmament to the very best boutiques in Paris. As the guests say goodnight, anticipating mouth-watering brioches the next morning before a day of cross-country skiing, one woman pauses. "Your inn is absolutely charming," she says. "Can you book the same room for my husband and me next fall? We'll be back for the foliage."

Bed-and-breakfast scene No. 2: Balancing a tray of orange juice in one hand and a coffee pot in the other, you smile bravely at the unshaven guest who is complaining loudly that there's no hot water for showers. Your partner abandons the stove to greet a new guest, despite the fact that check-in time isn't for another six hours. The newcomer turns out to be an unannounced travel writer, who wonders why smoke is coming from the kitchen.

Proprietors of bed and breakfast inns agree that the above scenarios are not only plausible, but might well happen at the same inn during the same week. More than most other small businesses, innkeeping represents a total life-style commitment. It's almost like a marriage—the vows of "for richer or poorer, in sickness and in health," come true every day for innkeepers of about fifteen hundred B&Bs across the country.

BUYING A LIFE STYLE

Many B&B converts are corporate fast-trackers who equate the deed to an inn with a ticket away from urban hassles. Many husband-and-wife teams see innkeeping as a way to spend more time with their families. Pat Hardy bought the Glenborough Inn in Santa Barbara, California, in 1981, after running a twenty-four-hour crisis hotline. "I was trying to figure out how I could be a working parent and still be present for a teenager," she recalls. In addition to working in-house, Pat has a full-time housekeeper who doubles as a babysitter when the need arises.

Innkeepers say they can mold their lives to suit their business needs—within limitations. You might take in a matinee on a lazy weekday, or host your daughter's scout troop. Pat Hardy sometimes sneaks weekday ski trips; Joan Wells, who operates the twelve-room Queen Victoria in the New Jersey seaside resort of Cape May, devotes afternoons to community projects.

The trick is to arrange your free time to the flow of the business. For example, Joan and her husband Dane Wells are not beach people. So, during their busy summer period, they don't long to hit the beach just minutes from their door. Says Joan: "If you're a skier, open an inn in Cape May. Then go to Vermont during your slack season."

Note: The expense of that Vermont getaway could well be on the business if you stay in a B&B. Accountants say visits to competitors fall under the category of research. Also, you can claim meals in neighborhood restaurants as business expenses. After all, you've got to be able to tell guests about area attractions.

WHAT MEASUREMENTS?

Because innkeeping is a way of life as well as a business, throw out all the regular sales and profit measurements when considering a B&B. Factor in the purchase of a home as well as a company when you figure startup costs. A plus, however, is that you're allowed business deductions for such everyday costs as heating and air conditioning. Kate McDill and Deborah Sweet structured the Chambered Nautilus Bed & Breakfast Inn in Seattle as a partnership, which allows them to deduct 90 percent of their overhead. "If we were a corporation, we could write off 100 percent," says Kate, but then the partners would each pay taxes as well as the corporation. The Chambered Nautilus, whose six guest rooms and four porches overlook snowy Cascade Mountain peaks, grossed $100,000 in 1986 with net expenses of $85,000.

"We have a few personal expenses—some clothing, a few groceries, some medical bills," explains Joan Wells. "But the company pays for everything else, including the upkeep on our car, a pension, and most of our food. You just get taxed on what's left over anyway."

Joan Wells's Queen Victoria supports a better living than most inns, with a 1986 take of over $200,000 and expenses of $150,000. Even though most B&Bs operate on skinny profit margins, they don't give rooms away. The Queen Victoria's rate sheet resembles a train schedule, with rates varying with the season and the size of the room. A carriage house on the property that includes a Jacuzzi, wet bar, and separate parlor rents for $220 a night during peak season.

Many innkeepers devise secondary incomes to complement their room rates. Pat Hardy and her partner JoAnn Bell operate a consultancy for new innkeepers called Inn Transition. Carl Glassman sells the work of local artists from the Wedgwood Inn, which he operates in New Hope, Pennsylvania. Kate McDill uses her kitchen for catering, and opens the sitting room during the day for corporate retreats.

WHERE DOES IT ALL GO?

Income evaporates in a B&B faster than water in a hot skillet. "Things you think will cost hundreds of dollars cost thousands," sighs Joan Wells, who spends $3,000 every three years or so to replace worn towels and sheets. "There are two things you don't mess around with," she instructs: "lumpy beds and no hot water." Joan constantly upgrades expensive antique furnishings, such as iron and brass beds that she covers with colorful quilts. "People are particularly hard on chairs," says Joan, a one-time executive director of the nonprofit Victorian Society, referring to her "graveyard of Victorian chairs stored in the basement."

And neither budget nor time allows more outside help. "My partner and I joke about calling maintenance when the toilet breaks," says Kate McDill, a restaurant chef before opening the Chambered Nautilus in 1983. "It helps to have a rudimentary knowledge of electricity and hammers and nails. Otherwise you spend a lot of money you can't afford."

EAST VS. WEST

The cost of an inn usually parallels other properties in an area. Kate McDill and Deborah Sweet spent $210,000 for their circa-1915 inn, followed by $50,000 to remodel, plumb, wire, and furnish it. Pat Hardy figures $20,000 to $30,000 per guest room buys an inn in an out-of-the-way East Coast or mountain locale, compared with $30,000 to $60,000 on the pricier West Coast, where suitable property is rarer. Most buyers secure a mortgage on top of a down payment.

In addition to the purchase, Pat assumes renovation will cost $20,000 to $50,000 per room. A typical inn is a drafty old mansion that was not built to host overnight guests. So, makeovers generally add baths, refurbish the kitchen, and decorate. Since spending $165,000 to buy The Queen Victoria in 1980, Joan and Dane Wells have laid out $200,000 for building improvements as well as

$100,000 for furnishings. Hint: Check the tax laws, which often favor renovation of older structures.

Mary E. Davies, editor of *innkeeping newsletter* and proprietor of Ten Inverness Way, says a California inn can get away with four or five guest rooms, because year-round good weather produces 60- to 70-percent occupancy rates. "In New England," she says, "you need a minimum of eight to ten rooms because occupancy is more like 40 percent." You have to be prepared to take care of the demand when it arises; otherwise you won't reach profitability. According to a 1983 Laventhal and Horwath study of California inns, city properties that attract business travelers during the week fill their rooms 70 percent of the time, compared to 50-percent occupancy at rural inns where Monday-to-Friday vacancies are common.

Your first requisite as an innkeeper is flexibility. "If you can't deal with crisis and change hats with aplomb, do not get into the business," advises Pat Hardy, who points to tasks that run the gamut from bookkeeping to housekeeping. While being a good cook helps, breakfast is an easy meal to make—which makes B&Bs easier to run than country inns, which serve dinners. Says Pat: "I know people who bring in croissants and serve fresh fruit and coffee."

The Queen Victoria's six-person staff alleviates some of the pressure on its innkeepers. But one member of the Wells team tries to be on hand at all times. They hire an "innsitter" to run things during occasional family getaways, and they also take separate vacations. "It's hard to get away together because someone needs to mind the store," says Joan. "Also, we work together all the time, so it's not a bad idea to get away alone."

DICKENS

Kate McDill lists creativity as another necessary trait: "You have to create a feeling. Atmosphere is why guests come to a bed and breakfast instead of a Holiday Inn."

Innkeepers' creative juices particularly flow when it comes to attracting guests into their homes. Most B&Bs budget little for advertising beyond guidebook listings, which everyone says is essential. However, Joan Wells sends a steady stream of press releases to travel sections of newspapers and magazines; as a result, each year her scrapbook grows by fifteen to thirty articles that mention The Queen Victoria. One annual gala began when a Dickens scholar read The Christmas Carol to a few guests beside the Inn's Christmas tree. By 1986, seven neighboring inns had joined in the Dickens Extravaganza. Area restaurants offered Victorian feasts, artisans demonstrated how to make Victorian Christmas tree ornaments, guests trimmed trees, and The Queen Victoria boasted a full house during a week that once was quieter than Scrooge's Christmases.

SPLIT PERSONALITY

Many inns maintain a dual identity: turn-of-the-century quaintness in their public rooms and stainless steel kitchens and personal computers behind closed doors. With the help of a computer containing the tidbits she picks up from guests in casual breakfast chit-chat, Joan Wells targets particular guest types. For example, she mails announcements of Cape May birdwatching weekends to former guests she knows are birdwatchers. In addition to bookkeeping, the computer also serves as a word processor on which Joan composes a newsletter which guests receive twice a year.

Innkeepers are people who like people, and most say they haven't been disappointed. "It's a very personal business and you get to know some wonderful people," says Kate McDill, who became best friends with a woman who stayed in the Chambered Nautilus before moving to Seattle. "About once a week someone leaves us a gift."

Innkeepers rarely complain about obnoxious guests. "The kind of person who agrees to share a bathroom is comfortable with other people," guesses Kate, who also speculates that types who commit credit fraud prefer the anonymity of a large hotel. "I've had only two things stolen in two years," she reports. "One woman took a washcloth by mistake and mailed it back."

RESEARCH

Before shelling out a life's savings to buy an inn, stay in as many B&Bs as possible. You may get better results if you visit during the week or off-season when the innkeeper has more time to answer questions. You also can offer a consulting fee. Courses on innkeeping are taught by consultants and some community colleges. The Wedgwood Inn offers an apprenticeship program; a kind of "hands-on" internship that runs from three days to two weeks, the program is a more formal way to follow the advice that innkeepers always offer: "Go to work for an inn before you buy one."

Before setting your heart on a particular property, check the local chamber of commerce or visitor's bureau to determine tourist traffic. Are area occupancy rates high enough to support your mortgage? Make sure local zoning ordinances permit B&Bs. But don't be afraid of other B&B competition. "It works like a shopping mall," says Joan Wells, referring to the score of inns that make up Cape May. "A critical mass builds that attracts customers."

Speaking of a critical mass, Mary Davies estimates six to eight hundred B&Bs clustered in California in 1986—compared with just two hundred three years before. Consultant William Oates suspects Vermont hoards well over two hundred B&Bs, or double the number a few years ago. The proliferation has helped travelers to view an inn as a legitimate alternative to mass-market hotels rather than a novelty vacation experience.

And bed and breakfasts are not just your Victorian mansion, complete with widows' walks if not ghosts. As those properties become harder to buy, proprietors have converted yachts, a lighthouse, and a Louisiana plantation into B&Bs.

SOURCES

Publications

Innkeeping newsletter, P.O. Box 267, Inverness, Calif. 94937 (415) 669-7304

Inn Review: Country Inns & Small Hotels, 105 E. Court, Kankakee, Ill. 60901 (815) 939-3509

Consultants

Inn Transition, 1327 Bath St., Santa Barbara, Calif. 93101 (805) 965-0707

The Inn School, Wedgwood Inn, 111 W. Bridge St., New Hope, Pa. 18938 (215) 862-2570

William Oates & Associates, P.O. Box 1162, Brattleboro, Vt. 05301 (802) 254-5931

Chanticleer Inn, 120 Gresham St., Ashland, Ore. 97520 (503) 482-1919

Limousine Service

> *"We drive celebrities—Stevie Winwood, all the prominent corporate execs. You get a vicarious thrill."* – Ron Goldman, Presidential Limousine Ltd.

Low Startup Investment: $10,000 (downpayment on one car)

High Startup Investment: $100,000 (a three-car fleet and drivers)

Time Until Breakeven: Three months to one year

Annual Revenues: $50,000-$500,000 (low end for a part-time operation; high end for a five-car, full-time fleet)

Annual Pre-tax Profits: $30,000-$325,000

Staffers Needed for Startup (including founder): One

"On St. Patrick's Day, one of our corporate accounts rented two stretches," relates Ron Goldman, who runs Presidential Limousine Ltd., in Chicago. "They really did the town from 4 P.M. until 4 A.M. The bill was well over $1,000—that's $1,000 for riding around in a *car*, mind you. But the client called the next morning saying he had a great time. So many other fields are thankless, even when you do a great job. But we get accolades."

There are more accolades to go around these days. According to *Limousine & Chauffeur Magazine,* forty thousand or so limousines purred down highways in 1987, about double the number five years earlier. "40 percent of the people now in the business have been in less than two years," says Maurice Sutton, publisher of *Limousine & Chauffeur.*

THE GREAT LIMOUSINE PROLIFERATION

Why the hoopla? To borrow an economics term, the business is supply driven. Maury Sutton points out that the six manufacturers churning out stretches in the late 1970s produced just sixteen hundred limousines a year; now about fifty so-called coachbuilders buy Lincolns and Caddys, saw them in half, and add the three to eight-foot inserts that make them stretches. These new suppliers have pushed production to six thousand limos a year.

Not only are there more cars, but they are cheaper. "In 1975, the markup was tremendous," says Maury Sutton, who estimates a fifty-four inch stretch Lincoln Towncar cost about $45,000 in the "old days." A 1987 model of that same car cost about $38,000— "and it's probably a better vehicle," he says. If you pay in $1,200 monthly installments, you can get into the stretch limo business today for under $10,000. That sum includes a down payment, license, insurance, a car phone, and some advertising. If you start with a three-car fleet, triple those expenses. Since you pay drivers only when they are on the job, salaries aren't a major concern. If you decide to pay for the cars up front and claim depreciation, startup costs could run $45,000 per car, depending on the options you collect. Another route is to buy snazzy used limos.

Your permit will often be lower than a taxi permit. For example, a New York City medallion cab license costs abut $75,000, while a livery license cost a mere $100 or so.

STRETCH STATUS

But no matter how accessible the limousine business is, operators wouldn't make it out of the garage if the public saw limousines as just for the rich and famous. Increasingly, however, all those thirteen-foot celebrity wagons roaming the streets act as their own advertisements for the public at large. *Limousine & Chauffeur* says 75 percent of the limousines sold today are bought by livery services rather than individuals. Instead of wiring mom and dad flowers, the kids are chipping in to charter a limousine to take them to an anniversary dinner. More important, corporations are opening up limo accounts. "You can work weekends doing weddings," says Maury Sutton. "If you charge $50 an hour, you can gross $3,000 a month driving part-time. But if you decide to make it a business, you've got to get the corporate accounts."

Corporations call more regularly than a consumer who uses limos as vehicles to fantasy land. Ron Goldman, who says 65 percent of his business comes from regular corporate clients, points to one three hundred-member law firm that charters a presidential limo two to three times a day. "The lawyers are always going to the airport, or clients are coming in," he explains.

MARKETING LUXURY TO THE MASSES

Advertisements in the Yellow Pages bring in the consumer crowd. "We run the largest ad we can get in the Chicago Yellow Pages," says Ron. "That ad pays for itself by the second month. The phone rings off the hook with people wanting to take Grandma to her seventieth birthday party in a limo." Let caterers and party planners know you're available for their clients as well.

You can also hook up with other merchants and jointly advertise in newspapers or on the radio. For example, one Los Angeles service arranges "Cuisine by Limousine." Flat-rate packages start at $80 a couple, and include a cocktail in the car, a rose for the lady, and a three-course meal at a restaurant. Although three-quarters of the tab goes to the restaurant, an organized chauffeur can shuttle diners back and forth all evening.

THE BREAD-AND-BUTTER BUSINESS

Tracking down corporate business involves writing and calling executives to bid on jobs. You may have to knock $5 or $10 off the hourly rate to land the big users, whom you bill just once a month. "In effect, it's a sales business," says Ron Goldman. His sales pitches underscore the convenience a limousine brings. For example, he stresses to real estate agents that a limo frees them to sell a property rather than worry about traffic and parking. The practice can be extended in any number of directions. If a salesperson plans to drive customers around in your car, the prestige factor will be at work, so mention your well-stocked wet-bar. High-pressure firms in congested cities view limousines as offices that drive down the street. Some fleets outfit the passenger compartment with desks, telephones, and even computers rather than televisions and compact disk players. Entertainer Ed McMahon says limousines, with their roomy compartments and tinted windows, are great for changing into a tuxedo.

THE OUT-OF-TOWN CROWD

Many executives become attached to limousine luxury and book the stretches on out-of-town junkets. Presidential's ten-car fleet stays busy with convention business. "Not just picking them up at the airport," says Ron Goldman, "but driving them and their sales reps and clients around while they're in town." As a member of the convention bureau, his company gets a list of all exhibitors at Chicago's conventions. Presidential shoots out letters to each, inviting them to hire a limo at $50 an hour. One exhibitor at a recent Home Improvement Show hired two limos for the three full days of the event to ferry its sales staff and customers around town. The bill: $3,500. The customer expressed such satisfaction with the squeaky-clean cars and affable drivers that Ron expects him to come back with the same arrangement annually.

Satisfied customers likely will recommend your company to their friends. You can also join a formal referral network through the National Limousine Association. Developing your own contacts by calling limo services in other cities also has a good return rate. You can collect a finder's fee from customers you refer, or just expect grateful entrepreneurs to reciprocate when their clients visit your town.

At $50 an hour, a busy limousine brings in $100,000 a year, from which an owner/operator can expect to collect $65,000 in pre-tax profits, not counting tips. A second car will cost you a chauffeur's salary (often not much above minimum wage, since the driver expects to make most of the income from tips). However, that second and third limo assures extra business. Each time a potential client calls when your car is in the shop or is already booked, you run the risk of losing future business. Some entrepreneurs make their entire living by taking care of another company's over-flow business. Generally, the referring company bills the client and keeps 20 percent of the hourly rate.

CHARLOTTESVILLE, VIRGINIA, AND JUNO, ALASKA

The limo business started with New York corporate execs, then leapfrogged to California producers and stars, and is now appearing in other major cities. Even small towns support limo services, particularly if they have an airport and industry or a wealthy population. Maury Sutton says several operators make a nice living in Florida by escorting wealthy matrons to the supermarket once a week. David John, Cadillac's director of Fleet and Leasing, expects annual improvement in the market as tougher drunk-driving laws steer more partygoers toward limos and as parking costs rise in big cities. He also points out that couples continue to spend lavishly on weddings and proms.

The trend is toward longer and more elaborate limousines. Although an understated, thirty-inch stretch was once *de rigeur,* Maury Sutton says sixty-inch (that's five-feet!) of stretch added to a typical Fleetwood is now the norm. One New York outfit includes among its fleet two white Lincolns, each with three bars, two TVs, two video-cassette recorders, and one laser disk. The forty-foot-long monsters seat twelve passengers inside, and two in an outside rumble seat. Even though your chauffeur will never find a parking space, customers who rent the mobile-home sized limo expect to spend $1,800 to get to a New Year's Eve bash. The services of a hostess who pours complementary drinks is included.

SOURCES

Industry Association

National Limousine Association, 1625 I St., N.W., Suite 625A, Washington, D.C. 20006 (202) 223-5466

Publication

Limousine & Chauffeur Magazine, 2512 Artesia Blvd., Redondo Beach, Calif. 90278 (213) 376-8788

Miniature Golf

> *"Being in the accounting field, I saw a lot of businesses. By far miniature golf is the easiest operation I've ever seen. You hire somebody to clean the grounds and somebody to sell tickets. It's a cash business so you don't even worry about collection."* — Tommy Crouch, Gator Golf Inc.

Low Startup Investment: $100,000 (for a modest course)

High Startup Investment: $900,000 (for an elaborate thirty-six-hole facility on purchased land)

Time Until Breakeven: One to three years

Annual Revenues: $75,000-$1.2 million

Annual Pre-tax Profits: $10,000-$700,000

Staffers Needed for Startup (including founder): Two

Tommy Crouch and his family saw fantastic miniature golf courses when vacationing in Myrtle Beach, South Carolina. The brightly colored, life-sized fiberglass animals towered above the palms in places with names like Jungle Lagoon. According to Charles Grove, who designs such courses and supplies twenty-foot-tall pirates and giraffes that drink from running streams, Myrtle Beach has sixty-four mini-golf courses up and down its main strand. Says Charles: "It's not unusual to see forty people in line to get in, just like at the finer restaurants."

A GATOR GOLF EMPIRE

Tommy Crouch had succeeded at several careers, beginning with accounting. "But I kept thinking about those golf courses," says the Hope, Arkansas, proprietor of Gator Golf Inc. "I knew Silver Dollar City, a tourist town on the Arkansas/Missouri border, didn't have a golf course, so I teamed up with a partner to put one in." When the partners asked for $150,000 to build on leased land, "The bank said, 'First of all, we don't know how you could spend that much on miniature golf, and secondly, if you did, we don't know how you'd make any money.'"

Tommy and his partner chipped in and literally built the first Gator Golf course themselves in 1983. They hired construction employees and followed plans supplied by Charles Grove. Tommy ran the tractor himself. "Well, that first year we made $154,000 in profits," he recalls. "I sold my interest to my partner and did it all over again in another tourist area, Pigeon Forge, Tennessee. Then I decided to go big time, so I sold that one and built a $350,000 mini-golf course in Orlando, Florida. I didn't like Florida, so I sold that one and now I'm buying land to do another in Hot Springs, Arkansas."

Tommy cleared $75,000 for his interest on the first putting course he sold, $50,000 on the second, and $200,000 on the third. This time around, the bank finally decided to back him with $500,000. Is there money to be made in miniature golf? Just ask Tommy Crouch.

MANAGING FROM A HAMMOCK

As he approaches fifty and wants to slow his life style a bit, Tommy plans to operate the Hot Springs Gator Golf Course himself—sort of. "I'll continue living in Hope, which is seventy-five miles away. I can get an assistant manager and be home most of the time."

According to those in the industry, not much can go wrong when you run a miniature golf operation. "A water park needs about sixty employees," says Charles Grove, who analyzes clients' locations and will help secure funding and walk the client through a host of local zoning permits. "Even a big putting course can get by with a half-dozen employees. A husband and wife can do it alone, except for the long hours. So I suggest you hire a couple of presentable teenagers. Insurance is minimal compared to other amusements. The operation is just real simple."

But the best part of the cash-only business is the profits. Putt-Putt Golf Courses of America Inc. says its relatively modest thirty-six or fifty-four-hole franchises average 16.06-percent profits from ticket sales (any concessions are gravy), excluding debt service. More elaborate theme courses do far better. Charles Grove tells clients, "As a rule of thumb, an ideal location with a good customer draw should gross the cost of the facility during the first year." Depending on how much interest land and construction loans eat up, Charles figures the owner of a $300,000 facility will keep pre-tax profits of 40 or even 60 percent of revenues—$120,000 to $180,000. Tommy Crouch says he knows people who do better than that. "If you have a $300,000 gross, your operating expenses are only about 20 percent of revenues, so you have $240,000 left over from which you pay out the principal."

HERE'S THE HITCH

Ah, but that principal . . . To support the colorful theme courses Tommy and Charles operate, expect high entry costs. The monster pelicans and cascading waterfalls require a large tourist population to pay for them. Land costs for the two acres that Charles considers minimal for an eighteen-hole course and parking usually run in the half-million-dollar range in high-traffic tourist areas. You can often lease land, but course construction still adds another $200,000 to $350,000.

Even so, Charles says it's not unusual for a young couple with about $42,000 to build one of his facilities by rounding up the rest from outsiders. "They get their in-laws involved, and a couple of neighbors, which creates a viable financial base to approach the banks. The couple sets up a corporate structure with the provision to buy their partners out in a few years."

Of course, the couple must eventually pay for the entire cost of the park, plus interest. You can buy into the more traditional mini-golf course with fewer filigrees for under $100,000. The less expensive parks need fewer players to reach breakeven, so you can look for less expensive landlords. Putt-Putt says a thirty-six-hole course needs thirty-thousand people living within a three-mile radius, or sixty-thousand within five miles. Including land and a franchise fee of $10,000 (you also pay 5 percent of gross ticket sales to the parent), "you could reasonably expect to open a thirty-six-hole course for approximately $130,000 and a fifty-four-hole course for $195,000."

Smaller courses cost less, although Putt-Putt discourages sale of its eighteen-hole variety these days, saying return on investment is better with the larger variety. In addition, some entrepreneurs have experimented with mini-miniature courses in shopping malls, although the owners also complain of high rents.

YOUR OWN BILLBOARD

Regardless of the type of course you build, you must be accessible and visible. Rhett Sandsburg doesn't bother to advertise Doublegolf in Myrtle Beach, South Carolina, since 99 percent of his business is from tourists. "We're between two stop lights, so traffic slows down in front of the course. People can see us because we have a lot of frontage on the road." Drivers can't miss props like the ten-foot mama elephant and her eight-foot baby, so Doublegolf acts as its own advertising.

Unless you operate in the deep South, miniature golf is a seasonal business, which doesn't bother successful operators one bit. Rhett Sandsburg uses Doublegolf's four-month recess for maintenance. "That's when we redo drainage on some holes, put back shrubbery, reshingle any huts, repair animals, or replace carpeting," he says.

Besides, after all that hard work, you could probably use a break. "You're open fifteen hours a day, seven days a week during the season," says Tommy Crouch, who, incidentally, doesn't like to play either golf or miniature golf. "So even though it's easy, you tend to burn out. But on the last day of October, you close and enjoy Thanksgiving and Christmas. In February you take care of any repairs and, by April 1, it's time to open again."

SOURCES

Industry Association

International Association of Amusement Parks & Attractions, 4230 King St., Alexandria, Va. 22301 (703) 671-5800

Publications

Amusement Business Magazine, 14 Music Circle E., Nashville, Tenn. 3703 (615) 748-8120

Fun World, 4230 King St., Alexandria, Va. 22301 (703) 671-5800

Consultant

Charles Grove; Dave Sherwood, P.O. Box 2435, Myrtle Beach, S.C. 29578 (803) 236-4733

Party Planner

> *"It's Fantasy Island."* – Patricia Watson, Magic by PTS
> Inc.

Low Startup Investment: $1,000 (pure planner functions)

High Startup Investment: $50,000 (for props and warehouse space)

Time Until Breakeven: Two weeks to one year

Annual Revenues: $100,000-$5 million

Annual Pre-tax Profits: $50,000-$2 million

Staffers Needed for Startup (including founder): One

"Last week we planned a kidnaping," relates party planner Patricia Watson, who runs Magic by PTS Inc. "The seventy Dean Witter executives knew they were going to a party, but they didn't know they'd arrive at a speakeasy (our warehouse) in a fire engine."

When Patty Watson says, "let's plan a party," don't expect Chuckles the Clown and ice cream for a dozen six-year-olds. "We arrange the unusual—that's what makes us Magic." Her $2 million-a-year Dallas-based firm stages "a couple hundred" parties a year, primarily for corporate and convention clients. The extravaganzas range from a Chinese New Year in June (complete with a dragon parade and rice-eating contest) to Mardigras costume parties. Magic's warehouse full of props holds a full-sized merry-go-round and fifteen-foot-tall toy soldiers. In addition to local entertainment, Patty has booked Dolly Parton and Tanya Tucker. For show business blasts, she contracts with a Joan Collins or Tom Selleck lookalike. Chow runs the gamut from *haute cuisine* to barbecue. It seems no true party planner is limited by anything other than imagination—either your own or your client's.

THE WHOLE MAGILLA

Using her own definition of a party planner as someone "capable of dotting every 'i' and crossing every 't,' " Patty Watson estimates only about five hundred true party planners operate across the country. So, if you're in an area that likes to throw parties, there's probably room for another party planner. Magic started as an off-shoot of a tour business Patty ran for conventioneers and their spouses in the 1970s. But before that, she was a mother and teacher, professions which "basically prepare you for the impossible," she says.

What does Patty mean by "the impossible?" Well, "Party planners conceptualize the whole thing," she explains. "We create the props, arrange the location, send invitations, handle the RSVPs, line up caterers, flowers, food, entertainment, and absolutely anything else that's necessary."

Party planners either plan the entire bash, or plan and execute. If you're restricting activities to pure planning, the price of admission to the business involves lining up customers and subcontractors, such as balloon decorators and caterers. Lease props from a rental store, let the caterer provide the serving personnel, and you can also hire freelancers of all sorts: a fifties party might need a cheerleader to lead cheerleading contests, or a part-time actor to host bubble-gum blowing tournaments. Since the client pays the planner who doles out the various fees, be sure to ask for a hefty enough deposit to cover whatever up-front commitments you make for entertainment, decorating, food, and so on.

If you have some expertise and capital, decide whether you want to handle some functions in-house. For example, many planners also cater, plan business meetings for corporate clients, or rent anything from tents to coffee pots. Each additional operation brings in revenues—but also requires expensive equipment and personnel. Most planners accumulate some props, which, if you grow large enough, will need to be stored in a warehouse. Also, you'll need office space.

While you can certainly start from home, some party planners create magical offices with props stashed in every corner. When you reach this stage, invite clients to your premises before planning their parties. The setting will spark all kinds of ideas.

Likewise, as you grow, you'll need vans to transport all those props to party sites. Splash the vans with a logo that you also use on your correspondence, business cards, and on the back of such party favors as photographs. While you should fade into the background during the party, you can advertise your presence as you set up.

PARTY PEOPLE

To get started, call folks all over town involved in parties. Those same photographers or florists you book for your parties can provide leads on clients. Let hotels know you can either help out their banquet managers on elaborate projects, or work directly with their customers. Call on convention planners and ask if you can assist them—or any of their exhibitors who might want to throw a private party. If you have an idea of which corporations throw the most elaborate to-dos, send them a brochure or call office managers to suggest they throw a Winter Wonderland theme party this Christmas. You'll not only create ski-slopes in their corporate dining room, you'll also pick up the key executives in horse-drawn sleighs.

Try to get commitments months in advance so you can plan in a more leisurely fashion and get better prices for your clients. Patty Watson likes to have eight months notice for $100,000 parties, although Magic has staged parties for hundreds of people in a couple of weeks. "They just cost more, not only because we have to put more people on the arrangements, but because you can't buy in quantity and you pay exorbitant freight costs," she explains. "For instance, if we know we're going to need one hundred dozen white roses six months ahead of time, we buy a field and get a better deal."

Set your charges by working backwards. Determine how much each element—from catering to props—will cost. Then tack on the cost of your own overhead and profits of 20 to 40 percent, depending on what the market and your client allows.

Before booking a $100,000 party—or even a four-figure wedding reception—clients want references and examples of what you do, so you have to build a reputation. Ask influential contacts to stop by before or during the murder mystery to see the Victorian set you created. Offer to help a charity plan its next luau, and take pictures of the affair. You could split the cost of a professionally produced video tape with a bride and groom if they'll let you use an edited version as a sales tool. The expense of planning a party for free and taking photographs or videos of the event will pay off when you land that big account. If you can put aside a few thousand dollars, kick off your own business with a gala.

MAKE THEM REMEMBER YOU

The key to repeat business from corporate clients and references for future business is to make the events fun. And the key to fun, says Patty Watson, is participatory events. Take, for example, Magic's "M*A*S*H" bashes.

First, Patty sets the stage with three-dimensional props rather than chintzy backdrops: The big olive drab O.R. tent set to the side of the dance floor contains hospital beds and IV-bottles. The guests ladle their own mashed potatoes and corn bread from large aluminum pots heated by sterno, and drink from tin cups with "M*A*S*H" stenciled on them. Second, get the guests to anticipate the event: Ask them to come costumed as Hot Lips or Corporal Klinger. Now comes the action: As the siren sounds, "doctors" wearing scrub suits whisk people off the dance floor in a gurney. After the "doctor" sets a splint and takes pictures, the "patients" line up for wheelchair races. Finally, give them something to remember you by. Patty doles out dog tags with guests' names on them.

THE CLIENT'S ALWAYS RIGHT

To create the right mood and get the touches right, ask the client what they hope to accomplish with the party. If you host a new-product kick-off, perhaps strolling fortune tellers might end each palm-reading with visions of the Caribbean vacation that the corporation will award to the top sales team. If you plan a retirement party, ask about the guest of honor's hobbies and interests, and make theme suggestions around those.

Be sure to outline in detail any outrageous ideas. For example, a gorilla serving during the coffee break might enliven the dullest seminar. But a client who hopes to sell financial services to customers intrigued by what they've just heard on the podium might not appreciate the disruption.

A couple of character traits spell disaster for party planners. If you're a rigid "go-by-the-book" sort, forget party planning. Not only will your imagination at its best be challenged before every party, but you'll have to improvise around unexpected glitches during each event. Also, since you deal with a myriad of details and various subcontractors, disorganization is death. Patty Watson sums it up nicely: "If you've ever planned a fiftieth Wedding Anniversary, a dinner party for a hundred guests, a graduation, a wedding, and an inaugural ball—and if they've all occurred on the same day —and they've all occurred in the same place—you can do this. You can be a party planner."

Source

Publication

Special Events Magazine, 2048 Cotner Ave., Los Angeles, Calif. 90025 (213) 477-3963

Party Rental Store

> *"It's an 'up' business. Oh, sometimes on Monday morning somebody returning an item has a hangover. But you mostly deal with people who are looking forward to having a good time at a party."* – Patrick Chose, San Francisco Party

Low Startup Investment: $40,000 (small store that warehouses items off-premise)

High Startup Investment: $100,000 (large center in prime location)

Time Until Breakeven: Nine to eighteen months

Annual Revenues: $80,000-$500,000

Annual Pre-tax Profits: $12,000-$150,000

Staffers Needed for Startup (including founder): Two

According to Patrick Chose, who runs San Francisco Party rental center and C&M Party Props in nearby Walnut Creek, the "Cabot-Smythe" family does a lot of entertaining. "Mr. Jenkins, the man-servant will call, and in his proper British accent, say; 'Mrs. Cabot-Smythe just informed me she is having eighty of her dearest friends over tomorrow night.'—Their dining room is just large enough to accommodate eighty," Pat adds as an aside. "The first thing he always orders is eighty of our $8 chairs for a rental fee of $640. The Cabot-Smythe mansion is large, but nobody's got room to store eighty chairs."

Patrick Chose, as a matter of fact, has seventeen thousand square feet of showroom and another eight thousand for warehouse space. And that's enough room to store five thousand chairs. Not to mention commercial-sized tents that conventions rent for $10,000 a day and all the decorations you need to transform your living room into an oriental theme party. "If you count the linen I stock in thirty-four colors and all the frilly toothpicks as separate items," he shakes his head, "I've no idea how many items we stock."

IT'S A GOOD LIVING

He does know that running a party rental store is a business for imaginative people who like to have fun and want to make a good living.

Pat Chose's two stores brought in profits "higher than the 16-percent" industry norm on 1987 revenues of about $1.6 million. Pat, who is one of the granddaddies of what the industry calls "pure party rentals" (no tools or other general-rental items offered), opened his Walnut Creek store in 1959 and a second store twenty-five years later in San Francisco, which his oldest son Jay now manages. Younger son Andy oversees the Walnut Creek shop.

San Francisco Party sits just around the corner from Moscone Center, and that prime location plus a large stock of inventory contributed to top-of-the-line startup costs of $100,000. Consultant Donald Charbonnet figures you can open the doors to a small store for $40,000. Compared with general rentals (see Rental Center), "party is more profitable, and you can break even quickly," he says. "You can rent a chair you bought for $8.50 for between 50 cents and $1. The rent pays for the chair quickly and there's little that can go wrong with a chair. But a general rental store stocks an electric jackhammer that might cost $1,000 and is a delicate piece of machinery. Even though you rent it for $50 day, the return on investment is not as fast." Because party renters usually keep items twenty-four hours or less, Don says a store with $50,000 worth of inventory should shoot for $100,000 in annual revenues, or twice what a general rental center could hope for on the same inventory base. In party, your inventory buck buys a lot more.

SWITCH TO PURE PARTY

Those numbers suggested why numerous general-rental stores either switched entirely to party, or added party sections to their lines. According to Richard E. Detmer, director of membership services for the American Rental Association (ARA), party is the fastest-growing segment of the rental industry, particularly since the recessionary years of the early 1980s. While contractors might not rent construction equipment as frequently during sad times, rentors reasoned people always entertain. Indeed, instead of holding the wedding reception at a hotel, they may move it to the backyard. A rental center can provide everything from dinnerware for one hundred to a parquet dance floor. Pat Chose says an average wedding reception rents $2,000 to $2,200 worth of goodies from his store.

HIT THE SPOT

Keith and Pat Klarin, who operate the Party Corner in Shrewsbury, New Jersey, and Party Line (which son Ronald manages) five miles away in Eatontown, say their Jersey Shore patrons are great party throwers. Summer and holiday times keep busy a twenty-person staff consisting primarily of college students. During slower winter months, ten people run the business. Before you open a party store, make sure you can count on an affluent clientele. For the most part, you should locate in well-to-do suburbs or business districts. "Party rentals won't support an entire store in some suburban communities," warns New Orleans entrepreneur Don Charbonnet, although they may still represent profitable segments of a general-rental business. Rather than waste valuable retail space on items that don't command large volume, Don's thirteen general-rental centers display samples of party goods and stock rental items in a central warehouse. "We can deliver to the customer's house in an hour." Also, some party centers take highly visible shopping mall cubbyholes just big enough to exhibit one of each rental item that they warehouse in low-rent districts.

Pat Chose says his suburban and urban customers represent two entirely different animals. "The San Francisco store does a tremendous commercial business through the week, but not much on weekends. At Walnut Creek, individuals throw the parties on weekends." This difference allows Pat to swap merchandise between the two stores as the need arises.

THE MIX

Pat Chose's two stores also emphasize different inventory. In Walnut Creek, C&M Party Props stocks a dozen garment racks, and most of the time keeps eleven on the floor. Most people attending parties in homes stash their minks in closets or in a spare bedroom and don't need garment racks. But in San Francisco, where offices hold parties in commercial settings, "we own one hundred garment racks, and most are gone all the time." Also, commercial clients paying with corporate bankrolls spring for higher ticket items. "They want our $8 chairs, not those that rent for $2," says Pat.

Party rentors shop trade shows to come up with inventory, a job that's become easier the last few years. "Manufacturers like silver companies looked down their noses at rental centers until they began to see the potential of selling to us," says Pat. "Now they take booths at the trade shows." He says the 1987 ARA trade show devoted a hundred and forty booths to party exhibitors, compared to zero eight years earlier.

Pure party centers may get 40 percent of revenues from disposable items they sell rather than rent. Keith Klarin calls paper goods "a very lucrative business," pointing out that they don't need maintenance. Pat Chose pays particular attention to the colors paper manufacturers feature, and often buys rental inventory in matching shades. "The manufacturers featured lavender a year before every bride knew she had to have that," he says. "The manufacturers do the research for you."

Coming up with inventory to amuse all your customers is as much art as science. Rather than buy items that you may lend out just a couple of times a year, you may want to tap colleagues. For example, for Mardigras nights, you may want to sub-rent roulette wheels (and occasionally even blackjack dealers) from a theatrical supplier. Shop your competitors and offer to trade novelty equipment back and forth.

Customers will suggest some of your most imaginative items. One client wanted an unusual buffet, so Pat Chose asked a prop house to build a "Winter Wonderland" table, complete with icebergs and various levels where dishes perched. "The client virtually pays the cost on the first rental," says Pat. "Then the friends see it and maybe pay a fee 20 percent of the original charge the next time around." Given two weeks notice, Pat will consider customizing anything that's practical for storage.

One of Pat's favorite rental items is coffins—real ones that he rents for $35 a day. "We have eight coffin bars that are mounted on sawhorses and hold ice and bottles. The fraternities love them. For coffin buffets, we suggest they put in things like cold cuts and headcheese."

CONSULTING

Anyone in party rental takes consulting seriously. "The average person planning a reception for one hundred has never had more than a couple of people over for dinner," he points out. "We suggest things, like do you have enough coffee servers." In addition to winning grateful thanks from customers, such guidance also lands the rental center another $2.50 (for a stainless steel pitcher) to $45 (for a hundred-cup silver samovar).

Pat Klarin acts as the Party Corner's resident party consultant. In addition to helping customers pick out the china-and-linen combinations, she recommends caterers, entertainment, and photographers. She typically visits the client's home to case the layout and offer aesthetic counsel if tents are involved. For a fee, the Party Corner even decorates. "There is a 15-percent surcharge if you want us to do the whole party, which involves lining up the caterer, the band, the flowers, etc.," says Keith. "But if you just want some random recommendations, the advice is on the house."

Rentors consider consulting just one of the services, along with deliveries and tent-raisings, which command fees on top of the rental price. Keith Klarin gives customers a number where they can reach someone from the Party Corner day or night. "Maybe the caterer didn't order dessert plates. They panic. We'll get a call at eight o'clock while the entrée is being served and we rush the dessert plates over."

Such accommodation makes good business sense. Each reception for one hundred people represents a potential selling ground for future parties any one of those hundred people may mount. This is your chance to show people who never considered renting how nice the experience can be.

As far as advertising goes, list under both "Parties" and "Rentals" in the Yellow Pages. Pat Chose sends "what's new letters" describing innovative rental items to banquet managers at hotels and clubs. He also scans the newspaper society columns. "If the Symphony Committee is throwing a kick-off party in June, we call to see if we can be of service. If they cater it, we call their caterer."

CATERING TO CATERERS

The real business comes not from the occasional bar mitzvah, but from frequent party throwers like the Cabot-Smythes and, especially, from caterers. "Once you get a caterer, they're with you for life," says Don Charbonnet. "They bring lots of repeat business."

Pat Chose set aside a special caterer's conference room when he designed his San Francisco store. The room, available free of charge, is chockablock with samples from the store's floor to encourage impulse sales. "Most caterers work out of their back pockets and never want the client to see their small kitchens," he reasons. Because caterers book the room eight to ten times a week, San Francisco Party profits not only from the caterer's business, but also from the extras clients pick up on the way out of the store.

A few party rental centers have grown to legendary proportions. For example, Don Charbonnet speaks in awe of one forty-thousand-square-foot pure party rental center in Chicago. "Of course they service McCormick Place [one of the largest convention centers in the country]." The company's revenues aren't published, but Don can guess: "They have union drivers that make $30,000 a year."

SOURCES

Industry Association

American Rental Association, 1900 19th St., Moline, Ill. 61265 (309) 764-2475

Publications

Rental Age, 1900 19th St., Moline, Ill. 60265 (309) 764-2475

Rental Equipment Register, 20048 Cotner Ave., Los Angeles, Calif. 90025 (213) 477-1033

Rental Products News 36 S. 3rd West, Fort Atkinson, Wisc. 53538 (414) 563-6388

Special Events Magazine, 20048 Cotner Ave., Los Angeles, Calif. 90025 (213) 477-1033

Consultants

Serr/Charbonnet & Assoc., P.O. Box 13607, New Orleans, La. 70185 (504) 837-9500

Ducky Firnberg Consultants, 16004 Chalfont Circle, Dallas, Tex. 75248 (214) 934-1677

Tour Operator

> *"I can't imagine burning out like a doctor from stress. It's enjoyable to offer people a cross-cultural experience that changes their lives—and be compensated at the same time."* – Will Weber, Journeys International Inc.

Low Startup Investment: $0 (leading a bicycle or rafting tour, using existing equipment)

High Startup Investment: $500,000 (a swank windjammer)

Time Until Breakeven: First tour to one year

Annual Revenues: $25,000-$10 million

Annual Pre-tax Profits: $2,500-$1 million

Staffers Needed for Startup (including founder): One

On a brilliant Vermont spring day in 1972, John Freidin and a couple of other professors from Middlebury College embarked on a biking weekend. As the sun splashed through the delicate new leaves, making a dappled pattern on the road ahead, John breathed the crisp air and reveled in the exertion of pedaling the Vermont hills. He could practically taste the contrast to his work-day life: his sedentary duties as a professor of history and education. His only conscious thoughts concerned the scenery around him, with a slight anticipation of the good meal and pleasant night's sleep at the country inn still hours down the road.

The next moments changed John Freidin's life. "In the middle of the first afternoon, I got a flash that people would like to ride like this if they could stay in a cozy inn and get lots of good food." He reasoned that not everyone knew Vermont's country roads as well as he, and would welcome help in plotting routes and booking inns the right distance down those roads. Voilà! Vermont Bicycle Touring was born.

In 1986, John sold his Bristol, Vermont–based company for an undisclosed sum but, he says, "a price I was very happy with." Now he's taking time off to consult, sail, and visit family and friends he neglected while he was nurturing his business to annual revenues of $1.6 million. During those years, he was indeed busy: In 1986, Vermont Bicycle Touring escorted fifty-two hundred people on bike treks throughout Vermont and bordering states. Most clients come from the Northeast megalopolis, but John's fame has spread throughout the fragmented tour operator network. "Freidin did it right," says a somewhat reverential Will Weber, founder of Journeys International Inc., Ann Arbor, Michigan, an "adventure tour" outfit that arranges Tibetan treks and East African safaris.

TRIAL-AND-ERROR-MANAGEMENT

By "doing it right," Will Weber refers to managing a tour operation like a business. John Freidin went so far as to write his own fifty-page rule book that he distributed to employees. In it he explains what to do in unusual situations, such as when a cyclist fails to bring a check. (Two possibilities: Either call Western Union with the client's credit card to get cash wired directly to Vermont Bicycle for a fee charged to the client; or show the customer how to write a perfectly legal check on a blank piece of paper.)

For the most part, the far-flung tour guide industry has few rules and a seat-of-the-pants management style. Unlike the related travel-agency business, tour operators have no industry associations trade publications to guide them. Each new operator invents what works for the particular tours he or she conceives, which can range from two-hour mule rides in Southwestern parks to round-the-world sails in schooners. Some plot "mundane" tours like six stops in ten days on a European vacation for schoolteachers. Others take scuba divers to the Great Barrier reef. But all operators devise boiler-plate itineraries and orchestrate all the details, from air travel to accommodations. Entrepreneurs either lead expeditions themselves or arrange for guides. Successful tours shoot for 10-percent pre-tax profits after salary, but the revelation that you can make money doing what outsiders consider a continual vacation can be slow in coming.

ALL THIS AND MONEY, TOO?

Many dabblers lead excursions for the sheer fun of it, or as a way to pay for their own trips. They simply fail to recognize they can make a respectable living from a kayak, and therefore don't pursue such business concerns as advertising or employee relations. Many operators are either young with few financial obligations, or have other sources of income. Let's see how John Freidin did it.

After the weekend of the fateful "flash" John acted decisively: "I immediately researched my first bike route and ran classified ads in *New York Magazine* and *Saturday Review of Literature.*" From the few inquiries he received, he persuaded three New Yorkers to take a début trip in early August; approximately seventy-five cyclists signed up over the rest of the season, which lasts as long as Vermont's stunning fall foliage does. "Fortunately," he says wryly, "I was still drawing a salary and didn't have to make a living." The next year, Vermont Bicycle Touring made a little money, and by 1974, "I was making more than I could as a teacher."

THE POWER OF THE PRESS

What happened to John is a boon to most entrepreneurs, but almost a necessity to success in the travel field: Vermont Bicycle Touring got publicity. One cyclist told a friend about his trip—a friend who happened to be the editor of the *New York Times* travel section. Soon blurbs appeared in travel sections of the *Boston Globe* and other publications. John admits the publicity "fell into my lap," but you can prod notices by sending press releases and invitations to travel writers. Advertising helps too, especially if you pinpoint publications that appeal to your particular clientele. Will Weber, for example, prefers *Natural History Magazine.*

WHO WANTS TO GO?

Unlike travel agents, who compete for the greatest possible volume of *local* clientele, tour operators see the world as their neighborhood. If you offer helicopter ski tours in British Columbia, for example, you may be better off advertising in *Ski Magazine* than in the Vancouver newspaper. Knowing only a tiny percentage of the locals will ever book from them, Journeys International does not even list in the Ann Arbor phone book. "Our clients are from all over the world—Mexico, Hong Kong, Japan," says Will Weber. "It's the old global village thing." While such a far-flung clientele may be hard to round up in the first place, it represents a more stable base. "If the largest local business should close down, we don't worry that it'll affect our market," says Will.

Most operators court steady repeat business, whether they lead $300 bike trips or $3,000 adventure tours. "On every trip, at least a couple of people have been with us on previous trips," says Will. "We really try hard with the final dinner to leave a good impression." The best leads on new vacationers are referrals of satisfied clients. Journeys International asks participants which friends might be interested and adds their names to its mailing list.

SEND US $3,000 . . .

Will Weber's complicated operation, with revenues "of more than $1 million," began in 1978. He and his wife had just started graduate studies after returning from Nepal, where Will had been in the Peace Corps. "There was nothing at the time that was affordable and offered the cross-cultural experience. All the groups stayed in Western hotels. Our idea was to experience the everyday life you can only get if you mix with the culture," explains Will, who later received his Ph.D. in natural resources.

Will and Joan Weber posted announcements on University of Michigan bulletin boards and landed a radio interview. The process took months. "When two grad students suggest people send them a $3,000 check and offer to take care of all the arrangements . . . well, you just don't have much credibility," admits Will. But ten people eventually signed up, which "basically paid our way back to see friends in Nepal." Unless you are prepared to be satisfied with only the free trips and can forsake financial profits, Will recommends "either money for lots of advertising, or patience."

You also need contacts. "I remember trying to get help from the airlines" in booking a group rate, says Will. "Nobody was interested in talking to us until a man from Air India came out in his big car and took us to lunch. He asked why we didn't advertise, and we admitted we had no money. But he liked our enthusiasm and believed we were worth a gamble. So he gave us $50—'Here, take this and run an ad,' just like that." Needless to say, Journeys International not only booked that first trip, but many subsequent flights on Air India. When trying to drum up clients or contacts, dress the part and act as professional as your budget permits. Printed brochures, for example, add to your credibility.

WHO WILL LEAD YOUR TOURS?

Once you grow beyond leading all tours yourself, you must find knowledgeable employees who stay around for more than a year. Many operations are seasonal, providing income only during the six-month tourist season, or for the half-dozen sixteen-day safaris a tour group books. If you're the owner, you either stockpile enough profits to see you through the dry months or book counterseasonal tours. But if you're an employee, your options are more limited.

To keep employees aboard, John Freidin created a byzantine bonus system, based on the number of days a tour guide worked and the number of people taking trips. More seasoned operators earned higher salaries, says John, who now consults for others interested in starting tour operations. Many Vermont Bicycle employees hold traditional jobs during the week and lead tours on weekends for the joint motives of additional income and the opportunity to pursue their cycling hobby.

John Freidin found local newspaper ads attracted appropriate guides, probably because "the type of person who chooses to live in Vermont likes exercise and the outdoors." In addition, don't neglect your own customers. They've already demonstrated their love of your business by paying money to participate, and the most knowledgeable or athletic may be good employee prospects. John says he got a surprising number of unsolicited inquiries "from people who took tours and decide they'd like to work for us."

Familiarity with your territory—whether it's Kenya or Colorado —helps in finding employees. The Webers tapped sherpas they knew in Nepal who arrange local travel and accommodations, in addition to serving as guides. Some operators contract with established guide operations, or book part of a tour through travel agencies. But Will maintains that such profit-sharing eats at margins and also crowds you out of the experience you're trying to provide. "How can you recommend a particular guide whom you don't even know?" he asks. Journeys International employs only locals. The practice keeps costs down, even if you pay American wages. And natives bring a wealth of intimate knowledge no outsider can ever attain. A U.S. guide leading Americans leaves vacationers with an American experience, Will argues.

While you should probably understand birdwatching before you lead a group of birdwatchers to the Galapagos Islands, you don't have to live in Bangkok to offer tours in Thailand. Just hire someone who knows the territory. Before Journeys International establishes a new destination, Will visits the country, sometimes taking a tour with an existing company. Such scouting serves two purposes: "You need some personal credibility—the ability to talk to people about your own experiences." Also, visits allow him to shop for the right local employee.

YOU CAN BUY A BOAT OR START WITH ZIP

No average startup cost exists in tour operations. Will estimates he spends $10,000 to set up a new trip, including $2,000 for promotion and mailings, and $2,000 for an on-site visit. He already has a computer that helps him write itineraries and sort mailing lists, as well as contacts with airlines and travel agencies through which he writes tickets. Launching windjammer cruises off Maine could be far more expensive; you must buy, rent, or (if you're really handy —and patient) build a seaworthy vessel.

However, many operators start with no capital at all, using deposits from customers to finance early costs, and profits from the first trip to buy additional equipment and advertising. Let's assume you are an experienced white-water expert who leads excursions down the Snake River. Your basic equipment includes a raft, life jackets, and cooking implements. After a couple of springs building a reputation in Idaho, you might put together an expedition to the Rio de la Plata in Argentina. If you are unsure of details, subcontract with an existing operator: You provide the river expertise and, on that first trip at least, let the old hand arrange travel and accommodations. Next time around, pull the entire package together without the partner. Eventually, you may establish a local office and employees while you scout out new rivers and new expeditions.

THE AGENCY CONNECTION

Most tour operators are not travel agents, although a growing number of agencies also devise tours. In order to collect airline fees and issue tickets, an agent must meet certain standards of financial responsibility, business experience, and personnel requirements, which may be beyond most tour startups. However, you may want to strike up relationships with various travel agents. If you agree to fork over a share of your bookings, agencies will book their customers on your tours. Or you can turn one specific aspect of your tour, like airfare, over to an agency. Journeys International writes airline tickets through agents, splitting the commissions fifty-fifty. Because it gets a cut of the airfare, the company can hold land costs to about $50 a day.

It's true you will get your share of freebies, although most operators turn down more trips than they take. Will Weber, who led three trips in 1986 and participated in another two, says that's fewer than he once took. He cites as reasons both business demands as the company grows and the desire to spend time at home with wife Joan and five-year-old daughter Robin. However, the whole family came along on a sixteen-day family excursion in 1986. The experience was so successful from both business and personal standpoints that Will plans to schedule one or two family outings a year from now on. When the founder of Journeys International speaks of family trips, he's not talking about a week at Disneyland. His Family Trek was to Nepal.

Journeys International's local representatives met the ten-person group in Kathmandu. After two days in a small local hotel, the participants took land vehicles two hundred kilometers to the Himalayas. "Every night we set up camp after an easy walk—three, four, or five hours," recalls Will. They eventually climbed to a comfortable eight thousand feet. The weather was balmy, although snow one night added to the experience. "The villagers had seen Westerners, but never Western kids, so they were real curious. Every afternoon we tried to learn Nepali songs and teach them English ones." At dusk, the group moved into tents where they talked about the majestic vistas and hospitality of their new friends, and played games with the children. Nepalese chefs who were part of the expedition prepared five-course dinners. Soon, the group went to sleep, anticipating a wake-up call in time to see dawn frame the mountains.

SOURCE

Consultant

John Freidin, RD 3, Box 950, Bristol, Vt. 05443 (802) 388-4011

Waterpark

> *"People say running a waterpark is a labor of love. Certain people have recreation in their blood." – William Haralson, William L. Haralson & Associates*

Low Startup Investment: $1 million (small flume park)

High Startup Investment: $10 million (regional park with multiple attractions)

Time Until Breakeven: Two to four years

Annual Revenues: $500,000-$5 million

Annual Pre-tax Profits: $75,000-$2.2 million

Staffers Needed for Startup (including founder): Ten to twenty

---

You stand at the precipice overlooking a five-story free fall. Despite the eighty-five-degree summer sun, goosebumps are pimpling your arm as you grip a flimsy foam mat. The giggles and screams of hundreds of people in bathing suits blend with your audibly pounding heartbeat as you lie headfirst on the mat, perched atop the water slide. You grit your teeth, press your eyes closed against the icy water that splashes in your face, and plunge into your umpteenth ride of the day.

Waterpark operators admit to taking occasional dives down their own slides, or surfing in their own olympic-sized wave pools. But they say they have more fun than Huck Finn on the Mississippi just watching the kids—and the parents who become kids again. "Running a waterpark is a business of entertaining," says Al Turner, executive director of the World Waterpark Association. "It's a business that makes people happy."

It's also a business where you can make pools of money, if you operate those flumes and pools like the income producers they are. You can run the business yourself or hire an experienced manager or contract with a management company that receives a percentage of the profits. But Bill Haralson, who runs the William L. Haralson & Associates consulting firm out of Dallas, advises entrepreneurs to "forget the fantasy stuff. Remember that any commercial recreation facility sells time and space. Just like a motel or an office building, you sell people the right to occupy your facilities. You run an income property."

MAKE A SPLASH

In a 1986 survey, World Waterpark Association found large waterparks (defined as a major pool and three other water attractions holding a capacity of three thousand people at any one time) reported 44-percent net income before depreciation and taxes on revenues of $9.81 million; in real numbers, that's annual profits of $4.32 million. Smaller flume parks only made 37 percent on $5.04 million. Even so, that's a healthy $1.86 million in annual profits. Those figures sound even better when you consider these facilities operated an average of just one hundred days a year. A seasonal business only hurts when you don't make money, points out the operator of a Colorado ski resort, who runs a waterpark in the off-season.

The waterparks industry is still new. In 1976, Wet 'N Wild opened as the country's first waterpark in Disney World's Orlando, Florida, backyard. A decade later, the World Waterpark Association spoke of six hundred small parks—some just a single flume—and sixty-five major facilities. That year, 30 million people went to waterparks, up 17 percent from the 25 million attendance of the previous year.

The growth, which should include another ten major parks a year "ad infinitum," says Al Turner, has not been faster for two reasons:

One, manufacturers have developed the best equipment only through trial and error. Now that they have finally worked out most of the kinks, vendors are creating new thrills, such as "river" rides that accommodate whole families in one inner tube.

Two, the parks are expensive. Major aquatic parks averaged $7.8 million startup costs in 1986, and small flume parks cost an average $1.1 million. "Most are put together as partnerships," says Al Turner. For a $7-million project, a fourteen-person partnership may come up with $3 million, and a bank might finance the rest based on the park's assets. In a few scattered cases, equipment manufacturers contribute a pool in exchange for a percentage of ownership.

MONEY TO MAKE MONEY

You can only get into a park with a plump bank book, but observers see a trend toward smaller $2-million and $3-million parks. "Operators have already cherry-picked the markets that can support the big parks," says Bill Haralson. "They also are realizing that a $15-million park is not the way to optimize their investment."

You can get into the business with less ($1 million or so) through a couple of strategies. High-volume tourist areas can support single water slides that cost $300,000 to $600,000 (not counting land). "If you own a spring-fed lake, put in a couple of slides, create a beach area, and emphasize picnics," suggests Bill Haralson.

Another strategy is to ask the government to be your partner. Raging Waters parks in Salt Lake City, Utah, and San Jose and San Dimas, California, all built on public land. "A lot of park land is poorly maintained and inaccessible to the public," says Bill Haralson. "A public/private joint venture defers land costs for the developer and gets the public sector a gold star for providing recreation facilities." Also, you can ask a municipality to provide tax-free bonds as financing. Or, to make operation more profitable, ask for tax breaks.

But if no particular cost-cutting strategy applies, you really need several million clams to create what Bill calls "a critical mass, a sufficient level of entertainment." That diversity might mean a wave pool, a kiddie pool and play area, slides, and maybe another attraction, such as a mini-golf facility. As Bill explains it, you can't get people to drive more than fifty miles for a single slide, and you need to attract people from all over the region in order to pay for your park.

HOME SWEET HOME

The key element of a good location is people. You need either a large residential population (World Waterpark Association suggests one hundred thousand people per flume), or a tie-in with a major tourist attraction. Your major customer will be under twenty years old, so look for families. Bill Haralson says not to worry too much about affluence, although you should avoid low-income neighborhoods. "In very high-income areas, the kids might be elsewhere during the summer." Although warmer and dryer climates seem more logical, some parks do just fine in northern climes. "Dallas gets eight to fifteen more good days a year than Cincinnati," says Bill. "But figure everybody gets Memorial Day to Labor Day. School is in session before then, so you only get weekends. And tradition keeps people from swimming in September."

Once you build the park, count on collecting just two-thirds of your take at the gate. World Waterpark's 1986 survey found parks charged an average general admission of $8.30 for each child and $9.71 per adult. On top of that, operators sold food and rented all manner of beach and fun time extras. Don't neglect lockers and umbrellas as sources of income. Also, dry facilities, such as batting cages and go-carts, add income and overcome at least some of a park's weather sensitivity.

Another third of the take—and probably a greater percentage of profits—comes from group sales. Offer schools, scouts, churches, and business groups discounts for volume sales, particularly during the slower weekdays. "They've prepaid, so groups come no matter what the weather," says Al Turner. You might spend half of your advertising budget attracting these lucrative groups. Overall, Bill

Haralson suggests putting aside 10 percent of expected revenues for all advertising and promotion.

BABY IT'S COLD OUTSIDE

Waterpark operators who recognize they are in the business of entertaining people, rather than just making them wet, experiment with some income-producing innovations. The main objective is to extend the season. Some parks promote such out-of-season events as Easter Egg hunts on the property. That way, your facility still makes money without ever turning on the water.

A waterpark inside a shopping mall opened in Winnipeg, Manitoba, in 1985, despite the city's seven-month winter. The park is considered a success, but not without some headaches. Thanks to minus forty-degree outside temperatures, lifeguards spend twenty minutes each morning defrosting the inside of the flumes. Because the dome traps chlorine fumes, the developers had to build an elaborate exhaust system.

"We still don't know how to do indoor parks," allows Al Turner, particularly in regard to overcoming the psychological aversion to swimming when the snow falls. But urban waterparks are just a few years away, he predicts. "I'd bet a bundle if you could find a vacant three- or four-story building and had the millions to develop it, a New York City waterpark could be super successful."

SOURCES

Industry Associations

World Water Park Association, 7474 Village Dr., Prairie Village, Kans. 66208 (913) 362-9440

International Association of Amusement Parks & Attractions, 4230 King St., Alexandria, Va. 22302 (703) 671-5800

Publication

Splash, 7474 Village Dr., Prairie Village, Kans. 66208 (913) 362-9440

Consultants

William L. Haralson & Associates, 13601 Preston Rd., Suite 118 E., Dallas, Tex. 75240 (214) 385-9542

Con-Serv Associates, 581 Humboldt St., Denver, Colo. 80217 (303) 733-2409

"Whodunit" Producer

> *"I'm actually getting paid to do this?"* – David-Michael Kenney, DMK Productions Inc.

Low Startup Investment: $2,000 (an inexpensive one-night production)

High Startup Investment: $20,000 (an elaborate Equity performance staged over a weekend)

Time Until Breakeven: One month to one year

Annual Revenues: $50,000-$300,000

Annual Pre-tax Profits: $20,000-$60,000

Staffers Needed for Startup (including founder): One

It's 1927 . . . the Jazz Age. Flappers in short skirts and strings of pearls sip champagne from teacups (Prohibition, remember?) and dance with escorts wearing striped trousers and morning coats. One hundred friends and assorted characters are welcoming world-famous musician Rock Barrett back to his home town. Rumors circulating about the attempt made on Rock's life don't dim the festive mood—that is until gunshots leave Rock in a pool of blood. Stretcher-bearers whisk away the dying musician, followed by his hysterical fiancée and his old friend Henri De La Mer, the famous French detective. Murder is afoot.

SIX HUNDRED A YEAR

You're in a murder mystery weekend. Created to entice armchair sleuths to English seaside resorts during the off-season, murder mystery weekends crossed the Atlantic in the 1970s. In addition to strictly amateur productions, at least half a dozen professional troupes stage whodunits in hotels, trains, cruise ships, resorts, restaurants, and even trade shows. David-Michael Kenney guesses professionals commit six hundred such crimes a year. His Philadelphia-based company, DMK Productions Inc., produces the *Jazz Mystery,* in which Henri De La Mer solves the murder described above.

DMK alone produced sixty-six mysteries in 1986, contributing about a third of the company's $175,000 in revenues. (The company also stages operas, cabaret shows, and other forms of entertainment for corporate clients.) Murder mysteries that involve the audience as unscripted characters are a form of entertainment David-Michael Kenney calls "participatory special events." David-Michael, who has been a stage manager since age seventeen, explains: "People watch a hundred and twenty-five satellite stations on TV, not to mention video tapes. You can even shop at home through the tube. There's no reason to leave the house. We bring people into your establishment."

PULLING IT ALL TOGETHER

To be sure, not all murder mysteries are as elaborate as DMK's which writes all its scripts specifically for the occasion. For $7,000, DMK gives a client seven Equity actors who stage five acts between Friday evening and Sunday brunch. The guests—sometimes as many as one hundred—receive their own character bios with hints on costumes and personality type. For the first-night soirée, DMK provides a five-person jazz combo; on the second night, a ragtime pianist performs.

While creativity is the absolute key to devising an outstanding whodunit, attention to professionalism adds the polishing touches. For example, the wireless microphones that the actors wear during the prime-rib dinner, cocktail parties, and Sunday brunch alone cost DMK $400 per weekend. Lighting to focus attention on the proper action runs another $100. Now that David-Michael Kenney amortizes the cost of costumes, props, and scripts over all his performances, he keeps 20 percent or $1,400 as pre-tax profits from each performance. But, not counting marketing, a startup company might need $15,000 to pay for all the essentials for that first production, including the renting of facilities for rehearsal and the buying of costumes.

Of course, some mysteries are far less expensive to stage. Amateur actors rounded up from local universities don't command Actor's Equity wages. Some productions follow a basic outline, but no real script, so royalties to playwrights are not a consideration. (The plot can't duplicate a famous Agatha Christie novel, however; the guests would already know the murderer.) You can ask the hotel to provide its own music. And single-evening performances need fewer props and costumes than do three-day affairs. But the more elaborate the production, the more a hotel or cruise ship can charge its guests, and therefore the more you charge as a production company. In 1987, The Palace Hotel in Philadelphia levied $490 a couple for its weekends.

PUBLICITY STUNTS

The Mystery at the Palace weekends began in 1984 as a publicity vehicle to create an image for the newest jewel in the Trusthouse Forte chain. "Mystery weekends spread the word of who we are and what we do in an upscale way," explains the director of public relations for Philadelphia's elegant Palace. "Mysteries started as a PR event, and now they are a profit center." The hotel has other expenses on top of the $7,000 fee to DMK, such as salaries for hotel employees, food and beverage costs, and advertising. But at nearly $500 per couple, the Palace brings in $25,000 for each of the seven to nine mystery weekends it stages each year, not counting what guests spend on such extras as cocktails when they meet to compare clues in the lounge.

"But I warn hotels they won't make money until they commit to at least three weekends," says David-Michael Kenney. "People don't respond to the first advertising as well as they do after word spreads. Also, collateral costs are high. Printing alone runs $1,500 for items like name tags, notes we slip under doors, and bios for one hundred twenty different characters."

SELLING THE SIZZLE

David-Michael Kenney says you have to sell the benefits once a hotel manager or cruise ship entertainment director realizes the actual cost of the extravaganza. "I recommend they borrow from their advertising and promotion budget to pay for the weekend. The event brings people in to sample the accommodations and meals, which generates long-range business. The Palace has found many of its guests are decision makers for corporations. They're involved in selecting meeting facilities or accommodations for VIP guests. Mysteries showcase the hotel." They also generate publicity. Two networks have filmed segments of the Palace's weekends; David-Michael screens those videotapes as a selling tool.

If all goes according to plan on the initial mystery, managers and employees get hooked and usually come back for more. "It's a morale builder," says David-Michael. "We use a real waiter who has been paid to kill the detective. He says: 'Henri, I have something for you,' and pulls out a gun." Employees fight over who gets to work weekends, and can't wait for rehearsal. David-Michael, who assumes the role of Slim, the Maintenance Man, to allow him to cue hotel employees unobtrusively, says getting the manager involved is a key to repeat business. "If the manager has the personality to pull off the role of manager in the script, jump right in and ask him to play the part."

ALL THE WORLD'S A STAGE

David-Michael expects murder mysteries to survive a long run, and points to contracts he has gotten from clients just discovering the concept. Corporations book hotels or restaurants for one-night Christmas parties or sales incentive dinners, and spring the murder unannounced. One corporation hired DMK to devise a two-act script that takes place over dinner and breakfast the next morning. The event was an ice-breaker to integrate a new forty-person research staff into the corporation. Another corporation asked for a seven-day cruise ship mystery with parts for four hundred people. Instead of cocktail parties where everyone gravitates to their own cliques, the mysteries throw people together in a unique way.

DMK sees murder mysteries as just one phase of interactive entertainment. "We're developing a tradeshow script that requires everyone to go to each booth and exchange a business card for a piece of the puzzle," says David-Michael. "Another participatory event is the scavenger hunt. Or Ben Franklin takes families on a tour of Philadelphia. When they get to the Liberty Bell, some of his friends happen to be there from other colonies and together they act out history."

In the age of the passive boob tube, interactive entertainment provides involvement. "We're a catalyst," says David-Michael, "a device to get people involved."

SOURCES

Industry Association

Actor's Equity Association, 165 W. 46th St., New York, N.Y. 10036 (212) 869-8530

Publication

Backstage Publications Inc., 330 W. 42nd St., New York, N.Y. 10036 (212) 947-0020

ABOUT THE AUTHORS

SHARON KAHN, former senior editor and regular contributor to *Venture* magazine is a business writer and editor.

THE PHILIP LIEF GROUP is a New York book-producing company whose previous books include *The 200 Best Franchises to Buy* and *How to Beat the MBA's to the Top*.